Ariane Goetz
Land Grabbing and Home Country Development

Political Science | Volume 61

This open access publication has been enabled by the support of POLLUX (Fachinformationsdienst Politikwissenschaft)

and a collaborative network of academic libraries for the promotion of the Open Access transformation in the Social Sciences and Humanities (transcript Open Library Politikwissenschaft 2019)

Bundesministerium der Verteidigung | Gottfried Wilhelm Leibniz Bibliothek –Niedersächsische Landesbibliothek | Harvard University | Kommunikations-, Informations-, Medienzentrum (KIM) der Universität Konstanz | Landesbibliothek Oldenburg | Max Planck Digital Library (MPDL) | Saarländische Universitäts- und Landesbibliothek | Sächsische Landesbibliothek Staats- und Universitätsbibliothek Dresden | Staats- und Universitätsbibliothek Bremen (POLLUX – Informationsdienst Politikwissenschaft) | Staats- und Universitätsbibliothek Carl von Ossietzky, Hamburg | Staatsbibliothek zu Berlin | Technische Informationsbibliothek Hannover | Thüringer Universitäts- und Landesbibliothek Jena (ThULB) | ULB Düsseldorf Universitäts- und Landesbibliothek Düsseldorf | Universitätsbibliothek Erfurt | Universitäts- und Landesbibliothek der Technischen Universität Darmstadt | Universitäts- und Landesbibliothek Münster | Universitäts- und Stadtbibliothek Köln | Universitätsbibliothek Bayreuth | Universitätsbibliothek Bielefeld | Universitätsbibliothek der Bauhaus-Universität Weimar | Universitätsbibliothek der FernUniversität Hagen | Universitätsbibliothek der Humboldt-Universität zu Berlin | Universitätsbibliothek der Justus-Liebig-Universität Gießen | Universitätsbibliothek der Ruhr-Universität Bochum | Universitätsbibliothek der Technischen Universität Braunschweig | Universitätsbibliothek der Universität Koblenz Landau | Universitätsbibliothek der Universität Potsdam | Universitätsbibliothek Duisburg-Essen | Universitätsbibliothek Erlangen-Nürnberg | Universitätsbibliothek Freiburg | Universitätsbibliothek Graz | Universitätsbibliothek J. C. Senckenberg an der Goethe-Universität Frankfurt | Universitätsbibliothek Kassel | Universitätsbibliothek Leipzig | Universitätsbibliothek der LMU München | Universitätsbibliothek Mainz | Universitätsbibliothek Marburg | Universitätsbibliothek Oldenburg | Universitätsbibliothek Osnabrück | Universitätsbibliothek Siegen | Universitätsbibliothek Vechta | Universitätsbibliothek Wien | Universitätsbibliothek Wuppertal | Zentral- und Hochschulbibliothek Luzern | Zentralbibliothek Zürich

This publication is compliant with the "Recommendations on quality standards for the open access provision of books", Nationaler Open Access Kontaktpunkt 2018 (https://pub.uni-bielefeld.de/record/2932189)

* * *

Ariane Goetz (PhD) is a political scientist. Her research focuses on the political economy of land use, agriculture, energy and the environment in the context of international organization, national development, and global restructuring.

Ariane Goetz
Land Grabbing and Home Country Development
Chinese and British Land Acquisitions in Comparative Perspective

[transcript]

Bibliographic information published by the Deutsche Nationalbibliothek
The Deutsche Nationalbibliothek lists this publication in the Deutsche Nationalbibliografie; detailed bibliographic data are available in the Internet at http://dnb.d-nb.de

This work is licensed under the Creative Commons Attribution-NonCommercial-No-Derivatives 4.0 (BY-NC-ND) which means that the text may be used for non-commercial purposes, provided credit is given to the author. For details go to
http://creativecommons.org/licenses/by-nc-nd/4.0/
To create an adaptation, translation, or derivative of the original work and for commercial use, further permission is required and can be obtained by contacting rights@transcript-verlag.de
Creative Commons license terms for re-use do not apply to any content (such as graphs, figures, photos, excerpts, etc.) not original to the Open Access publication and further permission may be required from the rights holder. The obligation to research and clear permission lies solely with the party re-using the material.

© 2019 transcript Verlag, Bielefeld

Cover concept: Maria Arndt, Bielefeld
Proofread by Peggy Whitfield
Typeset by Francisco Braganca, Bielefeld
Printed and bound in Great Britain by Marston Book Services Ltd, Oxfordshire
Print-ISBN 978-3-8376-4267-4
PDF-ISBN 978-3-8394-4267-8
https://doi.org/10.14361/9783839442678

Table of Contents

Abstract | 9

Acknowledgements | 11

List of Abbreviations | 13

List of Tables | 19

List of Figures | 21

**Chapter 1: Introduction and Overview—
Land Grabbing from a Home Country Perspective** | 23
1. The "Land Grabbing" Debate | 23
2. The Research Project | 33
3. Synopsis of Key Arguments | 38
4. Structure of the Book | 40
5. A Note on Methodological Issues and the Framework of Analysis | 41

Chapter 2: International Land Acquisitions Today | 53
1. Introduction | 54
2. Why "Land Grabbing" Made It Onto The
   International Research Agenda | 54
3. On Terminological Ambiguity | 57
4. The "Land Grab" Debate Since 2008 | 59
5. What About Policy? Influential Frames and
   Paradigms in the Debate | 65
6. Conclusion | 74

**Chapter 3: Historical Perspectives on Overseas Land Acquisitions
in the South** | 77
1. Introduction | 77
2. Imperialism and Colonialism—Key Theoretical Explanations | 80

3. The International Parameters of 19th-Century
   European Imperialism | 86
4. Finding an "African El Dorado"? The Scramble for Africa, 1870-1914 | 92
5. Decolonization and Globalization | 107
6. Conclusion | 112

**Chapter 4: Chinese Investments in Africa—
"Create Infinity, Benefit Mankind"** | 117
1. Introduction | 117
2. Background on China in Africa | 118
3. Key Characteristics of Chinese Land-Consuming
   OFDI in Sub-Saharan Africa | 121
4. The Investments in the Recipient Context:
   Stated Goals and Multifaceted Reality | 141
5. The Issue of Labor | 145
6. Conclusion | 149

**Chapter 5: The Chinese Context—
Investments from a Home Country Perspective** | 153
1. Introduction | 153
2. Home Country Measures | 154
3. Guiding Ideology | 164
4. Political Economy | 171
5. Development Context | 178
6. Conclusion | 183

**Chapter 6: British Investments in Africa—
"The Last Frontier to Find Alpha?"** | 189
1. Introduction | 189
2. Background on the UK in Africa | 191
3. Key Characteristics of British Land-Consuming
   OFDI in Sub-Saharan Africa | 193
4. The Investments in the Recipient Context:
   Stated Goals and Multifaceted Reality | 213
5. Investment Funds for Agriculture | 216
6. Conclusion | 221

**Chapter 7: The British Context—
Investments from a Home Country Perspective** | 225
1. Introduction | 225
2. Home Country Measures | 226
3. Guiding Ideology | 239

4. Political Economy | 245
5. Development Context | 253
6. Conclusion | 257

Chapter 8: Land Grabbing and Home Country Development— Conclusion and Outlook | 263
1. China in Africa: Resources, Alliances, Markets, and Globalization | 264
2. UK in Africa: Growth Regions, Climate and Energy Security, Reindustrialization | 269
3. Difference as Variation: A Country-Case Comparison | 273
4. Chinese and British "Land Grabs" in Historical Perspective | 278
5. Land Grabbing for Home Country Development? A Synthesis of Observations | 283

Appendices | 287
Appendix A: Chinese Investments in Africa (19 investigated projects) | 287
Appendix B: British Investments in Africa (22 investigated projects) | 295

References | 305

Abstract

The role of investor countries remains poorly understood in the contemporary "land grab" debate. This book provides a comparative historical-institutional and politico-economic account of "land grabbing" from a home country perspective. Specifically, the book investigates large-scale land acquisitions from two investor countries: the UK and China. The regional focus is on Sub-Saharan Africa, a major target of such land-consuming investments since 2000. The assessment provides an empirical-analytical account of 40 Chinese and British "land grab" projects that occurred during 2000-2015. It also reviews the specific details of the home country's industrial set-up, development challenges, ideological framing, political economy, and significant events critical to understanding what is happening.

The book advances three arguments: Firstly, it shows that Chinese outward foreign direct investment (OFDI) mentioned in the "land grab" literature reflects the demands of the country's resource-intensive and market-dependent manufacturing industry, and is part of economic upgrading. In the case of the UK, large-scale land acquisitions occur in response to reforms in the host countries, to international and domestic energy and climate policies, and to reindustrialization efforts.

Secondly, the comparative analysis reveals that in spite of their politico-economic differences, both countries share many similarities, such as the multiplicity of agencies, structures, and events involved, the guiding ideology in place, and the institutional framework supporting such OFDI projects. Notably, both countries' governments consider outward foreign direct investments (of which "land grabs" form a part) as a strategic instrument to pursue particular national development ambitions. These projects allegedly *"push the limits"* of profitable business and/or social mobility in an increasingly globalized economy, and serve as a tool to *"fight the limits"* of national development trajectories that cannot provide sufficient (and good) jobs, erode the national resource base, and are strongly vulnerable in their reliance on export markets.

Thirdly, the book reviews the main features of late 19th century colonial and imperial practices, to be aware of important factors and dynamics in the evaluation of contemporary land acquisitions. From this historical perspective, it shows that contemporary land-consuming OFDI activities have novel and "old" features in comparison to the Scramble for Africa. On the one hand, core institutions, ideas, and structures that emerged in the 19th century are still part of the fabric of today's global society. The multiplicity of motives, actors, and sectors at play also strongly resembles that of the past. On the other hand, a more detailed assessment of those features reveals that their characteristics have changed with regard to key aspects: Corporations have gained discretionary power vis-à-vis the state; host country governments proactively seek to attract foreign capital (rather than it being forced upon them); existing institutional structures supporting OFDI have been strengthened domestically and internationally, both at home and in the host countries. Moreover, contemporary capital exports by newcomers such as China reflect processes of global economic restructuring of which these overseas investments form a part.

Ultimately, the book shows that the risks associated with overseas investment projects—which tend to be minimised or overlooked by public and private actors—remain high. In many of the investigated cases, the expectations attached to going overseas have not been realized. Moreover, many projects have resulted in "loss-loss" scenarios for the host and home country. Finally, the findings suggest it is useful to leave behind the polarized framing of investment as land grab *or* development. Instead, it can be both, in the sense that the "land grabbing" investment is the material expression of a particular idea of modern development whose socioeconomic promises and developmental potential needs critical revisiting.

Acknowledgements

I would like to extend my deepest gratitude to colleagues, family, and friends, whose generous support, genuine interest, and insightful critiques have been invaluable throughout this research project.

Since this book was borne out of my dissertation, I am deeply indebted to my committee, namely Frederick Bird, Derek Hall, and Jennifer Clapp: Thank you for everything, I will never forget! I would also like to thank Patricia Goff, Dan Gorman, Randy Wigle, Gerry Boychuk, Haroon Akram-Lodhi, Ricardo Tranjan, Vic Yu Wai Li, Kim Burnett, Jennifer Jones, Ola Tjornbo Hany Besada, Aneta Nowakowska, Chrisa Hoicka, Nina Lichtenberg, Dorota Cygan, Maja Mann, Ina Richter, the Park Street housemates, Tracey Wagner-Rizvi, Masaya Llavaneras Blanco, Corinna Bobzien, Hartmut Gruber, Marco Scherbarth, Jan Bauer, Barbara Then, Stephan Kadelbach and the colleagues of the Normative Orders research group at Frankfurt University for thought-provoking discussions and enduring support. Special thanks to Franz J. Goetz, Astrid Mayer, Donald Blondin, Neva Nahtigal, Anneli Götz and Peggy Whitfield for their extremely helpful feedback on different drafts of this book. Also thanks to Jennifer Niediek and Kai Reinhardt from transcript for their support and patience. Several people prepared the ground for this project to grow on: thank you to Horst Denkler, Inge Kaul, and Markus Jachtenfuchs. Moreover, I would like to thank the Institute of Advanced Sustainability Studies (IASS Potsdam) for financially supporting this publication.

Last but not least, I would like to thank my parents, Anneli Götz and Franz Josef Götz, and my brother Christopher Götz, for all the love, empathy, interest, and support throughout the years; and Oliver Eß for being there throughout it all! This book is dedicated to you.

List of Abbreviations

ACP	African, Caribbean, and Pacific Group of States
ACP-EU	Refers to development cooperation between the ACP and EU
AfDB	African Development Bank
AFTi	Africa(n) Free Trade initiative
AIM	Alternative Investment Market of the London Stock Exchange ("International market for smaller growing companies")
AoA	WTO Agreement on Agriculture
AOCABFE	Assoc. Overseas Chinese Agricultural, Biological, and Food Engineers
AUC	African Union Commission
BAT	British American Tobacco
BIS	Department for Business, Innovation & Skills (UK) (est. 2009)
BIT	Bilateral Investment Treaty
BRICS	Refers to Brazil, Russia, India, China, and South Africa
C/IPE	Combination of comparative political economy and international political economy as an academic discipline
CADFund	China-Africa Development Fund
CAITEC	Chinese Academy of International Trade and Economic Cooperation
CAJCCI	China-Africa Joint Chamber of Commerce and Industry
CCP	Chinese Communist Party (also Communist Party of China [CPC])
CDB	China Development Bank
CDC	Development finance institution (formerly Commonwealth Dev. Corp.)
CDM	Clean Development Mechanism
CER	Certified Emission Reduction credit (equivalent to one tonne of CO_2)

CIF	China International Fund Limited
CO2	Carbon Dioxide (primary greenhouse gas emitted by human activities)
COMPLANT	China National Complete Plant Import & Export Corporation (Group)
CSFAC	China State Farm and Agribusiness Corporation
DECC	UK Department of Energy & Climate Change
DEFRA	Department for Environment, Food & Rural Affairs (UK)
DFID	Department for International Development (UK)
DRC	Democratic Republic of the Congo
DTI	Department of Trade and Industry (UK) (Formed in 1970, replaced in 2007 by the Dept. for Business, Enterprise and Regulatory Reform [BERR] and the Dept. for Innovation, Universities and Skills [DIUS]; these two departments were merged to create the Department for Business, Innovation & Skills [BIS, see entry above] in 2009)
EC	European Commission
ECGD	Export Credits Guarantee Department (UK)
EIB	European Investment Bank
EPO	Equatorial Palm Oil Company
EU	European Union
FAO	Food and Agriculture Organization of the United Nations
FCECCPLP	Forum on Economic and Trade Cooperation between China and Portuguese Countries
FCO	Foreign & Commonwealth Office (UK)
FDI	Foreign Direct Investment
FIAN International	Formerly, Food First Information and Action Network
FOCAC	Forum on China-Africa Cooperation
GATT	General Agreement on Tariffs and Trade
GDP	Gross Domestic Product
GEF	Global Environmental Fund (a firm focusing on clean tech operations; not to be confused with the Global Environment Facility)
GLP	Global Land Project
GOANA	Grand Agricultural Offensive for Food and Abundance (Senegal)
GTZ	German Agency for Technical Cooperation (Merged into the German Agency for International Cooperation [GIZ] in 2011)
HA	Hectare(s)

HCM	Home Country Measure
HK	Hong Kong
IAASTD	International Assessment of Agricultural Knowledge, Science and Technology for Development
ICBC	Industrial and Commercial Bank of China
IDE-JETRO	Institute of Developing Economies
IFAD	International Fund for Agricultural Development
IFDI	Inward Foreign Direct Investment
IFPRI	International Food Policy Research Institute
IIED	International Institute for Environment and Development
ILC	International Land Coalition
INKOTA	*Information, KOordination, TAgungen*
IO	International Organization
IPE	International Political Economy (as an academic discipline)
IPO	Initial Public Offering
IRAD	*Institut de Recherche Agricole pour le Développement*
ISS	International Institute of Social Studies (The Hague)
JV	Joint Venture
MAI	Multilateral Agreement on Investment
MNC	Multinational Corporation
MNE	Multinational Enterprise
MoD	Ministry of Defense
MOFA	Ministry of Foreign Affairs of the People's Republic of China
MOFCOM	Ministry of Commerce of the People's Republic of China (succeeded MoFTEC in 2003)
MoFTEC	Ministry of Foreign Trade and Economic Cooperation (preceded MOFCOM)
MoL(SS)	Ministry of Labor and Social Security of the People's Republic of China (established on basis of the former Ministry of Labor in 1998)
MoU	Memorandum of Understanding
NDRC	National Development and Reform Commission (China)
NEPAD	The New Partnership for Africa's Development
NFCFPA	National Federation of Communal Forests and Pastures of Albania
NGO	Non-governmental Organization
NIEO	New International Economic Order
NPC	National Planning Committee
ODA	Official Development Aid

OECD	Organisation for Economic Co-operation and Development
OFDI	Outward Foreign Direct Investment
ONS	Office for National Statistics (UK)
POE	Privately Owned Enterprise
PRC	People's Republic of China
RAI	Responsible Agricultural Investment
RFA	Renewable Fuels Agency (UK)
RMB	Renminbi (the official Chinese currency)
RFTO	Renewable Fuel Transport Obligation
SAFE	State Administration of Foreign Exchange
SAP	Structural Adjustment Program
SASAC	State-owned Assets Supervision and Administration Commission
SBF	Sun Biofuels
SEPA	State Environmental Protection Administration (China)
SEZ	Special Economic Zone
SLIEPA	Sierra Leone Investment and Export Promotion Agency
SME	Small and Medium Enterprises
SOE	State-owned Enterprise
SSA	Sub-Saharan Africa
TNC	Transnational Corporation
UEMOA	West African Economic and Monetary Union (French acronym; Union includes Benin, Burkina Faso, Cote d'Ivoire, Guinea-Bissau, Mali, Niger, Senegal, and Togo)
UK	United Kingdom
UKTI	UK Department for Trade & Investment
UN DESA	United Nations Department of Economic and Social Affairs
UN	United Nations
UNCCD	United Nations Convention to Combat Desertification
UNCTAD	United Nations Conference on Trade and Development
UNDP	United Nations Development Programme
UNECA	United Nations Economic Commission for Africa
UNEP	United Nations Environment Programme
UNESCO	United Nations Educational, Scientific and Cultural Organization
UNFCCC	United Nations Framework Convention on Climate Change
UNIDO	United Nations Industrial Development Organisation
UN-REDD	United Nations Collaborative Programme on Reducing Emissions from Deforestation and Forest Degradation

USD	United States Dollar
WB	World Bank
WFP	United Nations World Food Programme
WHO	World Health Organization
WTO	World Trade Organization

List of Tables

Table 1-1: Standard Explanations of Foreign Land Acquisitions: Prominent Examples from Academia, NGOs and Development Agencies | 26
Table 1-2: A Note on Terminology | 34
Table 1-3: Evolving Listings: May 2012, September 2012, and April 2014 (Land Matrix) | 43
Table 1-4: Categories and Sub-Questions Guiding the Assessment of Land-Consuming FDI | 46
Table 3-1: Main International Lenders and Borrowers, 1913 (Percentage shares, Bairoch and Kozul-Wright 1996) | 88
Table 3-2: Commodity and Geographical Composition of Exports, 1913 (Percentage shares, Bairoch and Kozul-Wright 1996) | 89
Table 3-3: Statutory Restrictions on Foreign Ownership of Equity across Regions and Sectors (where 100 = full foreign ownership allowed, WB 2010) | 110
Table 4-1: The Case of the China State Farm and Agribusiness Corporation (China.org.cn) | 132
Table 4-2: Chinese Special Economic Zones in Africa (Brautigam and Tang 2011; Brautigam (February) 2011) | 134
Table 4-3: Project Projections from the CIF's Website (CIF) | 137
Table 4-4: China in Africa: Actors involved in Land-Consuming OFDI (selected) | 139
Table 4-5: Review of the Empirical Characteristics of Chinese OFDI | 152
Table 5-1: Key Documents Outlining China's Development in Relation to the Chinese Presence in Africa (selected) | 166
Table 5-2: Guiding Principles and Objectives of "China's Africa Policy" (MOFA 2006) | 169
Table 5-3: Three Levels of Chinese Engagement in Africa (Jansson 2009) | 175
Table 5-4: Brief Review of the Home Country Context and Chinese OFDI in SSA | 187
Table 6-1: Discrepancies between Announced, Acquired, and Planted Land Areas in Selected Projects | 205

Table 6-2: The UK in Africa: Actors involved in Land-Consuming OFDI (selected) | 212

Table 6-3: Examples of UK Financial Companies Investing in Africa (Merian Research and CRBM 2010) | 220

Table 6-4: Brief Review of the Empirical Characteristics of UK OFDI | 224

Table 7-1: Key Documents Outlining the UK's Development in Relation to UK in Africa (selected) | 242

Table 7-2: Brief Review of the Home Country Context and British OFDI in SSA | 261

List of Figures

Figure 4-1: Distribution of China's Direct Investment in African Industries (State Council 2010) | 123
Figure 5-1: China International Fund Information Material (CIF 2011) | 170
Figure 6-1: UK OFDI in Africa by Industry, 2008 (in USD millions, ONS 2008) | 196
Figure 6-2: Three Examples of Crashes in Share Value, 2008-2012 (www.iii.co.uk.uk | 200

Chapter 1: Introduction and Overview
Land Grabbing from a Home Country Perspective

1. THE "LAND GRABBING" DEBATE

To understand the contemporary debate on "international land acquisitions" or "foreign direct investment (FDI)," it is necessary to revisit the years of 2007/2008. This was a period of multiple crises of food, energy, and finance, where rising commercial pressure on land and agriculture gained international attention under the headings of "land grabbing," "international land acquisitions," or "land deals." The term "land grabbing" was first applied by the international non-governmental organization (NGO) GRAIN to describe events of dispossession, privatization, and ownership concentration in the form of FDI in agriculture.[1] Since then, hundreds of studies have been published underlining the dramatic empirical dimensions of this phenomenon, both with regards to the affected lands and project scales. The International Land Coalition (ILC), for instance, suggested that approximately 71 million hectares (ha) of land were under negotiation during the 2000 to 2012 period (confirmed);[2] research by the World Bank (WB, 2011) concluded that approximately one quarter of such land-consuming projects were larger than 200.000ha, while only one quarter of the reported "land deals" involved less than 10.000ha;[3] and as of July 2018, the global land monitoring initiative Land Matrix lists a total of 1,591 concluded "land grab" projects in their observatory database, involving roughly 49,193,878 ha of land.[4]

Importantly, the debate about "land grabbing" has been constantly evolving. While the initial focus by GRAIN (2008) lay on the agricultural sector and

---

1 | GRAIN (2008).
2 | ILC (2012), 4.
3 | WB (2011), 51.
4 | See the website of Land Matrix at https://landmatrix.org/en/ (last accessed: 13 July 2018). Note: Section 5 discusses the data problems associated with the Land Matrix's global observatory.

related dynamics threatening the livelihoods of peasants in the form of dispossession, farmland-use change and ownership concentration, later, the body of empirical research on the topic of commercial pressure on land came to include non-agricultural forms of "land grabbing." Accordingly, the 2012 report by the ILC about international, large-scale investments in land has demonstrated that these occur in multiple sectors, such as tourism, industrial production, forestry, and mineral extraction.[5] At the same time, the ILC report has indicated great differences across regions, both with regards to the share of total land-consuming FDI and to the origin of related FDI flows. The position of Africa is unique, as it has received the largest overall share of land-consuming FDI flows, which have reportedly implicated 134 million ha (34 million of which have been confirmed).[6] The major share of FDI in Africa has come from outside the continent, while intra-regional capital flows have predominated in "land grabbing" events in Europe, Latin America, and Asia.[7]

Related analyses focus largely on the host country dynamics and oscillate between descriptions of "development opportunity" *or* "land grab," depending on the particular framing underpinning the respective study.[8] However, the empirical evidence lends urgency to the topic, with a large number of case studies reporting negative effects of such "land deals" for the recipient country's[9] social, economic, or ecological development. Even the World Bank report (2011) concludes that contrary to the (liberal) theoretical promises of job creation, diffusion of technology, capacity building, productivity increases, and/ or food security improvements associated with capital imports in the form of FDI, many projects seem to have "contributed to asset loss and left local people

---

5 | ILC (2012), 4. While FDI flows in agriculture seem to make up the largest share, representing 78% (by value) of total investments during 2000-2012, approximately three quarters of these investments have targeted biofuels rather than food production. These figures are confirmed by data from the Financial Times database (2011). Accordingly, during 2003-2008, an increasing share of global FDI in primary agriculture went into the alternative/renewable energy sector (in 2003: USD 7.9 billion; in 2008: USD 90.7 billion; in 2010: USD 42 billion). During the same time period, only a moderate growth of FDI could be observed in the food and tobacco sector (in 2003: USD 1.4 billion; in 2010: USD 1.6 billion). See Heumesser and Schmid (2012), 13.
6 | It is followed by Asia, with 29 million ha (confirmed). See ILC (2012), 4.
7 | ILC (2012), 22. Note: Given the complex set of data constraints that the Land Matrix, as well as other databases on the topic, is confronted with, the argument that Asia is the largest provider of FDI to Africa seems questionable.
8 | IIED/FAO/IFAD (2009).
9 | To ensure terminological clarity, please note that the terms "recipient country" and "host country" are used interchangeably.

worse off than they would have been without the investment."¹⁰ The findings of this book support this observation, particularly in view of the many instances in which projects failed due to unrealistic business models, financial constraints, or fraudulent behavior. Furthermore, research on sustainable resources management emphasizes that the process of privatization of communal or public lands, which often accompanies land-consuming FDI projects, may constrain a country's future land planning capacity, thereby curtailing its ability to manage and provide for key social needs, such as housing, food, energy, and water, in the face of rising eco-scarcity and climate change.¹¹

But why do these land-consuming investments occur in the first place? In contrast to the diverse set of analyses of the impact of land-consuming FDI projects in the target countries, explanations about why these projects happen from a home country and investor perspective—the focus of this book—remain surprisingly homogeneous and superficial.

The general reasoning of standard explanations assumes that the aforementioned crises of food, finance, and energy in 2007/2008¹² triggered the global "land rush."¹³ Alongside the crises, continues the narrative, "more immediate drivers" were the rising "market demands for food, biofuels, raw materials, and timber" and the resultant scarcity that drove up commodity prices. In addition, carbon offset markets and capital flows speculating on an increase in the value of land have been important.¹⁴ Take, for example, the widely cited analysis by McMichael which states that "the land grab is both a response to food price reversals generating export bans and government initiatives to secure offshore food and biofuel supplies and reflects a speculative interest in food and biofuel futures and associated land price inflation on the part of finance capital" ¹⁵ (see Table 1-1 for more examples).

---

10 | WB (2011), 51.
11 | Home (2009), 107.
12 | For a detailed and orthodox explanation of the interdependency effects of rising food and energy prices, see Headey and Fan (2010), xii-xvii.
13 | E.g., GRAIN (2008); and Arezki et al. (2013), 1; ILC (2012), 4; and Weingärtner (2010), 13.
14 | ILC (2012), 4.
15 | Mc Michael (2012), 683.

Table 1-1 – *Standard Explanations of Foreign Land Acquisitions: Prominent Examples from Academia, NGOs and Development Agencies*

Source	Quotation
	Quotes from Academia:
Ingwe et al. (2010), 29-30.	"Some attempts to explain the motives and forces driving these MNCs to grab land IN [sic] DCs have presented two major agenda [sic] thought to be behind their quest. The first agenda has been linked to food security problems in their home countries. It has been posited that due to the dependence of the populations of such countries, on food imported from abroad and the tightening of the global food markets, they have been forced to embark upon a new programme of outsourcing their national food production to other countries where MNCs provide a suitable platform for implementing the food production projects. Some of the countries that have been listed under this category are: Saudi Arabia, Japan, China, India, Korea, Libya, and Egypt. The second agenda is linked to profit making potential or favorable financial returns that the MNCs have overseen in the outsourcing of food production. It is argued that under the context of the ongoing global financial meltdown and economic recession, MNCs think that land acquisition presents a good strategy for making higher and reliable profit. Two strategic thoughts or considerations have emerged in the debate on land grabbing in developing countries (DCs). Some attribute the new scramble for Africa to the collapse of derivatives markets that were involved in the management of investments, private equity funds, investment houses, and so forth before the global financial and economic crisis of 2008. Therefore, the new thinking by investors in land is that food production constitutes a business sector that guarantees fast and stable turnover. Second, the investors in land in DCs, think that land serves multiple purposes of profit making, including its other uses (e.g. for the production of either food or bio-fuels and so forth)."
R.Hall (2011), 194.	"China, India, South Korea and the Gulf States are among those at the forefront of this agricultural expansion, as they seek to produce food overseas for their growing populations. Most deals are private investments [...]. Among these are European and North American banks and financial investors seeking alternatives to volatile international financial markets."
White et al. (2012), 627.	"High world food and fuel prices in 2007-08 led to a wave of protests and anti-government riots in more than 60 countries [...], precipitating protectionist measures by those with food production capacities and expansionist strategies by those without. The combined effects of global climate change, agro-industrial development, natural resource extraction, neo-liberal austerity policies and rapid urbanization have increased insecurity and vulnerability in rural areas across the globe."

Cotula (2012), 649.	"These acquisitions involve outright land purchases or, more commonly, long-term leases mainly on government-owned land. It is widely thought that private sector expectations of higher agricultural commodity prices and government concerns about longer-term food and energy security underpin much recent land acquisition for agricultural investments."
McMichael (2012), 681.	"Land grab appears to be a phenomenal expression of deepening contradictions in the corporate food regime. In particular, the end of cheap food (signaled in the 2008 'food crisis') has generated renewed interest in agriculture for development on the part of the development industry, matched by a rising interest in offshore land investments, driven by governments securing food and fuel exports and financiers speculating on commodity futures and land price inflation."
Brown (2013), 1.	"Saudi Arabia, South Korea, China, and India are among the countries that are leading the charge to buy or lease land abroad, either through government entities or through domestically based agribusiness firms. Saudi Arabia's population has simply outrun its land and water resources. The country is fast losing its irrigation water and will soon be totally dependent on imports from the world market or overseas farming projects for its grain. [...]. Investment capital is coming from many sources, including investment banks, pension funds, university endowments, and wealthy individuals. Many large investment funds are incorporating farmland into their portfolios. In addition, there are now many funds dedicated exclusively to farm investments. These farmland funds generated a rate of return from 1991 to 2010 that was roughly double that from investing in gold or the S&P 500 stock index and seven times that from investing in housing. Most of the rise in farmland earnings has come since 2003."

Quotes from NGOs and Development Agencies:

GRAIN (2008), 1.	"Today's food and financial crises have, in tandem, triggered a new global land grab. On the one hand, "food insecure" governments that rely on imports to feed their people are snatching up vast areas of farmland abroad for their own offshore food production. On the other hand, food corporations and private investors, hungry for profits in the midst of the deepening financial crisis, see investment in foreign farmland as an important new source of revenue. As a result, fertile agricultural land is becoming increasingly privatised and concentrated. If left unchecked, this global land grab could spell the end of small-scale farming, and rural livelihoods, in numerous places around the world."

Shepard and Mittal (2009), 3-4.	"A number of factors threatening food security [...] have led many nations, particularly in the Middle East and Asia, to reexamine domestic food security policies. Many governments are looking to stabilize supplies by acquiring foreign lands for food production in the hopes of averting domestic social unrest and political instability over food price and supply. [...] nations such as China, Japan, and South Korea are also seeking to acquire land as part of a long-term strategy for food security. China, which aims to increase its rice production from 100.000 tons to 500.000 tons in the next five years, has looked abroad to other Asian and African states, purchasing 101,171 hectares in Zimbabwe in June 2008 and investing 800 million dollars in Mozambique to modernize agriculture for export rice production."
GTZ[16] (2009), 12, 14-15.	"The biggest deals are negotiated with investors from Saudi Arabia, other Gulf States and some Asian countries (China, South Korea, India). These countries are characterised by a shortage of fertile land due to unfavourable climate conditions or population growth on the one hand and sufficient financial means on the other hand. [...] Based on available information, it seems that the investors from oil rich and emerging countries mainly are governments or state enterprises or state funds respectively. In contrast, investors from industrialised countries primarily are private companies investing mainly in agro-fuel projects. When governments try to follow their food or energy strategies by investing in foreign lands, they usually set up investment contracts with the governments in the target countries themselves or with companies through which they act. While private investments are mainly driven by the goals of the companies (especially short and long term profit, sustainable development of the firm), public investments can result from different objectives."
UN DESA[17] (2010), 1; and UN DESA (2012), 146.	"Foreign Land purchases: Private investors and governments have recently stepped up foreign investment in farmland in the form of purchases or long-term lease of large tracks [sic] of arable land, notably in Africa. [...] Importantly, the new investment strategy is more strongly driven by food, water and energy security than a notion of comparative advantage in the large scale production of indigenous crops for global markets, which has been more characteristic of foreign owned plantations since the end of the colonial era. The current land purchase and lease arrangements are about shifting land and water uses from local farming to essentially long distance farming to meet home state food and energy needs. It is, in practice, purchasing food production facilities. The growing scale of this practice today, combined with the increasing economic and environmental concerns that are motivating this surge, are creating a new dynamic of global importance. "

---

16 | GTZ is the acronym for German Agency for Technical Cooperation (merged into the German Agency for International Cooperation [GIZ] in 2011).

17 | UN DESA is the acronym for United Nations Department of Economic and Social Affairs.

The quotes (presented in Table 1-1) also highlight that standard explanations tend to further differentiate between two types of economies to elucidate how and why "land grabs" occur from a home country perspective. In the case of the state-capitalist countries, (i.e. countries where the government plays a central role in the economic system), the state is said to be the main actor in large-scale land acquisitions, and often state-owned enterprises and sovereign wealth funds are seen as major facilitating mechanisms.[18] Accordingly, the increase of commodity prices, together with the implementation of export bans by major food exporting countries, brought resource-scarce state-capitalist countries to focus on land-consuming investments as a way to secure resources "offshore" for consumption back home. This narrative is often applied when describing China's activities in Sub-Saharan Africa.

Simultaneously, land-consuming investment activities of actors from liberal countries are described as profit-driven and seen as a response to the wealth destruction of equity investments during the 2007/2008 financial crisis. This narrative is used to describe overseas investments originating from the UK. Specifically, large-scale land acquisitions are what Hall and Soskice have (in another context) called "equilibrium outcomes of firm behavior"[19] in a free market system, outcomes based on market factors such as demand/supply and/or capital-rich/resource-rich rationales. For example, a "land grabbing" panel at the 2014 academic conference of the European Consortium for Political Research announces that "increasing concerns about scarcity of water resources and arable land have incentivized investor groups from capital-rich, resource-poor countries to engage in large-scale land acquisitions [...] in resource-rich, capital-poor countries."[20] Similarly, Odusola argues that "the primary factor pulling investors to grab land on the continent is that Africa is home to 600 million ha of uncultivated arable land — about 60 per cent of the world's total [...]."[21]

---

18 | Martin (2010), summary; Magdoff (2013), 1.
19 | P. Hall and Soskice (2001), 8.
20 | Haller (2014). Also, see Rulli and D'Odorico (2014), 1; and Odusola (2014), 9. The projections about land availability that led to the above framing of countries as land-scarce and land-abundant largely stem from modeling exercises. Consequently, these figures about arable land reserves available for cultivation are highly contested. It is safe to say that these models are problematic, as many of them only assess the potentially suitable land as measured by irrigation or climatic conditions, without considering its actual use, or the socioeconomic and ecological repercussions of land use change. See, for instance, the models used by the FAO (Bruinsma, J. (2003)).
Odusola (2014), 9.
21 | Odusola (2014), 9.

The problem is that these typical explanations, which run through major academic publications of otherwise different framing and outlook, deviate from the emerging empirical evidence on the topic. They also diverge from historical explanations of economic expansion, and/or suffer from serious analytical incoherence. The following paragraphs will briefly highlight each of the explanatory shortfalls that sparked this research's interest in assessing "land grabbing" dynamics from a home country perspective.

Most importantly, the growing number of studies that do provide a detailed empirical assessment of investor countries[22] all cast doubt on the stereotypes and presumptions on which this standard explanation relies. For instance, research on Chinese "land grabbing" projects in African countries highlights that they are not intended for food security back home, as would be expected from the common narrative about state-driven investments, but serve multiple purposes and involve numerous actors, both public and private.[23] Moreover, a study on Japan suggests that even though the country should rank among the major investor countries—with its levels of foreign exchange reserves and dependency on food imports—this seems not to be the case.[24] Even the case of South Korea, whose failed investment project by Daewoo in Madagascar has become a prominent example of offshore farming in the debate, the dynamics are more complex, the scale exaggerated, and the whole undertaking only marginally related to the 2007/2008 food crisis.[25] The standard explanation also fails to account for agency in the recipient countries, while empirical evidence suggests this to be a significant component of how and why these investments take place.[26]

From a historical perspective, this common narrative is surprising, if not puzzling. Implicitly, it proposes that contemporary land acquisitions differ from past ones in fundamental ways. Contemporary "land grabs" are portrayed as an outcome of purely economic factors. Historical evidence about international land acquisitions in the past, however, highlights that many factors were not economic in character, but rather related to particular ideologies (e.g., civilizing mission),[27] actor constellations, or incidents of great power competi-

---

22 | Please note that the terms "investor country" and "home country" are used interchangeably to refer to the country and the related context from which land-consuming FDI is originating.
23 | Ekman (2010); Rosen and Hanemann (2009); and Brautigam (2011a). Also, see Chapters 4 and 5.
24 | See D. Hall (2012).
25 | Lee and Riel Müller (2012).
26 | Boamah (2014); Kragelund (2009); Brautigam and Ekman (2012).
27 | See extended version of a speech on socialism and colonial policy by Kautsky (1907).

tion.[28] Moreover, contemporary explanations often assume that international land acquisitions are driven by a rational choice interest in land as a natural resource, whereas historical research shows that other functions of land as a territory, strategic post, sphere of influence, or mythical promise were equally important in previous "grabs." So, does this mean that contemporary "land grabs" together make up a historically unprecedented phenomenon, and if so, in which way would this be the case? Unfortunately, the available literature does not provide a detailed historical comparison, nor does it offer any evidence for its implicit claims. Instead, most descriptions either reveal an unawareness that the alleged resource focus of contemporary land acquisitions would make them different from the ones in the past, or they tend to oversimplify key traits of historical land acquisitions.[29]

Finally, this narrative builds on presumptions and dichotomies that stem from mainstream economics[30] (e.g., liberal vs. illiberal economy; state vs. market; supply and demand; pricing signals), the prevailing operative paradigm of (inter)national economic governance. Yet, this frame cannot meaningfully explain the "accumulation of anomalies"[31] that these land-consuming capital flows represent for it. Why, for instance, would rational actors prefer to acquire

---

28 | See Chapter 3 for the historical review.

29 | Explicitly, some authors argue that the "land grabs" in Africa, the continent that has been most affected by the phenomenon since 2000, resemble strongly the Scramble of the late 19th century. At that time, European powers brought most of the continental territory under their control. Many infer the historical similarity on the basis of particular empirical traits, such as poor labor conditions, resources focus, and/or asymmetric trade relations (e.g., Jauch (2011)). Chapter 3 provides a critical discussion of this narrative against the background of historical evidence on late 19th century colonialism and imperialism.

30 | This book follows the assessment and definition of mainstream economics provided by Lavoie (2014). Accordingly, mainstream economics can be used interchangeably with orthodox economics, neoclassical economics, marginalism, and/or the dominant paradigm. Distinct from heterodox economists, "mainstream economists exhibit great confidence in the ability of uninhibited markets to deliver stability and full employment, and to deliver solutions to any economic or social problem. The most extreme versions of neoclassical theory claim that instability and unemployment can prevail only when government interferes in the operation of markets, thus hampering the price mechanism from achieving equilibrium" (Lavoie (2014), 5-30). Regarding international organization, the World Bank (WB) and the International Monetary Fund (IMF) are the two most prominent institutions whose policy advice has been informed by and promoted mainstream economic theory. For a detailed overview of key parameters and theoretical proponents, see Lavoie (2014).

31 | P. Hall (1990), 9.

land in countries with weak governance and/or a deteriorating context of political stability, a particular characteristic of international land acquisitions since 2000?[32] And why would governments back these capital exports in some cases, particularly at a time of financial crisis when capital markets are tight? In fact, explanations that try to accommodate such "anomalies"[33] within the reasoning of the mainstream economics framing are rare, empirically unsound,[34] and tend to contradict themselves analytically. For instance, the 2011 report by the WB argues that land acquisitions are a function of "commodity price volatility, growing human and environmental pressures, and worries about food security."[35] Interestingly, all of these factors are key indicators of a failure in the liberal paradigm, despite its promotion as the best alternative for the effective and efficient provision and use of cheap resources. Yet, the WB recommends further liberalization as a remedy to the crises and promotes the creation of land markets.[36] This approach screens out the analytical incoherence, while ignoring the question of the degree to which the operative paradigm might have contributed to the commercial pressure on land through policy advice and/or theoretical framing, as critiqued by Olivier De Schutter.[37]

Apparently, the context of crises, the high-risk environment of recipient countries, and the supporting role of states, as well as the multitude and diversity of actors and events that together compose the global "land grab" phenomenon, render an international assessment of what is happening impossible. Having to rely on aggregate-level conceptualizations of actors and events, and/or having to draw on broad theoretical frames for explanatory purposes, such

---

32 | For instance, Africa Confidential (18 October 2013) suggests deteriorating security situations in countries that have been favored by investors during recent years, such as Ethiopia, Rwanda, Nigeria, and the DRC. Also see WB Worldwide Governance Indicators, 1996-2011 (http://info.worldbank.org/governance/wgi/sc_chart.asp);the Ibrahim Index of African Governance (http://www.moibrahimfoundation.org/iiag/). Concerning the regional distribution of land-consuming FDI, see ILC (2012), 4.
33 | P. Hall (1990), 9.
34 | The case of Ethiopia is particularly interesting. It has been argued that Ethiopia is a major target of foreign investments in land and agriculture due to its comparative advantage of land-related resource abundance. However, according to research in the field of ecological economics, Ethiopia is categorized as a country with an "ecological deficit." This implies that it belongs to the bulk of countries identified as "net-exporters of biomass and sink-capacity" whose ecological capital is "eroding already due to local overuse of available biocapacity," a fact that is worsened by the external factor of trade. See Andersson and Lindroth (2001), 116. Also, see Zebregs (1998).
35 | WB (2011), xiii.
36 | WB (2011).
37 | De Schutter (11 June 2009), 15.

assessments necessarily fail to fully capture how and explain why these investments take place. More specifically, they cannot explain why the investments take place in some country cases but not in others, why different countries display different patterns in view of these international land acquisitions, or the significance of different actors in these investments.

Thus, this book argues that the phenomenon of "land grabbing" cannot be meaningfully understood through a deductive analysis that assumes unitary actor groups and states that exhibit rational (choice) behavior, and relies on predefined ideas about causal mechanisms in the form of demand and supply to explain what is happening. Clearly, rational (choice) and economic motivations and/or circumstances play a role in this phenomenon, as do international events. However, they do not *a priori* define actor motivations, policy outcomes, and/or land uses as is commonly hypothesized. Instead, contemporary, as well as historical, research about decision making and foreign (economic) policy indicates that non-rational (choice) and non-economic factors, such as ideas, political economy, development ambitions, events, or power politics might be equally important factors.

2. THE RESEARCH PROJECT

This research project provides a comparative historical-institutional and politico-economic account of "land grabbing" from a home country perspective. It also explains the specific roles of land-consuming FDI in home country development. Specifically, the project explores the global phenomenon of "land grabbing" from the comparative perspective of two central investor countries, the United Kingdom (UK) and China, and does so in the context of their political economy and development. The regional focus is on Chinese and British projects in Sub-Saharan Africa (SSA)—a region which appears to be a major target of large-scale, land-consuming investments (see Table 1-2 for an explanation of terminology).[38] Throughout, the research project is guided by the two overarching questions it aims to answer: How do these investments occur? Why do these investments take place? The timeframe of the analysis focuses on Chinese and British land-consuming FDI projects from 2000 to 2015. Through process tracing, the main empirical characteristics evident since 2000 are presented, connecting project-level data with insights about relevant aspects of the home country's political economy, ideology, and development. The empirical assessment of contemporary "land grabs" since 2000 is complemented by a historical review of land acquisitions during the late 19th century to clarify to

---

38 | ILC (2012), 4. For a discussion and explanation of the term "land-consuming investments," see Table 1-2.

what extent and in which ways today's land-consuming FDI projects differ from past ones.

Table 1-2 – A Note on Terminology

> **FDI in Land, Land Grab, or Land Acquisitions?**
>
> The terminological ambiguity that characterizes the "land grab" debate represented a conceptual challenge for this project. Hereafter, the book will primarily use the term "land-consuming FDI" to refer to listed "land grab" projects of over 100 hectares in scale. The use of other terms will be identified by quotation marks, inserted to remind the reader about the diversity of terms that are characteristic of the contemporary debate. The term land-consuming FDI highlights a major finding of this research project, namely that the primary purpose of many investments mentioned in the "land grab" debate is neither the acquisition of land nor the investment in agricultural production. Instead, "land grabs" occur due to investments in all sectors and industries of a host country. Often, these investments have commercial opportunities or the acquisition of financial assets as a primary driver. However, what is characteristic of these investments is that they consume large areas of land in their operations.
>
> Importantly, the use of these terms does not mean that the book subscribes to the assumptions of the particular framework that usually accompanies them. Instead, the conceptual choice of referring to these activities as capital flows and FDI is due solely to the fact that under the contemporary operative economic paradigm that is embedded in domestic and international institutions, as well as programs of economic governance, these flows are framed and treated as FDI. At no point does the use of this terminology imply that the assessment and explanation follows the normative statements of many policy makers and/or theoretical discussions about FDI.[39] For reasons of clarity in terms of the direction of FDI flows from a country perspective, the book also uses the terms "outward foreign direct investment" (OFDI) and "inward foreign direct investment" (IFDI) where it is deemed necessary. OFDI refers to capital exports, IFDI refers to capital imports. For a more detailed discussion of the political dimension of "land grabbing" terminology, see Chapter 2 (Section 3).

The timeframe from 2000 onwards has been chosen for two reasons: to investigate whether the 2007/2008 crises that orthodox explanations cite as having triggered the "land rush" actually led to a dramatic rise in land-consuming outward FDI (OFDI); and to account for the circumstance that the debate about "land grabbing" arose in relation to land-consuming FDI projects that occurred at the beginning of the 21st century. In fact, the most

---

39 | For a discussion of mainstream economic assumptions about FDI costs and benefits, see, for instance, Sornarajah (2010), 49-53; and Moran (2011), 1-9.

comprehensive database on "land grabs," the Land Matrix, lists projects from 2000 onwards.

The case selection of China and the UK stems from several considerations. Both countries appear among the central "land grabbers" according to the existing databases (measured by the total scale of their companies' operations overseas), which makes their study significant for a more meaningful understanding of what seems to be happening.[40] Moreover, they are also commonly framed as embodiments of the aforementioned antithetic investor country model (i.e., state vs. market) running through standard explanations, meaning that a comparative study of these contrasting cases enables the research project to systematically explore alternative explanations of the political economy of "land grabs," in view of the case-specific factors and dynamics at play, as well as regarding those that apply across the two cases.

In addition, the choice of China and the UK as comparative cases is particularly compelling in terms of the research project's aim to consider the role of land-consuming FDI in the context of home country development. This is because the countries differ in their industrial set-up and socioeconomic orientation and history. They allow us to explore the ways in which international land acquisitions are reflective of a home country's particular setting and development context in and over time. On the one hand, Chinese (land-consuming) OFDI is interesting because of the country's newcomer status as a source of capital exports. Such exports have to be understood against the background of the opening up of China in the late 1980s, which turned the country into an increasingly powerful international actor in the group of so-called "emerging economies." Therefore, any study of Chinese land-consuming investments in Sub-Saharan Africa has to take account of the potential processes of international development, such as the global economic and political restructuring, that these investments might reflect. The rise of China since the 1990s has been closely associated with a domestic development path that Jiang summarized as "heavy industrialization, labour- and capital- intensive manufacturing industries, export-led growth, low labour cost and high environmental damage."[41] In 2013 (est.), the industrial sector continued to represent the largest share of gross domestic product (GDP) at 45.3%, compared to 45% for services and 9.7% for agricultural activities.[42] With respect to the benchmark of genuine and sustainable development, this economic success has come at a high price in the form

---

40 | See Land Matrix (http://landmatrix.org/en/get-the-idea/web-transnational-deals/).
41 | Jiang (2009), 587.
42 | US Central Intelligence Agency (20 June 2014).

of low wages and worker welfare, plus contentious issues associated with "the eco-system and political reforms."[43]

On the other hand, and quite removed from China's emergence as the "Workshop of the World"[44] since the 1990s, the UK, as a former empire, has a long (industrial) history of economic presence worldwide, both as an investor and trading country. After the empire's disintegration post-WWII, the UK has remained a 'cosmopolitan' economy, whose operations are integrated in, and dependent on the world economy. Domestically, its economic development after WWII was characterized by deindustrialization and the post-oil-crisis collapse of the manufacturing sector during the late 1970s, the financialization[45] of the economy, and the adoption of neo-classical development policies that slowed reinvestments by the private sector which would have been needed to modernize the UK's industrial base.[46] As a result, the tertiary sector features prominently in the UK's development context: financial and other services make up 78.9% of GDP (est. 2013), and related (overseas) earnings have become an increasingly important revenue source for the state, compensating for the negative terms of trade that result from the economy's great dependence on foreign inputs and its relatively small secondary and primary sectors, which represent 20% and 0.7% of total GDP, respectively.[47] The political economy of UK development since the 1980s, characterized by an "embedded financial orthodoxy"[48] and a financialization-led growth model, has come at the high price. The country faces an escalating private and public-sector debt, rising wealth inequality, an employment crisis, and a growing fear that heightened international economic competition might weaken the positional ability of the country to "punch above its weight" in world politics. Alongside the financial

---

43 | Jiang (2009), 587.
44 | See, for instance, Martin and Manole (June 2004).
45 | Financialization describes the increasing importance and dominance of actors, instruments, and rationalizations of the financial sector in processes of the real economy. Stepping stones towards this shift of power from industry towards financial capitalism were the deregulation and liberalization of financial markets, the increasing marketization of financial relations, the dramatic increase in financial instruments, and the rise of the shareholder value ideology (amongst others). The phenomenon has begun to attract attention following its effects on the real economy of countries, and, in the case of "land grabbing," due to novel forms of engagement by actors from the financial sector in many land-consuming FDI projects, and related problems of speculation, short-termism, and unrealistically high profit expectations. See, for instance, Heires and Nölke (2014).
46 | The New Political Economy Network (2010), 14, 11-12.
47 | US Central Intelligence Agency (20 June 2014).
48 | Cerny and Evans (2004), 51.

sector crisis, which has led to a prolonged stagnation of the home economy, the Cameron-led government of the period began to consider the possibility of modifying economic policy to rebalance the distribution of economic sectors through reindustrialization.

In both countries, the costs of these development challenges have become a matter of concern for the political elite due to a dramatic increase in domestic protests over working conditions and pollution (China), and public concerns over inequality, economic recession, and the consequences of the latter for the country's international positional status (UK).

A major challenge that this research project was confronted with was the collection of data to give an overall empirical sense of overseas land-consuming investments. The details of most investment projects are shrouded by secrecy, corporate reports are often vague, the projects themselves are constantly changing, and there exists no (accessible) land deal inventory that registers every investment that occurs. To deal with the problem of data, this research project used the 2008-2010 project listings of three influential "land grab" reports, published by the International Institute for Environment and Development (IIED)/United Nations Food and Agriculture Organization (FAO)/International Fund for Agricultural Development (IFAD), the Global Land Project (GLP), and the International Food Policy Research Institute (IFPRI), as a starting point (not endpoint) of the research process (see Appendices 1 and 2 for the finalized list of process-traced projects by British and Chinese actors in Sub-Saharan Africa).[49] In addition, this research project monitored Chinese investment activities and relevant home country developments that occurred thereafter.

The process tracing of over 40 Chinese and British outward foreign direct investments, and the continuous observation of both countries' investment activities until 2014 made it possible to capture and understand the main empirical characteristics of what is happening and why in both country cases. The findings presented are the best estimate of the main trends and periods of Chinese and British land-consuming OFDI from 2000 to 2015.

The approach taken in this book results in three contributions to the debate on "land grabbing,"[50] all of which are effectively alternative interpretations of what happened. Firstly, the study provides an empirically grounded overview and meaningful understanding of Chinese and British land-consuming FDI in Sub-Saharan Africa. Secondly, the study contributes to the existing body of research through its comparative design, which allows it to identify similarities and differences between the two cases. It highlights that the differences of political economy between the two investor countries are exaggerated,

---

49 | IIED/FAO/IFAD (2009); GLP (2010); and IFPRI (2009).
50 | For a detailed discussion, see Chapter 2.

and it suggests that they are not necessarily significant for the explanation of "land grabbing," as is often assumed. Thirdly, the comparative study of two contrasting cases contributes to the broader debate about the role that these land-consuming capital exports play in the context of home country development. It also develops a framework that could also be utilized to study other cases.

Finally, it is important to note that due to the emphasis on investors and home countries, their perspectives, and the role of these investments in the context of home country development, empirical evidence about the impact of land-consuming FDI in host countries, or the role that host country actors play in this phenomenon are mentioned throughout the book only insofar as they provide for a better understanding of the nature of these projects. This approach is largely due to time and space constraints, and not reflective of any conclusion that the actors, institutions, and other host country factors are unimportant with regard to a comprehensive explanation of what is occurring. To the contrary, there is ample empirical evidence in the form of reports and case studies which highlights the importance of host country actors, dynamics, and institutions in these investment processes—they often shape what takes place and how.[51] In practice, these analyses do not mutually exclude each other, but call for more research on the linkages, overlaps, differences, and broad structures that together compose the global "land grab."

3. Synopsis of Key Arguments

The book argues that specific details of the home country's industrial set-up, development challenges, ideological framing, political economy, and significant events are critical to understanding what is occurring, as well as contingency.[52] Both country cases are characterized by a complexity of (f)actors at play, rather than a single masterplan.

---

51 | See, for instance, Sikor (2012); Fairbarn (2013); McCarthy et al. (2012); Visser et al. (2012); and Wolford et al (2013b). See also the papers presented at the conferences "Global Land Grabbing I" in 2011 (Sussex University) and "Global Land Grabbing II" in 2012 (Cornell University).

52 | Importantly, the book's central argument that a comprehensive assessment of "land grabs" has to account for the domestic political economy context of outward FDI activities is (at best) country-centric, not state-centric. While the analysis of Chinese and British land-consuming FDI activities in Sub-Saharan Africa takes note of the particular foreign economic policy, it does not primarily focus on the activities of the state.

In the Chinese case, OFDI, of which "land grab" projects form a part, reflects the interests of the country's resource-intensive and market-dependent manufacturing industry, and is part of economic upgrading. Consequently, the land-consuming investments are intended to diversify the country's energy and industrial minerals' supply, open new export markets, and facilitate the internationalization of Chinese companies' production chains. At the same time, private actors are involved, hoping for livelihood improvements or business opportunities that are lacking back home. Also, Chinese diplomatic engagement with Africa aims to establish or maintain international political alliances.

In the case of the UK, large-scale land acquisitions occur in response to reforms in the host countries, to international and domestic energy and climate policies, and to reindustrialization efforts. This means they occur because companies make use of the business opportunities offered to them in the form of divestiture programs in host countries, or the creation of markets by (inter)national climate and energy policies. Moreover, the expectation that Africa will be the new growth region drives the investments to the continent at a time of the financial crisis and economic stagnation back home. The latter perception also led the previous UK government to promote land-consuming OFDI to Sub-Saharan Africa as way to economic recovery and international political power through rising exports and industrial activity.

In historical comparison with late 19th century Scramble for Africa, contemporary land-consuming OFDI has novel and "old" features. On the one hand, core institutions, ideas, and structures that emerged in the 19th century are still part of the fabric of today's global society and the multiplicity of motives, actors, and sectors at play also strongly resembles that of the past. On the other hand, a detailed assessment of those features reveals that their characteristics have changed with regard to key aspects: Corporations have gained discretionary power vis-à-vis the state; host country governments proactively seek to attract foreign capital (rather than it being forced upon them); and existing institutional structures supporting OFDI have been strengthened domestically and internationally, both at home and in the host countries. Moreover, contemporary capital exports by newcomers such as China reflect processes of global economic restructuring of which these overseas investments form a part.

Ultimately, the book advances the broader comparative argument that these investments are reflective of international developmental regimes, national development trajectories, and transnational development imaginaries. In fact, the rhetoric by governments and investors frames these capital exports as a strategy of national and individual development. On the one hand, they allow a range of diverse actors to *"push the limits"* of profitable business and/or social mobility in an increasingly globalized economy. This includes the observation that land-consuming FDI projects are often about controlling or consuming "land-based wealth (stemming from different land uses and activities)."[53] On the other hand, they serve as a tool to *"fight the limits"* that different actors face at home in view of advancing their economic, political, and/or ideology-driven interests, as well as national development trajectories that cannot provide sufficient (and good) jobs, erode the national resource base, and are strongly vulnerable in their reliance on export markets. This explains why Chinese and British land-consuming OFDI projects are pursued, even when they are not at all economically successful. A substantial number of projects do not live up to the promise of extraordinary returns, and many projects collapse in the medium term, resulting in "loss-loss" scenarios for the home and host country. Nevertheless, they seem to serve the interests of diverse agents (firms, governments, individuals) who are involved with them, (geo-) politically and/or economically. This is true for both countries, in spite of the quite different forms of these investments. At last, this means to revisit the divided perception of investment as land grab *or* development. Instead, land-consuming FDI projects can be both, in the sense that investments that grab land are the factual expression of a particular ideology of development embedded in institutions, agencies, and practices of (inter-)national organization.

4. Structure of the Book

The remainder of Chapter 1 describes the research approach in terms of methodological issues and the framework of analysis.

Chapter 2 provides an analytical review of the contemporary body of research on "land grabbing" that has emerged since 2007. It explains gaps in the literature, offers an overview over influential policy paradigms, and concludes by highlighting the key aspects that this project contributes to the debate.

The review of historical literature on international land acquisitions in Chapter 3 complements the introduction of the contemporary debate, which remains inconclusive and relatively imprecise in view of the questions of how, and in which way, contemporary "land grabs" differ from or resemble those of the past. The discussion of the central features of "land grabs" in the late 19th century, often referred to as the high watermark of globalization, aims to contribute a meaningful summary of key empirical characteristics and explanations. To that end, the categories studied are similar to the ones applied in the empirical assessment process of the case studies in order to ensure comparability of data.

Following this introduction of contemporary debates about and past experiences of "land grabbing," Chapters 4 to 7 then present the empirical-ana-

---

53 | Goetz (2015), 180-181. Also, see GRAIN (2008); Borras and Franco (2010).

lytical assessment of Chinese and British large-scale land-consuming investments from a home country perspective. Together, Chapters 4 and 5 compose the China case study. Chapter 4 shows the main empirical characteristics of Chinese land-consuming FDI in African countries. The chapter is structured according to the same categories that guided the historical review and process tracing. Additionally, this chapter incorporates a section on the role of Chinese labor in these projects, a hotly debated phenomenon that requires clarification for a meaningful explanation of what is happening.

Chapter 5 complements the empirical evidence presented in Chapter 4. It explains these investments' characteristics in light of China's political economy; OFDI policy framework (called "home country measures"); guiding ideology; and development context. The chapter discusses how and why these investments are taking place from a home country perspective; and it explains what makes them Chinese, rather than British, in nature.

The UK case study is also divided into two chapters. Chapter 6 presents the key empirical characteristics of British land-consuming FDI in African countries since 2000. Again, it does so according to the categories outlined previously. Similar to the China case study, this chapter contains a country-case-specific section on the role of British investment funds active in agricultural investments. This allegedly novel phenomenon features prominently in the "land grab" debate and seems to represent a significant share of the UK investments. Therefore, it is important to clarify misconceptions about these cases.

Chapter 7 explains these investments and their characteristics in view of the UK's political economy; OFDI policy framework ("home country measures"); guiding ideology; and development context. The chapter addresses how and why these investments are taking place from a home country perspective and explains what makes them British.

Chapter 8 compares the key findings of both country cases, and contrasts them with both historical evidence on international land acquisitions and the standard explanations in the contemporary "land grab" debate. It concludes with a discussion of what these findings tell us with regard to the linkage of OFDI and home country development.

5. A Note on Methodological Issues and the Framework of Analysis

The empirical characteristics of land-consuming FDI projects by Chinese and British actors in various countries in Sub-Saharan Africa were explored by using the method of process tracing and triangulation. Consequently, and building on these empirical findings, alternative analytical explanations of why particular actors have been involved in these activities were investigated, largely by evaluating key empirical characteristics in the context of the home country's political economy and in view of its social, ecological, political, and economic development context. The comparative research design, as well as case selection, allowed for differentiation between common and unique patterns of each country's land-consuming outward foreign direct investment (OFDI) activities. The selection of dissimilar cases also challenged standard typologies of investor countries previously outlined and explored the role of land-consuming OFDI from a home country perspective.[54]

The next section will discuss the database constraints that this project was confronted with; explain the project's heuristic framework of analysis; and introduce relevant literature that has guided the study of political economy, as well as OFDI, in the context of home country development.

Database and Data Collection

This project's assessment and analysis of land-consuming FDI has drawn on a wide range of data accessible via desk review, including official documentation, corporate reports, speeches, field reports, semi-scholarly literature, statistical accounts, academic publications, and interviews. The following paragraphs recapitulate the particular nature of database constraints that this research on "land grabbing" was confronted with, and that shaped its research approach and design.

A central challenge has been the unreliable nature of the data available on the topic, together with its high degree of politicization.[55] While the latter results in a biased focus on large-scale FDI in farmland in the available "land grab" literature, the first feature means that existing databases can only serve as starting points of research, because they contain false reports, double postings, and outdated information. They also obviously suffer from the unwillingness of many governments and corporations to share information about investment deals. Even the World Bank was unable to overcome this lack of transparency and ultimately had to rely on the scattered information available in NGO-led databases.[56] Against this background, Oya's methodological critique of the

---

54 | For a methodological discussion, see, for instance, Falleti (2006). Goldstone (2008); George and Bennett (2005), 27, 19; Khan and Van Wynsberghe (2008), 5.

55 | The multiple epistemological and methodological challenges that researchers as well as available "land grab" databases (provided by Land Matrix and GRAIN) are confronted with have been discussed in detail by Oya (2013b); Edelman (2013); Anseeuw et al. (2013); GRAIN (2013); Scoones et al. (2013a).

56 | The WB report primarily relies on the collection of data available on the blog hosted by the international NGO GRAIN (www.farmlandgrab.org). Contrary to the WB Managing Director Ngozi Okonjo-Iweala's promise that the report would help to lift "the "land grab" literature warns us that many "authors' conclusions have an air of scientific rigour" that "represent[s] an instance of 'false precision'," particularly in those cases where "the underlying data are actually riddled with uncertainties," and where selection biases and/or prevailing assumptions go unchallenged.[57]

The assessment process of this research project has confirmed that most databases seem to lack rigid fact checking of reported projects. Take, for example, the Land Matrix, which is the most comprehensive database on large-scale land acquisitions. Since it went public in 2012, it has constantly faced the problem of incorrect listings, resulting in great deviations of the number of "land grabs" over time (due to corrections, changes in categorization, and new listings, see Table 1-3).

Table 1-3 – Evolving Listings: May 2012, September 2012, and April 2014 (Land Matrix)[58]

Country	May 2012 (Land Matrix)	Sept 2012 (Land Matrix)	April 2014 (Land Matrix)
UK	46 projects, 3,008,472ha	41 projects, 2,736,104ha	98 projects, 2,232,547ha
China	51 projects, 3,482,616ha	46 projects, 2,068,796ha	90 projects, 1,342,034ha

Overall, it must be acknowledged that no complete list of total hectares by sector and/or country could be found—nor does it seem likely or even feasible for such a list to exist in the future, due to terminological inconsistencies of what constitutes a "land grab," the lack of administrative data by states and companies, and/or the constant changes to project details during a project's lifecycle. Consequently, the figures of, and information about the phenomenon of "grabbed land" are only a proxy for commercial pressure on land, and they vary greatly across databases and reports, as a brief comparison of the total number and scale of assumed "land grabs" highlights: as of 2012, GRAIN listed 416 land deals in the agricultural sector that had been reported since 2006.

---

veil of secrecy that often surrounds these land deals," the report does not provide any information (data) in addition to that available on the blog. Moreover, instead of introducing 30 country case studies, it only includes 14. Out of these, not a single contract was published at the time. See WB (2011). Also see GRAIN's critique of the report (8 September 2010).

57 | Oya (2013b), 503-504.

58 | These listings are taken from the Land Matrix at different points in time, namely May and September 2012, and April 2014.

Altogether these were using "35 million hectares of land in 66 countries."[59] In comparison, The Land Matrix, which lists land-consuming investments from multiple sectors, including tourism, agriculture, mining and petroleum, and forestry, since 2000, counted 924 land deals covering 48,829,193ha of land.[60] Lastly, the "grassroots environmental network"[61] Friends of the Earth has been quoted as saying "that anywhere from 80 to 227 million hectares of rural, often agrarian land, typically in poorer countries hungry for foreign investment, have been taken over by private and corporate interests in recent years."[62]

In addition, the ahistorical, *in time* approach of these databases ignores land banks accumulated by foreign companies *over time* and prior to 2000. This posed a particular challenge for the comparative research design of this study with its focus on new and established investor countries, specifically China and the UK. For example, a rough investigation of the situation in Kenya (based on a review of corporate reports) showed that between 1999 and 2010, British food companies controlled approximately 22.000ha of agricultural land in the form of plantations or outgrower schemes under a fully integrated supply chains system—some being present in the Kenyan economy since 1869, as the case of Williamson Kenya illustrates.[63] Yet, none of these projects or hectares existed in the aforementioned databases and while these figures might seem insignificant in view of the scale of some contemporary FDI projects, they do highlight that investor (country) legacy, and the related foreign control over land banks accumulated before the year 2000, deserve greater scrutiny to ensure a balanced comparison of emerging powers and Organization for Economic Cooperation and Development (OECD) countries.

Finally, the method of crowdsourcing to collect data that is applied across databases and reports aggravates the problem of false and/or biased data on the phenomenon, as the active contributors that function as the "crowd," such as international media outlets, governments, and NGOs, often appear to give skewed attention to certain countries and phenomena, such as emerging countries' investment activities or biofuel projects. As a result, it seems that some countries' activities or certain investment types are potentially underreported in the aggregate.

---

59 | GRAIN (23 February 2012).
60 | Land Matrix (http://www.landmatrix.org/en/, accessed 21 November 2012).
61 | Friends of the Earth website (http://www.foei.org/).
62 | Biron (23 April 2012).
63 | Based on information from IDE-JETRO (n.d.); Mwega and Ngugi (2006), 119, 138-140; Kariuki (1999); British American Tobacco (BAT) (http://www.bat.com/); Williamson (https://www.williamsontea.com/); and Wei and Balasubramanyam (2004).

Heuristic Framework

The process of data collection and analysis is guided by several categories (see Table 1-4).[64] Accordingly, each land-consuming FDI project in Sub-Saharan Africa, and the associated country case, was assessed in view of 13 categories, namely the *actors, institutions,* and *sectors* involved throughout the project cycle; particular *timelines* of the projects; the *role of land* in the investments; the *purpose* of the investments; and the role of the projects in the *recipient country context*. Key outcomes of this process are documented in the appendix tables on Chinese and British investments since 2000. These also provide the final list of projects that this research project investigated in great detail.

Moreover, the empirical findings were discussed in view of the *political economy* and social, economic, and ecological *development context* of the home country. Particular attention was given to relevant *home country measures*[65] and *guiding ideologies*; specific *events* significant for investor choices, investment outcomes, and/or OFDI-relevant regulations; and the role played by *investor legacy* in these investments, in the form of linkages, quality of connections, and foreign policy traditions (see summary in Table 1-4). In order to enhance comparability of empirical findings over time, the historical review of international land acquisitions at the turn of the 20th century was also structured according to these categories. To complement the very detailed information obtained during process tracing, the study incorporated an extensive literature review about the history of the OFDI regimes, foreign economic policies, development trajectories, and the political economies of the home countries. To the degree necessary, it accounted for the political economy in host countries.

---

64 | Collier (2011), 824.
Collier (2011), 824.
65 | Home country measures refer to the policy frameworks of the investor country that support OFDI activities of the domestic industry. See, for instance, Sauvant et al. (2010).

Table 1-4 – Categories and Sub-Questions Guiding the Assessment of Land-Consuming FDI

Empirical Characteristics of FDI in SSA	Home Country Context
Actors • Who is involved? • At which stage of the project? • To which end?	**Development context** • What is the social, economic, and ecological state of home country development?
Institutions • What institutions play a role in these projects?	**Home country measures** • What is the institutional framework that OFDI is embedded in? • Do these institutions play a role in OFDI in SSA?
Sectors • What sectors do these projects go to? • What are core characteristics of this sector in the host country?	**Guiding ideologies** • How are capital exports rationalized by actors involved?
Timelines • What does the project life-cycle look like? • When did the project start? • How does the project develop?	**Investor (country) legacy** • Does the investor legacy play a role in how these investments occur?
Purpose • Is the project producing for export markets?	**Political economy** • What are relevant features of state-market relations?
Role of land • How is land used? • How is land governed? • How is land accessed?	
Recipient country context • What is the official position towards inward FDI? • Is the project embedded in national development plans?	**Events** • Which events were significant in the context of OFDI? • In which ways were these events significant?

Consequently, this research project's analysis of land-consuming FDI is the result of a trying decision-making process in respect of which information to include and which to exclude. Throughout, the research has been determined to depict the diversity of factors at play, and to weigh them according to their importance. Therefore, it presents the empirical and analytical findings of each case study in two distinct chapters. This structure provides the space to highlight the multiple factors that are part of the main empirical characteristics of each case and, in a second step, to draw broader analytical conclusions about why they occur from a home country perspective.

Political Economy, Outward Foreign Direct Investment, and Development

The research project is inspired by three sets of literature: comparative political economy, FDI, and development. These will be introduced in this section in order to elucidate the premises upon which this study's assessment and analysis of Chinese and British land-consuming FDI is built.

Political Economy

Firstly, the study of the comparative political economy of these projects was influenced by the work of key historical institutionalists. Drawing on the theoretical work of C/IPE[66] scholars such as Katzenstein, Hall, and Rueschemeyer and Mahoney, the project has not assumed that the interests of involved actors are exogenous, fixed, or necessarily material. Instead, it was based on the assumption that any study of the political economy of land-consuming FDI would have to be open to potentially new factors and variables that might shape relevant policy, project, and/or actor rationale, including the decision-making environment itself, psychological factors, international factors, domestic factors, and economic reasoning.[67]

Additionally, the study's interest in OFDI from the viewpoint of political economy was influenced by Katzenstein's argument that the "management and the analysis of interdependence must start at home."[68] Conventionally, IPE scholars accentuate the role of international factors in the form of international regimes, trade, FDI, epistemic communities, and civil society, while comparative political economists concentrate on domestic factors to explain policy outputs and outcomes. In the case of land-consuming OFDI, however, neither approach can fully capture what is happening. Instead, the literature review[69] suggests that national and international factors are at play, and that distinct domestic developments together make up the global phenomenon. In this context, the work by Katzenstein exemplifies a third way to study land-consuming FDI. He bridges the outlined divide between C/IPE scholars in his

---

66 | C/IPE refers to scholars that combine comparative political economy (CPE) and international political economy (IPE) research.
67 | See, for instance, Katzenstein (1977a; 1978); P. Hall (1990); and Rueschemeyer and Mahoney (2003). Other disciplines have acknowledged the multiplicity of factors in decision making. See DeRouen and Mintz (2010).
68 | Katzenstein (1977b), 606.
69 | See Chapter 2.

research on the foreign economic policy making of advanced industrial states, highlighting that it is the outcome of "the interaction of international and domestic forces."[70]

This research project's assessment and analysis of land-consuming FDI has adopted Katzenstein's argument that it is not possible to understand societies without examining the regional and global contexts within which they exist. At the same time, this logic suggests that one cannot understand regional and global phenomena without considering the distinctiveness of the societies (and the domestic structures of the nation-states) involved. Katzenstein's work also underlines the importance of accounting for differences in national responses to international challenges, such as the food or energy crisis in 2007/2008, even at a time when international interdependence and "the pervasiveness of transnational relations" are important phenomena in the reality of nation-states.[71] The above implies that the assessment of *how* international land acquisitions are actually carried out by actors from two major investor countries provides for a better understanding of *why* they might be happening in the home country context, how they relate to issues of crisis, and what their implications could be for international economic and political relations. Moreover, the institutional assessment differentiates between means (instruments) and ends (objective) while remaining aware that "means can become an end in itself, and ends can become a means in the attainment of other objectives."[72]

With regard to actor analysis, the study starts out by sorting actors into major interest groups of production relations (such as industry, finance, commerce, labor and agriculture) and political action groups related to the structures of political authority (state bureaucracy and political set-up). However, neither actor group should ultimately be seen as unitary during the process of assessment and analysis; nor should a strict normative distinction between private and public actors be upheld during process tracing and analysis. State power itself is made up of particular individuals belonging to a particular group in society, and their strategic considerations for foreign (economic) policy might end up conflicted between national interests (as state power held by particular groups) and the public good. Also, private actors within the same field might pursue very different interests and experience highly dissimilar outcomes. Furthermore, with regard to influence, *a priori* presumptions are not helpful for a meaningful understanding of how and why land-consuming FDI occurs. While interest groups, particularly in the field of economic policy, are important

---

70 | Katzenstein (1977b), 587, 591.
71 | Also see, for instance, Dore (2000).
72 | Katzenstein (1977b), 588.

in influencing public preference and choice, it can also work the other way around, with public policy influencing private preferences.[73]

More broadly, the analysis of land-consuming OFDI from an investor perspective treats agencies, clusters of ideas that perform ideological functions[74] (hereafter: guiding ideologies), structures, and events as co-determinant, and it does not assume variable independence. Consequently, the emphasis has been on studying in-depth "these interactive effects of the interdependence of multiple causal variables"[75] in the Chinese and British cases. The study has accepted that "history and ideas matter," that "institutions structure actor choices but are subject to change by actors themselves," and that actors "make decisions that are not always efficiently or purely self-interested."[76]

Concerning the aspect of power in the study of the two home countries' political economy, the assessment was influenced by the theoretical work of Barnett and Duvall. The authors developed a heuristic model of power as a social relation.[77] Accordingly, power transpires in the interaction of actors ("power over"), as well as in the structural setting within which this interaction takes place ("power to").[78] Therefore, the book has taken note of the home countries' development trajectories and political economies, as well as the existence and application of a particular discourse or cluster of ideas and refer-

---

73 | Katzenstein (1977b). Also see Levy and Prakash (2003) on transnational corporations in global governance or Chandler and Mazlish (2005).

74 | Ideological functions refer to the fact that ideologies tend to justify and reflect powerful interest structures. The assessment of Chinese and British OFDI from a home country perspective takes note of such powerful clusters of ideas that play a role in the promotion and rationalization of these investments. However, Gouldner (1976, 33) stressed that ideologies differ from propaganda which is purely strategically in nature. Instead, ideologies "are intended to be believed in by those affirming them publicly and by all men, because they are "true," and they thus have universal character." The universal appeal of ideologies, such as the claim that they serve the national interest, conceals the interest formation that they represent in their "concern for What is and by their world-referencing 'reports'." In this sense, then, the clusters of ideas supporting OFDI to Africa fulfill an ideological function: they mobilize support, conceal the interests of the particular political economy that drives them, and appear to be universal in character. Moreover, these guiding ideologies justify as well as create the institutions and purposeful agents at play in OFDI activities to Africa.

75 | Steinmo (2008), 166.

76 | Steinmo (2008), 178.

77 | Barnett and Duvall (2005).

78 | Barnett and Duvall (2005), 48. Clearly, this distinction should only be understood as a heuristic tool, because in practice, both power dimensions are intertwined.

ence systems that determine the subjectivities of actors, their capacity, and that shape preferences and perceptions.[79]

FDI Research

Secondly, the study has drawn on FDI research in its consideration of potential links between OFDI flows, domestic development, and foreign economic policy. OFDI research largely comprises economic-historical and legal-institutional studies on OFDI in and over time, and it bridges the analytical divide between micro-level OFDI activities and macro-level economic development by documenting the empirical correlations between them. Accordingly, "OFDI is one part of the country's overall strategy of economic development," i.e. "a means to an end, not the goal itself."[80]

The essay by Lall was particularly helpful, as it provides important findings on the significance of particular development challenges in influencing government policies on FDI activities. Lall's research documents the use of "FDI flows for furthering the growth of national ownership and locational advantages," mostly in cases of market failure, and it reveals the relevance of the home country context for explaining the large OFDI variations between and within investor countries in and over time.[81] The documented cases are not confined to state-capitalist countries, as the orthodox description of "land grabbing" countries would suggest, but include liberal economies such as the UK, whose statistics from 1973-2002 show that investment-related bilateral aid to improve the host country's investment environment positively correlated with OFDI flows over time.[82]

Also, the comparative study on OFDI by emerging economies, edited by Sauvant et al., was useful. It identifies key frameworks and elements of OFDI regulation by emerging economies, as well as OECD countries; and it outlines their emergence in the context of their economic development process. From its legal-institutional standpoint, the antithetic framing used in the contemporary debate on "land grabbing" (e.g., state vs. market) is not helpful in explaining what seems to be happening, since the resulting contrastive description of Chinese and British political economies does not correspond with the actual institutional frameworks in place in both countries, which are relatively similar with regard to OFDI regulation and promotion.[83]

---

79 | Gouldner (1976), 33.
80 | Broadman (2010), 331; Sauvant et al. (2010); Te Velde (2007); Hyam (2010); Nunnenkamp (2006); and Dumett 1999.
81 | Lall (1996), 324-325.
82 | Te Velde (2006), 24-25; and Te Velde (2007), 96.
83 | Sauvant et al. (2010).

At the same time, these works indicate that any implicit or explicit claims about the benefits of OFDI for domestic development need to be critically probed against empirical evidence. In practice, particular cost and benefit rationalizations by investors and governments often do not materialize, and capital exports might not turn out to be in the best interest of the country. Prominent examples are the "hollowing out" of the Japanese manufacturing industry,[84] the export of jobs, or cases of wealth destruction through project failure.[85] Historical FDI research also raises awareness of the fact that the contemporary promotional policy stance towards OFDI that is characteristic of China and the UK (since 2000) is unique. Over time, governments have shifted back and forth between restricting and/or liberalizing such capital flows, which emphasizes the need to be aware of potential changes in the respective policy landscape and guiding ideology over time.

Home Country Development

Thirdly, this project has studied Chinese and British land-consuming investments in view of home country development through the lens of four dimensions: the ecological dimension (pollution; resource availability and access); the social dimension (unemployment; education; lack of skilled personnel; demographic change; inequality of wealth and opportunity); the political dimension (public policies; political landscape; state-market relations); and the economic dimension (crisis; debt; job creation; sectoral distribution; productivity; external vulnerability; ambitions). These factors have been derived from a body of literature that discusses the trajectories, dynamics, potentials, and challenges of development approaches since the late 19th century.[86]

---

84 | Also see Moran (2011), 124.
85 | See Lall (1996); Moran (2011); Snyder (1991); and Cottrell (1975).
86 | E.g., Gillespie (2001); Bird and Velasquez (2006); Robbins (2004); Victor (2008); Hirsch (2005); Snyder (1991); Jackson (2011); Cato (2011); Ekins (1993); and Saeed (2008). Also see the literature review in Chapter 3 on the historical dynamics of home country development and overseas investment.

Chapter 2: International Land Acquisitions Today

A new international division of labour in agriculture is likely to emerge between countries with large tracts of arable land—and thus a likely exporter of biomass or densified derivatives—versus countries with smaller amounts of arable land (i.e. biomass importers, e.g. Holland). The biggest biomass export hubs are expected to be Brazil, Africa and North America.
(World Economic Forum 2010)

Like trade, foreign direct investment (FDI) has occurred throughout history. From the merchants of Sumer around 2500 BCE to the East India Company in the 17th century, investors routinely entered new markets in foreign dominions. In 1970 global FDI totaled $13.3 billion. By 2007 it was nearly 150 times higher, peaking at $1.9 trillion.
(WB 2010)

Importantly, the new investment strategy is more strongly driven by food, water and energy security than a notion of comparative advantage in the large scale production of indigenous crops for global markets, which has been more characteristic of foreign-owned plantations since the end of the colonial era. The current land purchase and lease arrangements are largely about shifting land and water uses from local farming to essentially long-distance farming to meet home state food and energy needs.
(UN DESA 2010)

1. INTRODUCTION

Diversity of frames and perspectives characterize the contemporary debate on "land grabbing" since 2007. While the emerging empirical evidence about dynamics in host countries is growing, meaningful assessments of land-consuming FDI from a home country perspective remain limited. The more nuanced assessments that have emerged all highlight the complexity of home-country-specific political economies involved, plus the significant share of non-resource focused, yet land-consuming OFDI projects.

This chapter introduces central concerns, trends, and paradigms of the "land grab" debate since 2008. It proceeds as follows: Firstly, key factors will be discussed that might explain the unexpected surge of international interest in, and research on the topic of "land grabbing." Secondly, the main terminological challenges will be outlined. Alongside the data challenges presented in Chapter 1, these are important in understanding the constraints and pitfalls that confront research on this topic. Thirdly, a review of major publications since 2008 will be presented, highlighting core explanations, and summarizing how the debate has evolved over time, analytically and empirically.[1] Fourthly, the three most influential framings that shape the policy debate and the research literature will be discussed. Aside from their significant role in identifying the problems of "land grabbing," and, on that basis, recommending potential remedies, these framings also mirror core actor constellations and paradigmatic contestations that affect what is being discussed in the academic literature on the topic. Finally, the contribution made by this research project to the debate will be briefly outlined.

2. WHY "LAND GRABBING" MADE IT ONTO THE INTERNATIONAL RESEARCH AGENDA

Before going into the debate on "land grabbing" itself, it seems important to reflect upon its basic parameters on a broader scale, namely the factors that put this topic on the international research agenda in the first place as well as the terminological ambiguity that characterizes it. These prior considerations about the context and terminology of the debate will allow us to identify potential interests, dynamics, and events that might be important for a better understanding of the "land grab" phenomenon. Clearly, processes of dispossession, concentration of ownership, and other aspects of commercial pressure on land

---

[1] | For clarification: While the "land grabbing" debate begun with the framing by GRAIN (2008) in 2008, it is important to note, that the projects that are referenced in the debate often trace back to the year 2000, or even further back.

that are discussed under the heading of "land grabbing," "international land acquisitions," or "FDI in land and agriculture," are by themselves nothing new, nor do the authors who contribute to the respective literature and policy debate seem to make a particular effort to understand whether anything about the phenomenon differs from the past. What exactly does the broader context of timing, actor constellation, or terminology then tell us about the renewed popularity of land issues?

It appears that the interplay of five factors has prepared the ground for new interest in the phenomenon. These factors can be described under the headings of framing, empirical evidence, crisis, competition, and opposition.

Firstly, the "land grab" framing itself seems important. "Land grabbing" has not only become the title under which a huge body of interdisciplinary research on the topic is emerging, but it also provides international NGOs such as GRAIN[2] with a powerful diagnostic tool and political platform to pool and jointly articulate their discontent with the predominant policy paradigms of the national and international development institutions and agencies that initially supported these "investments" and related policy reforms in the name of "development," "poverty reduction," and/or "food security."[3]

Secondly, in this process of paradigmatic contestation there is growing empirical evidence of the often high social, environmental, and/or economic costs of "land grabs" at the local level, which has been admitted by the WB.[4] Together with the sheer, unheard of scale of the projects, this has lent practical credibility to the alternative framing that challenges the widely institutionalized policy paradigm of mainstream economics over its failed promises—pointing, for instance, to the poor job creation and skills transfer, limited taxation, dispossession, displacement, pollution, and ownership concentration.[5]

Thirdly, the context of the financial, energy, and food crises of 2007/2008 has increased interest in the topic. On the one hand, the rise of FDI in land and agriculture, especially at a time when investments elsewhere were declining, generated attentiveness to the phenomenon on a general level—first from a quantitative angle by UNCTAD, and increasingly from a qualitative angle.[6] On the other hand, the crises had governments worldwide worrying about political and economic regime security in the face of food riots, high energy and food prices, unemployment, debt pressure, and lagging growth. These concerns

---

2 | GRAIN (2008).
3 | WB (2007); De Schutter (2011a); Caffentzis (2002); De Angelis (2005).
4 | WB (2011).
5 | WB (2011).
6 | UNCTAD (2009).

redirected their attention towards issues of food, job, and energy security, all of which are issues linked to land-consuming investments.[7]

Fourthly, the renewed attention to "land grabs" was also fueled by the widespread concern among public and private actors in old investor countries over heightened international competition and global economic restructuring.[8] This is evidenced by the high research output of OECD-based institutions on the rise of new economic powers as well as the officially documented fears of old economic powers over their declining international influence.[9]

Finally, the opposing interests and paradigms of dominant institutions, such as the WB, the FAO, or the UN Special Rapporteur on the Right to Food, have led to a lively, global-level policy debate on the issues of "land grabbing," food security, and the role of agriculture for development.[10] In this context, a well-prepared civil society, which had pushed the FAO since 2002 to change the course of its agricultural policy stance towards smallholder farming, also played a prominent role. It made productive use of the 2007/2008 food crisis and its established institutional linkages with the Rome-based agency once the crisis hit.[11]

In sum, these elements point to the political side of the debate, and they call attention to the fact that not everyone who engages in it does so out of an interest in "land grabbing" itself. Instead, part of the discussion taking place under the label of "land grabbing" seems to be the result of media diplomacy and the furthering of other agendas. This is highlighted by the great discrepancy between empirical facts and rhetorical claims about what is happening. This discrepancy, which this research project witnessed in many cases during process tracing, cannot be explained by the complex set of data constraints alone.

---

7 | Against this background, the observation by Ayoob (2005) that the securitization of an issue is preceded by its politicization seems important.

8 | See UNCTAD (2009, 124), especially regarding the rise of transnational corporations (TNCs) from Asian countries among the top 25 TNCs globally. Also see Dicken (2007), 33-69.

9 | See Chapters 6 and 7.

10 | See WB (2007); IAASTD (2008); De Schutter (2011a); WB (2011); and IIED/FAO/IFAD (2009).

11 | Personal communication, Steering Committee member of the Committee on World Food Security, November 2013.

3. ON TERMINOLOGICAL AMBIGUITY

The politics of the discourse on "land grabbing" that were discussed in the previous section are also reflected in the history of its terminology. The "land grab" terminology was brought to life by GRAIN's publication "Seized," which first applied it to describe an allegedly new global trend, namely the securing of large tracts of (farm)land by foreign governments and private actors. While the term "land grabbing" had previously been used to describe historical incidents of "arbitrary seizure of land either by military force or through dishonest or illegal means,"[12] GRAIN's reframing of international investments in land as "land grabs" pointed to the similarities between contemporary events and those of the past for the affected populations in the form of "the brutal expulsion of indigenous communities" and intensifying "struggles over land."[13] At the same time, it put the spotlight on the prevailing economic approach's "accumulation of anomalies,"[14] such as misleading assumptions about the benefits of such investments for the social and economic development of host countries. These assumptions did not match the empirical evidence and were plagued by an analytical inability to explain these investments meaningfully: why would investors target primarily countries with particularly low governance performance?

Subsequent reports by international institutions,[15] NGOs (e.g., Action Aid[16] and Oxfam[17]), and academia followed up on the core questions raised by GRAIN's alternative framing by assessing whether *farm*land acquisitions constituted a "land grab" or a "development opportunity."[18] Yet, these reports continued using different terminologies to describe land-consuming investments, such as "FDI in land,"[19] depending on their respective framing. In addition to the resulting pluralism of terms and frames to describe foreign investments in *farm*land, academic research broadened the focus of "land grabbing" to include "radical changes in the use and ownership of land" through FDI in sectors other than agriculture, such as tourism or industry.[20] The resulting termino-

---

12 | UNCCD (2010).
13 | GRAIN (2008), 1-2.
14 | P. Hall (1990), 9.
15 | IIED/FAO/IFAD (2009); WB (2011).
16 | Action Aid has a thematic work area and several publications on "Biofuels and Land Grabs" (http://www.actionaid.org/eu/what-we-do/biofuels-and-land-grabs).
17 | Oxfam produces research on the political economy and outcomes of land policy (http://oxf.am/4LX).
18 | IIED/FAO/IFAD (2009).
19 | Weingärtner 2010; WB (2011); and WB (2010).
20 | Zoomers (2010).

logical ambiguity led Borras and Franco to conclude that "the 'global land grab' has become a catch-all to describe and analyze the current explosion of large scale (trans)national commercial land transactions."[21]

At the same time, the analytical value of the concept came under increased scrutiny: as not all "land grabs" are the same, R. Hall argued that the concept's primary value was for activist rather than analytical purposes, because it ignored the context-specific dynamics and processes at play in the host countries.[22] Moreover, an increasing number of case studies began to question certain presumptions at the core of the "land grab" framing that were related to its peasant activist origin.[23] Studies on international farmland acquisitions in Russia and Ukraine challenged, for instance, the common supposition that peasants are inherently opposed to large-scale investments and farming models.[24] Instead, large-scale investments in farming can encounter a relatively positive expectation of production and expansion in country contexts where uncultivated land has a negative connotation as a further retreat of the state. This clearly highlights that research on "land grabbing" must account for the host country's specific development practice and history, rather than assuming a unitary peasant culture. Moreover, D. Hall's research on South East Asian crop booms advises "that we need to pay attention to smallholders as potential *agents* of land grabbing,"[25] instead of assuming (*a priori*) that they are all necessarily victims in the process. At the same time, the shortcomings of the "land grabbing" frame's narrow focus on smallholder farming and food sovereignty in particular institutional contexts and in view of de-peasantization have been highlighted.[26]

As of 2016, this struggle over the adequacy of the terms and frames used to describe what seems to be happening in the context of "land grabs" continues. How significant this struggle is for the assessment of "land grabbing" becomes obvious when considering that under the existing terms and frames, it is impossible to clearly identify whether a "land deal" is a "land grab" or not.[27] While GRAIN used the term to refer to any *foreign* investment in *agriculture*, over time research has challenged this definition, which only captures a minor

---

21 | Borras and Franco (2010), 2.
22 | R. Hall (2011), 193.
23 | Borras et al. (2011).
24 | Steggerda and Visser (2012); Mamonova (2012). Also see special journal editions on "Global Land Grabs" by *Third World Quarterly* 2013 (Volume 34, Issue 9) (see Edelman et al. (2013)); and "Land Grabbing and Global Governance" by *Globalizations* 2013 (Volume 10, Issue 1) (see Margulis et al. (2013)).
25 | D. Hall (2011), 838.
26 | De Master (2013).
27 | See also D. Hall (2013), 1592.

share of the total dynamic, ignoring, for instance, the significant dynamics of land dispossession and ownership concentration attributed to domestic investors of the respective host countries. The importance of the latter has resulted in case studies assessing "land grabbing" through a focus on the political economies of the host countries. Similarly, attempts to update the "land grab" terminology in line with the empirical evidence, such as the Tirana Declaration,[28] tend to forget that even under democratic methods, compensation and deliberation procedures might not solve the underpinning conflicts of land use and land struggles. Again, the definition is not precise enough to differentiate what is *not* a "land grab." Yet, such a definition would be needed to discuss "land grabbing" in the broader development context, especially in view of the fact that it is both part of and symptomatic of pressure on land in the form of economic upscaling, growth, and/or economic liberalization.

For the purpose of this research project, it is important to remember that it largely uses the term land-consuming FDI. This term best captures a common feature of many "land grab" projects that matters when assessing them from a home country perspective—namely, that their primary purpose is neither the acquisition of land nor the investment in agricultural production. Instead, what is characteristic of these investments is that they consume large areas of land in their operations.

4. The "Land Grab" Debate Since 2008

In spite of the widespread and growing academic criticism of "false precision," it is important to note that in the ongoing debate, as well as the public perception about the topic, a set of empirical facts continue to form a sort of "empirical fiction"[29] about the phenomenon.[30] Borras and Franco argue that the predominant empirical storyline about "land grabbing," which runs through

---

28 | The Tirana Declaration (ILC (2011), 8-10) was the outcome document of an international multi-stakeholder conference organized by the National Federation of Communal Forests and Pastures of Albania (NFCFPA), the Government of Albania, and the ILC on the theme "Securing land access for the poor in times of intensified natural resources competition" (24-26 May 2011).

29 | This term does not mean to argue that the empirical observation of a concentration of land ownership, access, and control is false. Instead, it wants to highlight that available reports and databases often pretend to provide precise figures in view of land "grabbed" by project or in aggregate (e.g., Land Matrix), even though these figures might frequently be incorrect for various reasons.

30 | For a detailed critique of the data foundation of the "land grab" debate, also see Rulli and D'Odorico (2013a) and (2013b); Scoones et al. (2013b); and Oya (2013b).

many scholarly, as well as para-scholarly, publications from the beginning, basically consists of five hypotheses: (1) land used for domestic consumption changes into land used for export production; (2) the main investor countries are "the Gulf states, Chinese and South Korean governments and companies;" (3) land deals also "involve finance capital, partly leading to speculative deals;" (4) they "are often shady in character, being non-transparent, non-consultative, and fraught with corruption involving national and local governments;" and (5) "land grabs" necessitate better regulation to prevent negative, and generate positive, outcomes.[31] In light of the growing and increasingly differentiated research on land-consuming FDI since 2008, this simplified empirical narrative is predominantly an ossification of the original theme of 2008, when the topic attracted international attention. The remainder of this section will provide an overview of the main themes, publications, and perspectives that have been characteristic of the evolving debate on land-consuming FDI over time.

The key milestones in the literature are reports by NGOs[32] and international institutions;[33] research papers submitted to conferences on "Land Grabbing" and "Food Sovereignty;"[34] and articles in particular journals, such as the "Global Land Grabs" issue of the journal *Development*;[35] the *Journal of Peasant Studies*, which not only published selected papers on the topic,[36] but also special issues covering specific aspects of international land acquisitions (e.g., green grabbing; the peasant in relation to the state and class; biofuels, land, and agrarian change);[37] the *Globalizations* journal (e.g., land grabbing and global governance);[38] or *Third World Quarterly* (e.g., agrarian reform).[39] In addition to this increasingly multi-faceted body of literature, numerous books on the topic have been written.[40]

---

31 | Borras and Franco (2012), 38. ILC (2012), 4.
32 | GRAIN (2008); and ILC (2012).
33 | IIED/FAO/IFAD (2009); WB (2011).
34 | See the conference documentation of the international conferences on Land Grabbing I (6-8 April 2011 at University of Sussex) and II (17-19 October 2012 at Cornell University), and the conferences on Food Sovereignty: A Critical Dialogue (14-15 September 2013 at Yale University; and 24 January 2014 at the International Institute of Social Studies (ISS), The Hague).
35 | Harcourt (2011).
36 | E.g., Zoomers (2010).
37 | Fairhead et al. (2012); *JPS* (Vol. 34, Nr. 3-4, 2007); McMichael and Scoones (2010).
38 | Margulis et al. (2013).
39 | Edelman et al. (2013).
40 | Fritz (2010); Pearce (2012); and Liberti (2012),

When starting off in 2008, the discussion of "land grabbing" focused largely on investments in *farm*land made by *foreign* agribusiness or financial investors in the context of the global food and financial crises.[41] Based on over 100 cases of "offshore food production," GRAIN argued that the governments of food importing countries, namely China, Saudi Arabia, Japan, China, India, Korea, Libya, and Egypt, were "snatching up vast areas of farmland abroad for their own offshore food production" and food security, as the food price crisis and food export bans in 2008 indicated the market's failure to provide for cheap and secure food commodities. Foreign agribusiness and private investors were also identified as acquirers of farmland, but for different reasons, namely the search for profitable investment opportunities at a time of financial crisis.[42]

The empirical description of investments in farmland has become more detailed and complex. Institutional and academic publications largely followed the original description of what seems to be happening,[43] but added the energy alias "peak oil"[44] crisis and the climate crisis to the range of "land grab" triggers—with the argument that these had resulted in domestic legislation with land-intensive (trans)national consequences.[45] Under the header of "green grabbing," a growing number of publications study the implications of biofuel policies, the REDD scheme,[46] and/or other policy regimes and cases "where 'green' credentials are called upon to justify appropriations of land for food or fuel—as where large tracts of land are acquired not just for 'more efficient farming' or 'food security', but also to 'alleviate pressure on forests'."[47]

At the same time, the 2009 report by FAO/IIED/IFAD emphasized the importance of domestic investors. It suggested that government-backed deals could be more about investing profitably than securing food, and stressed that the terminology of land acquisition might be misleading overall, as many land

---

41 | See more about the interrelation of food prices and financial sector speculation in the joint report by UNCTAD and Arbeiterkammer Wien (2011).
42 | GRAIN (2008); also see Table 1-1.
43 | Shepard and Mittal (2009); Smaller and Mann (2009); IIED/FAO/IFAD (2009); WB (2011).
44 | International Energy Agency (2013).
45 | Seiwald and Zeller (2011), Matondi et al. (2011).
46 | See the United Nations Collaborative Programme on Reducing Emissions from Deforestation and Forest Degradation (UN-REDD) website (http://www.un-redd.org/).
47 | See the introduction of the special issue of *JPS* 2012 (Vol. 39, No. 2) on Green Grabbing: a new appropriation of nature?, written by the editors Fairhead et al. (2012), 237. For an overview of relevant green grabbing publications, also see Steps Centre (25 April 2012).

deals—depending on the regulatory context of the host country—were in effect land leases rather than purchases.[48]

With time, more sub-themes emerged. For instance, the definition of "land grabbing" was broadened by some authors to include a wide range of land-consuming investments, such as tourism, infrastructure, and mining.[49]This broader definition illuminates the land-use competition dynamics at play. Additionally, the notion of "grabbing" was taken up by (often environmental) researchers and applied to other resources whose "grabbing" seemed to be part of the "land grab" package, particularly water and forests. The briefing by Skinner and Cotula, titled "Are land deals driving 'water grabs'?" is an example of this discursive shift from a focus on peasant struggles and food security to the topic of comprehensive and integrated resource management.[50] The publication highlighted that the Malian government transferred water (use) rights together with land (use) rights to large investors, "with little regard for how this will impact the millions of other users—from fisherman to pastoralists."[51] It also warned about the potential consequences of such transfers, namely the corresponding inflexibility and exclusiveness that would hamper future attempts to implement comprehensive resource management in the affected countries.[52] The latter aspect has been underlined by research on the relation of population, land use, and land ownership; for example, a study on the UK concludes that private land ownership at a time of rising eco-scarcity and climate change is unsustainable and might necessitate a public intervention in the medium term in order to regain the land planning capacity needed "for the successful management and security" of key social needs, namely "housing, food, energy, water, waste, ecosystems, transport and utilities."[53]

Simultaneous to the build-up of empirical case studies and the diversification of the debate, there has also been a rising number of distinct analytical approaches observable in the academic "land grab" debate. The phenomenon has been investigated using (multiple) theoretical frames and related concepts of political ecology,[54] Marxism,[55] world system theory,[56] mainstream econom-

---

48 | IIED/ FAO/IFAD (2009); D. Hall (2013).
49 | See GLP (2010) and ILC (2012).
50 | Skinner and Cotula (2011).
51 | Skinner and Cotula (2011), 1. Also see Smaller and Mann (2009) and Bizikova et al. (2013), 1.
52 | Skinner and Cotula (2011).
53 | Home (2009), 107.
54 | White et al. (2012).
55 | Oya (2013a).
56 | Baumann (2013).

ics,[57] human rights,[58] peasant studies,[59] gender studies,[60] political economy,[61] discourse analysis,[62] and/or (global) governance.[63] This varied body of analytical approaches has contributed to a more comprehensive understanding of what seems to be happening by studying the object from multiple angles.

However, these assessments largely focus on the host country and IFDI-side of "land grabbing." Moreover, the existing explanations of what is happening, and why, remain divided between two analytical trends. On the one hand, fairly structuralist approaches address transnational zero-sum dynamics, but neglect to account for more complex or less clear dynamics on a case by case basis. Take, for example, the Marxist or political ecology delineations, which often limit their focus to instances of, and pre-assumed ideas about "accumulation through dispossession"[64] and/or the transnational, socioeconomic, and environmental consequences of land-intensive policies, such as the renewable energy policies.[65] On the other hand, when examining more case-based analyses in the area of human geography[66] that do examine the details of local politics and the concrete business models of particular investors, they lack a structural outlook that would place the findings in the broader context of (trans)national developments and home country dynamics that they are part of—including economic restructuring and/or geopolitical strategizing.[67]

Overall, the debate about "land grabbing" still suffers from being "both wide and narrow," not only with regard to analytical explanations, as highlighted above, but also in terms of focus on investments in farmland.[68] FAO case studies, for instance, account merely for "broad processes of rural land and capital concentration in the context of neoliberal globalization,"[69] and confine the assessment to themes of food security, foreign government involvement,

---

57 | WB (2011).
58 | Bernstorff (2013); and Golay and Biglino (2013).
59 | Jansen (2014).
60 | Zetterlund (2013).
61 | Chasukwa (2013).
62 | Li (2012).
63 | Margulis et al. (2013).
64 | Harvey (2003), 137-182; also see the critical commentary on this framing by D. Hall (2013).
65 | Ariza-Montobbio et al. (2010); Borras et al. (2010); and Fairhead, et al. (2012).
66 | Boamah (2011).
67 | The special issue "Governing the Global Land Grab: The Role of the State in the Rush for Land" in *Development and Change* 44:2 (Wolford et al. (2013a)) tries to address this problem.
68 | Borras et al. (2012), 847. Amanor (2012), 731-49.
69 | Borras et al. (2012), 847.

and the significance of scale. Environmental groups[70] primarily focus on the problem of resource security, often without consideration for social implications, while land governance research[71] tends to leave out the ecological implications of "land grabs."

Moreover, studies generally do not account sufficiently for the differences and commonalities between and within regions, while the emphasis on conflictive land deals in Africa has yielded a particular understanding of the "land grabbing" dynamics that does not seem to be applicable to other parts of the world.[72] Take, for instance, "land grabbing" in Latin America, where empirical evidence shows that land acquisitions are largely made by regional or domestic actors rather than extra-regional actors as in Africa, and that they mostly occurred prior to the year 2000. Due to the narrow focus on foreign investors, these trends often remain invisible in many of the aggregate accounts on the phenomenon which center on foreign investments since 2008.[73]

Finally, a large share of the research output concentrates on host countries and the implications of capital imports, whereas the depiction of investor countries relies strongly on preconceived notions of their motivations.[74] Home country governments and corporations, so goes the narrative, acquire (farm) land overseas to produce food and other primary resources for export back home; or speculate on rising land values and commodity prices. The few (yet rising number of) studies that do provide a detailed assessment all call to question related stereotypes.[75]

---

70 | Bizikova et al. (2013).
71 | ILC (2012).
72 | See the interview with Saturnino Jr. Borras on *The Water Channel* (http://www.thewaterchannel.tv/en/videos/categories/viewvideo/1387/food-security/5-ways-to-re-think-land-grabs).
73 | Borras et al. (2012), 847.
74 | Again, these preconceived notions about investor country's rationales largely reflect on the predominance of themes of the first "land grab" publication by GRAIN (2008).
75 | See, for instance, D. Hall (2012) on Japan; and Alden (2007); Brautigam (2009); Ekman (2010); Rosen and Hanemann (2009); Smaller et al. (2012); Cotula (2012) on China.

5. WHAT ABOUT POLICY? INFLUENTIAL FRAMES AND PARADIGMS IN THE DEBATE

The range of analytical approaches to study the "land grabbing" phenomenon has diversified with time, particularly regarding the dynamics in the host countries. At the same time, standard narratives that framed the debate in the beginning remain influential concerning investor and home country perspectives.[76] It is in this context that the policy debate comes into view: not only is the policy debate a major component of the overall body of research on "land grabbing;" it also is one of the factors explaining the normative outlook of the debate.

Specifically, the policy debate is characterized by a competition of different framings regarding the problem definition of "land grabbing." The focus remains largely limited to investments in agricultural production, in spite of the empirical evidence that emphasizes the importance of other land-consuming activities in the global "land grab,"[77] such as tourism, infrastructure, manufacturing, and mining. In addition, most documents have a reductionist explanation of why international land acquisitions are occurring at this moment in time, based on economic notions of supply, demand, and international crises/resource scarcities that are also a core part of many academic explanations.[78]

In practice, the academic and policy debates overlap in view of framings and persons, making it often impossible to clearly differentiate between scholarly and policy-related research outputs. For instance, the NGO publication by GRAIN set the tone and focus of the debate on "(farm)land grabbing," and the original assessment and problem definition continues to inform a significant share of academic research or media output.[79] Moreover, the work of certain actors, such as Deininger from the WB, is published and widely cited in academic as well as policy channels. Deininger's publications are referenced in the "land grab" literature as a source of empirical evidence, and/or

---
76 | Borras and Franco (2012), 38. ILC (2012), 4.
77 | See, for instance, Skinner and Cotula (2011).
78 | Accordingly, the increasing food commodity demand (e.g., population growth and rising middle class), declining food supply (e.g., climate change and biofuel production), and the financial crisis (e.g., search for new speculative assets and biofuel production reducing food production) have led to a rise in food prices. As a result, there has been a surge in "FDI in land, agriculture, forestry" motivated by the profit rationales of private investors, and a strategy by investor countries to engage in "offshore" production to increase global supply and/or secure resources for import back home. Time-wise, the international food and financial crisis in 2007/2008 has become the marker to explain the occurrence of "land grabbing" in time. See ILC (2012), 4. Also, see Weingärtner (2010), 13.
79 | Simantke (12 August 2013).

discussed regarding their conceptual validity.[80] In particular, the World Bank report[81] on large-scale land acquisitions,—produced under the lead authorship of Deininger and Byerlee—has stirred a conceptual and highly normative debate in the "land grab" literature. In this context, Starr writes that Deininger and Byerlee "are among a handful of authors who have built typologies of land deals."[82]

This section will present key framings of the policy debate and their respective actor constellations. The debate has at its core a process of contestation or defense of the prevailing operative paradigm of (inter)national economic governance; and is shaped by (the interests behind) the three predominant analytical approaches. The next paragraphs will discuss these approaches under the labels of peasant activism, mainstream economics, and Right to Food.

Peasant Activism

Central to the policy debate on "land grabs" is the corresponding framing by GRAIN that is a function of a peasant activist worldview and shared by other civil society organizations, such as the international NGO, La Via Campesina. Its recommendations are closely aligned with the policy advice of the final report of the International Assessment of Agricultural Science and Technology for Development, an intergovernmental panel under the co-sponsorship of the FAO, Global Environmental Fund (GEF), United Nations Development Programme (UNDP), United Nations Environment Programme (UNEP), United Nations Educational, Scientific and Cultural Organization (UNESCO), the WB, and the World Health Organization (WHO) (2005–2007) which was entrusted to assess how agriculture, science, and technology could contribute to a rural development process that was socially, economically, and environmentally sustainable.[83] This peasant activist framing challenges the predominant frame of mainstream economics (see below).

According to the peasant activist worldview, the fundamental complex of problems identified with regard to international land acquisitions relates to the fact that "fertile agricultural land is becoming increasingly privatized and concentrated," a tendency that "could spell the end of small-scale farming, and rural

---

80 | Voget-Kleschin and Stephan (2013) referencing Deininger's work as empirical input. Also, see critical discussion of Deininger's work in view of concepts and norms in Li (2011); Wolford et al. (2013a); McMichael (2014).
81 | WB (2011).
82 | Starr (2013), 6.
83 | IAASTD (2008). See more under the internal NGO website on the International Assessment of Agricultural Knowledge, Science, and Technology for Development, IAASTD (http://www.agassessment.org/).

livelihoods, in numerous places around the world"—"[i]f left unchecked."[84] In particular, four problems stand out as worrisome: firstly, the securing of food supplies overseas by state-capitalist countries that have lost faith in the market and are bypassing existing market structures to reduce food import costs, thereby aggravating the world food crisis. The second problem is the loss of access to, and control over land by local communities and governments, and the prioritizing of "large industrial estates" that are connected to world markets – all of which will undermine the future ability of countries and communities to implement the concept of food sovereignty. The third issue is the lack of sustainable investment planning by host governments in two areas: a long-term vision of economic activity and agricultural development, both of which are necessary to ensure that agricultural investment contributes to rural development. Then fourthly and finally, there is the difficulty of food insecurity in host countries that are themselves net food importers, which might be growing as a result of these investments, particularly as the policy leaning in these countries heads towards an industrial model of export-oriented agriculture with a track record of "creating poverty and environmental destruction, and exacerbating loss of biodiversity, pollution from farm chemicals and crop contamination from modified organisms."[85]

Food sovereignty is a central concept in this framing, and it takes on multiple functions as analytical tool, as well as vision, depending on who is promoting it.[86] Going against the descriptive concept of food security which remains silent about how and by whom such security should be achieved, the concept of food sovereignty deliberately "puts the aspirations and needs of those who produce, distribute and consume food at the heart of food systems and policies rather than the demands of markets and corporations"—to use the words of the Declaration of the Forum for Food Sovereignty.[87] It provides an antithetic frame to the mainstream economic paradigm and the related "corporate trade and food regime,"[88] and it also represents part of a mobilizing rhetoric that passes the "revolutionary agency [...] from the proletariat to the

---

84 | GRAIN (2008), 1.
85 | GRAIN (2008), 7-8.
86 | See, for instance, the papers presented at the Agrarian Studies Conference "Food Sovereignty: A Critical Dialogue" at Yale University, 14-15 September 2013 (http://www.yale.edu/agrarianstudies/foodsovereignty/) and at the ISS in The Hague, Erasmus University Rotterdam, 24 January 2014 (http://www.iss.nl/news_events/iss_news/detail/article/57242-food-sovereignty-a-critical-dialogue/).
87 | At the first multi-stakeholder Forum for Food Sovereignty in Mali in 2007, participants endorsed the Declaration of Nyéléni, which sets out the core principles of food sovereignty. See Nyéléni (2007); Rosset (2011); and Clapp (2015).
88 | Nyéléni (2007).

peasantry."[89] The latter aspect differentiates it from Marxist framings,[90] and it re-politicizes the questions of resource management in view of use, access, control, distribution, and location.[91]

In practice, the actors that use this food sovereignty perspective, such as FIAN and GRAIN, have cooperated with the FAO in an initiative to develop guidelines for the governance of land tenure and natural resources which are supposed to ensure "adequate and secure access to land and natural resources by the rural and urban poor" and *serve as* "an instrument for social movements, marginalized groups and civil society at large democratizing land and natural resources tenure for the well-being of the whole society."[92] In May 2012, after three years of negotiations between multiple stakeholders (governments and civil society organizations) the FAO's Committee on World Food Security recognized suitable principles and practices under the "Voluntary Guidelines on the Responsible Governance of Tenure of Land, Fisheries and Forests."[93]

Overall, the peasant activist framing has questioned the notion, widespread in mainstream economics, that the location of capital ownership is irrelevant to assessing its potential impact or related implications for the host country. It has also mobilized widespread political support. However, from a methodological and analytical point of view, the framing has several shortcomings. For instance, it reflects a certain degree of peasant essentialism.[94] This is necessary for ascribing "revolutionary agency"[95] to the peasantry, but it also poses a methodological challenge. According to Bernstein and Byres, this challenge lies in the "argument (or assumption) that the core elements of peasant 'society'—household, kin, community, locale—produce (or express) a distinctive internal logic or dynamic, whether cultural, sociological, economic, or in some combination,"[96] which is oppressed by external actors and factors.[97] This assumption does not match empirical evidence on "land grabbing," which calls into question the unitary (essentialist) peasantry presumption, as highlighted before.[98] So far, the food sovereignty concept does not sufficiently explain how it can be gradually realized and implemented in countries where corporations

---

89 | Brass (1997).
90 | For a comparison of Marxism and peasant populism, see Brass (1997).
91 | Nyéléni (2007).
92 | Suárez et al. (2009), 1.
93 | See PANAP (2013) (http://www.panap.net/en/fs/page/food-sovereignty/77); and FAO (2012b).
94 | Bernstein and Byres (2001).
95 | Brass (1997), 27.
96 | Bernstein and Byres (2001), 6-7.
97 | Bernstein (1977), 73.
98 | D. Hall (2011); Steggerda and Visser (2012); and Boamah (2014).

are already important actors in food production and trade activities; in countries where peasants are integrated in the corporate food and trade system through outgrower schemes and/or processes of de-peasantization are at work; or against the background of a global setting in which the prevalence of private governance schemes (i.e. transnational supermarket chains) has led to the systemic marginalization of local voice and/or representation, while agriculture has become part of the food business within the global governance structures.[99] From a systemic point of view, the primary focus on the Global South underestimates equal processes in the Global North, while perhaps overemphasizing the role of foreign investors in the "land grab" dynamics.

Mainstream Economics

The second worldview, the one challenged by the peasant activist framing of "land grabbing," is composed of the models and assumptions of mainstream economics. It refers to "land grabs" as "international land acquisitions" or "investment projects," and it applies a supply/demand market lens to the phenomenon. Compared to the activist peasant framing, which supports an agro-ecological model, the mainstream economics framing promotes a productionist agricultural model with life science elements.[100] It associates the transition from small- to large-scale farming with economic development, often constricts the analysis of poverty to an evaluation of income levels, and supports the coexistence of genetically modified and organic, peasant and industrial farming. In the policy debate, the mainstream economic frame is applied by key policy entrepreneurs and policy makers, such as the WB,[101] bilateral development agencies,[102] many host governments' national development plans, and/or private actors.

The most influential framing in (inter)national economic governance since the 1980s, this mainstream economic worldview does not identify "rising global interest in farmland" by corporate investors or government companies as itself problematic.[103] Instead, international land acquisitions are proof of the underpinning assumption that the "market" is driven by supply and demand and that it has a natural "tendency toward convergence, toward equilibrium"[104]

---

99 | Konefal et al. (2005).
100 | Classification taken from Lang and Heasman (2004), 126-167.
101 | WB (2007); WB (2011).
102 | Weingärtner (2010).
103 | WB (2011), xxv.
104 | This argument rests on Harvey's Marxist reflection on conventional economics: "So conventional economics is always talking about the tendency toward convergence, toward equilibrium, and that equilibrium is possible provided the right mix of policies

of the factors of production. International land acquisitions are seen as part of a market process in which land-scarce but capital-rich countries (or their corporations) invest in land-abundant but capital-poor countries, creating a "win-win" scenario and development opportunity. Importantly, this assessment is a core component of the standard explanations of investor motives.

According to the theoretical appraisal of FDI under the liberal paradigm, benefits for host countries come from multiple factors. FDI projects make domestic capital available for other uses of public benefit; transfer and diffuse technology; create new employment; build capacity (new job profiles); transfer skills (labor); and build necessary public infrastructure.[105] Against the background of decreasing aid flows and tight public budgets, such capital imports allow the host countries to increase productivity and efficiency levels in the agricultural sector and to improve food (supply) security both domestically (due to corresponding increases in food supply and income levels) and globally.[106] This narrative is supported by a technical discussion that identifies "yield gaps" (i.e., the difference between the potential and the actual amount of crops grown in a country) as problem that these investments help to close.[107]

The problem then is empirical. Emerging evidence about "large-scale land acquisitions" highlights that in practice, many investment projects do not live up to their theoretical promise. In its 2011 report, the WB admits that in addition to low job creation, many projects turn out to be economically unviable, do not improve food security or productivity levels significantly, and have a negative impact on rural livelihoods.[108] Consequently, good governance mechanisms are suggested as the solution to the negative side effects of the commercial pressure on land. These take the form of a voluntary set of "Principles for Responsible Agro-Investment" that corporate investors should abide by; the establishment of "effective consultation" that comprises representation, administration, and monitoring; the development and improvement of transparent land transfer mechanisms; the introduction of an open land market; and the negotiation of terms of investment that distribute the benefits more equitably in the recipient context.[109] Moreover, Deininger, lead economist in the rural development

---

and as long as there isn't anything external that disrupts the whole system. External problems would be so-called natural disasters, wars, geopolitical conflicts, and protectionism. Crisis would then arise because of these external interventions, which take us away from the path to equilibrium, which is always possible." See Harvey, D., & Rivera, H.A. (September 2010).

105 | WB (2011), 2.
106 | WB (2011).
107 | E.g., WB (2011); also see Li (2012).
108 | WB (2011), 51; WB (7 September 2010).
109 | WB (2011), xiiv, xxv.

group within the WB's Development Research Department, argues that the focus should be on raising the productivity of land under cultivation, rather than focusing on land expansion.[110]

Overall, this framework runs into several problems that have been outlined before when trying to assess or solve what is happening in the context of "land grabbing." The narrow focus on productivity and efficiency in the context of food security, and on transparency and good governance in view of land deals, prevents the identification of structural problems that might greatly impede the multiplier effect of agriculture. For instance, the assessment leaves aside aspects of political economy, and it argues for the coexistence of peasant and corporate farming, thereby masking asymmetric power constellations in the global food and trade regime.[111] Moreover, the fact that FDIs are not only capital flows but also part of "a process whereby residents of one country (the investor country) acquire ownership for the purpose of controlling the production, distribution and other activities of a firm"[112] and/or land in another country is left outside the mainstream economic assessment of productivity and governance. Yet, it is exactly this aspect of international investment that has been critiqued for its political, environmental and socioeconomic implications.

Consequently, assessments using this frame tend to negate the problematic history of FDI in the form of colonialisms and imperialisms, and they are in constant danger of continuing the disreputable "tradition of imperial historiography,"[113] with its uncritical description of the first wave of globalization.[114] At the same time, such analyses remain inconsistent. It is, for instance, unclear why such reports end on overly optimistic notes by suggesting that the benefits of international land acquisitions can be captured through good governance, even though major host countries show deteriorating governance performance

---

110 | WB (7 September 2010).
111 | WB (2011).
112 | Moosa (2002), 1.
113 | Mann (2012), 406.
114 | See, for instance, the WB (2010, 2) on overseas investments. The report refers to the East India Company as a (positive) example of FDI: "Like trade, foreign direct investment (FDI) has occurred throughout history. From the merchants of Sumer around 2500 BCE to the East India Company in the 17th century, investors routinely entered new markets in foreign dominions." Such a narrow framing of capital flows obscures the very violent history of FDI enterprises, such as the East India Company. It also fails to mention that this example is hardly suited to the promotion of "free market" policies, as the empirical reality of that time was characterized by trade monopolies and/or alien investment restrictions. Also see the historical review of late 19th century colonialisms and imperialisms in Chapter 3; Mann (2012); and Davis (2002), 11-13.

according to the WB's governance assessment method.[115] Most problematic, however, is the unwillingness or failure to engage in more profound reflection about the sources of the current crises in the fields of agriculture, environment, and governance,[116] and one that constitutes a general problem in the available body of research on land-consuming FDI and commercial pressure on land.

Right to Food

The third framing in the policy debate about "land grabbing," the Right to Food approach, has been promoted by both civil society and the UN Special Rapporteur on the Right to Food, Olivier De Schutter (2008-2014). Focusing on the human rights challenge represented by increased commercial and speculative interest in land, the *right to food* framing considers issues of access, culture, and livelihood that are impacted by shifts in access to, and ownership of land.[117]

De Schutter criticizes the widespread assumption that the problems associated with large-scale investments in farming can be solved simply through regulation based on (voluntary) principles and governance approaches, such as the above-mentioned Principles for Responsible Agricultural Investment (RAI) put forward by the WB, or the FAO's Voluntary Guidelines.[118] These governance approaches were developed and promoted by the very same institutions whose policy advocacy has in the recent past contributed greatly to the "land grab;" for example, by advising host governments to "cut [...] down administrative requirements and consultations that might slow down or restrict investments" by foreign investors.[119] The question of regulation also ignores the "question of opportunity costs"[120] brought about by acquisition-related changes in land access and ownership. For instance, the *right to food* could be undermined since large-scale investments in farmland (and related processes of concentration of resources and power) tend to reduce the multiple favorable effects of agriculture in view of rural development. Meanwhile, regulation is likely to actually

---

115 | Worldwide Governance Indicators by WB (http://info.worldbank.org/gover nance/wgi2007/sc_chart.asp#).
116 | De Schutter (2011a), 274-275; De Schutter (2009), 15.
117 | The definition says that "the right to food is the right to have regular, permanent and unrestricted access, either directly or by means of financial purchases, to quantitatively and qualitatively adequate and sufficient food corresponding to the cultural traditions of the people to which the consumer belongs, and which ensure a physical and mental, individual and collective, fulfilling and dignified life free of fear." See United Nations Human Rights, Office of the High Commissioner for Human Rights (n.d.) .
118 | De Schutter (2011a); FAO (2012b).
119 | Compare also Shepard and Mittal (2009); quote from De Schutter (2011a), 254.
120 | De Schutter (2011a), 255.

increase the commercial pressure on land and other resources.[121] Moreover, the governance initiatives proposed by the FAO and WB are arguably marginal in comparison to pre-existing treaties, agreements, and related obligations which both restrict the performance requirements that can be imposed on foreign investors[122] and severely limit the leeway of host governments to negotiate and steer investments in their interest or seek alternative investment models that do not result in changes of access or ownership, for instance, through contract farming.[123]

Thus, the human rights framing identifies the absence of (a broader debate about) a strategy and long-term vision of rights-based resource management as a key problem that needs to be addressed—particularly in view of growing commercial pressures, of which "land grabbing" is one.[124] Accordingly, the question is how to invest in a way that best takes into consideration the "context of ecological, food, and energy crises."[125] In practice, the approach proposes Minimum Human Rights principles.[126] These define states' obligations on the basis of already existing human rights instruments "to clarify the human rights implications of land-related investments, in order to make it clear that governments had obligations they could not simply ignore for the sake of attracting capital."[127] The key elements of the principles are related to the right of self-determination and the right to development, both of which call for governments to ensure that investments do not weaken food security by generating a dependency on foreign aid or volatile markets if the produced food is intended for export (to the home country or the international market); that they do not dispossess local populations from productive resources indispensable for their livelihood; and that they protect workers' rights and tenure rights.[128]

The human rights approach provides a comprehensive analytical basis for questioning the limitations of the predominant policy frame of mainstream economics in terms of solving the relevant problems, as it accounts for aspects of political economy and ecology, but goes beyond the strong producer-rights-orientation of food sovereignty. However, and this is due to the nature of the

---

121 | De Schutter (2011a), 249.
122 | The legal agreement on Trade-Related Investment Measures (TRIMS), for instance, regulates the treatment of foreign investors by host countries. The agreement is part of the WTO regime, and it bans local content requirements and trade balancing rules from the (industrial) policy framework of signatory countries.
123 | De Schutter (2011a), 250, 266.
124 | De Schutter (2011a), 275.
125 | De Schutter (2011a), 250.
126 | De Schutter (2011a), 253.
127 | De Schutter (2011a), 254.
128 | De Schutter (2009).

UN Special Rapporteur on the Right to Food's mandate, it continues to focus primarily on investments in farmland, even though commercial pressure on land comes from multiple sources, namely industrialization and urbanization. Moreover, while putting the role and responsibility of host country governments in the spotlight of analysis, the responsibilities of investor countries remain largely ignored. Given that land-consuming domestic policies in the form of renewable energy policy for biofuels, as well as unsustainable consumption and production patterns in home countries,[129] are among the factors driving "land grabs," it seems that a crucial link in the rights-based resource management approach is still missing. As long as this aspect remains unaddressed, home country governments will continue to make unsustainable policy choices that have global repercussions. Notably, the rights-based approach itself might pose more challenges than solutions. While ideally delivering a strong analytical and legal instrument to judge the performance of states in fulfilling their obligations towards their citizens—revealing an important aspect that should be part of the responsibility that comes with sovereignty—its reliance on legal structures might prove ineffective in countries with weak legal capacities, limited rule of law, and a high degree of corruption.

6. Conclusion

The rising number and increasingly differentiated body of empirical studies and analytical approaches on the topic contributes to a more nuanced yet comprehensive understanding of what seems to be happening with regards to the empirical phenomenon of "land grabbing." Concurrently, it points out the political nature of the debate which takes place in academia as well as policy circles; and in which competing frames seem to be as important as empirical facts in shaping the perspectives, narratives, and responses towards land-consuming OFDI. This is also evidenced by the politics of terminology that sometimes cloud our understanding of what is happening.

---

129 | Analyses of society-nature interactions show that industrialization led to a dramatic increase in the material use per capita. In fact, the material use doubled in the global economy, even though the material intensity (i.e. materials used per unit of GDP) declined over time. Overall, the material use "increased 8-fold" on a global scale from the beginning of the 20th century to 2005. A closer assessment highlights distinct trajectories of consumption of different materials: while "biomass use hardly keeps up with population growth," mineral use increases dramatically, indicating that "an increase in material productivity is a general feature of economic development." See Krausmann et al. (2009), 2696; and Krausmann et al. (2008).

Overall, the review underlines the need for a critical handling of data and potential explanations throughout the research process. It has also become evident that certain aspects of "land grabbing" and commercial pressure on land are often absent from the academic and policy debate. Take, for example, the historical transformation of institutions, ideas, and political economies at the national, local, and international level that has resulted in natural resources, such as land and forests, being relatively accessible through economic mechanisms in many countries' economies today.[130] This constitutes a fundamental change from previous approaches and institutions that restricted foreign access to food and land, framing these resources as critical infrastructure to meet a society's basic social needs.[131]

In addition, the policy debate, which is largely reflective of the contemporary actor constellation in the area of agriculture, needs to start incorporating non-farming aspects of commercial land pressure highlighted in the "land grab" literature, as these impact farming in the form of land use and ownership changes, soil erosion, or migratory pressures (as a side effect of extractive industry). Interestingly, these aspects have so far primarily entered the policy dialogue through broader development debates outside the issue of "land grabbing," such as the negotiations over the Post-2015 Development Agenda, or the development and application of certain methods of measurement (e.g., virtual land imports).[132] Moreover, more academic and policy-relevant research about the implications of land-consuming FDI and related changes in rural development for regions, urban populations, and local, national, and global food systems would be important to grasp the multiple repercussions in terms of food security, conflict, exodus, health, and demographic development that this trend might be part of or cause.

Regarding the investor countries, the following assumptions persist about how and why "land grabs" occur, particularly in the large majority of reports that study the host country context: foreign governments and corporations are involved in land-consuming OFDI through land-intensive policies (e.g., green grabbing); the launching of offshore agricultural production to secure resources for consumption back home; and/or the search for profitable business at a time of financial crisis.[133]

---

130 | WB (2010), 25-26.
131 | This fact is, for instance, reflected in governance systems that restricted alien land ownership at the time of the last international food crises in the 1970s; and it calls for case-based research on how this transition towards liberalizing access to primary resources occurred in different countries. Compare Weisman (1980) and WB (2010).
132 | E.g., Tortajada (2013); and Marmo (2013).
133 | Borras and Franco (2012), 38.

It has been argued earlier that this explanation does not offer any evidence on the home country and/or project-specific (f)actors at play. Moreover, this explanation easily undervalues the role of host country actors, institutions, and contingent events in the commercial pressure on land. Therefore, the following chapters present rich empirical data about project timelines; the role of land in these investments; the markets they produce for; the range of actors involved in a single project throughout its lifecycle; the role of the ecological, financial, food and/or other crises; the political economies; and/or the cluster of ideas that are part of Chinese and British land-consuming OFDI. On the basis of the rich empirical accounts of the two countries' overseas investments, the book identifies the main country-specific as well as cross-country dynamics and factors at play, compares the findings with the above assumptions, and deliberates on the role of OFDI from a home country perspective.

Chapter 3: Historical Perspectives on Overseas Land Acquisitions in the South

1. Introduction

In view of the question of what differentiates the allegedly new "global land rush" from those of earlier times, the "land grab" debate since 2008 remains inconclusive. The ILC report argues that the international timelines can only explain the surge of acquisitions, while "[t]he dispossession and marginalization of the rural poor are nothing new."[1] Accordingly, the "land rush represents an acceleration of ongoing processes, and one that appears set to continue."[2] A UN Briefing states that the novelty of the phenomenon is to be found in the details, namely the trend towards offshore production by major investor countries "to meet home state food and energy needs."[3] This largely follows the argument presented by GRAIN.[4] Meanwhile, a study by the Woodrow Wilson International Center argues that details such as their scale and their focus on "staples instead of cash crops" distinguish contemporary land investments from previous ones—together with the fact that they occur on a contractual basis "instead of through the barrel of a gun."[5] Excepting these very broad references to historical incidents of foreign investments at a time of colonialism and imperialism, there are few detailed comparisons of institutional or other empirical characteristics. Alden Wily, for instance, studies the legal practices of "land theft" during the Irish and English enclosures of the 17th to 19th centuries, the processes of dispossession in North America, and the Scramble for Africa in the late 19th century. She concludes that the historical use of legal

---

1 | ILC (2012), 4.
2 | ILC (2012), 4.
3 | UN DESA (2010), 1.
4 | GRAIN (2008).
5 | Kugelman (2009), 4-5.

instruments by the state to dispossess traditional land owners strongly resembles current practices.⁶

This chapter assesses the main empirical characteristics of, and key theoretical explanations for colonial and imperial relations in the late 19th century – a period of European imperialism (1870-1914) that is often referred to as the "high-water mark of nineteenth century globalization."⁷ As such it shares many features that are characteristic of the contemporary world, namely large and growing "transfers of commodities, people, capital, and ideas between and within continents."⁸ The period was also shaped by imperial expansion through colonization and continues to strongly inform the common notions of colonialism and imperialism prevalent today. Moreover, core ideas and practices of contemporary development approaches can often be traced back to that era.⁹ The focus of the review is largely on the perspective of the imperial powers.

As a result, the review critically interrogates simplified references to imperialism/colonialism in the contemporary "land grab" debate. While some researchers argue that ongoing land-consuming FDI is the "new age" version of colonialism characterized by deregulated markets and state involvement, other analyses conclude that colonial "land grabbing" has been replaced by a form of corporate "land grabbing."¹⁰ Yet, the respective allusion to colonialism or imperialism seems largely a function of political sentiment rather than the outcome of a careful conceptual and empirical comparison of land-consuming investments over time. Take, for example, the article on Chinese investments in Africa by Jauch in which the author compares these to colonial undertakings on the basis of their poor labor records and strong resource orientation.¹¹ Clearly, such a reduced understanding of what constitutes imperial or colonial phenomena is problematic, and any comparison of the past and present that rests on such a limited set of criteria—i.e. one that could be applied to many contemporary contexts within and across countries worldwide—will prove rather meaningless. Thus, this review aims to present a more useful theoretical and empirical basis for later discussion of the extent to which the imperial or colonial framing adequately captures what is happening today.

The key findings of this chapter are that the late 19th century trade and investment relations, which followed earlier imperial expansion in the Americas and India, differ greatly from contemporary explanations of "land

---

6 | Alden Wily (2012).
7 | Daudin et al. (2010), 6.
8 | Daudin et al. (2010), 6.
9 | Kegley and Raymond (2011), 110-112, and Craggs (2014), 5-9.
10 | See, for instance, Jauch (2011); Broughton (6 November 2012); Liberti 2012; Aziz (15 April 2011); and Sadeque (2012).
11 | Jauch (2011).

grabbing." While the latter seem to assume that land acquisitions made since 2000 resemble colonial undertakings due to their primary rational interest in land as a natural resource, historical evidence highlights that factors and motivations extended well beyond a narrow focus on natural resources. From an investor country perspective, colonial and imperial relations between the North and South, and related "divisions of labor," were driven by domestic development processes, such as the process of industrialization in the home countries and the economic crisis of the 1870s, which led to the search for new (exclusive) markets. Moreover, the dynamic was a reflection of the political economy of aristocracy in which losses in land value, an outcome of industrialization, led landed elites to secure their wealth status by investing overseas. Other enabling or influential factors at the time were breakthroughs in technological and medical capacity, especially innovations in the transport sector and malaria medicine; and external events, such as the European state formation, and the great power competition dynamics in Europe.

This means that while the search for gold and the extraction of resources for domestic consumption back home were important characteristics of colonial and imperial expansion, the latter was also about the (violent) opening of consumer markets, the acquisition of strategic assets, the facilitation of planned settlements, and the search for profitable business opportunities and financial services. More broadly, the rationalization of these enterprises in the home country context claimed that they would improve the state's international positional status relative to others; or, as in the case of Belgium, the enterprises simply reflected an individually felt need by the ruler for self-aggrandizement in comparison to other nations.[12] This diversity of interests and factors is also evident on the policy level. Home countries' imperial economic policies were biased towards, yet not exclusively focused on, the production of raw materials overseas. Government actors but also business associations had very different understandings of imperial politics, resulting in a lack of any clear-cut strategy or plan for colonial development.[13]

In addition to this complex character of imperial and colonial undertakings, historical research questions the widespread assumption, present in many theoretical explanations (and visible in contemporary government and corporate rhetoric), about the utility of international land acquisitions for the home country and/or investor. Contrary to the accompanying rhetoric of efficiency, profit, necessity, or significance used by actors in the past and present to justify, motivate, or explain territorial and/or economic expansion and related capital exports, empirical evidence illustrates that in practice a high percentage of overseas investment projects did not generate profits or failed, and that

---

12 | See, for instance, Olukoju (2002); Green (1999); and Davis (1999).
13 | See Schmitt (1979); and Davis (1999).

projects did not automatically promise higher returns than investments back home. Instead, they were often the outcome of a metropolitan bias or non-economic interest constellations. This makes it very difficult to assess whether the benefits of these endeavors outweighed the costs for the home country.[14] At a minimum, the expansion overseas provided temporary career and income options for those involved in it, and in doing so may have contributed to political regime stability in the home countries. Most importantly, the historical and theoretical research underlines the importance of studying OFDI in the context of a home country's political economy, ideology, and development in order to achieve a better understanding of what is happening.

The remainder of this chapter will proceed as follows: starting with the key theoretical explanations (Section 2) and main international parameters (Section 3) of international land acquisitions between 1870 and 1914 in the South, the review will then look more closely at the "Scramble for Africa" due to the relevance of contemporary investment flows to Africa, but also because the Scramble has become synonymous with the imperial expansion of that era (Section 4). It will also highlight key aspects of institutional path dependency and change post-WWII whose consideration is important for a meaningful understanding of the 'novel' character of what is happening today (Section 5). The chapter concludes with a brief summary of core findings (Section 6).

2. Imperialism and Colonialism— Key Theoretical Explanations

Historical materialist, liberal, world systems, and political theories are relevant for the study of international land acquisitions insofar as they: (1) outline various factors and potential causal mechanisms to be taken into account during the process of assessing "land grabs;" (2) underline the importance of systemic dynamics that the individual cases under study might be reflective of or embedded in; and (3) provide an overview of prevailing narratives about imperialism that are present in the public perception and academic debate about "land grabbing" (e.g., media).[15] Ince, for example, has emphasized that "[o]ne line of inquiry approaches land grabs as instances of "primitive accumulation of capital" whereby lands in the Global South are "enclosed" and brought within the ambit of global capitalism."[16]

---

14 | Argument by Cottrell (1975), 47-53.
15 | Makki and Geisler (2011).
16 | Ince (2013), 104. Also see D. Hall (2013) for a historical materialist interpretation of the "land grab" phenomenon.

Historically, imperialism appeared in many regions, if we consider the Chinese, Roman, and British empires, and it comprised sets of very different features—from the commercial dominion of some countries over others to violent territorial expansion. As a result, multiple definitions and understandings of imperialism exist, reflecting these distinct forms of dominion. At a maximum, imperialism is conceptualized as the "policy or practice of extending a state's rule over other territories," one form of which has been colonialism, defined as "the policy or practice of a power in extending control over weaker peoples or areas."[17] At a minimum, imperialism takes place in indirect forms of "extension [...] of authority, influence, power, etc."[18] Most imperialist undertakings combine(d) multiple forms of dominion, territorial as well as non-territorial, whereas "[o]ver time, the social and political mobilization of opponents of territorial rule in the colonies simply outstripped advances in the technologies of coercion."[19] Non-territorial sources of power related, for instance, to the "dynastic and religious affiliations" of the Habsburg and the Ottoman empires prior to WWI; ideologies of supremacy in the case of European empires prior to and during WWII; and, later, to liberal ideologies (American Imperium) or anti-fascist "ideological capital," in the case of the Soviet Union.[20] Over time, the continuous political and economic power discrepancy between industrialized and developing countries became referred to as a type of imperialistic relationship, with the former dominating the latter.[21]

For the purpose of reviewing experiences of international land acquisitions in the South during the late 19th century—the focus of this chapter—it is important to keep in mind that imperialism and colonialism describe related yet different phenomena. While imperial expansion might involve colonialism as a territorial source of power, it goes beyond this particular form of dominion and includes a specific outlook on world politics/policy. As a result, colonies were not only purposes in themselves for the imperial powers, but they were also used as pledges in global power games, particularly during the late 19th century when the great powers used colonies as potential weights with which to rebalance intra-European power struggles. During that time, colonies were

---

17 | Collins English Dictionary (5th edition, first published in 2000), and Collins A-Z Thesaurus (1st edition, first published in 1995).
18 | Collins English Dictionary (5th edition, first published in 2000), and Collins A-Z Thesaurus (1st edition, first published in 1995).
19 | Katzenstein (2005), 4.
20 | Katzenstein (2005), 4-5. Originally understood as a state strategy, the rise of the American Imperium post-WWII, with its emphasis on free markets and global economic integration, led to the perception that certain phenomena constituted forms of dominion of corporations over states, framed as corporate imperialism.
21 | Prahalad and Lieberthal (2003).

exchanged amongst the great economic powers, and latecomers to the circle of great powers needed to achieve recognition of their new status and/or to negotiate the right to colonize.[22]

Several theories have tried to explain why the "imperial landrush"[23] that characterized the "second wave of European imperialism"[24] in general, and the colonization of Africa in particular, occurred from a home country perspective and in the context of home country development. These shall be briefly introduced in the remainder of this section to raise awareness of potential causal mechanisms in the empirical assessment and analytical explanation of Chinese and British investments in African countries.

One of the most prominent works on the economic, social, ideological, and political dimensions of late 19th century imperialism and colonialism is the study by Hobson,[25] which heavily influenced the subsequent historical materialist treatises on imperialism.[26] In particular, Hobson's economic argument that "excessive powers of production, [and] excessive capital in search of investment" were drivers of British imperialist expansions became (and remained) very influential.[27] Yet, Hobson's study differs greatly from the large body of functional explanations that argues for the inevitability of imperial expansion along these lines. Instead, he suggested that imperial expansion could be prevented by addressing the concentration of wealth in the home country, namely Britain. Accordingly, high inequality combined with increasing productivity composed the "economic taproot of imperialism" in the form of lagging domestic demand, over-saving, and overproduction.[28] This, however, could be remedied through equality-promoting public policy which would balance domestic demand with domestic production.[29] Interestingly, Hobson's related argument about the importance of qualitative rather than quantitative growth efforts—which could be placed under the heading of "inclusive growth"[30]—is very topical again today (as of 2015) in view of the rising inequality within and

---

22 | Rough translation of an argument made by Osterhammel (2009), 27.
23 | Davis (2002), 12.
24 | Kegley and Raymond (2011), 110-112.
25 | Hobson (1965).
26 | Siegelman (1965), v.
27 | Siegelman (1965), xiii.
28 | Hobson (1965), 71-93.
29 | Hobson (1965), 85-92.
30 | See, for instance, the respective OECD initiative on Inclusive Growth (OECD (2015a)). According to the WB (2009), the "difference between pro-poor and inclusive growth is that the pro-poor approach is mainly interested in the welfare of the poor while inclusive growth is concerned with opportunities for the majority of the labor force, poor and middle-class alike." See WB (2009), 1.

across developing and industrialized countries (measured by income and accumulated wealth).[31] Back in his time, Hobson's study clearly offered a counterpoint to influential contemporary voices that justified imperial expansion by referring to it as a national necessity and whose basic rhetorical elements are still common today (see Chapters 5 and 7):

> However costly, however perilous, this process of imperial expansion may be, it is necessary to the continued existence of our nation; if we abandon it we must be content to leave the development of the world to other nations, who will everywhere cut into our trade, and even impair our means of securing the food and raw materials we require to support our population. Imperialism is thus seen to be, not a choice, but a necessity.[32]

While Hobson's study has been criticized by historians for exaggerating the importance of industry and the financial sector in the British empire, his empirical observations about imperialism and colonialism seem noteworthy. Indeed, they provide useful parameters for studying overseas investments from a home country perspective, such as the importance of examining the particular domestic political economy in home countries to understand their foreign economic policy; the significance of ideology in this process; the questionable utility and benefit of these overseas activities for the home country; the importance of public-private partnerships in facilitating overseas economic expansion, with public money used for private gain;[33] and, finally, the fact that the process of economic expansion also has repercussions back home. Moreover, he pointed at the multiplicity of motivations and actors at play, in the form of "patriotism, adventure, military enterprise, political ambition, and philanthropy," all of which constituted the "fuel" for imperial expansion.[34]

Other historical materialist assessments of imperial and colonial relations largely followed Hobson's outlook on the phenomenon, locating the agency in the home country's capitalist development context, though with a deterministic twist. Consequently, imperialist expansion was framed as an inherent component of capitalism, and assumed to be profitable for the home country, which, according to historical evidence, was (often) not the case.[35] Informed by Marxist thought about the crisis of capitalist systems in the form of over-accumula-

---

31 | Hobson (1965), 92. Also, see OECD (2015b) on "social and welfare issues;" and Raghavan (2000).
32 | Hobson (1965), 73.
33 | Hobson (1965), 96-97.
34 | Hobson (1965), 59.
35 | Snyder (1991).

tion,[36] "[t]he consequence of the development of industrial capitalistic societies is a pressure for expansion which may lead to military or political acquisition (colonies) or to maintaining economic dependence (developing countries)."[37] While the various imperialism theories differ in their explanation of the particular reason for "the pressure of expansion," they do share the understanding that imperialism is the "result of the inability to cope internally [i.e. within the spatial limits of the nation-state] with the consequences of permanent technological innovation and their effects on society."[38] Moreover, distinct from the liberal frames with their arguments of efficiency gains, comparative advantage, or the international division of labor, imperialism theories focus on zero-sum dynamics—nationally and internationally—between capital and labor, states, and ecologies.[39]

Another strain of imperialism theory emerged after WWII. In view of the persistent gap in living standards between industrial and developing countries after decolonization, and following the failure of modernization theory's[40]

---

36 | Over-accumulation means that excessive investment occurs and goods cannot be sold profitably. This results in capital increasing in some sectors or speculative endeavors, instead of being re-invested in productive enterprise. Moreover, this may lead to unused plants and equipment, large build-up of unsold commodities, rising unemployment, or the rise of financial markets as alternative outlet.

37 | Kuhnen (1986), 20.

38 | Kuhnen (1986), 20.

39 | Basically, classical imperialism theory (e.g., Luxemburg (1913) and Lenin (1975)) argues that imperialism is not benefitting the development of the colonies. Instead, the "establishment of new markets in underdeveloped areas destroys traditional markets and production relations of these areas. While the expansion creates employment back home, it signifies an export of unemployment to these underdeveloped areas. At the same time, capital exports to these countries are reflective of interests of industrial countries, and not the needs of the recipient areas. Given that profits of these investments are remitted to home countries, this then highlights that these forms of economic expansion are at the core exploitative relationships between industrial and so-called underdeveloped areas, whereas the exploitation of the latter serves the development of the home country." See summary by Kuhnen (1986), 20.

40 | At the core, modernization theories assume that "industrialized countries are the model for economy and society," whereas deviations from this model are framed as "backwardness." Definitions of development as "an increase of production and efficiency," its measurement as GDP and "per capita income," and the analytical dualism promoting the "suppression of the traditional sector by concentrating on and expanding the modern sector," all still inform many programs and policy recommendations of multilateral and bilateral development organizations today. See Kuhnen (1986), 12-13; and Lepenies (2008). Also, see the development narrative of the WB (2007), which development policies to solve this problem, structural difference and related forms of disadvantageous "technological-industrial dependence" were seen as causing the persistence of exploitative relationships between industrial and developing countries.[41] This form of structural dominion occurred through "[i]ndustrial countries invest[ing] in the production and export of raw material in developing countries, influenc[ing] with their potential of power the terms of trade in their favour, and thus perpetuat[ing] the international division of labour" with detrimental effects for developing economies and societies.[42]

At their core, these new imperialism theories, similar to dependency theories, presume that post-WWII underdevelopment is a function of the historical legacy of violent and "asymmetric integration" of developing countries into an international division of labor defined by industrial countries.[43] The economic structure of developing countries—namely the dominance of the primary sector and the export orientation—together with co-opted elites and changes in culture, has contributed to sustaining the international asymmetry characteristic of colonial relations, as well as the pattern of overseas investments by industrial countries. Similarly, Wallerstein's world systems theory differentiates between a wealth and power-related core and periphery of regions, and argues that "the *dependencia*-style linkage between development at the core and underdevelopment in the periphery (uneven development) remains integral to the system and persists through alternating periods of growth and contraction."[44]

---

equates rural development and poverty alleviation with increases in production, efficiency and per capita income.
41 | Kuhnen (1986), 21.
42 | Kuhnen (1986), 21.
43 | In more detail, dependency theories that explain the genesis of underdevelopment in developing countries argue that the asymmetric trade relations of dominion result in "deteriorating exchange relations between industrialized and developing countries (and, as well, between the industrialized and the agricultural sector in developing countries)." Meanwhile, industrialized countries gain from international trade due to the rise in productivity, together with elastic demand for value added products in the world market, both of which result in increasing incomes and positive terms of trade. Developing countries as producers and exporters of primary products cannot reap the assumed benefits from trade. To the contrary, rising productivity in primary production suppresses prices due to an inelastic demand for such products in the world markets, and results in deteriorating incomes as well as terms of trade. At the same time, the falling prices in world markets result in increasing exports to compensate for the worsening terms of trade. See summary of major authors of dependencia theory by Kuhnen (1986), 19-20.
44 | Wolfe (1997), 404.

Deviating from these largely economic accounts of imperialism is, for instance, the political theory of imperialism developed by classical realists. Morgenthau perceives imperialism as a foreign policy of the state. Accordingly, imperialist undertakings aim at increasing a state's power status within the status quo and, in comparison to other states, thereby enhancing the relative security of the more powerful state in the international realm.[45]

3. The International Parameters of 19th-Century European Imperialism

This section complements the previous theoretical review by providing a brief overview of the most important international parameters of 19th century European imperialism. In particular, it will look at the configuration of capital and trade flows during that era in order to assess the quantitative and qualitative dimensions of that era's imperial and colonial relations. That is, what significance did capital exports and trade flows to the colonies have from the perspective of the home country? And what did the trade and investment policies of that time look like? The historical evidence on these questions allows us to derive a meaningful comparison with contemporary capital flows and foreign economic policies that—as this book argues—"land grabs" reflect. It also highlights their role in the context of home country development.

Empirically, the time between 1870 and 1913 has been branded by historians as the "first wave of globalization,"[46] due to the (largely rhetorical) credo of free trade and the laissez faire approach to capital mobility. Geopolitically, this time is referred to as "Pax-Britannica with London constituting the financial center of the world and the British pound the dominant currency in the context of the international gold standard."[47] At the same time, it was also a period that witnessed massive migration flows, reflecting the pressures of industrial development in the home countries and the hopes attached to moving to new lands.[48] Between 1870 and 1914, approximately "60 million people emigrated from [...] Europe to [...] countries of the New World including Argentina, Aus-

---

45 | Morgenthau (2005).
46 | Solimano and Watts (2005), 14.
47 | Solimano and Watts (2005), 14. It is against this background that Bairoch and Kozul-Wright (1996) argue that the myths about 19th century globalization are primarily built on experiences of the British empire, but even in this case they fail to capture the complex character of this era.
48 | Solimano and Watts (2005), 14.

tralia, Brazil, Canada, New Zealand and the United States."[49] A smaller share of migrants also targeted East Africa, Southeast Asia, the Pacific Islands, the Caribbean, and the West Coast of North America.[50]

The historical evidence on overseas investment during the 1870-1914 period stresses three important characteristics, namely the asymmetric significance of trade and investment for the countries involved; the complexity of the sectoral composition of investments that went beyond natural resources; and the interrelation of trade and investment activities with home country events and public policies rather than "free markets."

Firstly, the different significance of imperial/colonial relations for the home country and colony is reflected in the asymmetric regional distribution of investment and trade flows. Empirical data on the regional composition of European capital and trade flows demonstrates that trading and investing primarily happened between the wealthiest countries, including the New World.[51] At the same time, and quite surprisingly, the so-called Scramble for Africa (1876-1914), which is often alluded to in the contemporary "land grab" debate, is not reflected in European investment trends in the form of any significant shifts.[52] Available data on the main international lenders and borrowers shows that in 1913 the major capital exporters were Britain (with 41% of total overseas investments), followed by France (20%) and Germany (13%). Moreover, Europe, North America, and Latin America were the main recipients of the total overseas investment flows, receiving 27%, 24%, and 19%, respectively (Table 3-1).

---

49 | The US was the main destination. Until 1920 about 26 million migrants arrived from "core Europe" (e.g., England, Germany, and France) and "peripheral Europe" (e.g. the relatively poorer Scandinavian countries; Spain, Italy and Portugal in the south; Poland, Russia, Romania to the east; and the former nations of the Austro-Hungarian empire). Also countries in Latin America, such as Argentina, Uruguay, Cuba, Mexico, and Chile absorbed a significant share of European migration. Solimano and Watts (2005), 14.
50 | Solimano and Watts (2005), 16.
51 | Bairoch and Kozul-Wright (1996), 12-13. According to Cottrell (1975, 27), in the case of Britain, "temperate regions of recent settlement" such as Canada and the US received the largest share of the total capital exports, amounting to 68% of the total share between 1865 and 1914.
52 | Cottrell (1975), 27; Cain and Hopkins (1987), 14.

Table 3-1 – Main International Lenders and Borrowers, 1913 (Percentage shares, Bairoch and Kozul-Wright 1996)[53]

Lenders			Borrowers		
	Total overseas investment	FDI	Region	Total overseas investment	FDI
Britain	41	45.5	Europe	27	17.71
France	20	12.2	Latin America	19	32.7
Germany	13	10.5	North America	24	16
United States	8	18.5	Asia	14	20.9
Others	18	13.3	Africa-Oceania	16	12.6

The picture of asymmetric significance that emerges for trade relations is closely related to the one seen above for overseas investment flows. Even in the case of Great Britain, the country with the most globalized economy at the time, trade with the "poor and precarious markets" from the seized tracts of territories lagged behind trade volumes with other great economic powers.[54] The largest share of trading occurred between Northern countries, both in manufacturing goods as well as primary commodities. As of 1913, approximately 60% of total world trade took place among industrial economies, and 40% of total world trade was intra-European (see Table 3-2).[55]

---

53 | Bairoch and Kozul-Wright (1996), 12.
54 | Bairoch and Kozul-Wright (1996), 9. It is important to note that the UK's trading pattern during the late 19th century, characterized by exports of manufactured goods to, and imports of primary commodities from the South, which has become a defining criterion of imperial/colonial relations, was "the exception rather than the rule" at that time (see Table 3-2).
55 | Bairoch and Kozul-Wright (1996), 9.

Table 3-2 – *Commodity and Geographical Composition of Exports, 1913 (Percentage shares, Bairoch and Kozul-Wright 1996)*[56]

Countries	Share of world exports	Trade with the North	Exports of manufactures as share of total exports	Exports to other industrial economies as share of total manufacturing exports
UK	22.8	37.9	76.6	31.8
France	12.1	68.2	57.9	63.8
Germany	21.4	53.4	71.7	53.5
Other Western European	15.0	70.3	49.4	62
United States	22.1	74.5	34.1	63.2

Secondly, the sectoral composition of colonial trade and investment relations points to the case-specific quality and overall complexity of colonial relations from a home country perspective. Empirical evidence from Britain and France shows that a large share of lending went to social overhead[57] and related business rather than resources.[58] Also, manufacturing enterprises were scarce, receiving "less than 4 per cent of total subscriptions to overseas issues" during the 1865-1914 timeframe.[59]

Food processing (milling and meat-packaging), transport improvement, and public utilities were key sectors of interest. Particularly, railway bonds featured prominently: in 1914, approximately 70% of British and French long-term foreign investment went into this area.[60] Apparently, most investors were "rentiers" rather than providers of risk capital, and non-resource sectors under straightforward management, such as railway construction, appeared less risky, due to guaranteed returns. The risk aversion of European investors is

---

56 | Bairoch and Kozul-Wright (1996), 10.
57 | Social overhead refers to "capital goods of types which are available to anybody, hence social; and are not tightly linked to any particular part of production, hence overhead. Because of their broad availability they often have to be provided by the government. Examples of social overhead capital include roads, schools, hospitals, and public parks." See Black et al. (2009).
58 | See, for instance, Svedberg (1980), 29.
59 | Cottrell (1975), 40.
60 | Bairoch and Kozul-Wright (1996). 13.

also reflected in the fact that FDI only accounted for one third of all international capital flows between 1870 and 1914.[61] Except for the UK, the majority of overseas investment took the form of portfolio investments (see also Table 3-1 on the share of FDI of the total international investment).[62] This dissimilarity in composition compared to contemporary capital exports has been largely attributed to the fact that the 19th century investment environment was riskier, which together with "[i]nformational problems made investments in debt safer than those in equity."[63]

It should be noted that in contrast to the widespread rhetoric of liberalism and free trade now associated with that era, financial mechanisms were not (only) "dominated by the market sentiment of private investors" during that period; neither were trade flows nor international relations.[64] Instead, public actors and policies played a key role in setting incentives. As mentioned above, empirical data shows that "bond issues dominated other debt instruments (notably equities)" and prevailed over securities markets.[65] This means that although private actors and banks from industrial countries invested overseas in long-term liabilities (such as railways), the borrowers were colonial and foreign governments in need of external capital to both address acute financial needs and finance infrastructure projects whose costs greatly exceeded the revenues.[66] The associated obligation of the borrower to make fixed interest payments and/or to reimburse the investor made this formula appealing for foreign investors.[67] While those guaranteed rates of return are not part of contemporary land-consuming investment projects, the accompanying rhetoric and provision of investor-friendly conditions (e.g., tax waiver) to attract foreign capital seem fairly similar to contemporary host governments' strategies to attract foreign capital.[68]

---

61 | Bairoch and Kozul-Wright (1996), 11.
62 | Bairoch and Kozul-Wright (1996), 11. Interestingly, it was the FDI component of total capital exports that showed a sectoral bias towards projects in the primary sector from 1870 to 1914. To the extent that FDI was a part of a strategy of expanding companies to develop intra-firm trade and related intra-firm facilitated division of labor, these projects also clearly impacted on international development and reinforced uneven developments in the world economy, creating a three-tier world whose divisions are still felt. Bairoch and Kozul-Wright (1996), 20-21, 10-11.
63 | Bairoch and Kozul-Wright (1996), 3.
64 | Bairoch and Kozul-Wright (1996), 12.
65 | Bairoch and Kozul-Wright (1996), 12-13.
66 | Bairoch and Kozul-Wright (1996), 13; Cottrell (1975), 28.
67 | Cottrell (1975), 28.
68 | Cottrell (1975), 28.

Also, trading activities were often regulated.[69] In several independent Latin American countries, where "Western pressure had imposed [...] treaties [...] which entailed the elimination of customs and duties" at the beginning of the 19th century, governments began to introduce protectionist trade policies in 1870 to promote industrialization following independence.[70] Simultaneously, policy preferences in industrial countries were characterized by great "divisions of opinion and interest over the empire's economic function."[71] A case in point is the British Imperial Federation League (IFL), which emerged in 1884 to make recommendations on how to strengthen economic cooperation within the empire. This organization dissolved in 1893 due to an inability to find consensus on imperial economic policy, with a particular point of contestation being the promotion of "free trade" or imperial preference as the key norm of economic organization.[72]

Overall, however, it should be noted that, until 1913, free trade had a "doctrinal, quasi-religious status"[73] in the British Empire, to the extent that "its rules of multilateralism and non-discrimination have shaped the post-World War Two international order."[74] It was widely supported by (British) civil society and "helped soften people's earlier view of the state [...] as exploitative instrument of the ruling class"[75]—as popular notions of "Free Trade envisaged the social as relatively autonomous from state and market."[76] Simultaneously, the free trade doctrine reflected the growing reliance on foreign farmers and the rise in consumption.[77] At the same time, references to free trade always also had a strong rhetorical character, allowing the colonizers and imperial powers to unilaterally enter overseas markets and territories without having to fear retaliation back home, given the power asymmetries in place.

With time, the rise of a group of strongly growing countries impacted international economic governance and led to the emergence of an international monetary and economic framework tailored to these countries' investing and trading interests. However, this did not necessarily imply a more competitive organization of international and domestic economic, social and political rela-

---

69 | Bairoch and Kozul-Wright (1996), 8-9.
70 | Bairoch and Kozul-Wright (1996), 8-9.
71 | Green (1999), 47.
72 | Green (1999), 48.
73 | Trentmann (2008), 7.
74 | Trentmann (2008), 7.
75 | Trentmann(2008), 15.
76 | Trentmann (2008), 15.
77 | Trentmann (2008), 15.

tions.[78] Often, "imperial conflicts were related to and interconnected with the class struggles that characterized the expansion of industrial capitalism"[79] at that time. They reflected "feudal forms of organization; [...] monopolism, protectionism, cartelization and corporatism; and [...] rural, pre-industrial, and autocratic structures of power and authority."[80]

Against this background, it is not surprising to see that economic expansion by the great economic powers was largely an outcome of cooperation between the governments, financial institutions, and entrepreneurs. The countries that went down the industrialization path relatively late in comparison to the United Kingdom, such as Germany, were particularly characterized by close cooperation between these seemingly different actor groups, with the result that "[f]requently, interested bankers obtained government approval and support for the projects of others"[81]—not to mention diplomatic and military support. Yet, private sector capital exports were not necessarily embraced by most home country governments. Countries such as Germany and France tried to "discourage such outflows or at least sought ways to tie them more closely to export orders."[82] They were concerned about structural unemployment and foreign debt.[83]

4. Finding an "African El Dorado"? The Scramble for Africa, 1870-1914

The African continent ranked comparatively low with regards to European trade and investment activities during the late 19th and early 20th century. During the 1870-1913 period, the continent received 9.1% of British capital exports, 7.3% of French, and 8.5% of German foreign investment.[84] Nevertheless, the Scramble for Africa, i.e. the partition of and "run" onto the continent by European economic powers at the end of the 19th century has almost become synonymous with the popular notion of the "second wave"[85] of European imperialism. Since references to the Scramble are also common in the contemporary

---

78 | Bairoch and Kozul-Wright (1996), 24. Key aspects of this framework, for instance, the protection of foreign property or the imposition of the "open door" principle, have become key pillars of the contemporary international economic constitution.
79 | Halperin (2004), 76.
80 | Halperin (2005), 4.
81 | Bairoch and Kozul-Wright (1996), 24
82 | Bairoch and Kozul-Wright (1996), 24.
83 | Bairoch and Kozul-Wright (1996), 24; and Raghavan (2000).
84 | Daudin et al. (2010), 12 (Table 1-4).
85 | Bowden (2009), 25-26.

"land grab" debate that has emerged since 2000,[86] a more detailed summary of how and why it occurred from the perspective of the European colonizers will be provided.

In the early 1870s, the African continent remained unexplored and "mysterious" from the perspective of Europeans, who considered the region to be "'vacant': legally *res nullius*, a no-man's-land," except for the trading hubs and a few strategic colonies (South Africa, Algeria) on the coastline.[87] The African continent had never occupied an important spot on the European imaginary map prior to the Scramble, a "term [...] coined in 1884."[88] Therefore, it was surprising then, and still is today, that within "half a generation, the Scramble gave Europe virtually the whole continent: including thirty new colonies and protectorates, 10 million square miles of new territory and 110 million dazed new subjects."[89]

What happened? The historical literature remains inconclusive over why the Scramble occurred from 1876 to 1913. However, there is broad agreement that monocausal explanations that point, for instance, to surplus capital are insufficient to capture the multiplicity of events and factors at work.[90] Aside from mythical notions of an African El Dorado[91] that were inspired by the diamonds and gold mines in South Africa, there was the "lure of the unknown," which was stimulated by geographic sciences for which "Africa was still [...] one of those few great regions where cartographers still left white spaces in place of rivers lakes and mountains."[92] Moreover, the context of the economic crisis in Europe, which was experiencing its first Long Depression,[93] as well as international power shifts, such as the rise of the US, and great power competition within Europe over markets and the positional status in the European system of states were important. These all have been influential factors in the imperial expansion onto, and the colonization of, the African continent.[94] Technological and scientific innovations that lowered the transport and health barriers to explore the interior of the continent sped up the Scramble.[95] At the same

---

86 | E.g., Biney (2009).
87 | Pakenham (1992), xxiii. Also see Duignan and Gann (1969a), 2-3.
88 | In this sub-chapter the term is used to "embrace the whole hectic phase of the partition, beginning with a prelude in 1876 and ending in 1912," following the description of Pakenham (1992), xxvii.
89 | Pakenham (1992), xxiii.
90 | Pakenham (1992), xxiii-xxiv.
91 | See, for instance, Pearce (1984), 90.
92 | Duignan and Gann (1969a), 6-7.
93 | Hobsbawm (1989), 45. For a detailed explanation of this crisis, see Nelson (2008).
94 | See Pakenham (1992), xxiii-xxvi; Duignan and Gann (1969a); and Dumett (1999).
95 | Duignan and Gann (1969a), 2.

time, the Scramble relied on institutions developed during the first half of the 19th century, namely the international banking system, the reform of corporate governance, or strategic posts along the coastline that served as points of entry into the continent.

Historical research also points to the importance of country-specific factors and dynamics. In practice, different imperialisms of political and economic character were at play, and they depended on a country's particular political economy, ideology, and development setting, in addition to the international context.[96] For instance, British and French rationalizations of imperial expansion were influenced by their investor legacy. Accordingly, the key drivers of British interest in the African continent were "first to safeguard their [trade] passage to India and secondly to profit from economic opportunities." These interest priorities led Duignan and Gann to argue that the British participation in the Scramble occurred at the beginning out of "self-defense," i.e. out of a fear of losing political control in the context of the French-British rivalry over positional status within Europe.[97] The French expansion was pushed forward by diverse actor groups (e.g., "soldiers, merchants, geographic societies") "to promote the idea of empire" as a form of political power that would spread French culture and the allegedly "universal ideals of the Enlightenment."[98] The core empirical characteristics of the Scramble and how it occurred from a home country perspective are reviewed next.

To start, the Scramble timelines underline the procedural character of colonization and late 19th century imperial expansion. This process consisted of a gradual move from exploration and treaty-based forms of land acquisition and colonization, which were accompanied and often executed by imperial philanthropists (missionaries), to the use of force, the atrocities of which are well-documented.[99] In fact, "paper imperialism," such as the partition of Africa among European powers at the Berlin Conference (1884-1885), proved insufficient in the process of acquisition: "When effective occupation became necessary to establish a good title, conflict became inevitable."[100]

An assessment of the colonization timelines also shows that the strategies for gaining or staying in control changed with time. While killings and violence were widely applied at the beginning of the occupation, some colonial administrations shifted their focus from direct to indirect forms of exploitation to

---

96 | E.g. Duignan and Gann (1969a); Pakenham (1992); Dumett (1999); and Hobsbawm (1989).
97 | Duignan and Gann (1969a), 8.
98 | See Jones (2014).
99 | Take, for instance, the German extermination order against Hereros in Southwest Africa. Pakenham (1992), xxv.
100 | Pakenham (1992), xxv.

prevent further revolts (see, for instance, the governance of farmland below). Throughout, law constituted an important instrument of acquisition and colonization, as it "provided a far more comprehensive framework than did the others for recalibrating land and life on the colonizers' terms and without reference to indigenous antecedents."[101] The central role of law as primary tool to access the best land and govern colonial territory led Fahrmeir and Steller to refer to these practices as "lawfare" instead of warfare.[102] Interestingly, though, many aspects of "lawfare" had their origin in the commercial conflicts among European powers that they were meant to regulate—a point to consider when assessing contemporary legal approaches and voluntary initiatives in the context of governing land-consuming FDI.[103]

Importantly, the widespread narrative of primary-resources-driven colonialism, which the previous overview of key imperial parameters called into question for the majority of imperial projects, does apply to the African case. The empirical evidence on the sectoral composition of capital imports from 1870 to 1935 shows that the largest share of private foreign capital "went into mining and much colonial public investment was intended for developing mining."[104] In practice, this led to the establishment of enclave economies that were characterized by their export-orientation, as well as their strong reliance on foreign capital and the facilitating institutions in the form of colonial administration and law, infrastructures, and labor needed for the exploitation of resources.[105] In the process of acquisition and colonization, colonial governments made use of mining policies and marketing mechanisms to put African enterprises at a disadvantage compared to their foreign competitors, ultimately resulting in their elimination.[106] This was also true for cases such as the gold industry in Southern Rhodesia, "where the geological conditions favored small-scale producers and where African tradition and experience were considerable."[107] Also, following decolonization, foreign investments in Africa have remained biased towards the natural resource sector (agriculture, mining), which still made up 50% to 80% of total FDI flows as of 2005. At the same time, the positional status of African countries has remained evocative of the continent's colonial heritage: South Africa, which was a major, late 19th century target country of

---

101 | Harris (2004), 179; Alden Wily (2012).
102 | Fahrmeir und Steller (2013), 172.
103 | The Act of Berlin (1885), the "legislative vehicle for the Scramble for Africa," was as much about the partition of the continent amongst the European powers as it was about guaranteeing free trade in spite of the partition. See Gardner (2012), 43.
104 | Economic Commission for Africa, Africa Union (2011), 12.
105 | Stuchtey (2010).
106 | Economic Commission for Africa, Africa Union (2011), 13.
107 | Economic Commission for Africa, Africa Union (2011), 13.

foreign investments "with the other economies in its orbit,"[108] continues to be a major trading and investment hub on the continent.[109]

A core component of these processes of colonization and capital transfers was that they consumed land in its multiple forms, as territory, resource, and cultural landscape; by multiple means, namely legal and violent, direct and/or indirect forms of dispossession; for multiple reasons. However, it is important to remember that land as a resource only became a core issue at a later stage of colonization. Historical evidence on the "Conference of Berlin" (1884-1885) indicates that in the beginning European economic powers met to negotiate the future of the African continent as a way to ease competition pressures and conflicts over commercial routes and (exclusive) markets. These issues had been building up amongst themselves. And then they gained further significance during the Great Depression, and in the context of the declining possibility of expansion on the European continent due to the formation of nation-states.[110] Contributing factors to the focus on commercial and strategic interests during this partition process might have been that "many African colonies were short of [...] known mineral deposits,"[111] and that large parts of the continent were "terra incognita" and not intended for settlement.[112]

Over time, land played an important role as a sphere of influence and strategic territory for the home countries' commercial interests, as a resource, as a productive space of society, as an area of settlement, or as an asset (in cases where investors speculated on rising land values)[113]—a list that is similar to the functions of land in contemporary foreign investments. However, the initial neglect of, or ignorance about land resources on the African continent led to situations in which investors and colonial administrations had to realize that the acquired land (tropical soils) was not necessarily conducive to the colonial export economy they had envisioned. In addition, the colonized territories often faced a shortage of labor and lacked the infrastructure required for industrial export agriculture.[114]

Similar to the varying role of land within and across colonies, the governance of land was characterized by plural, complex, and evolving modes and events rather than a single approach. In view of access, the "ability to dispossess rested primarily on physical power and the supporting infrastructure of the state." [115]

---

108 | Economic Commission for Africa, Africa Union (2011), 12.
109 | Ezeoha and Cattaneo (2011), 2.
110 | Pakenham (1992); Anghie (2007).
111 | Austin (2010), 9-10.
112 | Austin (2010), 9-10.
113 | Hobson (1965), 63, 357.
114 | Austin (2010), 10; Duignan and Gann (1969b), 102.
115 | Harris (2004), 179.

At a later stage of colonization, the threat of military intervention and/or legal punishment by the colonial administration or the chartered company was often sufficient to acquire land through dispossession.[116] At the same time, the governance of land was shaped by commercial interests; concerns over lacking wage labor—in this case land dispossession together with taxation provided a mechanism to force Africans to work in the mines and plantations of colonial governments and corporations;[117] and the fiscal needs of the "colonial treasury."

Moreover, governance depended on how the respective colony was framed by the colonizer, namely whether it was deemed a "settler," "plantation," or "peasant" colony.[118] The framing was based on the utility of the soils and infrastructure for primary export production, and had significant consequences in view of the support that home country agents were receiving from the colonial government.[119] In the case of (British) Ghana, a "peasant" colony, British farmers were, for instance, allowed to get involved in cocoa production. However, they did not succeed in the competition with African producers.[120] A key factor for their failure was that these farmers did not receive the biased support from the colonial administration that British subjects were experiencing in "semi-settler" colonies such as Kenya and Southern Africa. Instead, the colonial government preferred to "rel[y] on the efforts of African small capitalists and peasants in growing and local marketing of export crops" for accommodating commercial projects and generating state revenues. This strategy proved very profitable, "yielding a 20-fold rise of foreign trade (measured in real value) between 1897 and 1960."[121] Another example is the case of Nigeria, also a "peasant" colony. Between 1906 and 1925, the colonial government turned down the advances of the soap manufacturer H.W. Lever (whose manufacturing companies today form part of the Unilever Corporation[122]) who asked permission to develop large oil palm plantations.[123] As a consequence, "African producers literally delivered the goods [...] through land-extensive methods well adapted to the factor endowment," resulting in the "continued African occupation of virtually all agricultural land."[124] However, these examples do not mean that

---

116 | Harris (2004), 179.
117 | Austin (2010), 9.
118 | Austin (2010), 9, 13.
119 | Austin (2010), 9, 13.
120 | Austin (2010), 8.
121 | Austin (2010), 9.
122 | Unilever (http://www.unilever.co.uk/aboutus/ourhistory/).
123 | Austin (2010), 9.
124 | These choices by colonial governments were largely a function of giving in to the resilience of "African production for the market" and/or resistance, and not outcomes of a greater strategy for colonial development. Austin (2010), 9, 13.

these farmers were free to grow what they wanted in the way they wanted. Instead, "the colonial administration completely discouraged the cultivation of food crops while encouraging cash crops production."[125] As a result of this economic policy, existing economic systems that ensured the food self-sufficiency of families were destroyed, resulting in rural households' starvation.[126]

More broadly, in the agricultural sector, three business models prevailed that are still popular today: plantations, contract farming,[127] and commercial farming.[128] In most colonies, preferential treatment was given to foreign-owned plantations, or farms owned by European emigrants.[129] Plantations reflected European visions of establishing an export economy in the colonies. However, in practice, this production and governance model often struggled for economic viability, and it never became the most common mode of production or land use on the African continent.[130] Until today, this model and related governance schemes are known for their detrimental social impacts in the form of slavery and indentured labor, violent expropriation, undervalued compensation for land; as well as their land-extensive and capital-intensive nature. In practice, plantations depended strongly on colonial administration to govern the economy and territory in a way that defeated the competition from African smallholder producers or facilitated the forced labor supply to meet their labor demands.[131] Usually, plantations were set up close to ports by settlers or corporations (like Del Monte, Firestone); and they had the widest application in settler colonies such as Kenya, Zimbabwe, and South Africa.[132] In the case of settlers' commercial farms, the other business model characteristic of the late 19th/early 20th century on the continent, the colonial administration allocated specific land areas to settlers.[133] In contrast to plantations, with their focus on monoculture and their operation by multinational corporations, these farms tend(ed) to be less integrated in the world economy, to plant multiple crops, and to raise livestock.[134]

---

125 | Shokpeka and Nwaokocha (2009), 57.
126 | Shokpeka and Nwaokocha (2009), 57.
127 | This form has been promoted as a way to integrate small-scale farmers in the plantation economy by turning them into suppliers to estate structures. See Smalley (2013), 11.
128 | Smalley (2013).
129 | Smalley (2013), 3.
130 | Smalley (2013), 21.
131 | Smalley (2013), 9.
132 | Smalley (2013), 21, 9.
133 | Smalley (2013), 11.
134 | Smalley (2013), 11.

The descriptions above highlight two things about the colonial administration of land: colonial land governance did not necessarily displace African producers in every case; however, colonial administration used other means of control, such as economic policies, to steer what was being produced and it also used biased agricultural marketing methods that treated European producers with partiality.[135] These subtleties have to be kept in mind when assessing contemporary land-consuming FDI projects. At the same time, land governance depended strongly on the respective administration's perception of local realities—from the framing of a colony as peasant, settler, or plantation colony, to the establishing of land markets for African land-owners. Moreover, land governance changed with time. Kenya is a case in point. Colonial administration had prevented "the emergence of land markets in areas controlled by Africans."[136] However, much later, in the post-WWII period and more than a decade prior to Kenya gaining independence (in 1962), there were controlled cases of land registration "in response to the *de facto* emergence of land sales and individual proprietorship."[137] An important reason was that the colonial government saw this as a way to strengthen its control by empowering conservative African land-owners.[138] More broadly, historical records show that public colonial spending "was concentrated on a combination of administration, defense, and infrastructure," and governed to both "promote expansion of primary export industry" and service debt.[139] Hardly any of the state budget was made available for social investments in schools, hospitals, pension, or other welfare areas of state action that were rapidly expanding in Europe at the time.[140]

While the governance of lands and colonies focused strongly on favoring Europeans and installing a primary export industry, it would be wrong to think of actors and institutions in the target regions as passive objects in this process. In practice, their responses lay somewhere between the two poles: strategized cooperation as a means to exert their own influence on the ground and resistance.[141] Consequently, the particular response on the ground, together with

---

135 | Austin (2010), 12.
136 | Austin (2010), 12-13.
137 | Austin (2010), 12-13.
138 | Austin (2010), 12-13.
139 | Gardner (2012), 36-40.
140 | Gardner (2012), 34, 234.
141 | For instance, anglicized Africans in Nigeria "possess[ed] a sense of the British 'imperial mission'" from their religious point of view; while some traders in Senegal hoped to protect their trade against competitors under French rule. In some cases, "[l]iterate Africans looked for promotion in the local public services." At the same time, some groups of the African aristocracy, whose cooperation imperial control depended on, established a kind of 'sub-imperialism,' securing and even expanding their influence

the political institutions in place in African regions, which ranged "from stateless societies [...] to city states and extensive kingdoms" with monarchies,[142] partly shaped the interaction between European and African actors.[143]

From a home country perspective, the Scramble involved a wide range of actors and institutions, such as state officials, adventurers, missionaries, and entrepreneurs, but also landed elites and bankers. Moreover, it relied on important institutions that emerged during that time of great power competition, including the forms of international law mentioned above,[144] commercial treaty standards,[145] and/or principles of the international economic system, particularly the Most Favored Nation principle. A particularly prominent institution of that time, which could be traced back to the 16th century, was the chartered company with its "dual roles of entrepreneur and representative" of the respective home government.[146] It allowed merchants to pool resources in order to invest and trade overseas, sometimes to the extent of administering the colonies as proxies of the home country state politically, economically, and

over and control of the territory and the population within the colonial framework (e.g., Lozi in Gambia, Ganda in Uganda). See Duignan and Gann (1969a), 4, 13, 16; Duignan and Gann (1969b), 109, 122; and Boamah (2014).

142 | Duignan and Gann (1969a), 11.
143 | Austin (2010), 15. Also see Halperin (2005).
144 | Anghie (2006, 739-742) describes the "evolution of international law from the 16th century" as a discipline of European origin, "consist[ing] of a series of doctrines and principles that were developed in Europe, that emerged out of European history and experience, and that were extended to the non-European world which existed outside the realm of European international law." Accordingly, law was an institutional mechanism in facilitating imperial expansion, but it was at the same time shaped by it, with colonialism being "central to its formation," and thus making it "universal." Key for this process of international law facilitating and legitimizing colonial enterprises was the "dynamic of difference." The assumed universality of the norms and principles of international law "posit[ed] a gap, a difference between European and non-European cultures and peoples." That gap then needed closing, and this legitimated the framings of imperialism as a "civilizing mission." To a certain degree, this was reflected also in "an aggressive variety of imperial philanthropy," that tried to "help [...] the unbelievers in the African bush." Also see Duignan and Gann (1969a), 9, 6-7.
145 | The incorporation of commercial treaty standards on the protection of alien property and the obligation of full compensation in case of expropriation into international law in the 19th century reduced the risk for internationally operating firms. As a result of property standards, "[u]ncompensated seizure [of alien property] was considered robbery, and the use of unilateral force was considered a legal and legitimate response." See Jones (2005a), 24-25.
146 | Moss et al. (2004), 6.

by means of military force. Usually, these companies were given a contract by the home country government, which in return expected to profit from the annual revenues in the form of royalties or intensified trade (exports), and/or hoped to maintain or gain a favorable positional status at the international level at relatively low cost.[147]

Institutionally, colonial undertakings also profited from the internationalization of the banking sector.[148] The British government, for instance, supported overseas investments and colonial administrations through loans and public spending in the form of grants-in-aid. These financial schemes needed the approval of the British Treasury, the main guarantor in most cases, which provided the colonies with lower interest rates.[149] Loans were granted in cases where the local colonial state revenue did not manage to cover the expenditures, even though the stated goal was for colonial governments to become self-sufficient and produce balanced budgets in the medium term.[150] While the colonized had to pay for their own subjugation, in practice, the case of Britain highlights that few colonies became financially independent.[151] Repeatedly, the already volatile financial situation of the colonies deteriorated with slowdowns in world trade and/or falls in commodity prices.[152] As a result, the colonial governments tried to build up financial reserves for these incidents of revenue declines through export trade, and they cut down on the size of their administrations to reduce costs. The interrelation of colonial governance and financial administration has been highlighted by Gardner, who argues that the British approach to "indirect rule" was less the outcome of an ideological choice than of financial constraints in view of limited revenues available to the colonial state in spite of their violent collection from the colonized in the process of conquest and colonization (e.g., taxes).[153]

With time, the support of home country governments for capital exports changed, as did the approach to colonial administration. While the governments had originally framed capital exports as beneficial (at least to a certain degree), suggesting them as a way to expedite the import of food and raw mate-

---

147 | Duignan and Gann (1969a), 17.
148 | Jones (2005a), 25.
149 | Gardner (2012), 40-41.
150 | Gardner (2012), 37-40.
151 | Gardner (2012), 32. It is important to note, however, that India, the largest and most important colony of the British empire, appears to have been financially profitable for Great Britain, which kept "draining Indian revenues to pay for an expensive bureaucracy (including in London) and an army beyond India's own defence needs" and to meet other financial interests in London. See, for instance, Kaul (3 March 2011).
152 | Gardner (2012), 6.
153 | Gardner (2012), 5-6.

rials, to promote exports and thus create jobs, and to ensure an annual state income in the form of commission fees and remittances, this "laissez-faire" attitude changed during World War I.[154] Even the British government began to fear that outward investments could have negative repercussions on the foreign exchange position of the motherland and pressure the internal capital markets. This resulted in tighter regulation designed to ensure the availability of capital for domestic development or the development of the colonies.[155]

In conclusion, the material presented above begs the question of utility, i.e. was the violent colonization of, and imperial expansion into African, but also Asian and Latin American lands, actually rewarded with the finding of an "El Dorado?" Historical evidence suggests that outcomes were complex, and not necessarily a success story. Contrary to the claims that outward investments would increase exports, create jobs, secure resources, and provide a stable source of annual state revenues in the form of commissions from issuing loans or remittances on profits, in practice, the impact was less obvious.[156] Particularly regarding the colonization of tropical Africa, the effects of overseas trade, migration, and investment were ambiguous, and "capital exports to colonies were important, but not dominant" for economic development back home.[157] For instance, it remains unclear whether overseas investment in the primary resource sector in the colonies or (in the case of Britain) the Empire was even necessary from the home country perspective. Europe was resource abundant with regard to major energy sources (coal), "and nearly self-sufficient in iron ore and other minerals."[158] Only industrial crops such as cotton constituted an important commodity, and they were largely supplied to European countries by the United States. Also, the acquired colonial territories that supposedly served as outlets for European capital and trade accounted for less than 15% of European countries' exports.[159] At the same time, there is an ongoing debate over the extent to which colonial tax and trade revenues from major colonies (e.g., India in the case of Britain) constituted vital inputs for the home country's

---

154 | Atkin (1970), 324-328
155 | Atkin (1970), 324-328.
156 | Colonial India, which is not covered in this chapter, seems to be an exception in this regard. Historical research suggests that it might have played an important role in British development and expansion. For instance, colonial tax and opium trade revenues were used to service the debt and facilitate the further expansion and maintenance of the British empire; and the colonization of India brought prestige to Great Britain. See Cain and Hopkins (1987); and Deming (2011).
157 | Daudin et al. (2010), 17.
158 | Daudin et al. (2010), 17.
159 | Daudin et al. (2010), 17.

development and imperial expansion.[160] While Cain and Hopkins have shown that colonization was a relevant factor, subsequent historical research underlines that the benefits are not straightforward.[161]

These basic colonial trade and investment figures, however, raise doubts about the usefulness of many of these undertakings from the home country perspective, particularly regarding resource security. They also highlight that other interests, be they commercial or geopolitical in nature, were equally relevant. At the same time, the project details emphasize that capital exports were not necessarily profitable. In fact, the "tropical treasure house myth"[162] that underpinned and legitimized colonial expansion in the home countries neither reflected the reality of mining projects nor that of agricultural projects. Instead, many enterprises, such as the chartered companies, turned out to be highly unprofitable, leading to their ultimate failure—in spite of the monopolistic concessions and coercive means at their disposal. Prominent cases in point were the British South Africa Company in Southern Rhodesia, as well as French activities in Equatorial Africa.[163] To attract foreign capital, these companies facilitated the "granting of large scale territorial concessions on easy terms" to foreign investors.[164] Since their business model relied heavily on foreign funding, these concessionary companies faced the problem that their "grantees usually failed to invest sufficient funds or to do much serious development work."[165] The shareholders often did not profit either. The British South Africa Company, for instance, which was active in mining, landholding, and railway construction, and was basically a chartered company constructed on the example of the infamous British East India Company,[166] "never paid a single penny to its shareholders and was generally unprofitable" (between 1890 and 1923).[167]

Contrary to the rhetoric of progress and efficiency, it also turned out that insufficient 'on the ground' knowledge and shortages of labor "did not make for efficient agriculture."[168] In the African colonies, European farming enterprises faced the same challenges as local farmers, namely "plant disease, floods, droughts and sickness," as well as poorly developed communication and trans-

---

160 | Cain and Hopkins (1987). See, also, footnote 376.
161 | E.g., Cain and Hopkins (1987); Gardner (2012); Dumett (1999).
162 | Duignan and Gann (1969a), 10.
163 | Duignan and Gann (1969a), 20.
164 | Duignan and Gann (1969a), 20.
165 | Duignan and Gann (1969a), 20.
166 | Regarding the East India Company, see for instance Britannica.com (http://www.britannica.com/EBchecked/topic/176643/East-India-Company).
167 | Duignan and Gann (1969b), 102.
168 | Pearce (1984), 90.

port routes, which made their projects relatively expensive and economically unviable.[169] At the same time, imported animals and plants often did not suit the climate, and the European farmers also "had to cope with the unfamiliar properties of African soils"—a fact that seems as pertinent today as it was back then. Often, this unfamiliarity with local conditions resulted in detrimental impacts in the form of declining soil fertility and rising soil degradation.[170] Even ventures in the mining sector (e.g., diamond and gold) that generated returns, nourished the public imagination on colonialism and imperialism, and came closest to the "concept of colonial super-profits" were encountering difficulties, and "large dividends in some mines were balanced by low profits or losses in others."[171]

Regarding job creation, it is impossible to clearly judge the impact of these undertakings. On the one hand, empirical evidence suggests an inverse relation between overseas investments and jobs available in the home countries.[172] On the other hand, the overseas territories, particularly those in the New World, created (even if they were moderate in most cases) some outlets for surplus production, capital, and labor. Cottrell argues that this allowed the ruling elite to uphold regime stability by opening new sources of profit to landed elites back home while offering avenues for social mobility through a military career or migration. Moreover, Daudin et al. highlight that "[m]igration was the dimension of globalization that had the greatest impact on European workers' living standards during this period" through its prompting of real wage rises in poor economies back home and provision of a way to bypass or leave behind domestic barriers.[173] In this latter sense, it provided an option to earn a higher income and/or evade religious or political oppression or persecution in the home countries.[174] In most cases, European migrants came from rural populations, but increasingly they also came from cities and industrial (i.e. deskilled, unschooled worker) backgrounds.[175]

At the same time, these very same elements that sustained stability also prevented domestic reform processes. Politically, the old elites were able to

---

169 | Duignan and Gann (1969b), 102.
170 | Duignan and Gann (1969b), 102; also see Kotschi and AGRECOL (2013); Goldsmith (1993), 2.
171 | Duignan and Gann (1969b), 108.
172 | Cottrell (1975), 53.
173 | Daudin et al. (2010), 21-23.
174 | Daudin et al. (2010), 21-23. See, for instance, the case of European migrant farmers in Argentina, Solberg (1974), 127; and Solimano and Watts (2005) for an overview of migration flows during the late 19th century.
175 | See, for instance, the description of the political economy of core countries by Halperin (2005); and Solimano and Watts (2005), 16.

secure their positional status, while economically, many overseas investments turned out to be harmful due to their wasteful and fraudulent quality[176] or the fact that their focus on primary resources abroad led to the neglect of domestic agricultural production back home.[177] More broadly, capital exports resulted in the stagnation of domestic industry productivity and export growth since "the bulk of the savings generated in the non-industrial sectors of the economy had been directed not into industry but into [...] secure investments" such as "government stocks, [...] agricultural mortgages, or after 1840, the railways."[178] Moreover, from 1880 onwards until 1914, the marginal returns of Britain's colonial investments were below those from (less risky) investments in industry back home. However, when taking a broader view of what the benefits might have been for the home country, research suggests that overseas investment facilitated an elite strata continuation at a time of economic transformation back home. Tax and trade revenues of key colonies also seem to have mitigated financial volatility and serviced debt in the British Empire.[179] This underlines the importance of looking at the nuances and the political economy of the home country's colonial undertakings for a meaningful understanding of how and why overseas investments occur when assessing contemporary acquisitions, rather than adopting the investor's framing or the rhetoric of efficiency and profit.

From the viewpoint of the colonies and/or the countries in the South that received FDI and other capital flows, these foreign funds were part of very violent processes of dispossession, suppression, and acquisition. Economically, they proved harmful for the host countries, because they destroyed local socio-economic institutions[180] and were mostly "unable to establish [...] a cumulative growth dynamic."[181] In particular, "speculative capital flows were [...] likely to become a destabilizing element," resulting in "deflationary pressures, debt crisis, reduction[s] in [capital] imports."[182] As a result, non-colonies also grew increasingly dependent on the orders of their European lenders, namely banks and governments, which cooperated with industry in this context to further joint interests at the cost of the borrowing countries.[183] The imported funds

---

176 | Cottrell (1975), 47.
177 | See Potter (2002), 124.
178 | Cain and Hopkins (1987), 4. Regarding the explanation of major investment trends during 1855-1914, see Cottrell (1975), 35.
179 | Cain and Hopkins (1987); Deming (2011).
180 | Shokpeka and Nwaokocha (2009); Davis (2002).
181 | Bairoch and Kozul-Wright (1996), 25.
182 | Bairoch and Kozul-Wright (1996), 25.
183 | Argentina is a case in point: following a crisis of "excess borrowing" in 1890, the State had to fulfill the "dictates of the international banks that imposed severe

extended the asymmetric export-import trading relationship, establishing a specialized economic structure that was not conducive to the debtor countries' economic development in the medium term, yet very difficult to overcome.[184]

The forming of an uneven development geography, which was characteristic of the Scramble, often went along with environmental degradation due to the concentration of land ownership and control. This concentration led to overcrowding and the use of less valuable land by dispossessed and/or relocated rural populations, and exceeding domestic biocapacity became a problem due to the focus on primary exports.[185] While "[d]e-industrialisation in colonies and developing countries predated the era of global integration," the process was "accelerated, during much of the period of global integration."[186] This process is evidenced by the low share of imperial borrowing in manufacturing:[187] between 1860 and 1913, "the developing country share of world manufacturing production declined from over one-third to under a tenth," a fact that has been closely linked to the dramatic rise of imports of European manufactured goods in the South.[188]

On the individual level, a large share of the local population, particularly in Africa, Latin America, and Asia did not benefit from these forms of "coercive development."[189] Instead, populations were evicted from their lands and then confronted with hunger and starvation[190] while concurrently being framed by colonial administrations as cheap "labour reservoir[s]."[191] Even farmers who produced for multinational corporations through new forms of outgrower schemes did not profit from integration of the agricultural sector in the international markets. To the contrary, they were confronted with dramatic declines in agricultural prices, had to bear all the risks such as currency fluctuations

---

financial conditions on both the national and the provincial governments in order to guarantee that they would recoup their loans and to assure the profitability of allied enterprises, such as British railways firms." At the same time, European banks turned the crisis into an opportunity, buying up Argentinean enterprises from the private and public sector and thereby furthering their economic position within the Argentinean economy. Bairoch and Kozul-Wright (1996), 25.

184 | Cottrell (1975), 41.
185 | Compare Andersson and Lindroth (2001); and Clover and Eriksen (2009).
186 | Bairoch and Kozul-Wright (1996), 16.
187 | Bairoch and Kozul-Wright (1996), 16.
188 | Bairoch and Kozul-Wright (1996), 16.
189 | See Bessant (1992), 39-50.
190 | Davis (2002).
191 | Bessant (1992).

and weather events, and lacked any political privileges under colonial administration.[192]

In retrospect, the legacy of the three-tier world that emerged during this era is still felt today. Its three tiers were, firstly, the "small group of rapidly industrializing economies" that is seen as having most profited from the international capital dynamics, while also playing the central role in the emergence of economic standards (gold standard); secondly, the few settler countries which managed to profit from primary resource exports and, over time, to begin to industrialize; and, thirdly, the large group of countries that "shared a tenuous position in the new international division of labour," and did not manage to industrialize sustainably, or—in the case of the colonies—were discouraged or even prevented from doing so.[193]

5. Decolonization and Globalization

For the assessment of the novel character of contemporary "land grabs" (or, in the terminology of this book: land-consuming investments), it is important to account for international structures as well as domestic developments in the home and host countries in the post-WWII period. The underpinning question is whether fundamental changes in agencies, structures, and ideologies are observable in the context of foreign land acquisitions after decolonization.

Regarding the situation in recipient and home countries, decolonization has not led to a radical break with colonial economic structures, ideas, policies, or legislation in the form of a zero hour:

Many of the ideas, policies, and priorities of postcolonial development can trace their genealogies to the colonial era, where they were shaped through metropolitan concerns to maintain and modernise colonies, and through contact with the local people, knowledge, and conditions.[194]

Instead, most African countries show a mix of path-dependent[195], as well as new, elements in areas relevant to land-consuming OFDI. As of 2016, it seems to be a combination of colonial-state legacy (state as nominal land rights

---

192 | See Hobson (1965), 113-116; Smalley (2013), 18, 30-52; and Clapp (1988).
193 | Bairoch and Kozul-Wright (1996), 19.
194 | Craggs (2014), 9.
195 | Path dependency is an analytical concept of social sciences. It basically assumes that history matters when trying to understand contemporary institutional developments, collective action, power asymmetries, and perceptions. See, for instance, the work of North (1990).

holder), the persistence of modernization ideas informing domestic and international development programs,[196] and the postcolonial history of Structural Adjustment Programs (SAPs)[197] that lays the institutional, ideological, and legal ground for these investments to take place.

A closer look at natural resource governance also shows that many countries' governments (North and South) have moved away from "state-led large-scale development" conceptions and the related "interventionist development policies" that were characteristic of colonial policies in the 1930s and continued for a certain period of time post-independence.[198] Today, many governments have adopted a neoclassical outlook on development characterized by the preference of private ownership of means of production, the promotion of minimum state intervention in sectoral governance, the assumption of rational actors, and the reduction of socioeconomic development to issues of efficiency and productivity.[199]

Consequently, many countries' national development plans put an emphasis on foreign capital attraction and liberalization, and reflect an ideology of development as a process of unlimited growth rather than a zero-sum process of resource allocation that was characteristic of rival systems and orders [200] in the

---

196 | Craggs (2014), 5-9. This particularly applies to large-scale agricultural investment projects by multilateral or bilateral development programs that focus on infrastructure, yield, and productivity improvement.

197 | See Chang (2003) for a detailed discussion of the track record of these policies in the form of an under-provision of public goods and services, or the failure to live up to their own standards (e.g., declining rather than rising growth levels during the 1990s). In practice, related development strategies resulted in a drop in public investment in the agricultural sector, the preference of private sector investment, and/or the liberalization of the primary sector. The country data on public expenditure on agriculture from 1980 to 2007 highlights that the total amount, as well as the share of agriculture in African governments' expenditures, dropped significantly from 1980 to 2007 (FAO (2012a), 4, 134-135).

198 | In fact, the plantation project that Unilever Ghana invested in during the 1990s is a perfect example of a formerly aid-funded, state-led, large-scale plantation program. Following the divestiture program in the 1990s, Unilever exploited this opportunity by buying the shares of this plantation on the Stock Market.

199 | Thomas (1994), 75-77; Kotz (2002), 64-66. For a critical discussion of mainstream economic theories that the neoclassical outlook on development is part of, see the publications by the heterodox economists Lavoie (2014, 1-30) and Cohn (2003).

200 | NIEO, short for New International Economic Order, was promoted during the 1970s, following decolonization. It aimed to replace the post-colonial order and establish an order that would be "based on equity, sovereign equality, interdependence, common interest, and cooperation among all States." See NIEO Declaration (1974), 1.

past.[201] In the governance of FDI, the ideological contestation of foreign investment by the recipient governments, which characterized the years during colonization and after decolonization, has largely disappeared.[202] Most countries in Sub-Saharan Africa have adopted a very liberal legal framework (as of 2010) that allows close to full foreign equity ownership in the agricultural, mining, or forestry sectors: "whereas countries used to list those specific sectors open to foreigner investment, the norm is now to assume a legally open regime with restricted sectors listed as exceptions" (see Table 3-3).[203] Moreover, several African governments have created investment promotion agencies and introduced favorable policies to attract investors, in the form of long lease terms, tax exemptions, and the promise of low labor costs.[204]

The trend towards deregulation and economic liberalization since the 1980s has increased the discretionary power of the private sector vis-à-vis the state. Regarding host countries, multinational companies have profited from the fact that "regional blocs and countries compete against each other for investments [...] by offering them best investment and climate conditions."[205] In addition, existing national and international laws are "not precise enough to account for diffused responsibility in multinational corporations between local subsidiaries and headquarters," enabling, for instance, practices of trade mispricing and tax evasion, both of which reflect and further reduce the decreased control and benefits available to state authorities. However, this tendency is not limited to the realm of host countries. The economic importance of multinational companies for job creation, supply sourcing, and trading activities has also expanded their power in negotiations with state authorities in home countries.[206]

---

201 | Informal interview with staff from the WB Inspection Panel, November 2011.
202 | Moss et al. (2004), 1.
203 | Moss et al. (2004), 3.
204 | Moss et al. (2004), 3. Also see Chapters 4 and 6.
205 | Kumar and Graf (1998), 133.
206 | Kumar and Graf (1998), 133.

Table 3-3 – Statutory Restrictions on Foreign Ownership of Equity across Regions and Sectors (where 100 = full foreign ownership allowed, WB 2010)[205]

Region/Economy	Mining, oil and gas ▼	Agriculture and forestry ▼	Light manufacturing ▼	Telecom ▼	Electricity ▼	Banking ▼	Insurance ▼	Transport ▼	Media ▼	Construction, tourism and retail ▼	Health care & waste management ▼
East Asia and Pacific	78.4	82.9	86.8	64.9	75.8	76.1	80.9	66.0	36.1	93.4	84.1
South Asia	88.0	90.0	96.3	94.8	94.3	87.2	75.4	79.8	68.0	96.7	100.0
Latin America and Caribbean	91.0	96.4	100.0	94.5	82.5	96.4	96.4	80.8	73.1	100.0	96.4
Eastern Europe and Central Asia	96.2	97.5	98.5	96.2	96.4	100.0	94.9	84.0	73.1	100.0	100.0
Sub-Saharan Africa	95.2	97.6	98.6	84.1	90.5	84.7	87.3	86.6	69.9	97.6	100.0
High-income OECD	100.0	100.0	93.8	89.9	88.0	97.1	100.0	69.2	73.3	100.0	91.7
Middle East and North Africa	78.8	100.0	95.0	84.0	68.5	82.0	92.0	63.2	70.0	94.9	90.0

207 | This table shows statutory restrictions on foreign ownership of equity in new investment projects (greenfield FDI) and on the acquisition of shares in existing compa-

At the same time, foreign land-consuming FDI continues to face other administrative barriers, such as limits "on the amount of equity owned by non-resident foreigners,"[208] or political interventions in the economies.[209] Importantly, public actors and interventions (in the form of state-owned enterprises and/or public approval processes) remain a key characteristic in many host economies characterized by high inequality.[210] While post-independence land reforms aimed to achieve greater equality through land redistribution, these have not overcome the legacy of the colonial period in the form of the concentration of land ownership and socioeconomic marginalization.[211] This means that "land grabbing" in SSA occurs in countries with a land crisis and a political economy characterized by highly unequal ownership structures, high socioeconomic inequality, and discriminatory legislation.[212]

A coexistence of novel and path-dependent elements also characterizes the international level. Core principles of imperial law, namely the most favored nation norm and the non-discrimination principle, have become key pillars of the post-WWII trade governance and legal structures that also govern FDI (General Agreement on Tariffs and Trade (GATT), then WTO).[213] At the same time, the institutional framework regulating FDI in general, and agriculture in particular, has changed—due to the extension of liberal principles and frames to this activity and sector. Under the WTO's Agreement on Agriculture (AoA), for instance, the approach towards agriculture has shifted from the notion of agri*culture* to agri*business*.[214]

In the home countries, many governments had shifted towards restrictive OFDI regulations after WWII to ensure that capital would be available for domestic reconstruction purposes (also see Chapter 7). However, since the 1980s, capital exports and trade activities have been deregulated again, and in some cases even pro-actively supported by policy makers. As a result of these

---

nies (mergers and acquisitions). One hundred equals full foreign equity ownership. The table is from the online database of the WB (2010) report (http://iab.worldbank.org/Data/Explore%20Topics/Investing-across-sectors).
208 | Moss et al. (2004), 9.
209 | Moss et al. (2004), 9.
210 | WB (2010); and Moss et al. (2004).
211 | Home (2012), 19.
212 | For a discussion of land reform problems, see Home (2012); and Borras and McKinley (2006).
213 | See collection of clauses in GATT and WTO in the database of the Japanese Ministry of Economy, Trade, and Industry (http://www.meti.go.jp/english/report/data/gCT9901e.html). Also see Anghie (2007) on the role of imperialism in realizing the universality of international law.
214 | Weis (2007).

processes of economic liberalization and deregulation, which have occurred almost worldwide since the 1990s, the most recent decades have often been characterized by an increasing corporate concentration, intra-firm division of labor, and market internationalization by TNCs, particularly in the food and energy sectors.[215] Against this background, Clapp and Fuchs have stressed the significant structural and discursive power of contemporary TNCs relative to the state and civil society.[216] Others, such as Murphy, have pointed to the importance of nation-states and governments in this process of private sector expansion.[217] From a historical perspective, it has become clear that these two seemingly contradictory observations might as well be complementary phenomena. At the same time, it seems that what is at least partly fueling the contemporary debate on "land grabbing" is the discontent with the social, economic, political, and ecological repercussions of this development trajectory, combined with a fundamental concern about how the state will be able to deliver core welfare functions in the future, considering the rapidly progressing privatization of access to, and governance of land and its multiple functions.

6. Conclusion

The review presented above outlined particular mechanisms that could be labeled as imperialist "best practices," such as the exertion of diplomatic pressure, use of military force, facilitation through legal instruments and corporate actors, or the provision of financial support by the state. Together, they showcase the strong role that was taken by the public sector in facilitating private sector expansion. Public actors promoted overseas investments, stating that these operations would provide the home country with revenues, jobs, and access to markets. Moreover, overseas investments were defined from a mercantilist viewpoint as a means to improve the home country's positional status in the system of states. Obviously, multiple imperialisms were at play; they were made unique by their particular country settings, actor constellations, and specific motivations.

References to (neo)colonialism and imperialism in contemporary explanations of "land grabs" since 2000 do not often match this diverse historical evidence on colonialism and imperialism; nor are they particularly meaningful. Rather than being solely about land, natural resources, or labor, colonial and imperial expansion was driven by a multitude of factors, including the protection of commercial interests; personal desire to achieve "self-aggrandize-

---

215 | See Clapp and Fuchs (2009); and Goldthau and Witte (2010).
216 | Clapp and Fuchs (2009).
217 | Dunning and Narula (1996); and Murphy (1994).

ment;" state desire to expand political influence as part of the European power game; or other events that resonated in the home countries, such as the Long Depression and processes of economic restructuring. Thus, both economic and non-economic aspects mattered, and "grabbed" land was important as natural resource, as well as territory, market space, strategic hub, or place of settlement.

The review also emphasizes the importance of accounting for the subtle changes that have occurred in political agendas, actor constellations, and corporate and resource governance post-World War II. Processes of economic liberalization and deregulation have yielded corporate concentration, intra-firm division of labor, and market internationalization by TNCs. Moreover, economic liberalization and deregulation has increased the discretionary power of corporate actors vis-à-vis the state. At the same time, governments in the host and home countries seem to embrace land-consuming overseas investments from the private sector and/or development agencies as a way to realize specific development agendas, even in sectors such as agriculture, where foreign access and ownership had been restricted in the past (also see Chapter 4-8).[218]

Importantly, the official support for land-consuming FDI raises questions about the accuracy of references to imperialism and (neo)colonialism in the literature and media, particularly in those cases where land-consuming OFDI is proactively sought after by the host countries. Do these concepts help to further our analysis and empirical understanding of what is happening in a particular "land grab" context, or to find effective ways to address the phenomenon? To highlight this problem, take, for example, the Oakland Institute's definition of "land grabbing" as "a neo-colonialism concept that has arisen in the midst of a severe food and economic crisis in the world in 2008."[219] Accordingly, it describes the "purchase of vast tracts of land by wealthier food-insecure nations and private investors from mostly poor, developing countries in order to produce crop for export."[220]

An article in the Somaliland Press rightly notes that such a "description is based on the assumption that the term of neo-colonialism is defined as a system that has been invented in place of colonialism, as a main instrument of oppression."[221] Accordingly, "the essence of neo-colonialism is that the state which is subjected to it, at least in theory, is an independent and has all outward features of international sovereignty [...]. However, in reality both its economic system and political policy are directed from outside."[222] Such references to (neo)colonialist traits of Chinese and British land-consuming OFDI have been

---

218 | See, for instance, Lavers (2011).
219 | Somaliland Press (19 May 2013).
220 | Somaliland Press (19 May 2013).
221 | Somaliland Press (19 May 2013).
222 | Somaliland Press (19 May 2013).

popular in the media. The National Post, for instance, writes the following about recent Chinese investment negotiations in the Ukraine:

Ukraine has agreed a deal with a Chinese company to lease 5% of its land to feed China's burgeoning population, it was reported on Tuesday.

It would be the biggest so called "land grab" agreement, where one country leases or sells land to another, in a trend that has been compared with the 19th century "scramble for Africa", but which is now spreading to eastern Europe.

Under the 50-year plan, China would eventually control 7.5 million acres, an area equivalent to the size of Belgium or Massachusetts, which represents 9% of Ukraine's arable land.

Initially 250.000 acres would be leased. The farmland in the eastern Dnipropetrovsk region would be cultivated principally for growing crops and raising pigs. The produce would be sold at preferential prices to Chinese state-owned conglomerates, said the Xinjiang Production and Construction Corp (XPCC), a quasi-military organisation also known as Bingtuan.

But KSG Agro denied reports that it had sold land to the Chinese, saying it had reached agreement for the Chinese only to modernize 7,500 acres and "may in the future gradually expand to cover more areas".

Any sort of "land-grab" deal can be sensitive politically. Madagascar was forced to scrap a plan to lease 2.5 million acres to South Korea in 2009 after protests against "neo-colonialism". The Philippines has also blocked a China deal.

"This reminds us of a colonial process even when there is no colonial link between the two countries involved," said Christina Plank, the co-author of a report by the Transnational Institute on "land-grabbing".[223]

However, this news article highlights two problems that apply to most descriptions of "land grabbing" as (neo)colonial. First, it seems that the concept of (neo)colonialism is used to weave a seemingly clear and coherent "land grab" story, rather than contribute to better data and an actual understanding of what is going on—in Ukraine, in China, or elsewhere. Second, as highlighted before, it remains unclear under what conditions such an investment transaction between two unequal partners would *not* be considered "land grabbing," nor qualify as a (neo)colonial relationship.

---

223 | Spillius (25 September 2013).

Chapter 3: Historical Perspectives on Overseas Land Acquisitions in the South

Concerning the subsequent assessment of Chinese and British land-consuming OFDI in SSA, all of the above stresses the need to generate rich empirical data and to account for the mix of structural and individual, strategic and contingent dynamics at work. At the same time, the case findings of this book suggest that contemporary references to imperialism and (neo)colonialism do not adequately capture the diversity of agency and political economies. In particular, these references seem to exaggerate the purposeful agency and strategic mastermind qualities of home countries, and to underestimate the agency of host countries regarding "land grabs."

Chapter 4: Chinese Investments in Africa
"Create Infinity, Benefit Mankind"

> The Chinese government encourages and supports Chinese enterprises with strength and good reputation to expand their investment in Africa, and has adopted necessary measures to guide them in this respect. The result is satisfactory.[1]
> (State Council 2010)

1. Introduction

The Yuan Long Ping High-Tech Agriculture Company, a seed company which is named after the "father of hybrid rice" and involved in investments in Africa, describes its managerial approach with the slogan "Create infinity, benefit mankind."[2] The company associates three aspects with this motto: to abide by the government strategy to upgrade and improve the sector's industry operations; to push ecological limits through technological innovation; and to expand business operations to profit from economies of scale. With regard to Chinese overseas investments in Sub-Saharan Africa, the motto seems to stretch beyond this originally operational context to capture major findings about these investments.

This chapter represents the first part of the two-part case study on China. It will present the core empirical characteristics of how (and partially why) Chinese land-consuming investments in Sub-Saharan Africa take place, in and over time. It proceeds as follows: Section 2 introduces the history of Chinese-African relations. These relations reach far back in time, but they have intensified since the 1990s. Section 3 then discusses the details of how these investments

---
[1] | State Council (2010).
[2] | Yuan Long Ping High-Tech Agriculture Company (2014), corporate website (http://www.lpht.com.cn/eng/company/Company.htm).

occur. In particular, it will focus on land-consuming FDI's sectoral composition and timelines, the role of land, the recipient context, and key actors and institutions. Section 4 briefly highlights the recipient context in which these investments occur, and Section 5 reviews the issue of Chinese labor exports that has attracted international attention. The chapter will conclude by summarizing the key empirical findings about Chinese land-consuming FDI in Sub-Saharan Africa (Section 6).

Core findings underline that the empirical characteristics of Chinese land-consuming investments in Sub-Saharan Africa are more multifaceted than standard explanations acknowledge. Despite a strong focus on resources, and the predominance of public actors, they involve a diverse range agencies and interests from the private and public sectors, home and recipient countries, and multilateral agencies; and they comprise investments in multiple sectors, from construction and mining to farming. Many projects predate the 2007/2008 crises, and some build on a long history of China-Africa cooperation. Distinct from orthodox explanations, investments in food production only made up a minor share of Chinese land-consuming FDI in Sub-Saharan Africa until 2015, and largely produced for regional consumption. Most projects apply market principles and mainstream managerial economics in their operations. Regarding the role of land, it is used in these projects as resource as well as productive space.

2. Background on China in Africa

While China-Africa cooperation began attracting international attention relatively recently, modern Chinese relations with the African continent trace back to the 1950s. However, China's engagement with African countries has only intensified dramatically in the last two decades. In 2010, China became the continent's third largest trading partner.[3] Additionally, Chinese OFDI activities in African countries rose from USD 317.43 million in 2004 to USD 2,111.99 million in 2010.[4] In 2016, China became the largest source of FDI in Sub-Saharan Africa, "totalling an investment outlay of 66.4 billion USD."[5] Moreover, Africa was receiving 46.7 % of all Chinese Official Development Aid (ODA) as of 2008, making the continent the primary focus of Chinese aid and economic cooperation.[6]

---

3 | State Council (2010).
4 | Ministry of Commerce (MOFCOM) (2011a), 81-87. Note: Data for 2004-2006 includes only non-financial OFDI flows.
5 | Bo (May 3, 2017).
6 | State Council (2011); and Li (2006).

The nature of the relations between China and Africa has also changed significantly: from the 1950s up to the 1970s they were characterized primarily by "unilateral economic assistance from China to Africa" to improve the "self-reliance" and "self-development abilities" of recipient countries, but these relations have grown more complex.[7] In the 1980s, the focus shifted from unilateral economic assistance in the form of aid towards "carrying out mutually beneficial cooperation with Africa."[8] The latter was supposed to benefit China's interests as much as Africa's (see below).[9]

Increasingly, aid came to resemble economic cooperation projects with the medium-term objective of profitability, whereas the focus on self-reliance and self-development was disbanded. While the eligibility to receive aid remained linked to the One China principle[10] of the past, at the same time, aid and economic cooperation became part of China's resources and, as this chapter argues, expansion diplomacy, in the search for export markets, business opportunities, and allies in international politics. In an interview in 2011, Lu Shaye, the Director-General of the Department of African Affairs in the Ministry of Foreign Affairs from 2009-2014[11], describes the driver for, and nature of these changing relations as follows:

With China's rapid economic development, there is a growing demand from China for Africa's market and resources. China's investment in Africa also grew rapidly. While taking away resources from Africa, we also give back to African countries. We helped African countries put in place a large number of infrastructure projects according to their economic development needs. It's all about each taking what he needs.[12]

Along these lines, the Ministry of Foreign Affairs states that the intensification of China-Africa relations has allowed China and African countries to satisfy their rising demand "for products and technologies from each other during the process of industrialization and urbanization." Moreover, Zhong Manying, then-chief of the Department of Western Asian and African Affairs in the

---

7 | See interview with Lu Shaye, then-Director-General of the Department of African Affairs, conducted by Gouraud (18 October 2011). Lu Shaye was Director-General from 2009-2014 (http://ca.china-embassy.org/eng/dsxx/dsjl/t1442216.htm).
8 | Gouraud (18 October 2011).
9 | Gouraud (18 October 2011).
10 | The One China policy is about the rejection of Taiwan as a sovereign state and the acceptance of Beijing as the sole legitimate representative of China. It is a precondition for entering into diplomatic relations with China. See, for instance, Winkler (June 2012).
11 | See the website of the Embassy of the People's Republic of China in Canada for Lu Shaye's biography (http://ca.china-embassy.org/eng/dsxx/dsjl/t1442216.htm).
12 | Gouraud (18 October 2011).

Ministry of Commerce, has been quoted as saying that "[t]here is [still] tremendous potential for economic cooperation."[13]

In practice, this mutual demand model has resulted in Chinese-African trade flows that largely follow the Western pattern. China imports primary commodities relevant for its economy, such as cotton, phosphates, energy, and mineral products, and exports value-added products, such as machinery, chemicals, food, and textiles.[14] To expand imports and moderate the negative trade balance of African countries, China has offered zero tariff treatment to some countries. Moreover, freight charges were reduced or annulled, and Chinese trade missions were sent to African countries "to help increase the continent's exports to China," particularly regarding primary commodities.[15] Still, data from 2011-2014 shows that the terms of trade have been deteriorating for Sub-Saharan African countries, particularly for China's key trading partners Angola, South Africa, Republic of Congo, Zambia, and Equatorial Guinea, as a result of increasing imports from China and declining exports to China due to "reduced external demand and lower commodity prices."[16] On the investment side, mining and manufacturing projects made up 51 % of Chinese OFDI in Africa in 2010, reflecting the country's industrial make-up and policy orientation, while hinting at the importance of looking more closely at the potential pull and push factors for these investments.

At the same time, it is essential to consider that even though Africa seems to have gained importance in China's development ambitions, by regional comparison, the continent still only ranks fifth as a destination of Chinese OFDI. It is preceded by Asia (Hong Kong in particular), Latin America, Europe, and North America.[17] The same kind of asymmetric significance holds true for China's top trading partners, the top five of which are the US, Japan, Hong Kong, South Korea, and Taiwan.[18] Yet, the details of these investments are much more complex than such a broad comparison suggests. On the bilateral level, for instance, Angola has become the second largest oil supplier to China after Saudi Arabia,[19] and China has become the primary export destination for Angola, followed by the US, with the greatest share of exports being crude oil (in 2009).[20]

---

13 | Ministry of Foreign Affairs (15 October 2010).
14 | See, for instance, Romei and Jopson (14 December 2010). The figures are from UNCTAD.
15 | CAITEC (2010), 3.
16 | Romei (December 3, 2015).
17 | State Council (2010).
18 | Dutta (2005), 222. Data from 2003.
19 | Salvaterra (13 May 2013).
20 | Sandrey (2009), 15, 17; Chinafrica.asia (2009).

3. KEY CHARACTERISTICS OF CHINESE LAND-CONSUMING OFDI IN SUB-SAHARAN AFRICA

Clearly, the empirical evidence on China-Africa relations suggests that the common narrative, according to which Chinese land-consuming investments are relatively new and meant to address energy and/or food security concerns back home following the 2007/2008 crises, might fall short of apprehending the diversity of factors and events at play. To facilitate a meaningful understanding of how Chinese investments in Sub-Saharan Africa (SSA) actually happen, this section will highlight their primary empirical characteristics, accounting for sector distribution and project timelines, and the role of land, stated goals, the issue of labor migration, and key actors and institutions.

The major findings of this section are as follows: Firstly, the investments include different sectors, and the agricultural sector makes up the smallest percentage of land-consuming investment projects in SSA. Secondly, most investment projects pre-date the 2008 crisis, and they have undergone an economic shift over time. Thirdly, the role of land in these projects is often secondary, as these investments are mostly about expanding business operations overseas rather than acquiring land. Still, what characterizes these investment projects is that they consume land in their operations. Fourthly, only a few incidents in which the Chinese government proactively tried to acquire land for agricultural or resettlement purposes have been reported. Fifthly, most investments are embedded in the respective recipient countries' national development plans.

Sectors

The investigated investment activities comprise multiple sectors, such as farming, attempted resettlement projects, mining, manufacturing, and construction. Some of these projects have failed while others have already been implemented. Looking at them in more detail, these investment projects aim to grow and process food, biofuels, cotton, or sugar; restore so-called farm wasteland; resettle Chinese farmers; produce cement; construct public infrastructure and irrigation systems; train farmers in particular agricultural technologies; or construct Special Economic Zones that serve as manufacturing, agribusiness, or IT hubs for Chinese and/or other foreign companies.[21]

---

21 | It is important to note that agricultural projects prevail in this research project's list of investigated projects (see Appendix A). However, compared to other assessments and official data by the Chinese government, this does not seem to be representative of the actual sectoral composition. Instead, it appears to be the result of biased reporting, and the research project has relied on related "land grab" reports to start investigating

While the international debate on Chinese investments in Africa focuses largely on investments in agriculture in the context of food security, a report by the State Council suggests that this sector only accounted for 3.1 % of total Chinese direct investments in Africa in 2009 (measured by value).[22] The predominant investment sectors were the mining industry (29.2 %) and the manufacturing sector (22.0 %), followed by construction (15.8 %) and finance (13.9 %) (see Figure 41).[23] It has been noted by Brautigam that the small percentage of OFDI going into agricultural projects is not as a result of a lack of opportunities. In fact, Chinese actors have continuously been offered land to invest in by African governments:

If Chinese investors wanted large land leases, they clearly could have signed some. After all, as a 2012 Oakland Institute study[24] showed, "Mozambique granted concessions to investors for more than 2.5 million hectares (ha) of land between 2004 and the end of 2009" almost entirely to European and South African investors—there were no Chinese investors in their list.[25]

Rather, the small percentage of agricultural projects reflects the low priority assigned to them by the Chinese government, as well as investors, in the past. In fact, agricultural investments since the 1990s have largely been undertaken as part of Chinese resource diplomacy, and upon the request of African governments.[26]

However, in the medium-term, it seems that the sectoral composition of Chinese land-consuming investments is likely to change. A declaration of the China-Africa Cooperation Forum in 2009,[27] a political platform that facilitates dialogue between China and African countries on matters of trade, aid, and investment, announced that the countries would explore new areas of investment, such as tourism, which might involve different kinds of land development.[28] Moreover, the previous marginalization of the commercial agricultural sector might be ending. In 2011, China's Ministry of Finance and Ministry of Commerce issued a joint notice[29] outlining their financial support for the

---

Chinese projects. In fact, the discussion about Chinese land-consuming FDI in the "land grab" literature has largely focused on food production and farming.
22 | State Council (2010). Also see remark in previous footnote 464.
23 | State Council (2010).
24 | Home and Mittal (2011), 2.
25 | Brautigam (12 January 2012).
26 | Alden (2007); Brautigam (2009).
27 | Shelton (22 December 2009).
28 | State Council (2010).
29 | MOFCOM (2011c).

overseas expansion of Chinese agribusiness.³⁰ Accordingly, special funds of a maximum of RMB 30 million (per annum and enterprise) were made available for investment projects in mining, agriculture, forestry, or fisheries.³¹ However, this general financial support for overseas farming is not necessarily intended for investments in Africa. Therefore, it is difficult to assess what impact it might have for African countries and farmers.³²

*Figure 4-1 – Distribution of China's Direct Investment in African Industries (end of 2009, State Council 2010, measured by value)*³³

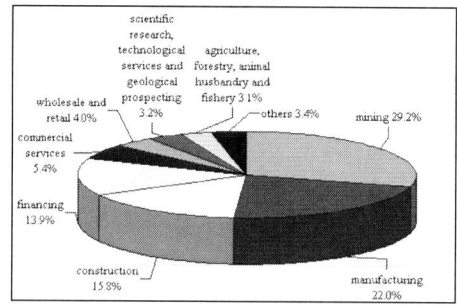

Timelines

The Chinese land-consuming investments that this research investigated (see Appendix A) often go far back in time, thereby questioning the widespread narrative of a "land rush" that began as a result of the 'international financial, food, and energy crises in 2007/2008'. Interestingly, this holds true especially for investments in agriculture, many of which are either a continuation of Chinese agricultural aid programs in Africa, the rehabilitation of former Chinese agricultural Friendship Farms, or related to other events pre-dating the 2007/2008 crises.³⁴ For instance, the project by SINO CAM IKO in Cameroon builds on the remnants of a formerly Taiwanese Cooperation Farm that was set up in 1972. After bilateral negotiations in 2005, the project officially began in 2006.³⁵ Also, the ZTE energy project in the Democratic Republic of the Congo (DRC) would have been part of an attempt to rehabilitate a plantation-based Sino-Congolese

---

30 | MOFCOM (2011c). Also see English.news.cn (18 August 2010).
31 | MOFCOM (2011c).
32 | For a list of MOFCOM-approved Chinese agricultural projects in African countries until 2013, see Brautigam and Zhang (2013), 1680.
33 | State Council (2010).
34 | See, for instance, Li (2006).
35 | Brautigam and Zhang (2013), 1684-1685.

cooperation project from 1972.[36] However, as of 2013, this palm oil project, which would have consumed up to 100.000 ha, and intended to convert palm oil into biofuels, has not materialized. Instead, the company operates a farm on 256 ha that produces maize, soy, meat, chicken, and eggs.[37] Meanwhile, the failed resettlement project in Mozambique, which is one of most frequently cited projects in the "land grab" literature, dates back to 1997 and the time of the Asian financial crisis.[38]

Similar to these agricultural investments, land-consuming projects in the manufacturing, construction, energy, and/or mining sectors also have histories that predate the crises in 2007/2008. For example, investments in the construction and mining sectors started to pick up speed in the 1950s and 1990s, respectively. While the rise in construction projects was associated with Chinese aid projects, the mining projects reflect China's rising external resource dependency. Even in the manufacturing sector, overseas investments date back to the 1980s, with approximately 200 investments taking place between 1979 and 2001.[39] However, investments in most sectors have only increased significantly in number and size since China's opening up in the 1990s, and particularly with the adoption of the "Go Abroad" (*zou chuqu*) policies in 2000 (also see Chapter 5 on home country measures).

Even though many projects have long histories, their conduct and purpose have changed with time in ways that are key to understanding the core features of contemporary Chinese land-consuming OFDI. Projects with a long history bear especially strong witness to the altered nature of the Chinese presence in African countries. Take, for example, the SUKALA S.A. project, a joint venture between the Chinese state-owned company CLETC and the Malian government.[40] In its current form, the project began in 1996, when the Chinese company—following a request made by the Malian government—bought a majority share in the Mali state company SUKALA S.A. through a debt-for-equity-swap. Tracing the project back to its beginnings in the 1960s reveals that it had started out as an aid and technical cooperation project under cooperative management. It then went through a phase of transitional management before becoming a joint venture.[41] This project's shifting character is in fact repre-

---

36 | See Putzel and Kabuyaya (2011), 34; and Brautigam and Zhang (2013), 1686.
37 | Officially, the company has said that high transport costs made the palm oil project unprofitable. See Brautigam and Zhang (2013), 1686.
38 | Brautigam and Ekman (2012), 5; and Ekman (2010), 30-31.
39 | Rosen and Hanemann (2009).
40 | Diaz-Chavez et al. (2010), 50; Aiddata.org (n.d.c); Feng (2010); and Baxter and Mousseau (2011), 19, 22.
41 | Moreover, the precursor factories date back even farther, having been built in the 1960s and renovated in the 1980s with Chinese government involvement.

sentative of the overarching trend in Chinese investments: most have changed from an aid basis to an economic (for-profit) rationale.

This change in the rationale of long-term projects in the context of home country reform is also characteristic of the construction sector. Until 1978, Chinese construction companies were part of unilateral technical aid programs, along with agricultural projects. Thereafter, following domestic governance reforms in China, construction companies were turned into sub-contractors and began bidding for contracts and financing from multilateral development programs, domestic development budgets, and bilateral "barter exchange deals" through which construction was undertaken in exchange for resources (to be exploited in the future).[42] These "barter exchange deals" were pre-financed by the China EXIM Bank following approval by China's Ministry of Commerce.[43] Africa is the second largest market after Asia for Chinese construction companies, while the percentage of turnover in Africa has more than doubled since 2001, rising from 14.1 % to 30.9 % (in 2011).[44] This story is again linked with, but not exclusive to, home country support, reforms, and resource diplomacy. According to a WB study, China has become a major financier of African infrastructure construction, covering a wide range of projects from dams, irrigation, and roads to schools, hospitals, and power stations.[45] Aside from their predominance in the construction sector across Africa, these companies fulfill multiple functions of significance for China-Africa cooperation. For instance, they are important agents in the export promotion of Chinese manufactured products and Chinese labor services.[46]

While this trend towards a market rationale seems to apply to land-consuming OFDI activities across sectors, the focus on timelines highlights that there are also peculiarities observable in each of the sectors over time. The recent renewal of agricultural (aid) projects, for instance, is often seen as an outcome of bilateral resource diplomacy and the proactive lobbying of African governments.[47] As a result, there are 20 so-called agricultural demonstration centers being established across Africa, as announced at the 2009 high level summit of the Forum of China Africa Cooperation (FOCAC) in Sharm-El-Sheik.[48] In 2012, at the fifth FOCAC meeting, it was agreed that China would build more agricultural demonstration centers in the future.[49] These demon-

---

42 | Asche and Schueller (2008); Yi and Yong 2011, 7-8.
43 | Asche and Schueller (2008).
44 | Yi and Yong (2011), 7-8.
45 | Foster et al. (2008).
46 | Shengjin (1995).
47 | Brautigam (2009); Alden (2007).
48 | See Li (2010).
49 | FOCAC (2012).

stration centers were initiated "all at the request of local governments [...] for their own agricultural purposes," with the aim of rehabilitating former aid projects. The estimated investment value is RMB 40-55 million per center.[50] Some of these centers have been listed in "land grab" databases.[51] The other category of agricultural investment projects, so-called "commercial agricultural enterprises investing in land and agriculture in Africa," is a rather recent one. The precursors, however, were again former agricultural aid projects that had been strategically re-orientated in the 1990s to run profitably and sustainably under market-oriented management.

Given the growing intensity and changing quality of China-Africa exchanges, how successful they will be remains to be seen. Looking at the time that passes from a company's first relevant statement until project completion, particularly in the agricultural sector, there often seems to be a great difference between announced project deadlines and what has actually been implemented by the time that deadline arrives.[52] This observation, which also holds true for many British land-consuming FDI projects,[53] is usually related to difficulties with administrative processes, funding problems, or other unexpected events. At the same time, it is hard to evaluate such projects given the lack of data on investment deadlines and the absence of follow-up reports on project outcomes. On a general note, statements made by representatives from various sectors suggest that it is possible to work profitably, but that it would be unrealistic to expect extremely high returns on investment. This is a feature to keep in mind when researching the projects of investment funds that promise above-average returns on their land-consuming investments in Sub-Saharan Africa.[54]

What can be said about the roles of the 2007/2008 food, energy, and finance crises that the orthodox explanations rely on? Regarding the financial crisis, it has so far had an ambiguous impact on Chinese overseas investments. On the one hand, it allowed some companies to 'go out' and get 'cheap bargains,' profiting from price sensitivity and declining asset prices. At the same time, the

---

50 | Brautigam (12 January 2012). Also see Ekman (2010), 33-35; and Li (2010), who support this assessment.

51 | Projects that appear in"land grab"listings have entered the database via crowdsourcing. This means they have been reported by NGOs or the media. This fact explains the relatively random (incomplete) listing of projects, such as the agricultural demonstration centers; and it warns to automatically equate a listed project with"land grabbing."Instead, it is necessary to review the individual cases and evaluate what is happening.

52 | See Brautigam and Zhang (2013) for a review of major Chinese agricultural projects, their timelines, and actual implementation status.

53 | See Chapter 6.

54 | See example in Table 4-1.

global economic crisis presented a challenge for potential Chinese investors.[55] In 2009, the total value of approved non-financial OFDI projects declined by nearly two thirds (USD 3.7 billion) from the value of the previous year (USD 10 billion); however, it has since been recovering.[56] Regarding the food crisis, China was largely food self-sufficient as of 2007,[57] when the crisis hit. Finally, external energy dependency has been a government concern since the mid-1990s. It is not a recent phenomenon.

Land: Its Role and Use in the Investments

The multiplicity of investment sectors and their changing character over time raises questions with regard to the role played by land in these investments. The following section will therefore briefly outline the extent and use of land in these investments. It will also highlight the major strategies of access and aspects of land governance observed in the projects under study.

Extent

In a 2011 interview, Lu Shaye, the Director-General of the Department of African Affairs within the Chinese Ministry of Foreign Affairs from 2009 to 2014, stated that Chinese investments in agriculture are small in scale and do not enclose land, contrary to "western countries [which] have enclosed a total of 30 million hectares of land, equivalent to the half of France."[58] This research's assessment of projects (see Appendix A), as well as reports[59] on more recent projects mentioned in the "land grab" literature, indicates that the Chinese land-consuming projects in Sub-Saharan Africa seem to range from 100 ha to 100.000 ha, with the majority using less than 10.000 ha. This means that compared to Chinese land-consuming FDI in other regions (e.g., Latin America and Eastern Europe), but also in comparison with British land-consuming OFDI in Sub-Saharan Africa, the average size of Chinese land-consuming OFDI projects in Sub-Saharan Africa seems to be smaller. Then again, it is all a matter of perspective: when, for instance, the 100 ha project size is compared to the average farm size in major investor countries, such as China, where the average amount of land available to farmers is 0.47 ha (in 2005),[60] or seen against the background of the

---

55 | Rosen and Hanemann (2009). 1.
56 | Rosen and Hanemann (2009), 1.
57 | FAO (2009), 33-35.
58 | Gouraud (18 October 2011).
59 | Brautigam and Zhang (2013); ILC (2012); Smaller et al. (2012).
60 | Kahrl et al. (2005), 11.

land crisis[61] and small-scale farming in the recipient countries, the amount of land claimed by some investments seems enormous.[62]

Overall, it is impossible to assess the total extent of land used by Chinese overseas investments, partially due to the lack of comprehensive data, and partially due to the great discrepancy between the announced or envisioned size of a project and the actual land under operation. The discrepancy seems to be particularly characteristic of land-consuming projects in agriculture. To provide several examples: even though negotiations had been completed in 2006, and a Memorandum of Understanding (MoU) had been signed between the Chinese SOE Shaanxi Agricultural Group and the Ministry of Agriculture (Cameroon), the Chinese subsidiary in Cameroon, SINO CAM IKO, was operating only 100-150 ha of the announced 10.000 ha five years later (in 2011).[63] In fact, the company was only able to build a rice demonstration center on the land of a formerly Taiwanese-aided farm that had been closed when Cameroon decided to engage in diplomatic relations with China instead.[64] As of 2010, operations were still being held back by the Cameroonian government, which had not approved the further expansion of this and other projects, contrary to the original investment agreement in the form of the MoU.[65] Also, the Chipata Cotton Company (now the China Africa Cotton Company),[66] which is a subsidiary of Qingdao New Textiles Ltd., operating in Zambia since 2004, originally only had 2,500 contract farmers out of the envisioned 20.000.[67] And the Hebei Hanhe Investment Company, a state-owned provincial company that has started in Uganda in 2009, and is targeting the development of around

---

61 | The land crisis in Sub-Saharan Africa is characterized by the highly unequal distribution of land, insecure tenure relationships, and rising land use competition (amongst other problems) that the respective host governments have not been able to resolve since independence in spite of the fact that land reforms have been a core component of political programs.

62 | See, for instance, Eastwood et al. (2004); or Agriculture Council of America. (2014).

63 | Li 2010; and Brautigam and Zhang (2013), 1684-1685.

64 | Putzel et al. (2011), 31.

65 | Brautigam and Zhang (2013), 1685; and Putzel and Kabuyaya (2011), 31.

66 | It seems that Chipata Cotton Company experienced profitability problems, leading to its temporary closure in 2007. It changed its name and re-opened in 2008 with the financial support of the China-Africa Development Fund of the China Development Bank, which invests in African companies. See Schoneveld et al. (2014), 25-27; and China Development Bank (31 May 2012).

67 | Tschirley and Kabwe (2009); *Times of Zambia* (14 June 2004); Chinese Embassy in the Republic of Zambia (10 September 2013); Phiri (11 September 2013); Wang (30 June 2014); and China Development Bank (31 May 2012).

17.000 ha in 10 years, had a total of 173 ha under operation as of 2011, growing maize, vegetables, and trees.[68]

These discrepancies point to the difficult and time-consuming nature of large-scale investment projects, particularly in the agricultural sector, where investors can run into political, ecological, social, and operative problems. At the same time, the discrepancy between the announced investment scales and the actual amount of land under operation underlines that in the near future an expansion of Chinese land-consuming investments in Sub-Saharan Africa is to be expected. This seems even more likely given the aforementioned (2011) policy turn and the new funds that were made available to Chinese agribusiness by the Ministries of Agriculture and Finance.[69]

Use and Purpose

There exist two main types of land use in these investments: its use as a resource with particular qualities such as limestone or arable land, and its use as a productive space for industrial or modernization projects. One observation is that the purpose differs across regions, at least with regard to investments in agriculture. In the case of Latin America and Eastern Europe, reports indicate that Chinese land-consuming OFDI projects might be producing for export to China in order to "circumvent the Chicago commodities exchange and secure direct grain and oil supply."[70] However, this does not seem applicable to most agricultural investment projects in African countries.[71] Instead, most of the investment projects in SSA that this research project has looked at seem to produce products that are intended for local and/or regional consumption. In the area of food production in particular, there is no evidence that these projects are intended to meet Chinese food demands.[72] However, the outputs of farming projects that produce biofuels or industrial crops such as cotton seem to be intended for export to international markets or China.[73] Moreover, some projects might affect food security not because they export food crops, but as a result of land-use competition, (*de facto*) ownership changes, and/or the diversion of food resources such as cassava to the production of biofuels.[74]

---

68 | Wang (10 October 2011); and Aiddata.org (n.d.b).
69 | Macquarie University and Free University Amsterdam Project (15 May 2011).
70 | Rasmussen et al. (2011); Finance.jrj.com.cn (May 2011).
71 | Rasmussen et al. (2011); Finance.jrj.com.cn (May 2011).
72 | Brautigam (2009); Ekman (2010).
73 | One example is the Chipata Cotton Company. It exports the surplus cotton that exceeds the capacity of its ginning factory to international markets and China. Schoneveld et al. (2014), 25-27; and China Development Bank (31 May 2012).
74 | The latter case has been reported from Benin. See details and organogram in Nonfodji (2011).

At the same time, other factors that relate to the use of land have to be accounted for when assessing the utility derived from these investments. This clearly extends beyond the question of production for local or international consumption. In the case of the agricultural demonstration centers, for instance, these projects support the internationalization of Chinese agribusinesses, allow for economies of scale, and create new markets for their services in the form of proprietary seeds and machinery. In the case of infrastructure or mining projects, these projects often support Chinese efforts to access resources and/or promote exports. This means that in many cases, the additional utility derived from the use of land overseas perfectly matches China's official development objectives, as outlined in its OFDI policy, the country's 11th and 12th Five Year Plans,[75] and/or Africa-relevant policies. A closer assessment of the question of how these investments relate to the interests of influential Chinese actors and broader development agenda will be provided in Chapter 5, where the country's political economy, ideology, policy, and development trajectory are considered.

Strategies of Access

Land for agricultural investments is usually acquired through leasing contracts, contract farming schemes, or through joint ventures with domestic companies that have direct or indirect access to land. The method used depends on domestic legislation and context. Ordinarily, the suitability of the land area has been identified through exploratory visits. Interestingly, there are hardly any known cases in which Chinese investors or officials explicitly tried to request large-scale land leases.[76] One such case has been reported from Mozambique, where the Chinese government negotiated a resettlement project of Chinese farmers that was first proposed in 1997. However, the project negotiations never left parliament and were discontinued due to political sensitivities.[77] Another case is the ZTE biofuel project in the DRC, where the company negotiated at least 100.000 ha for palm oil plantations with the DRC Ministry of Agriculture in 2007.[78] As of 2013, the palm oil project had not been implemented. Instead, the company was farming 256 ha as previously mentioned. The fact that a case which has been widely reported as the "land grabbing" case—a Chinese company's acquisition of 2.800.000 ha of land for the production of biofuels[79]—does not exist highlights the unsound quality of many "land grab" reports.[80]

---

75 | Chinese Government (2006); Chinese Government (2011).
76 | Brautigam and Zhang (2013).
77 | Ekman (2010), 30-31.
78 | Brautigam and Zhang (2013), 1686.
79 | E.g., GTZ (2009), 66; GLP (2010), 24.
80 | For comparison of different reports and their use of data, also see Giovanetti and Ticci (2011), 44 (Table A 1).

In many cases, the recipient governments' agencies have offered land for agriculture to Chinese investors. In Cameroon, for instance, the government presented the Chinese businessman Wang Jianjun (who manages the SINO IKO CAM company) with a long-term land lease option for 10.000 ha for the production of hybrid rice.[81] In Mozambique, several agricultural projects in the Zambezi valley, mostly in processing, were chosen and lobbied for by the Mozambique government.[82] In Mali, the SUKALA S.A. project, which owns an approximately 5.000 ha sugarcane plantation, was requested by the Mali government. This last investment took the form of a debt-equity swap that led to a joint venture between the Chinese SOE CLETC and the Malian government. The arrangement gave the Chinese side indirect control due to its majority stake (70 %) in the project.[83] The proactive attraction of Chinese investors also seems to be the case with regard to the agricultural demonstration centers mentioned earlier. [84] To obtain this type of cooperation project the recipient country has to submit an application. The agricultural demonstration center in Tanzania, for instance, comprises between 62 ha and 300 ha (depending on the estimate), and is run by the Chongqing Seed Corporation, a Chinese municipal state-owned enterprise. The land is used both to produce a hybrid rice variant that has the Chinese company's identifiable intellectual property and to train others in its cultivation. Apart from the demonstration site, the center grows rice through centralized outgrower schemes with local farmers, and expects to modernize Tanzanian agricultural production.[85]

The phenomenon of African governments offering land to investors for lease is far from unique to the Chinese case. An informal interview with two representatives of Saudi Arabia's Ministry of Agriculture in 2011,[86] as well as the very straightforward website announcements and, in some cases, overseas presence of Investment Promotion Agencies from host countries (e.g., Zambia), all reveal that this phenomenon seems to be common practice. At the same time, land lease processes remain tricky: the SINO CAM IKO project in Cameroon, for instance, was still awaiting approval of the land contract from the recipient government's presidential office, even though the China EXIM Bank had already transferred two thirds of the total (USD 62 million) announced in the signed

---

81 | Putzel et al. (2011), 31.
82 | Ekman (2010), 29-30.
83 | Diaz-Chavez et al (2010), 41; and Nolte and Voget-Kleschin (2013). 16-17.
84 | Li (2010).
85 | Tanzanian Affairs (1 January 2013); Brautigam and Tang (2012), 9-10; and China-Daily.com.cn (17 May 2008).
86 | Informal interview, Berlin, November (2011).

investment agreement.[87] In another case, reported by the China State Farm and Agribusiness Corporation, the Mauritanian government suddenly decided to raise the annual land rent by 20 %, which, together with other events, namely the fuel price rise and a host government induced price ceiling on agricultural products, led to a failure of the investment project (see Table 4-1).[88]

Table 4-1 – The Case of the China State Farm and Agribusiness Corporation (China.org.cn)[89]

The China State Farm and Agribusiness Corporation (CSFAC)

"Decades ago we were at the forefront of China's campaign to reclaim wasteland. Now we apply our skills in African countries."—Han Xiangshan, Vice President of the China State Farm and Agribusiness Corporation, and leader of its agricultural projects in Africa.

Currently, CSFAC operates on a total of 16.000 hectares in different countries in SSA, growing cash and food crops, and engaging in the whole range of agricultural production, processing and sales.

Success factors mentioned are (1) the political and policy support by African governments (e.g., preferential policies for expansion of the agricultural sector; tax exemptions on agricultural machinery and production material imports; tax rebates on fuel for agricultural use; reduction of annual land rent); (2) natural conditions such as the availability of fertile soil, favourable climate; (3) China's capability to provide adequate agricultural technology, management, machinery and other inputs.

Yet, political and natural risks remain, together with varying market potential, ideology gaps and differences in work efficiency. Han Xianshan refers to a former CSFAC project in Mauretania [sic], which had to close after three years despite a successful process of reclamation, experimentation and cultivation on the rented farm. However, the government raised the annual land rent by 20 %, and together with the domestic fuel price inflation, the annual expenditure rose by USD 100.000. When the local government then put a price ceiling on agricultural products, the state farm project ran high losses, and had to close."

For reasons of risk minimization and/or domestic legislation, most investment projects rely on indirect forms of access to farmland, including joint ventures, contract farming, and/or purchase agreements. If the data on the number of farmers under contract is correct, contract farming as a form of land access seems to be very common and must be affecting many rural households. Take, for example, the Malawi Cotton Company, a joint venture of the China-Africa

---

87 | See Khan and Baye 2008; Jansson (2009), 10; Brautigam and Zhang (2013), 1685; and Li (2010).
88 | China.org.cn (10 December 2003).
89 | China.org.cn (10 December 2003).

Development Fund[90] and the Qingdao Ruichang Cotton Cooperation. It is active in cotton production from farming to processing, and reportedly involves 110.000 rural households under a central farming contract scheme ("company + rural household"). This means that the farmers grow the cotton, whereas the company controls and provides inputs and reaps value-added margins by processing the harvest at the new spinning and ginning plant in Balaka for export to China.[91] Through the scheme, the company was harvesting close to 40.000 tons of cotton as of 2011.[92] In another project, a Chinese company appears to deliver fertilizer and other assistance to a peanut growing project in Senegal. There, the recipient country's farmer association organizes the production of the peanuts on 100.000 ha. It is envisioned that 30 % of the yield will be shipped to China, while the rest will be processed at local factories.[93] Finally, there are projects which mix direct and indirect forms of access as a strategy to ensure sufficient supplies for plant operation in the context of supply scarcities. For instance, the SUCOBE Company in Benin, which is an affiliate of the Chinese SOE COMPLANT, relies on external harvests to complement its own agricultural output. In addition to sugar cane production on 4,800 ha of land, which the company is leasing for 99 years (renewable), it buys cassava from local farmers for its plant operation.[94] As a result, there has been a cassava price hike in Benin.[95]

Aside from investments by agribusiness or mining corporations, the use of land usually plays out more indirectly in its function as a space where productive activities can take place. In the case of construction and infrastructure projects, for instance, the land is appropriated by the respective government and only of profit for Chinese companies in its use as a construction or rehabilitation site. And with regard to Chinese Special Economic Zones (SEZs), seven of which are currently operating across Africa, the land is leased and becomes the basis of a quasi-extraterritorial zone. Though special regulations apply within the zone, it remains under the control of the respective recipient government (see Table 4-2). China itself has used SEZs to serve as controlled areas of economic reform while retaining the old political system and it now seems to export its development experiences to countries that are officially striving to become emerging econo-

---

90 | See Chapter 5 for a more detailed description of this fund in the home country context.
91 | CDB (31 May 2012); and Chirombo (29 December 2009).
92 | See CDB (31 May 2012); and Chirombo (29 December 2009).
93 | Smaller et al. (2012), 16 (Note: While China imports significant amounts of peanuts from Senegal (e.g., China DSIC International Trade Co. Ltd 2014), this particular case has so far remained unconfirmed.)
94 | See Nonfodji (2011).
95 | Nonfodji (2011), 12.

mies.[96] In Mauritius, for instance, Chinese companies are establishing an SEZ which is intended to become a major manufacturing hub for Chinese light industrial products, medicines, textiles, and electronics. Built on an area of 200-500 ha, this SEZ is headed by Chinese companies, and it is expected to accommodate 40 Chinese companies and create 34.000 jobs, of which 8.000 shall go to Chinese contractors. It is claimed to generate USD 220 million through exports and attract an inflow of USD 750 million worth of investments.[97]

Table 4-2 – Chinese Special Economic Zones in Africa (Brautigam and Tang 2011; Brautigam [February] 2011)

Nr.	Special Economic Zone
1	Chambishi, Zambia: copper and copper related industries.
2	Lusaka, Zambia: garments, food, appliances, tobacco and electronics. This zone is classified as a subzone of the Chambishi zone.
3	Jinfei, Mauritius: manufacturing (textiles, garments, machinery, high-tech), trade, tourism, and finance.
4	Ethiopia: electrical machinery, construction materials, steel, and metallurgy.
5	Ogun, Nigeria: construction materials, ceramics, ironware, furniture, wood processing, medicine, and computers.
6	Lekki, Nigeria: transportation equipment, textiles, home appliances, telecommunications, and light industry.
7	Suez, Egypt: petroleum equipment, electrical appliance, textile, and automobile manufacturers. (completed in October 2010)

Aspects of Governance

A closer look at issues of land governance also highlights the importance of taking note of agency in host countries. In most recipient countries, land is owned by the state. Key ministries or government agencies are involved in these investments, often depending on the land's function. Arable land, for instance, frequently falls within the competency of the respective Ministry of Agriculture, whereas land suitable for mining is overseen by the respective Ministry of Land and Resources. At the same time, investments often take place under the guidance of Investment Promotion Agencies. The negotiation and approval process has sometimes included parliamentary consultations, while in other cases the investment has been approved by a single office within a Ministry

---

96 | See, for instance, Konijin (2013), 3 (Box 3).
97 | Brautigam and Tang (2011). For a more detailed story of the JinFei Special Economic Zone, see Alves (2011).

vested with extensive powers to decide over land leases, as, for instance, a report about the Office du Niger in Mali underlines.[98]

Many cases show an overlap of competencies, as well as an absence of effective governance structures, clear objectives, or a country-wide land-use or development plan. Often, the respective agencies do not know how much arable land is available in total and earmark territory for foreign investments based on assumptions which differ across agencies.[99] In some cases, the political elite seem divided on matters of land-consuming FDI.[100] From a more historical perspective that accounts for the context of the SSA land crisis in which these investments take place, these failures to effectively govern the land used by the investments are not surprising. Rather, they are closely related to the political economy of land in the respective host countries.[101] In this regard, a reporter commenting on the weak governance structures in Angola concluded that the foreign investments were the outcome of "a global alliance between the well-connected in Angola and get-rich forces in China, Brazil and Portugal," which in the case of Angola have come to form an alliance that is even "a threat to the former colonial forces in Europe and the speculators in Wall Street."[102]

Actors and Institutions

Obviously, on the recipient side, these investments involve various ministries and agencies from different levels of government, and that host country agency matters. Civil society groups and local community members remain largely on the sidelines in the ongoing negotiations. Being embedded in national development plans, some projects gain access to funding from national banks or multilateral programs, or are part of inter-governmental credit agreements or cooperation programs.

From the Chinese side, representatives of different levels of government and embassy personnel, as well as private or state-owned entrepreneurs

---

98 | See a detailed description of the Office du Niger, Mali, in Baxter and Mousseau (2011), 18-58.
99 | See, for instance, Baxter and Mousseau (2011), 1-3.
100 | The latter became obvious in the case of Ethiopia where Girma Woldegirogis, the Prime Minister from 2001 to 2013, wrote a public letter to the then Minister of Agriculture, Mr. Tafera Derbew, to stop a USD 4.4 billion investment deal in the Western Region by an Indian company intending to grow pulses and edible oil crops for export to India. The deal was likely to negatively impact the region's fragile microclimate, yet the Minister of Agriculture refused to react to the Prime Minister's request. See, for instance, Ethiopian Review.com (2 February 2011).
101 | Mosley (2012); Besada and Goetz (2012).
102 | Campbell (1 December 2011).

(central, provincial, municipal), are involved in these investment projects (see Table 4-4). Among the more unique public actors are the SOEs that belong to the so-called state farm system[103] and are subordinate to the Ministry of Agriculture's State Farm Bureaus at the central or provincial level. In the past, these SOEs have been used as "a mechanism for leading the way and for gauging the effect of national agricultural/rural policies."[104] At the same time, they represented the 'first wave' of Chinese agribusiness going global.[105] As of 2014, these companies run the agricultural technology demonstration centers on a for-profit basis. In fact, the previously mentioned example of SINO CAM IKO in Cameroon belongs to this system. The company is a subsidiary of a provincially managed Chinese state farm (Shaanxi Land Reclamation) that is currently engaged in the rehabilitation and operation of such a center in Cameroon, in collaboration with IRAD,[106] a national agricultural research center. These kinds of state farms highlight the important linkages between processes of home country development ambitions, the international context, and "land deals."

Unfortunately, there is hardly any information about the wide range of Chinese private actors and their projects in Africa. Among the few that have been assessed in great detail is the China International Fund Limited (CIF), which was established in Hong Kong in 2003, and has since begun investing in various construction projects in Angola.[107] The fund, which has a bad reputation as a "murky Hong Kong real estate, construction and investment company," has no reported connection to the Chinese government. However, it has pretended to act on behalf of the Chinese government to gain access to certain projects in the past.[108] The company is also involved in a joint venture with a company named SPI that is the business arm of the Liberation Front of Mozambique Party (Frelimo). This mining and cement production project began in 2012 (see Table 4-3). On several occasions, the Chinese government has distanced itself

---

103 | Established in 1947, China's "state-owned farming system today has expanded considerably—a sharp contrast to the decline of state-owned enterprises in the urban sector." State farms are a vital element in China's agricultural system, "operating in 30 provinces [...], occupying 39 million hectares of land [...], employing over 3.5 million people, [...] and contributing to 3.4 % of the country's total output" (Zhang [2010], 365). For a detailed description, see Zhang (2010). Also, see WB (1998), 55.
104 | WB (1998), 55.
105 | Brautigam (2009), 255-257.
106 | IRAD is the abbreviation for Institut de Recherche Agricole pour le Développement. The Institute conducts multi-disciplinary research on how to improve agricultural production. Its history traces back to the year 1889; however, it has been reformed since (http://iradcameroun.org/en).
107 | See the company's website (http://www.chinainternationalfund.com/).
108 | Brautigam (2 June 2010).

from the fund's activities, hinting at the conflict of interests of the different actors involved in Chinese land-consuming OFDI activities (see Chapter 5).[109]

Table 4-3 – *Project Projections from the CIF's Website (CIF)*[110]

Original Condition of the Construction Site	Future Condition of the Construction Site

In addition to such diverse individual interests that play a role in Chinese land-consuming OFDI, several institutions structure the political realm. The Chinese government has used the Forum of China Africa Cooperation (FOCAC), a high-level summit established in 2000 that is modeled after the French Summit,[111] to institutionalize relations with African countries and push for the implementation of projects on a bilateral basis. Similar forums, such as the Forum on Economic and Trade Cooperation between China and Portuguese Countries (FCECCPLP), have also been put in place for other regions in order to re-establish economic and political ties.[112]

Also, several financial institutions support these investments. Specifically, the two Chinese policy banks created in the 1990s, the China EXIM Bank and the China Development Bank (CDB), play an important role. For instance, the CDB supervises the newly created (in 2006) China-Africa Development Fund (CADFund), a stock equity fund that targets Chinese companies whose trade and economic activities will reach or take place in Africa.[113] Further, the Chipata Cotton Company in Zambia (now the China Africa Cotton Company) received financial support—in the form of equity investment through the CADFund – in 2008 after its temporary closure due to financial problems the previous year.[114]

---

109 | Shih (18 January 2010).
110 | See CIF website (http://www.chinainternationalfund.com/projects1.asp?Id=286).
111 | On the role and constitution of annual Franco-African Summits since 1974, see Chafer (2002), 3.
112 | Jansson and Kiala (2009), 3.
113 | CADF (2014).
114 | Schoneveld et al. (2014), 25-27; and China Development Bank (31 May 2012).

Importantly, the regulations of the CADFund ensure that African companies are able to acquire funding only through a joint venture with a Chinese company.[115]

In many cases, however, investments take place without official funding. Some SOE subsidiaries seem to profit from preferential loan access through their headquarters, while other projects receive national bank credit in the recipient country or multilateral funding, in particular in the construction area. In addition, some projects profit from the tripartite cooperation structure of FAO projects under the "South South Cooperation" umbrella program on food security.[116] Furthermore, in 2011, the Africa Development Bank (AfDB) signed a memorandum of understanding with the Agricultural Bank of China on "collaborative ventures in co-financing, technical cooperation for capacity building and knowledge partnership" in the areas of trade finance, infrastructure, agriculture and agribusiness, clean energy projects, energy conservation, non-traditional lending business (e.g., investment banking, consultancy, and advisory business), knowledge sharing and technical assistance, and, if necessary, other areas.[117] Moreover, the company ZTE was accredited as a UN World Food Programme supplier for an experimental plot of 10 ha near Kinshasa, where it has been growing food since 2008 in cooperation with the DRC Ministry of Agriculture.[118]

With regard to investments that are part of aid projects, the choice of aid instruments is largely context specific. While grants and zero-interest loans are spread across the continent, concessional loans are linked to the receiving country's capacity, which depends on its economic status, or the condition that the loan goes into a productive project whose generated income allows for repayment over time.[119] Brautigam has shown that basically all SSA countries

---

115 | Basically, the fund differs from aid because it provides market based funds, and it differs from credit because it invests together with the enterprise, increasing the latter's financial capacity. Since 2009, the CDB has an additional special fund for African SMEs, which will be made available on the basis of lending and tending. See CADFund website (http://www.cadfund.com/en/).
116 | Brautigam (2010), 31-33. Under the FAO Special Programme for Food Security, Chinese projects were implemented in Gabon, Sierra Leone, Caribbean Islands, Ethiopia, Bangladesh, and Ghana, among others. Projects have included the sending of agricultural technicians, training of local agricultural technicians, construction of agricultural schools, and building of general infrastructure, such as irrigation and road projects. In Angola, for example, over 120.000 farmers from 60 farming associations and cooperatives are benefiting from the construction of a dam and irrigation channel and training of agricultural technicians. See InSouth.org (2014).
117 | See AfDB (9 June 2011).
118 | ZTE Energy (n.d.b). The current status of this project remains unclear.
119 | Brautigam (2011b), 212. State Council (2011a).

that have diplomatic ties with Beijing (China) receive foreign aid to various degrees.[120] A precondition for diplomatic ties is adherence to the previously mentioned 'one China principle.' At the same time, there is no indication that resource rich countries, namely Nigeria and the DRC, are the recipients of larger amounts of aid.[121]

Table 4-4 – China in Africa: Actors involved in Land-Consuming OFDI (selected)

Actors Involved at Different Levels of Governance		Public	Private	Hybrid
INTERNATIONAL/ OTHER	International agents	• FAO South-South Cooperation Program • United Nations' World Food Program (WFP) Supplier Program • WB • AfDB	• Earth Rights Institute (NGO)	
CHINA AND HONG-KONG (HK)	National	• China EXIM Bank • SINOSURE • State Council • Ministry of Commerce • MoFTEC[122] and MoL • Ministry of Agriculture • China Development Bank -(CAD-Fund) • SOEs from central state • SUCOBE (Benin) is a subsidiary of China National Complete Plant I/E Corporation (Group) (COMPLANT) under supervision of State Council	• "Snakeheads"[123] • Private owned enterprises (POEs) (only a few are known) • China Africa Cotton Company (listed at Hong Kong Stock Exchange)	

---

120 | Brautigam (2011b), 212.
121 | See Gouraud (18 October 2011).
122 | The Ministry of Foreign Trade and Economic Cooperation (MoFTEC) preceded the Ministry of Commerce (MOFCOM).
123 | This term describes criminal organizations that smuggle people and drugs. See African Labour Research Network (2009), 27.

Actors Involved at Different Levels of Governance		Public	Private	Hybrid
CHINA AND HONG-KONG (HK)	Sub-national	• SOEs from provinces or municipality, • bureaucratic agents and agencies: • Chongqing Sino-Tanzania Agriculture Development Company, subsidiary of Chongqing Zhong Yi Seed Ltd. in Tanzania (outgrower scheme, hybrid rice) • Shaanxi Land Reclamation General Corporation (state-owned conglomerate) • Hebei Province Bureau of Foreign Trade Promotion • Shandong Province (Cement Factory) • Fuzhou Province Fishery Coop • Shaanxi State Farm (provincial actor), has a subsidiary (SINO IKO) in Cameroon • Guangdong Agribusiness Group	• AOCABFE (umbrella organization)[124] • China International Investment (investor umbrella organization for 260 Chinese organizations) • ZTE Energy, subsidiary of ZTE corporation[125] • China International Fund (Hong Kong) • Farmers • Workers • Labor Export Companies • Daitong (POE)	• Malawi Cotton Company (joint venture between CADFund and Qingdao Ruichang Cotton Company)
BILATERAL		• SUKALA (China-Mali) • Inter-provincial cooperation between Gaza Province (MOZ) and Hubei Province • CADFund office in Zambia • Friendship Farms	China International Fund (HK) and Frelimo's investment arm, SPI-Gestão e Investimentos (JV on cement in MOZ)	• Viscount Energy Limited • Nigeria's Ebony State government • Zambia Development Agency • China LongPing High Tec Company

---

124 | AOCABFE stands for Association of Overseas Chinese Agricultural, Biological, and Food Engineers.

125 | Formerly a state owned enterprise, ZTE Corporation has been turned into a private company (shareholding). See testimony in front of the Permanent Select Committee on Intelligence of the US Congress by ZTE's Senior Vice President for North America and Europe, Zhu (2012); and the report by the Permanent Select Committee on Intelligence, Rogers and Ruppersberger (2012).

Actors Involved at Different Levels of Governance		Public	Private	Hybrid
RECIPIENT COUNTRIES	National	• Senegal National Bank • Zambia Development Agency • IRAD (Institute de Recherche Agricole pour le Developpement, Cameroon) • (Cameroon) Office of the Prime Minister • Inter-Ministerial Committee • local authorities at Ndjoré • Tanzanian government • Mali National Assembly • DRC Ministry of Agriculture	• African Finance Corporation (Nigeria) • Nigerian Banks	
	Subnational			• Chief of Ndore (in Nigeria)

In order to further elaborate on the official perspective on land-consuming FDI in the recipient country context, the following section will briefly outline the stated goals of the investment projects on the project and country levels.

4. THE INVESTMENTS IN THE RECIPIENT CONTEXT: STATED GOALS AND MULTIFACETED REALITY

Host country agency and public policy are often ignored by orthodox explanations of land-consuming OFDI from an investor country perspective. Yet, overall, Chinese investments are embedded in the national (and international) development programs and rhetoric. Therefore, the next sections provide several examples that I have encountered during process tracing, focusing on the stated goals, development policies, and actual impact of Chinese land-consuming investments. The insights gained contribute to the exploration of alternative explanations of how (and why) Chinese OFDI projects take place, and they show that so-called pull and push factors coexist.

The stated goals of the investigated investments vary slightly across different levels of analysis. On the project level, the stated goal of many investments in both the agricultural and mining sectors is often to reduce imports and boost production of the respective product in order to promote food security and/or the industrialization goals of the recipient country. For instance, SINO CAM IKO in Cameroon envisioned reducing rice imports by increasing output from 50.000 tons to 400.000 tons per year,[126] and the CIF-SPI joint venture in Mozambique (called CIF-MOZ) allegedly aims to increase cement production and thereby support industrialization and modernization plans through reduced cement prices.[127] In the case of Nigeria, VISCOUNT Energy, the "Chinese-supported Nigerian firm" active in the biofuels sector claims that the project is intended to improve domestic energy security.[128]

On the recipient country level, many investment projects are embedded in national development plans that the respective government wishes to implement with the help and capital of foreign investors.[129] For instance, the detailed case study by Ekman on Chinese investments in Mozambique shows that the agricultural investment projects have been determined by the Mozambican government.[130] The same applies to other countries and projects. The previously mentioned VISCOUNT Energy project in Nigeria matches the Nigerian National Biofuel Development Policy.[131] The ZTE Energy investment in the DRC (status unclear) would be part of a project to restitute a former agriculture cooperation farm (DAIPN); it would involve Chinese investors as well as the African Development Bank and other foreign companies.[132] Moreover, the extension of the SUKALA S.A. project in Mali is part of the Malian government's acclaimed goal to turn the country into an "agricultural powerhouse."[133] Similarly, agricultural investments in Senegal are part of the Senegalese Growth Plan ("Grand Agricultural Offensive for Food and Abundance (GOANA)") that has come about as a result of the food crisis. It favors foreign investors through free repatriation of profit, tax breaks, or the provision of public subsidies[134] and the SUCOBE project in Benin matches the government's proclaimed goal of stepping up agricultural production and mechanization.[135]

These project level statements and domestic development programs are matched by programs and institutions at the regional level, such as the African

---

126 | Khan and Baye (2008), 7, 15; Wikileaks (2010a).
127 | Cementchina.net (27 August 2010); Cementchina.net (31 May 2011); Duran (2012), 20-22.
128 | Rothkopf (2007), 336.
129 | See, for instance, Baxter and Mousseau (2011) on Mali; and Lavers (2011, 2012) on Ethiopia.
130 | Ekman (2010).
131 | Shaad and Wilson (2009), 10; Galadima et al. (2011), 22-24; and This Day (28 August 2006).
132 | Baende (29 March 2010); and Braeckmann (September 2009).
133 | Xue (2010). See also Baxter and Mousseau (2011), 19, 24; Ministry of Agriculture, Republic of Mali (2009), 14.
134 | See, for instance, Stads and Sène (2011), 3.
135 | See Nonfodji (2011).

Union Commission (AUC), the New Partnership for Africa's Development (NEPAD) Secretariat, or the African Development Bank (AfDB). These organizations have, for example, started an initiative for the development of infrastructure in Africa, which is framed as a prerequisite for economic development and growth on the continent.[136] They are also promoting FDI projects in agriculture to boost food security and improve drought resilience. In fact, the AfDB's regional strategy for 2012 refers explicitly to "the mobilization of resources from China, India, Brazil and Argentina" as a means to address related challenges through modernization.[137]

Despite such claims about the developmental offerings of land-consuming FDI projects made by people and institutions involved in the relevant processes, empirical evidence underlines that for the host countries, as well as the home countries, the implications are ambiguous. For instance, from a social viewpoint, these investments are not necessarily a developmental success story: while they can create jobs and generate revenue, in many cases few jobs are generated, and these are characterized by poor labor relations and/or wage discrimination between Chinese and local labor.[138] Wages in some cases are reported to be below the domestic minimum wage, and in most cases, jobs are offered on a daily wage basis without social insurance. Employees earn about USD 1.5-2 per day.[139] Unfortunately, these unfavorable social conditions seem to be common to most foreign projects rather than being unique to Chinese ventures.[140] With regard to rural development, the large-scale implementation of central contract farming schemes seems unlikely to improve rural livelihoods given the weak legal environment, lack of risk insurance, and official corruption present in many host countries. Indeed, historical evidence about the developmental implications of such schemes suggests that they tend to reduce rather than strengthen the multiple positive impacts that agricultural work can have with regards to social, economic, political, or environmental aspects of society.[141]

Empirical (albeit anecdotal) evidence also suggests that the development policies in many recipient countries pose challenges for national economic development, for instance, by disadvantaging otherwise competitive indigenous enterprises that suffer from limited access to capital, technology, or global markets. The crowding out of such enterprises by these investments has been observed to a certain degree in the textile industry, though mainly through the

---

136 | See AfDB (2014).
137 | AfDB (8 February 2012).
138 | Baah and Jauch (2009), 330.
139 | Baah and Jauch (2009).
140 | See, for instance, Baah and Jauch (2009), 108.
141 | See, for instance, Smalley (2013); and IAASTD (2008).

intensified trade and import of textiles. Also, the strong presence of Chinese construction companies that manage to profit from government-facilitated 'resource for infrastructure' deals, seems to squeeze the operating space for local or regional firms.[142] Plus, the influx of Chinese small-scale entrepreneurs, a side effect of intensifying Chinese-African trade and investment relations, has proved challenging for local shop owners. Another concern raised in the context of national economic development is the issue of financial debt. It is true that "barter exchange deals" consider issues such as the "manageability of debt," often by requiring recipient country governments to repay it with the investment returns that are anticipated from the benefits of industrialization.[143] Yet, the high degree of corruption and poor governance record in most countries, together with the generally long period before repayment is due, provide valid reasons for concern over the sustainable management of debt.[144]

Aside from these economic and social challenges, some reports highlight the negative environmental impacts of some large-scale farming projects, specifically regarding regional microclimates or water security. Take, for example, the SINO CAM IKO's farming project in Cameroon that was mentioned above. In order to gain access to fertile ground in a moderate climate zone, the investor cut down trees, which might result in problematic changes to the regional microclimate. Another example is the sugar cane production project in Mali. A case study by the Oakland Institute mentions the problem of water diversion and the declining level of the Niger River as a project related challenge that is likely to intensify water insecurity and affect neighboring countries that depend on this river.[145] Also, Bosshard has pointed to the fact that key development finance institutions, such as the China EXIM Bank, have financed projects, including dam construction, for which the environmental pre-assessment did not meet international standards, yielding problematic results for the affected population and environment on the ground (Sudan).[146] Finally, the water-intensive character of Chinese agricultural projects in African countries has been highlighted as worrisome, since rice, sugar cane, and cotton rank among the 'thirstiest' crops.[147]

Regarding the public perception about Chinese investments within recipient countries it is interesting to note that this does not seem to differ from that about Western countries, according to a study by Gadzala and Hanusch (in

---

142 | Brautigam (2011a), 7; Chen et al. (2009).
143 | See Brautigam (2011a), 7.
144 | Brautigam (2011a), 7-8.
145 | Baxter and Mousseau (2011), 15-26.
146 | Bosshard (2008), 3-5. Also, see Tan-Mullins et al. (2017).
147 | See Davis' (2003) study on the water-intensity of the crops rice, wheat, cotton, and sugar cane.

2010).¹⁴⁸ These authors write that the "negative rhetoric emanating from much of the surrounding literature tells only part of the story, as African perceptions of China are found to be near equivalent to those held vis-à-vis Western countries."¹⁴⁹ Nevertheless, the Chinese presence in African economies has become politicized and entered the political discourse during electoral campaigning in some countries as the case of Zambia highlights (see below).

In some cases, rising and vocal discontent has emerged among third parties affected by Chinese investments through increased competition. A cable by the US Embassy in Mali, for example, reported that the US company Schaffer had complained about the strong Chinese presence in the country.¹⁵⁰ This was likely in relation to the SUKALA S.A. (Sino-Mali joint venture) expansion plans, which pertain to areas of land that had originally been promised to Schaffer by the host government. According to statements made by Schaffer, the expansion is part of a broader strategy to prevent other companies from entering the sugar market, thereby preserving the joint venture's quasi-monopoly position within this sector.¹⁵¹ In this context, it is interesting to note that since 2008 there has been a proliferation of Western funds set up by the development agencies of OECD countries to support Western agribusinesses in Sub-Saharan Africa.¹⁵² While difficult to prove, these funds seem to be inspired by the basic model of the China-Africa Development Fund, which was put in place by China in 2006. The Western funds are clearly aimed at strengthening the OECD economic presence on the continent. The impact of heightened competition through newcomers such as China is also well documented in the context of the Chipata Cotton Company in Zambia. Due to the company's presence, the previous informal pricing regime led by quasi-monopolists from France and Britain has been challenged.¹⁵³

5. The Issue of Labor

One phenomenon that has received widespread international attention is the issue of Chinese labor exports in these investments to SSA. The following section will provide a brief overview of the core issues to discern myths while deliberating on the dimension and background of this phenomenon. This step seems necessary for a meaningful understanding of the Chinese presence in

---

148 | Gadzala and Hanusch (2010).
149 | Gadzala and Hanusch (2010), 4.
150 | Wikileaks (2009a).
151 | Wikileaks (2009a).
152 | Miller et al. (2010), 146-165.
153 | Tschirley and Kabwe (2009).

SSA. Moreover, given the historical roles of migration and labor exports in political regime stability and social mobility, which were described in Chapter 3, this overview of the contemporary situation will provide valuable insights for comparison.

A study by Yoon Jung Park reveals that the number of Chinese migrants in Africa rose constantly over the 10-year period ending in 2012 and probably reached one million that year. It also reports that many of these migrants live in segregated communities:

In 2009, the Chinese population in Africa was estimated at between 580.000 to 820.000. Today, that number is likely closer to (or even over) 1 million, although exact counts are virtually impossible to ascertain due to the mobility of Chinese migrants as well as highly porous borders within Africa, high levels of corruption within some African government agencies, and inefficiencies within agencies tasked with immigration and border control.

While most Chinese in Africa are there only temporarily – as contract laborers and professionals – there are a growing number of Chinese migrants choosing to remain in Africa to explore greater economic opportunities. Recent research in southern Africa indicates that, although many Chinese migrants plan to eventually return to China, many in South Africa and Lesotho have already stayed years beyond their original plans.[154]

While it appears that China has no grand strategy of labor export in place, several factors in the home country do encourage it. These include official propaganda portraying Africa as the continent of opportunity,[155] the absence of sufficient unemployment protection in China,[156] widespread corruption, development and climate change related land loss, the problematic *hukou* system[157] which discriminates against rural workers wishing to migrate to urban areas, lax migration controls, and the negotiation of work visas for Chinese staff overseas by the Chinese government. The confluence of all of these features in the Chinese context definitely creates an environment of high migration pressure. This could be seen as the silent promotion of labor export, so long as conditions back home do not improve significantly for the rural population.

---

154 | Park (4 January 2012); also see Park (2009).
155 | Park (4 January 2012).
156 | Lee (2000), executive summary.
157 | *Hukou* refers to a household registration system that restricts rural to urban migration. In its current form it "discriminate[s] against poor migrant workers in favor of the wealthy and educated." For more details, see, for instance, Congressional-Executive Commission on China (2005), 1; also see Murphy and Tao (2006).

Moreover, Chinese companies continue to gain a competitive advantage over Northern competitors when using comparatively cheap but skilled Chinese labor.[158] One of the striking aspects of Chinese labor export is that it highlights the shortfalls of the country's economic development in view of social development. Research about Chinese construction projects shows that even in current times, (skilled) Chinese workers (in China) often do not earn significantly more than their African counterparts (in Africa) while working under harsh conditions and being denied basic social rights.[159] Brautigam argues that the use of Chinese workers in investments in agriculture is especially common in oil-rich countries with higher wage levels. In such places, Chinese labor provides companies with a competitive edge in contract bidding.[160] At the same time, the wages paid to Chinese staff in overseas projects can be higher than those paid in China, which explains why many workers decide to go overseas and work in projects in Africa to improve their family's welfare back home.

Overall, however, the cost competitiveness of skilled Chinese labor is only (a minor) one of several considerations that influence Chinese companies' choice of hiring Chinese rather than local staff. Equally important are cultural and social aspects. Hiring Chinese staff, particularly for managerial positions, allows the company to circumvent language barriers that arise from the lack of knowledge of foreign languages among Chinese technical experts, and makes it easier to implement Chinese work modes: "Using Chinese workers ensured fast communication within project teams and prompt completion of the work."[161] A contributing factor seems to be the (alleged) lack of skilled African workers, particularly in the construction sector. The resultant rise of skilled African workers' wages close to the level of skilled Chinese workers' wages, together with the perception that skilled African labor is less productive, has also motivated Chinese companies to import slightly more costly Chinese workers in the implementation of projects.[162]

Even though labor export is not a primary concern of the central government in China, the internationalization of the labor market is promoted for different reasons by different actors. The central government has endorsed it as a way for its companies to succeed in contract bidding by taking on the comparatively 'cheap (skilled) labor.' There are other voices, particularly at the provincial and municipal government levels (e.g., websites of provincial governments), that promote labor export as a way to address the social costs of the chosen development path, such as the problems of structural unemployment,

---

158 | See Alden (2007).
159 | Chen et al. (2009), 83-84.
160 | Brautigam (2011a), 7-8.
161 | Chen et al. (2009), 83.
162 | Chen et al. (2009), 83.

poverty, low social mobility, and land-loss-related displacement. In an interview in 2008, for instance, Li Ruguo, President of the China EXIM Bank, is quoted as saying that his Bank would assist 12 million workers who were to lose their land through modernization, industrialization, and urbanization to find work abroad.[163] Former President Hu Jintao has been quoted as saying that emigration was "a good way to lower demographic pressure, economic overheating, and pollution in mainland China."[164] Also, as mentioned above, wages can be from 30 % to 400 % higher in Africa for skilled workers in managerial positions.[165]

In practice, the increasing number of (un)skilled Chinese laborers, who often live in segregated communities, is perceived as a threat in recipient countries with high unemployment levels. The concerns of the host populations over these social aspects of Chinese investments have been politicized by some political actors during electoral campaigns, such as the former opposition leader and then elected President Michael Sata in Zambia (who was in office from 2011 until his death in October 2014). However, the case of Zambia also reveals that it might be too easy to blame these unfavorable conditions on foreign investors such as the Chinese. Undeniably, the previous Zambian governments actually abstained from governing whole sectors (e.g., cotton) and from negotiating local content requirements in the context of IFDI.[166] And the newly-elected President (and suddenly deceased), Michael Sata, has not undertaken reforms that will provide a better framework for the Zambian population to profit from these and other investments during his time in office.[167] Several case studies document that national policy and politics in recipient countries matter greatly in shaping how these investments take place. The labor report by Baah and Jauch, for instance, cites numerous incidents where the response by government agencies or trade unions improved conditions on the ground.[168] At the same time, the increasing risk awareness among Chinese government officials and the fear of huge investment losses overseas have led the government to offer CSR training to the corporate management staff of SOEs, and to implement the Equator Principles as evaluation criteria for public funding.[169]

From the official angle, the global repercussion of this trend towards internationalizing the Chinese labor market and its specific characteristics (e.g., segregated overseas communities) have been downplayed and/or explained in

---

163 | Coonan (28 December 2008); Patton (7 April 2008); Murphy and Tao (2006).
164 | Sege and Beuret (2009), 5.
165 | Park (2009).
166 | Tschirley and Kabwe (2009).
167 | Spilsbury (2012/2013).
168 | Baah and Jauch (2009).
169 | Leung (2010).

the context of China's development trajectory. Lu Shaye, Director General of the Department of African Affairs within the Ministry of Foreign Affairs from 2009 to 2014, partially dismisses labor related problems of Chinese investments to Africa by arguing that it is all a matter of perspective.[170] His point is that the low wage levels associated with the investments in Africa are high when compared to wage levels in the same sectors in China. The overseas wage levels result from the fact that Chinese companies' competitive edge is their low cost. Moreover, the segregation of Chinese workers from local communities is due to "a problem of cultural gap and language barrier" that leads the workers to "[...] build up their own social circle."[171] In his opinion, this trend is intensified by the fact that Chinese employees abroad work in harsh conditions to ensure a better life at home: "The Chinese employees work in tougher conditions than the employees of western companies. [...] They live a hard life, eat simple food and live in simple domiciles so that they can send home the money they earned to raise their families and improve their living conditions." Notably, all of this bears a strong resemblance to migratory patterns in the late 19th century.[172] At the same time, the number of Chinese labor disputes has increased, reflecting "attempts by China-based labor export agents to get extra income from the Chinese workers."[173]

6. Conclusion

This chapter has presented the main empirical characteristics of what is happening regarding Chinese land-consuming OFDI since 2000. The chapter has reported in great detail on agricultural projects. These were the most common in the "land grab" reports that served as a starting point of my research.[174] However, official data shows that agricultural investments only make up a minor share of total on Chinese (land-consuming) OFDI in SSA.

Importantly, the empirical findings point to the complexity of (f)actors at play and/or the different timelines involved. The following paragraphs will

---

170 | Gouraud (18 October 2011). Also see Buckley (2011) for an ethnographic description of the different perspectives involved in Chinese-Senegalese agricultural projects.
171 | Gouraud (18 October 2011).
172 | Gouraud (18 October 2011).
173 | Chen et al. (2009), 83.
174 | It is important to remember that the strong focus on Chinese agricultural projects that characterized early publications and project listings of the "land grab" debate is a result of two things: biased reporting; and the initial focus on *farm*land grabs. In the UK case, similar data problems led to an over-reporting of investments in biofuels. See Chapter 1 (Section 5).

summarize the core empirical findings for each of the categories that have guided this chapter (see Table 4-5). This implies a reduction of the complexity that has been characteristic of the main empirical traits identified, and it clearly means that certain features which are also part of Chinese land-consuming OFDI in SSA will be excluded. However, it is a necessary step to guide the reader and refresh the core results that the Chapter 5 will go on to explain.

The findings highlight that multiple actors are involved in Chinese land-consuming OFDI in SSA. However, they also show that public actors and agencies are predominant in (large-scale) Chinese land-consuming OFDI in SSA. SOEs, for example, run economic cooperation projects, regardless of the sector, and also search for profitable investment operations on their own. They are often involved—usually with a majority position—in joint ventures with host country companies or SOEs. Government officials of the home and host country are also active in these joint ventures, particularly in negotiating the terms of economic cooperation, which they frequently do at political forums (such as FOCAC) or through other (bilateral) exchange channels.

Importantly, these forms of state agency are composed of diverse "land grab" interests and strategies. Chinese official actors often pursue their own agenda rather than that of the central state. Moreover, Chinese SOEs rely on multiple institutions and financial sources (e.g., headquarters, host country national banks, and multilateral funding) in their operations, aside from Chinese development finance. They also apply mainstream managerial economics in their operations and are characterized by a profit orientation, even in cases where Chinese development finance is involved, or where resources are being exploited. The previous assessment also highlighted that Chinese land-consuming FDI projects are often pro-actively sought by African governments, and reflective of recipient countries' development policies.

Most companies produce for domestic and regional markets in SSA, particularly in the agricultural sector. However, the latter makes up only a minor share of total Chinese OFDI activities of which land-consuming investments form a part. The majority of investments go into mining, manufacturing, and financial services. With regard to the role of land, this means that land is used as a natural resource, but also as a space to open up profitable business opportunities in construction, manufacturing, and/or through SEZs.

The timelines of most of these investment projects can be traced far back. While China is a newcomer to the role of capital exporter, it shares a long history of cooperating with and providing aid to many African countries. Several actors, such as construction companies, have previously run aid projects on the ground, and have more recently turned into successful contract bidders due to their experience and cost advantage. The multiple crises of 2007/2008 have not been critical for what has been happening since 2000. Instead, their role in

Chinese OFDI activities has been ambiguous—preventing as well as enabling Chinese overseas investments.

In the case of China, Section 5 addressed the issue of labor migration and related claims of strategic labor export. These claims have regularly appeared in the media and led to political tensions in host countries, many of which suffer from high unemployment. It showed that while the central government has no pro-active strategy in place to promote labor export, it also does not have a strategy to curb the phenomenon, nor are the origins of the pressure to work abroad adequately dealt with by the home government.

In conclusion, several tendencies of Chinese land-consuming OFDI seem noteworthy and demand an explanation that assesses them in the home country context. In particular, the empirical findings show that Chinese investment projects in SSA establish new markets, access and secure resources, engage in profitable business undertakings, internationalize the operations of particular companies, and/or strengthen and expand the home country's political ties and powerful economic presence in African countries.

Table 4-5 – *Review of the Empirical Characteristics of Chinese OFDI*[175]

Category	Core Empirical Characteristics
Actors	Projects involve public actors from the recipient country and China; they are usually operated by Chinese SOEs, often in cooperation with host country SOEs; some actors have a long history on the continent (e.g., construction companies) because they began implementing Chinese aid projects in the 1950s; Chinese workers and experts are an integral part of Chinese investment projects: the experts are part of agricultural training centers that Chinese companies are rehabilitating and the workers are often employed by construction and energy companies in order to keep costs low.
Institutions	The main cooperation strategies are negotiated at FOCAC; regarding finances, companies rely on multiple sources, ranging from headquarter support and Chinese development finance to multilateral and host country funding.
Sectors	The majority of investments go into mining and manufacturing, followed by financial services; according to government data, agricultural investments make up only a minor share of total Chinese OFDI in SSA.
Timelines	Projects predate the 2007/2008 crises, often they can be traced back to Mao-Era cooperation with African countries; however, the way they are run has changed significantly over time; today, they are for-profit enterprises.
Role of land	Land is used as a natural resource, but also as a space in which to open profitable business opportunities (e.g., construction and manufacturing); in both cases, projects have a strong profit orientation, and are not necessarily producing for export to China.
Recipient context	Projects, particularly in the agricultural sector, have been requested by African host country governments; mostly, they seem to be the result of inter-governmental cooperation at different levels of government; the actors involved can have very different interests.

---

175 | This summary substantially reduces the complexity that has characterized the empirical findings of this chapter. However, it is intended to guide the reader by highlighting the core traits of Chinese investment projects that will be explained from a home country perspective in Chapter 5 and compared with British empirical characteristics in Chapter 8.

Chapter 5: The Chinese Context
Investments from a Home Country Perspective

1. INTRODUCTION

The empirical evidence casts doubt upon the widespread claims according to which Chinese land-consuming OFDI is for the country's food security. In practice, the comparatively small share of agricultural projects produces for domestic or regional consumption, and many projects can be traced back before the 2007/2008 crises. Moreover, Chinese projects target multiple sectors that use land not only as a resource, but also as a productive space for industrial and modernization activities. At the same time, the agency of the state is very diverse. And, a wide range of non-state actors, Chinese and other are involved.

This chapter looks at the how and why of Chinese land-consuming OFDI activities against the background of the investor country itself. In particular, it will discuss these activities in view of China's OFDI policy (Section 2), the guiding ideology of China-Africa relations (Section 3), and, finally, the country's political economy (Section 4) and development trajectory (Section 5). The multiple threads emerging from this discussion will be summarized in the conclusion (Section 6), which will be guided by the question of why these investments occur as they do in and over time. In addition to domestic dynamics and international contexts, this section will also briefly assess the investments' likely welfare implications.

It is argued that the following features are significant in explaining Chinese OFDI from a home country perspective: (1) these investments are embedded in an increasingly supportive OFDI framework that emerged as a result of the country's resource-intensive and export-oriented industrial set-up; (2) they are guided by a foreign policy ideology that is affected by the neoliberal terminology of "win-win" and embedded in the analytical frame of today's mainstream economics—representing a major shift away from previous concepts of autarky and self-reliance that informed China-Africa relations; (3) the very actors and institutions involved are reflective of a system of "neoliberal governmentality" that has emerged since 1978, and whose state-market relations are more complex than the concept of state capitalism usually assumes; and (4) the investments reflect the rising resource pressures, external dependencies, high international competition, and social costs of China's development trajectory since the 1990s.

More broadly, four drivers explain why Chinese land-consuming OFDI in SSA happens from the home country perspective. Accordingly, Chinese land-consuming OFDI projects are part of a long-term strategy to diversify supply and access to resources (mineral products), even if these are not consumed back home; a diplomatic strategy to foster political alliances and expand the country's soft power in international relations, through economic presence as well as commitment to host country requests; a commercial strategy to develop and open new markets for Chinese products; and a strategy to internationalize China's industrial base to address the competitive pressures back home, as well as the ecological and social challenges.

2. Home Country Measures

Institutionally, the investments in Africa reflect the full range of home country measures that have been implemented in China since the mid-1980s. This section will assess key timelines of the emerging policy framework underpinning Chinese overseas investments; deliberate on the framework's changing objectives in and over time; and introduce its key components that pertain to Chinese engagement with African countries. The discussion of Chinese land-consuming investments in the context of policy will be complemented by consecutive sections addressing the ideological and politico-economic specificities of Chinese "land acquisitions" from a home country perspective.

From a historical perspective, the increasingly supportive stance on OFDI flows and the related policy framework emerged in the 1990s. They then gained momentum in 2001 with the adoption of the "Go Out" (*zou chuqu*) policy framework.[1] While it built on existing aid projects and bilateral diplomatic relations, this framework also reflects the fundamental changes that the Chinese government has made towards its OFDI policy preferences since 1978. Outward investments had long been referred to as "poisonous grass"[2] in the domestic debate. They were portrayed as unfavorable for a domestic development strategy prioritizing the accumulation of foreign exchange reserves.

The transition from this OFDI-restrictive policy regime towards a supportive one has happened over several periods, stretching from China's opening up

---

1 | Bernasconi-Osterwalder et al. (2013).
2 | Xue and Han (2010), 310-320.

in 1984 until the present.³ Firstly, during the 1980s, the Chinese government prioritized the accumulation of foreign exchange reserves, and maintained a prohibitive stance towards OFDI. Capital exports needed the approval of the National People's Congress; foreign exchange earnings were only applicable for licensed companies in the export sector; and requirements established a USD 10 million limit, together with the obligation to remit all profits made overseas.⁴

Secondly, from 1991 until 2000, and particularly after Deng Xiaoping's famous trip to the South in 1992 and the victory of the economically liberal faction within the Chinese Communist Party (CCP) over the socialist faction, OFDI provisions and related regulations began to undergo far-reaching reforms. SOEs took on the status of monopolistic enterprises, which gave their management more leeway in operational decisions;⁵ foreign exchange regulations "changed from the previous 'earn to use' mode into a 'buy and use' mode;" and OFDI was framed in an official document ("opinion") by the National Planning Commission (NPC) as a strategic instrument for overseas expansion.⁶

Thirdly, since 2001, the Chinese government started implementing the "go out" framework, reflecting a more technical and increasingly supportive stance on Chinese OFDI (see below for a more detailed description of the framework). As a result, the overseas expansion of Chinese companies was supported by financial mechanisms and/or the provision of information about the host countries to the companies.

Since 2009, the regulatory framework has "further eased and decentralized the approval procedures," thereby encouraging the overseas activities of Chinese companies.⁷ Moreover, "[i]n July 2009, the PRC government launched a small pilot program to permit selected Chinese companies to settle their cross-border trades in select offshore jurisdictions in RMB."⁸ In this context, China's Central Bank has also begun to push the internationalization of the renminbi, for instance, in the form of an agreement with the trade hub Nigeria

---

3 | Xue and Han (2010), 310-320.
4 | Xue and Han (2010), 310-320.
5 | Wang (2002), 201-205.
6 | The NPC document was titled, "Opinion of the State Planning Commission on the Strengthening of the Administration of Overseas Investment Projects." (The NPC is now the National Development and Reform Commission (NDRC)). See Xue and Han (2010), 316-317.
7 | Rosen and Hanemann (2009). Of particular interest is Table 1 (p. 20) on "China's OFDI Policy Framework."
8 | King and Wood Mallesons (May 2014).

in Africa to include the RMB as part of its foreign exchange reserves from January 2011.[9]

OFDI: Development, Contexts, and Objectives

A closer look at the official OFDI documentation helps to break down the sequence of events and identify the objectives that led the government (under the given political economy) to perceive overseas investment as a useful instrument to realize particular interests. The following paragraphs will show that OFDI has been framed as a tool to facilitate the acquisition of resources, technology, and knowhow, promote exports, and create new markets. Specifically, OFDI is said to support the country's efforts to upgrade its industrial structure to reduce the negative environmental, ecological, and social impacts of the economic development strategy; enhance resource security through the diversification of supply; counter the negative impacts of the economic crisis in Asia (and Europe) on the Chinese export industry; strengthen and support the emergence of national champions (enterprises) in the context of liberalization and WTO accession; and, thereby, ensure the stability of the political regime whose legitimacy is seen to rely on economic growth (see Sections 3 and 4).

Historically, two events explain the changing attitude of the Chinese government in view of OFDI in the mid-1990s: firstly, the rise to power of the economically liberal faction within the CCP; and, secondly, the rising external resource dependency in the 1990s and the increasing inability of the domestic resource base to keep up with industrial demand. Consequently, in 1992, OFDI became part of the country's economic development plan, primarily in the context of encouraging the national oil companies to go abroad and diversify supply.[10] The official document of the National Planning Committee also stated that OFDI should be endorsed to "acquire resources, technologies and markets overseas."[11] These were all crucial elements that the formerly closed-off country was missing in its industrial set-up, which did not have a global production

---

9 | See Payi (September 2011) according to which "Nigeria diversif[ies] reserves into Renminbi" to moderate the currency volatility and inflation experienced between US and Naira (Nigerian currency). The negative US sovereign rating and the ongoing economic crisis in Europe have been influencing the decision by Nigeria to diversify its foreign exchange reserves as a strategy to improve security, liquidity, and returns. Also see the case of Zimbabwe, which has adopted the renminbi as legal currency under BusinessDaylive.co.za (30 January 2014).
10 | Adapted from Xue and Han (2010), 317. And Rosen and Hanemann (2009), 20.
11 | The NPC document was titled "Opinion of the State Planning Commission on the Strengthening of the Administration of Overseas Investment Projects." See Xue and Han (2010), 316-317.

network dimension. Consequently, changes in foreign exchange management made it easier for a greater variety of (SOE) enterprises to invest overseas.[12]

With time, additional dynamics played an important role. In 1999, the Asian financial crisis gave impetus to further reform of the existing OFDI regulations. The crisis had led to a huge decline in exports due to the relative appreciation of the renminbi, and this decline was negatively affecting the manufacturing industry, a major source of jobs and state revenues. In response, a first reference to the "Go Out" strategy appeared in the 1999 State Council document titled "Opinion on encouraging companies to carry out overseas material processing and assembly."[13] This document affirmed the use of OFDI to address the problem of a massive decline in regional export demand, and it encouraged overseas assembly and processing activities to profit from cheap labor and resources in the context of the rising international competition for markets. In this reform step, the economic emphasis was on export promotion and industrial restructuring.

Another event that impacted OFDI regulation was China's WTO accession in 2001. In anticipation of this event, the 5th Plenary Session of the 15th Congress of the CCP issued a "suggestion" for economic and social development in 2000, which mentioned four investment types that would be supported, namely "processing, trade, resources extraction, project contracting."[14] Among the policy support measures mentioned were credit and insurance services.[15] This "suggestion," which forms the basis of today's "Go Out" Strategy, was then embedded in the "Outline of the 11th Five Year Plan for national economic and social development."[16] It has become the foundation of ongoing reforms, such as the further simplification and decentralization of approval procedures regarding overseas investment,[17] particularly with regard to foreign exchange management and the provision of funds for market development and internationalization.

The underpinning story of this reform process, namely the association of overseas investment with domestic economic interests (framed as "needs" in the respective official documentation), has since become a common pattern of official rhetoric and action. For instance, at the 16th National Congress of the CCP in 2002, the then President Jiang Zemin stressed the importance of overseas investments for facilitating domestic reforms and liberalization in the context of WTO accession, and for creating competitive TNCs and brands with

---

12 | Xue and Han (2010), 316-317.
13 | Wilkes and Huang (2011), 9.
14 | Wilkes and Huang (2011), 9.
15 | Wilkes and Huang (2011), 9.
16 | Wilkes and Huang (2011), 9.
17 | Rosen and Hannemann (2009), 20; Wilkes and Huang (2011), 9.

the help of the export of commodities and labor services.[18] Ongoing reforms of OFDI management continue to simplify approval structures while freeing more financial resources in support of OFDI activities.[19]

Together, these multiple objectives, which have come to be associated with the Chinese perspective on OFDI projects and embedded in the contemporary policy framework, provide important parameters of Chinese development challenges, economic interests and paradigms that any assessment and explanation of Chinese land-consuming FDI has to take into consideration. The key institutional features of this framework in which Chinese OFDI in Sub-Saharan Africa is embedded will be outlined in the following section. At the same time, this positive framing of OFDI mirrors shifts in the country's guiding ideology and political economy that will be explained subsequently.

The "Go Out" Framework

Today, the set of home country measures that supports Chinese OFDI is cross-cutting in view of both sectors and policy fields (aid, trade, and investment). It incorporates a large range of encouragement policies in the form of tax relief, loans support, foreign exchange policy, expat insurance, bilateral investment treaty (BIT) agreements, and information services, as well as simplified approval processes, and regularized supervision.[20] While this OFDI policy framework is among the most elaborate when compared to those of the other BRICS countries[21], it still lags behind those of the OECD countries, and Chinese entrepreneurs will remain at a disadvantage compared to their Western counterparts as long as government and governance "largely function by way of the 'unwritten rules' of political life."[22] The framework also suffers from the overlapping responsibilities of the agencies involved, especially the Ministry of Commerce (MOFCOM)[23] and the NDRC, which coordinate the host country catalogue. That catalogue lists the countries in which Chinese inves-

---

18 | Wilkes and Huang (2011), 9-10.
19 | Xue and Han (2010).
20 | Xue and Han (2010), 305-323.
21 | BRICS refers to Brazil, Russia, India, China, and South Africa.
22 | Yu (2008), 23.
23 | MOFCOM, the Ministry of Commerce of the Government of the People's Republic of China, was established in its current form in 2003. It focuses on trade policies, consumer regulations, FDI, and foreign economic policies/agreements (e.g., bilateral and multilateral trade agreements).

tors are eligible for subsidies from their government.[24] Moreover, the transfer of approval authority over foreign investments of less than USD 3 million from central government agencies, namely SAFE[25] and MOFCOM, to the provincial level in 2003 resulted in what has been described as "an alphabet soup of agencies, bureaucrats, and businesses looking to regulate or profit from Chinese firms' overseas investments."[26]

With regard to Africa, the Chinese government has negotiated 26 bilateral investment agreements with African countries in recent years.[27] It has also put in place an information service platform, through which companies can report difficulties they are facing in different countries and learn from each other's experiences while retrieving legal and resource-related data on a given country. At the same time, formalized supervision has been introduced in the form of annual reporting by the investing company. All of these measures not only support OFDI, but also allow for the steering it.

In addition to the regulatory institutions, several political and financial instruments specifically directed towards investments in SSA are part of this framework of home country measures that play an important role in the facilitation of Chinese land-consuming investments. In the political realm, the Forum of China Africa Cooperation (FOCAC, *Zhong Fei hezuo luntan*) has become a central platform for inter-governmental exchange, coordination, and cooperation. Since its establishment in 2000, high level summits have taken place on a triennial basis.

Activities at FOCAC include the announcement of major economic and aid cooperation projects between China and Africa, such as the agricultural technology development centers, and the release of important white papers about the terms and principles of cooperation. Many heads of state and high level ministry personnel have attended the summits. For instance, the 4th FOCAC meeting in 2009 attracted heads of states and government officials from 49 African countries in addition to a big Chinese entourage. In his opening speech, Chinese Premier Wen Jiabao emphasized the significance of the forum:

Since its founding nine years ago, FOCAC has played a major role in guiding and promoting the development of China-Africa relations and become a bridge of friendship

---

24 | For a detailed description of responsible agencies, their competencies, and issued policies concerning OFDI management, see Wilkes and Huang (2011); and Han and Xue (2010).
25 | SAFE, the State Administration of Foreign Exchange established in 1978, is a government agency that administers the rules and regulations of foreign exchange market activities. It also manages foreign exchange reserves.
26 | Salidjanova (2011), 13; Xue and Han (2010).
27 | Takman (2004).

and a platform of cooperation between China and Africa. In the three years since the Beijing Summit in particular, the two sides have worked together to build the new type of strategic partnership featuring political equality and mutual trust, economic win-win cooperation and cultural exchanges. Together, we have opened a new chapter in China-Africa cooperation.[28]

Accompanying this form of strategic political cooperation are new forms of so-called development finance for overseas projects. In the case of Chinese investments in Africa, several financing sources which are embedded in the "Go Out" framework and located in the aid, trade, or investment policy fields are essential and will be highlighted in the following paragraphs.

Firstly, grants, zero-interest loans, and concessional loans support Chinese aid projects, which have been aligned to trade and investment objectives since a reform in the 1990s. Zero-interest loans and grants are taken from China's aid budget and overseen by MOFCOM and the Ministry of Foreign Affairs.[29] The China Development Bank (CDB) and the China EXIM Bank, created in 1994, provide most of this finance under MOFCOM supervision. Moreover, concessional loans were introduced as a new aid instrument in 1995 under the management of the China EXIM Bank. These loans have a long-term repayment period of 20 years, a fixed interest rate (2-3%), and a five-year grace period. Importantly, the aid funds are only used to cover the difference between the China EXIM Bank's rate and the fixed interest rate.[30] Using these new instruments to deliver development finance, the Chinese government could increase the total number of development assistance activities.[31]

Another financial mechanism is the Special Fund for Foreign Economic and Technical Cooperation (hereafter 'the Special Fund'), one of several under the supervision of MOFCOM that are meant to support Chinese companies "carrying out the needs of China's economic diplomacy."[32] It has, for instance, been used to back Chinese companies involved in the establishment of the Special Economic Zones mentioned in Chapter 4.[33] The Special Fund repays to companies active in African countries a share of their pre-investment costs and provides interest rate subsidies for bank loans. Importantly, the Special Fund is not part of the official aid budget.[34]

---

28 | Wen (2009).
29 | Brautigam (2011a), 3; State Council (2011a).
30 | Brautigam (2011a), 4.
31 | Brautigam (2011a), 4.
32 | Brautigam (2011a), 4.
33 | State Council (2010).
34 | Brautigam (2011a), 4.

Loans made by the two major policy banks, the CDB and the China EXIM Bank, are also important for Chinese land-consuming investments. While these loans are "heavily influenced by government policies and are not to operate in full compliance with market rules," they have to meet criteria of profitability.[35] Since these banks get the same credit-rating as the Chinese government, they can increase funds by issuing bonds with that favorable rating; and they can take a long-term perspective.[36]

In addition, export buyer's credits, a long-time feature of the OECD countries' OFDI frameworks, were introduced in 1998. They were initially for firms with projects in the construction sector overseas (Asia). Since 2005, the China EXIM Bank has offered such credits for investments in Africa. These export buyers' credits, which make up the majority of lending done by the China EXIM Bank, are not part of the foreign aid regime. Instead, they are issued in United States dollars using international standard rates like the London Interbank Offered Rate (LIBOR) or the Commercial Interest Rate of Reference (CIRR).[37] Moreover, preferential export buyer's credits are issued.

Aside from the aforementioned activities conducted by the so-called policy banks, financial activities in Africa also involve Chinese commercial bank activities, such as the China Construction Bank, the Industrial and Commercial Bank of China (ICBC), the Agricultural Bank of China, and the Bank of China. These banks have recently set up branches in African countries with the aim of supporting Chinese companies overseas. Take, for example, the ICBC, which purchased a 20% share in the South Africa's Standard Bank. The latter is active in 18 African countries, and it is a major financial actor with regard to loan services in Africa.[38] This means that increasingly, Chinese financial actors, both private and state-owned, are becoming influential actors in the financial sectors of key African countries and gaining the ability to facilitate investments through bilateral arrangements and beyond. This is also evidenced by the internationalization of the renminbi and its previously noted recognition as foreign exchange currency in some host countries (e.g., Nigeria, Zambia).

On the inter-governmental level, the China-Africa Development Fund, an equity fund established in 2006 at FOCAC, supports Chinese companies whose trade and economic activities concentrate on Africa. Rather than providing credits, this fund invests in these companies in order to raise their financial capacities. It also provides consulting services. It is overseen by the China Development Bank, and projects are chosen on the basis of China's diplomatic

---
35 | Brautigam (2011a), 4.
36 | Brautigam (2011a), 4.
37 | Brautigam (2011a), 4.
38 | See the report on China's financial institutions by Executive Research Associates Ltd. (2009), 77-91.

and economic policies towards the continent. In addition, in 2009, the China Development Bank announced a Special Loan for African SMEs in selected sectors (export orientation, agriculture), using the mode of direct lending and tending.[39]

In Hong Kong, the "Go Out" strategy was mirrored by the creation of the China-Africa Business Council on 21 April, 2007. The Council, at that time under the presidency of Mr. Hu Deping, was established by the China Society for Promotion of the Guangcai Program, together with the United Nations Development Program and the Ministry of Commerce/China International Centre for Economic and Technical Exchanges.[40] It seeks to explore business opportunities among Hong Kong, the Mainland, and African businesses.

Summary

Five observations regarding Chinese land-consuming investments in SSA can be derived from the OFDI policy framework and its emergence. Firstly, these investments are part of a general trend of growth in Chinese overseas investments that is related to the adoption of a supportive OFDI policy over time, particularly since 2000. According to China's Ministry of Commerce, at the end of 2010, 13.000 Chinese investors or institutions were operating 16.000 overseas enterprises in 178 countries.[41] By that year, China had become a major source of global OFDI flows, moving into fifth place among all investor countries (preceded only by the US, Germany, France, and Hong Kong).[42]

Secondly, the comparatively low levels of OFDI stock nonetheless reveal that China has just begun to catch up with the international standards represented by the OECD countries.[43] The ratio of Chinese IFDI-to-OFDI, which in 2011

---

[39] | Definition of "African SME:" solely African owned small and medium-sized enterprise (SME); Chinese owned SME in Africa; Joint African-Chinese private equity SMEs; contractual joint venture SMEs. Sectors supported: infrastructure, agriculture, tertiary industry. In 2009, the CDB developed and recorded 34 projects in Africa. These have a total value of USD 961 million in commercial or preferential loans, which does not count as aid but as market based financial support. See MOFCOM (2011b); and MOFCOM, Department of Western Asian and African Affairs (2010).
[40] | See China-Africa Business Council (Hong Kong) website (http://cabc.hkbu.edu.hk/news6.html); and Africa Confidential (2014).
[41] | MOFCOM (2011a), 79, 80.
[42] | See MOFCOM (2011a), 79, 80.
[43] | MOFCOM (2011a); 81. On the limitations of OFDI data from MOFCOM, see, for instance, Korniyenko and Sakatsume (2009), 3.

stood at a level of 1:0.09, was still below the world average of 1:1.11. In comparison, OECD countries have an average ratio of 1:1.14.⁴⁴

Thirdly, despite being part of a general trend, the instruments summarized above apply particularly to the Chinese investments in African countries. Yet, it is important to note that it remains unclear to which extent Chinese land-consuming FDI projects have actually accessed or profited from these political and financial support mechanisms.

Fourthly, while these investments are unique within the Chinese country context, they are not exceptional in comparison to other countries' practices. Comparative research on FDI regulations shows that the home country measures implemented in China are rather common worldwide, particularly among the highly industrialized countries.⁴⁵ Also, Chinese development finance is far from being extraordinary in international comparison.⁴⁶

Fifthly, the timeline of the emergence of China's OFDI framework underscores that it was a response to country specific developments and politico-economic constellations at certain points in time. These include the rise to power of the economically liberal faction within the CCP; the industrial demand surpassing the country's resource base; the increasing dependence on export markets; and the enhanced competition at home due to the IFDI-led growth strategy as well as WTO accession.

In summary, the above overview of frameworks, timelines, and objectives supports this research project's argument that it is crucial to account for the specificities of home country context and development in explaining why these investments are occurring. This section has done so by comparatively introducing the key features and events that have constituted and shaped the contemporary policy framework that supports Chinese OFDI in general and Chinese OFDI in Africa in particular. Such a detailed contextualization of the investments in country frameworks, timelines, and objectives also points to the importance of taking the structural (i.e. export dependency, limited resource base, or WTO accession) and contingent (i.e. Asian crisis or the victory of the liberal faction within the CCP) factors of a home country's development trajectory into account when assessing and analyzing land-consuming investments. As Marks so pointedly highlighted in his history of the modern world, in many cases events not plans shape great powers.⁴⁷ This insight emphasizes the limits of using highly functional theoretical approaches to capture why "land grabs" occur.

---

44 | Sun (2011), 8.
45 | Sauvant et al. (2010).
46 | See, for instance, Brautigam (2011a).
47 | Marks (2007)

3. Guiding Ideology

Chinese land-consuming OFDI projects do not transpire in an ideological vacuum. Rather, their facilitation and legitimation is embedded in an overarching and guiding set of ideas that is prone to shifts over time. This guiding ideology, basically a cluster of ideas that perform ideological functions, ranges over several policy sectors, taking the form of white papers, significant government speeches, or declarations at the end of FOCAC conferences. A closer look at the discourse surrounding these investments reveals the profound changes that have taken place in China's political landscape and development orientation since 1978. Instead of portraying the anti-capitalist and self-dependence dogma of Mao-era foreign policy, the new discourse is affected by the neoliberal terminology of "win-win" and embedded in the analytical frame of today's mainstream economics.[48] The latter has become entrenched in the thoughts of the different factions in the CCP,[49] and it is visible in official reports on China-Africa relations, such as the one by the Chinese Academy of International Trade and Economic Cooperation (CAITEC), which argues that the "sustained, rapid growth of China's economy has provided a broad and stable market for African products."[50] Phenomena that under Mao-era rhetoric would have been attributed to "imperialism" are now framed as "opportunities," and the exploration of resources is now referred to as serving both parties' "development needs" rather than representing unilateral "exploitation" and "plunder."[51]

However, this rhetoric is not confined to the realm of international economic relations. Instead, it reflects the 'trickle down' ideology that has been embraced by the political elite since the 1990s in national development programs. The strengthening of the (economically) liberal faction within the CCP led to the adoption of a development strategy that has become known as "playing two hands hard."[52] While one hand represents the ultimate power and political control by the party, the other hand has been used "to achieve economic growth by any and all means possible and available."[53] Under this development paradigm, economic growth has come to be seen as a guarantee of political regime stability, (allegedly) providing jobs and state revenues. Accordingly, it

---

48 | Compare, for instance, Deng (1974) and the whitepaper on peaceful development by the State Council (2011b).
49 | Cheng (2001).
50 | CAITEC (2010).
51 | The comparison is based on Deng Xiaoping's speech at the UN General Assembly (Deng (1974)) and contemporary government rhetoric of the Chinese Ministry of Foreign Affairs (MOFA) (MOFA (2006)).
52 | Oman (1 July 2011).
53 | Oman (1 July 2011).

is at the center of political agendas across all levels of government. In 2011, the mounting social unrest related to the high costs of this development approach led the Chinese government to change the principle of "strong state, wealthy people" into "wealthy people, strong state" (12th Five Year Plan),[54] indicating a new emphasis on social, environmental, and ecological aspects of development. Yet, in practice, the political control of the party still comes before the well-being of the people or the environment (see Table 5-1 for relevant publications articulating China's development ambitions and strategies).

Against this background, China's outreach to Africa since 2000 is seen in relation to China's construction of a "socialist market economy"[55] and is argued to be of "mutual benefit"[56] for the parties involved. While the first notion clearly establishes a linkage between domestic economic interests and development plans and overseas investments, the latter exposes the fundamental shift in China-Africa relations, from unilateral aid provision by China to Africa towards "mutually beneficial" cooperation, which is supposed to benefit Chinese economic interests as much as it does African countries (see Table 5-1 for key documents establishing this linkage).[57]

---

54 | Chinese Government (2011).
55 | State Council (2011a).
56 | State Council (2011b).
57 | Li (2006).

Table 5-1 – Key Documents Outlining China's Development in Relation to the Chinese Presence in Africa (selected)[58]

Speeches
1974 – Deng Xiaoping, Speech at the UN General Assembly
Government (White) Papers
2005 – White paper, "Peaceful Development Road"   2006 – White paper, "China's Africa Policy"   2006 – Strategy paper, "11th Five Year Plan, 2006-2010"   2010 – White paper, "China-Africa Trade and Economic Cooperation"   2011 – White paper "Peaceful Development"   2011 – White paper "Foreign Aid"   2011 – Strategy paper, "12th Five Year Plan, 2011-2015"
Official Notice and Frameworks
1991 – National Planning Committee "Opinion"[59]   1999– State Council "Opinion"[60]   2000 – CCP "Suggestion"[61]   Since 2001– Emerging "Go Out" Framework for Overseas FDI[62]
Reports
2010 – China-Africa Trade and Economic Relationship   2011 – Statistical Bulletin of China's OFDI 2010

---

58 | The documents can be found in the bibliography section as follows: Deng (1974); State Council (2005); MOFA (2006); National People's Congress (2006); Chinese Government (2006); State Council (2011b), State Council (2011a); National People's Congress (2011); Wilkes and Huang (2011); Chinese Government (2011); CAITEC (2010); Ministry of Commerce (2011a).
59 | See description in Xue and Han (2010), 316-317.
60 | See description in Wilkes and Huang (2011), 9.
61 | Wilkes and Huang (2011), 9.
62 | See description of major reforms and notices under Xue and Han (2010); Wilkes and Huang (2011); Bernasconi-Osterwalder et al. (2013).

China's Africa Policy

In 2006, for the first time, the Ministry of Foreign Affairs published "China's Africa Policy" (January 2006),[63] a white paper that "present[ed] to the world the objectives of China's policy towards Africa and the measures to achieve them, and its proposals for cooperation in various fields in the coming years, with a view to promoting the steady growth of China-Africa relations in the long term and bringing the mutually-beneficial cooperation to a new stage."[64]

The document starts out by portraying Africa as a post-colonial continent with a "long history, vast expanse of land, rich natural resources and huge potential for development," and continues by identifying the guiding principles of China-Africa relations as "equality and mutual benefit, solidarity and common development."[65] At the same time, the Ministry describes China as the "largest developing country in the world, [which] follows the path of peaceful development and pursues an independent foreign policy of peace."[66]

With regard to the guiding ideology, the complementary concepts of "peaceful development" and "common development" are of special importance. Already in 2004 (and again in 2011), a foreign policy whitepaper titled "Peaceful Development" outlined this concept against the background of rising international concerns over Chinese investment activities abroad. Basically, the concept of peaceful development claims that China's development trajectory is different from that of Western countries in the past, particularly regarding its foreign economic policy. Contrary to Western countries' episodes of economic expansion and industrial restructuring, which were characterized by violence, domination, and colonization, China is framed as a responsible "big country," managing its current industrial 'need' to expand overseas in a peaceful manner that allows for the realization of the development goals of all parties involved. Therefore, it allows for "common development," which again matches the guiding principles of China-Africa relations, namely "mutual benefits," "equality" and "solidarity," as mentioned in "China's Africa Policy" (see Table 5-2). Multiple statements made by government officials apply this narrative, including the earlier quote from 2011 by Lu Shaye, then Director General of the Department of African Affairs of the Ministry of Foreign Affairs, on the nature and driver of Chinese-African relations.[67] China-Africa relations are said to be complementary in nature, meeting China's interest in new markets, resources, and business opportunities, and African countries' interest to increase their

---

63 | MOFA (2006).
64 | MOFA (2006).
65 | MOFA (2006).
66 | MOFA (2006).
67 | Gouraud (18 October 2011).

primary commodity exports, import technology to improve their economies' productivity, and improve their representation in international fora.[68]

It is worth noting that the 2006 "China's Africa Policy" also provides a detailed account of measures to be implemented to realize the "mutually beneficial" cooperation. Measures named in the political realm include enhanced governmental cooperation at all levels of government between the African continent and China, as well as cooperation in international affairs, with China speaking up for African interests in international institutions. Objectives in the economic field are to establish a China Africa Joint Chamber of Commerce and Industry (CAJCCI),[69] stimulate trade, facilitate investment, enhance agricultural cooperation, boost infrastructure projects, and foster "resource cooperation" while continuing with FOCAC ministerial conferences, amongst other projects. In the case of Chinese land-consuming investments in agriculture, the document states that the "focus will be laid on the cooperation in land development, agricultural plantation, breeding technologies, food security, agricultural machinery and the processing of agricultural and side-line products."[70]

---

68 | Gouraud (18 October 2011).
69 | See the website of the China Africa Joint Chamber of Commerce and Industry (http://www.china-africajcci.org/english/about_us.asp) for more information.
70 | MOFA (2006).

Table 5-2 – Guiding Principles and Objectives of "China's Africa Policy" (MOFA 2006)[71]

> SINCERITY, FRIENDSHIP AND EQUALITY. China adheres to the Five Principles of Peaceful Coexistence, respects African countries' independent choice of the road of development and supports African countries' efforts to grow stronger through unity.
>
> MUTUAL BENEFIT, RECIPROCITY AND COMMON PROSPERITY. China supports African countries' endeavor for economic development and nation building, carries out cooperation in various forms in the economic and social development, and promotes common prosperity of China and Africa.
>
> MUTUAL SUPPORT AND CLOSE COORDINATION. China will strengthen cooperation with Africa in the UN and other multilateral systems by supporting each other's just demand and reasonable propositions and continue to appeal to the international community to give more attention to questions concerning peace and development in Africa.
>
> LEARNING FROM EACH OTHER AND SEEKING COMMON DEVELOPMENT. China and Africa will learn from and draw upon each other's experience in governance and development, strengthen exchange and cooperation in education, science, culture and health. Supporting African countries' efforts to enhance capacity building, China will work together with Africa in the exploration of the road of sustainable development.
>
> The one China principle is the political foundation for the establishment and development of China's relations with African countries and regional organizations.

In many cases, this rhetoric of mutual benefit, learning, solidarity, and common development is replicated when outlining inter-governmental project goals (see Chapter 4), but it is also present on the private firm level. For example, the "murky" China International Fund Ltd. (CIF) uses a Chinese allegory tracing back to the philosopher Laozi to show how its investments in Africa will serve the goal of "common development" and "mutual benefit" by transferring technology and know-how on the one side, and creating new business opportunities on the other: "Give a Man a Fish and you Feed him for a Day. Teach a Man to Fish and You Feed Him for a Lifetime" (see Figure 51).[72]

---

71 | MOFA (2006), part III.
72 | To learn more about the dubious reputation of this Fund, see a summary of critical reports on the blog by Brautigam (19 October 2011).

Figure 5-1 – China International Fund Information Material (CIF 2011)[73]

Summary

China's changing ideological orientation clearly correlates with the shifting interests of its growth and export-oriented and resource-intensive (political) economy. Undoubtedly, such an economy cannot function along the lines of an anti-capitalist ethics framework. That old framework, focusing on "self-dependence" and "autonomy" and assuming a zero-sum nature of international economic and ecological exchanges conducted on a capitalist basis, was the common Chinese standpoint prior to the opening up of the country. To the degree that the current ideology basically denies that there are zero-sum aspects in the above outlined bilateral relations that might make one of the two partners worse off—from an ecological, economic, and/or social point of view—the ideological discourse reveals an affinity with mainstream economics framings of development and cooperation that are embedded at the level of international economic and aid governance.

At the same time, the above presented information/publicity brochure of the China International Fund Ltd. (Figure 5–1) reflects the slightly asymmetric conception of this "mutual benefit" relationship that is outlined in "China's Africa Policy" and other significant publications mentioned before. It anticipates the exchange of resources from African countries for technology and

---

73 | "Give a Man a Fish and You Feed Him for a Day. Teach a Man to Fish and You Feed Him for a Lifetime." This saying is reported to date back to Laozi, a philosopher of ancient China who developed the strain of Taoism (dao-ism). Chinese characters displayed are as follows: 非洲 (feizhou) = Africa; 中国 (zhongguo) = China; 鱼 (yu) = Fishery; 渔(yu) = Fish. The sentence plays with the multiple meanings of the word "yu" (jade alias wealth; fish; fishery). The comic is taken from the information brochure of the China International Fund (2011), 27-28.

know-how from China. For the moment, this is largely a reflection of the economic set-up of the partnering countries, but historical evidence highlights that such asymmetric exchanges carry the danger of becoming permanent. At the least, they are hard to overcome, especially once they are locked into existing societal and economic structures. The following section will expand on the key characteristics of Chinese political economy because they are important to understanding the core traits of this shift towards liberalism presented above from the viewpoint of interests involved.

4. Political Economy

Given the complexity of actor constellations in the context of land-consuming investments, but also in view of the previously described discursive shift since the 1990s, it seems vital to outline the key characteristics of the investor country's political economy that might explain both phenomena in the larger context of home country development. Evidently, referring to the dominant role of the state in China's economy falls short of capturing the specificities and/or fails to account for conflicting interests.

In this section, the argument is made that three aspects of the political economy are of particular relevance when contextualizing and explaining—in the home country context—the guiding ideology, as well as the multitude of Chinese agents, involved in overseas investments in SSA. These aspects will be discussed under the headings of state fragmentation; the rise of bureaucratic entrepreneurs; and shifting state-market relations. The characteristic mixture of these three aspects has been summarized by Feng Xu under the concept of "neoliberal governmentality."[74]

State Fragmentation

Though this is often overlooked, the emergence of the OFDI framework has been the outcome of a process of political reform. That is, despite the absence of a reform in China towards a "multiparty system and the separation of powers,"[75] it was a political reform process which created the foundation for the economic transition outlined above. This reform process, which has yielded an increasing "fragmentation of the central government,"[76] as well as the "rise of sub[-]state actors," has taken place in the areas of "state governance and of the

---

74 | Feng (2009), 432.
75 | Yu (2008), 23.
76 | Bo (2011).

administrative systems of the state."[77] As a result, Feng Xu argues that a system of "neoliberal governmentality" has emerged:

> Although China is in broad terms an illiberal polity, the Chinese state is increasingly adopting a neo-liberal way of governing or neo-liberal governmentality. Following Michel Foucault, "governmentality" refers to forms of governance that utilize a network of state and non-state actors, with the specific aim of steering individuals (both individual persons and individual institutions) to govern themselves in the market economy.[78]

Increasingly, governance of areas such as energy, agriculture, investment, and labor, all of which are related to Chinese land-consuming OFDI, reveals forms of neoliberal governmentality in the way it is organized. Particular characteristics are the engagement of multiple actors from the public and private sectors, the decentralization of approval processes to lower levels of government, and the rising degree of "rule by regulation" in the governing of these policy areas.

Importantly, Foucault coined the term "neoliberal governmentality" to describe a middle ground of economic governance between laissez faire and state collectivism.[79] In addition, Lemke highlighted that the term defines the fundamental change in how a particular socioeconomic and political order is legitimized: "Collective wealth produced a social consensus on a state that was no longer defined in terms of a historical mission but legitimated itself with reference to economic growth. Economic prosperity revealed the legitimacy of the state for all to see [...]."[80] Moreover, from the perspective of liberal and neoliberal political and economic theories, the term 'neoliberal governmentality' seems to capture elements of both definitions. On the one hand, the economic liberalization processes underway since the 1980s have led to greater importance being placed on the rule of law and markets in the governance of China's economy; however, the (altered) state remains central in establishing these institutions and governing this process.[81] On the other hand, some areas have become increasingly deregulated, and (central) state control has been significantly reduced.

This transformation is reflected in the increasingly elaborate "Go Out" framework as well as in the composition of OFDI. Not only have approval processes been transferred to the provincial level, but provincial actors have also begun to act as foreign policy entrepreneurs and investors. For instance, a pilot farm in

---

77 | Yu (2008), 23.
78 | Feng (2009), 432.
79 | He attributed this form of governmentality to Germany, and acknowledged that different countries have different degrees of neoliberalism and governmentality in their socioeconomic orders. Foucault(2008), 192-194.
80 | Lemke (2010), 195-197.
81 | See, for instance, North et al. (2009), 45 (Footnote 16).

Mozambique is the result of inter-provincial cooperation between Gaza province and Hubei province.[82] In some cases, provincial overseas activities have even been in direct conflict with the foreign policy objectives of China's central government.[83] Moreover, the major actors and institutions of the OFDI governance system have been created rather recently in order to meet the administrative challenges posed by the new complexity of economic relations and international development objectives; take, for example, MOFCOM. This ministry was established in 2003 and given the responsibility of supervising Chinese OFDI in the domestic and international contexts while also coordinating foreign aid policy and instruments (funds and loans).[84] The institution is a merger of multiple functions that were carried out by other departments prior to its existence. Another example is the State-owned Assets Supervision and Administration Commission (SASAC). It was created as an 'ad hoc' institution in 2003 and tasked with the management of national SOEs, including supervision and approval of their OFDI projects. It operates on the premises of the Ministry of Finance,[85] and since its establishment, it has constantly advanced FDI related deregulation. Likewise, the acting Premier, Li Keqiang, and the State Council have asked government agencies to further deregulate and reduce "unnecessary administrative approvals."[86]

The Rise of "Bureaucratic Entrepreneurs"

It is crucial to understand that in spite of the aforementioned political reform process and the multiplicity of actors involved in land-consuming overseas investments, the state remains a dominant actor in both the domestic economy and outward investment activities. The political reform was the result of a choice by the ruling elite to transform the economic structure while ensuring the "continuation of the elite strata."[87] Similar to the industrial revolution in Great Britain and that country's subsequent overseas expansion, political actors in China gave up a certain portion of their political and legal privileges while becoming "new entrepreneurs and legislators" in a process that enhanced the intermingling of political office and economic opportunity.[88]

The concentration of economic power within the multi-level realm of the state is reflected by the fact that among the 500 largest Chinese enterprises, the so-called "China 500," almost all of the assets (96%) and profits (85%) were

---

82 | Chichava (2013), 2, 9-11.
83 | Chen and Jian (2009).
84 | See Xue and Han (2010), 308-309.
85 | See Xue and Han (2010), 308-309.
86 | Wildau (10 May 2013).
87 | Cheng (2001), 241.
88 | Cheng (2001), 241.

held by SOEs in 2006.[89] Currently, the Chinese government is also trying to increase its influence over the private sector, which is said to contribute more than two thirds of the annual growth in GNP.[90] A rising number of private enterprises feature a party cell in their organizational set-up.[91] However, it seems that in some cases, private companies undertake such CCP related activities primarily as a way to present themselves to relevant cadres and gain access to funding. This makes sense in the context of more than two decades of financial repression and a re-tightening of economic control by the political elite that has put the private sector at a disadvantage, both compared to state-owned enterprises and international competitors.[92]

Since China's opening up, this process of the "marketization of power"[93] has turned state officials into bureaucratic entrepreneurs. At the same time, the party has opened its membership regulations to allow private entrepreneurs in the CCP. By 2000, 20% of private entrepreneurs were said to have become party members. This trend enhances the synergetic relationship between public and private interests, particularly since a growing number of entrepreneurs belong to local party committees that exercise great influence at the local level.[94] At the 18th National Congress of the CCP in 2012, Liang Wengen, the billionaire entrepreneur, was elected as a delegate for the second time, the first occasion being in 2007. Wengen epitomizes this intermingling of political power and economic wealth, as he had originally been a government official before he became an entrepreneur.[95]

With regard to Chinese OFDI, this dominance of the state, together with the shifting interest structure of the actors involved, has several implications. On the one hand, overseas investments do reflect the dominance of state actors within the domestic economy: most (recorded) OFDI projects were still being undertaken by state-owned enterprises as of 2013.[96] In Chinese land-consuming OFDI in Africa, research by Jansson indicates that SOEs usually dominate large-scale investment projects in the oil and construction sectors, while private enterprises tend to have small-scale investments in agribusiness, manufacturing, and communication (also see Table 5-3).[97] Among the investments in the "land grab" literature that were studied for this book, the majority

---

89 | Rudman (2006), 34.
90 | BloombergBusinessweek.com (21 August 2005).
91 | English.news.cn (21 June 2011).
92 | Fewsmith (2001), 170-176.
93 | He (13 November 2012). Also see He (2002).
94 | Rudman (2006), 50.
95 | Tây Sơn News Wire (27 September 2011); and ChinaDaily.com.cn (12 November 2012).
96 | Davies (2013), 8.
97 | Jansson (2009), 3.

was undertaken by provincial and central SOEs in the mining or construction sectors, or by those SOEs active in the agricultural Friendship Farms. On the other hand, it is important to highlight the changing interest structure of state actors, which is reflected by the discursive turn outlined in the previous section on guiding ideology. State actors are increasingly in it for profit, which they then manage themselves.[98] Given that capital investments in Africa are said to have a 60% higher return than in Asia,[99] this detail seems essential for explaining why these investments take place as they do, particularly against the Chinese background of declining returns, domestic market saturation, limited economies of scale, and high wealth inequality.

Table 5-3 – Three Levels of Chinese Engagement in Africa (Jansson 2009)[100]

	ACTORS	ACTIVITIES
Level 1 – government	Primarily Chinese and African governments and embassies, government departments, banks (China Export—Import; China Development Bank), and other financial institutions	Bilateral relations and official visits, FOCAC, party to party relations, policy bank financed concessional finance agreements, donations (stadiums, parliament buildings, hospitals), development aid, debt relief.
Level 2 – larger company level	Chinese state-owned enterprises (SOEs) and larger private Chinese companies. These actors mostly have close relations with the Chinese Embassy in the respective African country, but they do not always work on projects financed by the Chinese government.	• Large-scale infrastructure undertakings financed either by Chinese concessional loans, the AfDB, the WB, the African government, or other financial institutions. • Extractive industries: oil, minerals, timber. • Larger manufacturing/ assembly plants.
Level 3 – small-scale economic activity level	Small-scale traders, owners of processing plants, and 'fast-moving' businessmen who entered African countries independently. Between these actors and the Chinese Embassy there is often very little interaction, assistance, and/ or control.	• Import and trade in consumer goods, mineral processing, timber export, other small-scale economic activities.

---

98 | Also see He (13 November 2012).
99 | Liu (4 November 2011).
100 | Jansson (2009), 3 (Table 1).

Changing State-Market Relations

The material presented above highlights two aspects of the changing state-market relationship that are critical to understanding how and why Chinese investments occur. Firstly, the central state is not necessarily in control of what is happening and, secondly, the strong position of the state does not imply that these investments are not for profit. Rather, the high degree of state fragmentation has provided discretionary power to the provinces, and the emergence of bureaucratic entrepreneurs has given rise to changing interest structures and an enhanced focus on profit, together with a development discourse that matches this interest structure and profit orientation.

Adding to these increasingly complex state-market relations is a third aspect: the SOE management reforms that began in the 1980s (these were briefly alluded to in the 'home country measures' section of this chapter). In fact, over time, the Chinese government and the CCP introduced a policy (*zhengqi fenkai*) that separated "government functions from business operations."[101] As a consequence, "state-owned companies of all kinds have gradually been losing some of the advantages once conferred by their relationship with the state."[102] While SOEs gained leeway in terms of choosing CEOs, and now can hold on to the profit they generate, they are also held accountable for their failures by state officials, who have increasingly become distanced from SOEs. As a consequence, a rising number of SOEs has gone out of business.[103]

This complex relationship is reflected in Chinese land-consuming OFDI in SSA, as even agricultural cooperation projects are operated by Chinese state farms on a for-profit basis, often without financial support from the government.[104] The complex nature of the relationship is also evidenced by the fact that construction sector SOEs have turned into contract bidders that pursue their own business strategies. Even in the case of China's policy banks, the marketization of state interests, as well as the effects of the SOE management reform, is of fundamental importance. While bank loans are "heavily influenced by government policies and are not to operate in full compliance with the market rules,"[105] as outlined earlier, banks are not permitted to accumulate debts and/or engage in unprofitable business. This also applies to the China-Africa Development Fund, which is expected to generate returns on the support it provides to Chinese businesses investing overseas.[106]

---

101 | Woetzel (8 July 2008).
102 | Woetzel (8 July 2008); Wang (2002).
103 | Woetzel (8 July 2008).
104 | Brautigam (2009).
105 | Brautigam (2011a), 4.
106 | Brautigam (2011a), 4.

Also, the assessment of private investors benefits from the differentiated analysis of state-market relations. While thus far private entrepreneurs have hardly profited from Chinese funding or state institutions when investing overseas,[107] research shows that their motivation to go abroad is often related to the state dominated political economy back home in two main ways. On the one hand, their motivation seems to be related to the crowding out effects of IFDI policies within China, together with domestic market saturation and unfavorable regulations.[108] On the other hand, a detailed study on the practices of Chinese companies in Angola has shown that Chinese privately owned enterprises (POEs) seem to operate in the periphery of SOEs, with the former taking on activities that the latter outsource from their overall production processes. This indicates that an isolated assessment of SOE and POE activity might miss the pull-and-push dynamics that link the two types of enterprises.[109]

Summary

The assessment of state-market relations underlines that key economic and political changes since the 1990s match the shifting development discourse in which Chinese land-consuming investments are embedded. The economic and political changes also explain the way these investments take place, namely their use of modern development finance, for-profit orientation, and/or the complex actor constellations.

The intermingling of political power and economic wealth, the rise of sub-state actors, and the linked dynamics between SOE and POE activity characteristic of China's political economy are easily overlooked by those explanations of Chinese land-consuming FDI that assume that these investments are primarily conducted by state agents with the intent to secure resources. Such a narrow description also tends to overemphasize differences in relation to liberal countries. Take the example of home country measures applicable to Chinese OFDI: from a comparative perspective, these are very similar to the institutional landscape that has been in place in industrialized countries for a long time. In fact, China is just catching up to the range of mechanisms that companies in OECD countries have at their disposal. The greatest finding of this section might indeed be the high degree of institutional similarity (rather than uniqueness or innovation) that characterizes Chinese engagement with African countries when compared to Western relations with the continent—a

---

107 | Jansson (2009); and Brautigam (2009), 257.
108 | Rui et al. (2010), 182.
109 | Action for South Africa (2011), 1; also see Belchior (2010). Overall, activities of privately owned enterprises (POEs) are under-researched, and POE projects are hardly mentioned in "land grab" databases.

fact that is particularly interesting with regards to the South-South cooperation rhetoric often applied not just by Chinese and African partners, but also by multilateral organizations, such as the FAO.[110]

5. Development Context

China has moved from close to zero OFDI activity to becoming an important investor country within less than three decades. From this historical perspective, but also with regards to China's more recent decision to proactively promote such capital exports, the linkage of development trajectories and OFDI promotion deserves closer attention. After all, OFDI has become an important component of the country's contemporary foreign economic policy as well as its diplomatic efforts. Also, FDI research has rightly noted that *"OFDI is one part of the country's overall strategy of economic development. It is a means to an end, not the goal itself."*[111] The next paragraphs will bring together the various threads about OFDI in the context of Chinese development that appeared in earlier sections. Ultimately, this section provides the foundation for the comparative discussion of role of OFDI in the context of home country development.

It is argued that Chinese land-consuming investments are part of a trend by the Chinese government to further internationalize development in the search for markets, resources, profitable business, and/or political allies, and in the face of rising resource pressures, external dependencies and high international competition.[112] In an international comparison, this globalization of Chinese development via its "emerging transnational companies" is nothing out of the ordinary. For instance, authors such as Hirsch have drawn attention to the fact that transnational or multinational enterprises play important roles in a home country's social and economic development.[113] Their foreign supply sourcing and embeddedness in international markets are, for instance, important in terms of facilitating international economies of scale in spite of the problem of domestic diseconomies of space. They also enable industrial upgrading and provide institutionalized access to resources looked for in the particular industrial setting:

The MNEs' value activities lower the barriers separating countries from their foreign sources of supply and their international markets. This enables home countries to increase the benefits they derive from the international division of labor, exploitation

---

110 | Goetz (2018) (forthcoming).
111 | Broadman (2010), 331.
112 | Wilkes and Huang (2011).
113 | Hirsch (2012), 1-2.

of economies of scale and the ownership advantages of their MNEs. Other things being equal, an extension of the global reach achieved through cross-border value activities is likely to compensate for the tax loss and the diminution of sovereignty implied by outward FDI.[114]

At the same time, of course, it can be argued that the wave of deregulation in the 1990s, together with advances in transportation and communication, has changed the nature of state-market relations, thereby rendering the home country's advantages that it can obtain through its companies' OFDI activities (even) less feasible. For instance, transnational enterprises increasingly threaten governments to exit their country's economy and relocate their production activities to other countries in the case of unfavorable policy measures. Moreover, corporate actors pursue a narrow shareholder value objective, and tax evasion is widespread. Yet, it seems that in many cases, the perception that the paybacks of the "extension of the global reach achieved [by companies] through cross-border value activities" outweigh the costs still prevails among policy makers. Perhaps this is partly due to the lack of theorized alternatives, but it also partially results from the fact that policy makers are often closely interlinked with corporate actors and interests, as the specificities of China's political economy have perfectly illustrated.

According to the outline of the 11th Five Year Plan (2006-2010), which has become the foundation of China's evolving OFDI policy framework, the policy stance towards OFDI seeks to promote five developmental objectives.[115] First, going overseas shall raise companies' competitiveness through enhanced international economic and technical cooperation, which will provide them with new opportunities, economies of scale, and knowhow. Second, OFDI shall support the export sector by means of "overseas project contracting and labor service cooperation."[116] Third, the sourcing of domestically scarce resources overseas is seen by the government to address the dramatic environmental impact of China's development trajectory while securing stable and efficient supplies. Fourth, overseas research and development activities are intended to improve the technological base and upgrade relevant sectors. Fifth, OFDI is framed as a means to globalize the economy by internationalizing production chains and business operations. This (foreign) economic strategy is complemented by an IFDI strategy that aims both to regulate IFDI such that it becomes "greener" and advances the technology and knowhow transfer (see also the 12th Five Year Plan, 2011-2015).[117]

---

114 | Hirsch (2012), 1.
115 | Wilkes and Huang (2011).
116 | Based on information provided by Wilkes and Huang (2011), 9-10.
117 | Chinese Government (2011).

Clearly, the above-presented policy choices and official rhetoric that Chinese land-consuming FDI projects are reflective of and embedded in cannot be fully captured without looking more closely at the specific development challenges that the country has faced and that increasingly threaten the political elite. China's development path since opening up has been summarized by Wenran Jiang as "heavy industrialization, labor- and capital- intensive manufacturing industries, export-led growth, low labor cost and high environmental damage."[118] By 1993, the country had turned from petroleum exporter to petroleum importer.[119] Moreover, the development trajectory has resulted in low worker welfare, the stagnation of political reforms, and a burgeoning rise in social (wealth) inequality in a context where economic opportunity is linked to public office.[120] Together with the intense environmental consequences[121] of the country's rapid urbanization,[122] industrialization, and modernization processes, these factors have come to pose a challenge for the country's social stability, as well as its food security,[123] and they are viewed as matters of national security that have the potential to threaten the stability of the political party regime.

The IFDI-led export growth strategy has also had a negative impact on domestic enterprises. In many cases, these struggle to compete with foreign companies because they lack access to credit services, they have to deal with political interference, and are less embedded in international markets. As one entrepreneur going overseas put it: "The best food has all been eaten up by the global giants and what we can do is to have those leftovers."[124] At the same time, the country's overall industrial productivity and efficiency did not necessarily improve all that much through foreign investment.[125] To a certain degree, China has been locked in the existing international division of labor, and it has become the workshop in the international production line of foreign compa-

---

118 | Jiang (2009), 587.
119 | Vissers (June 2013), 1-7.
120 | Jiang (2009), 587.
121 | WB and SEPA (China) (2007).
122 | Liu et al. (2005), 450.
123 | While China managed to maintain a self-sufficiency rate of 95% with regard to food security, defined as grain security, it became a net importer of certain crops and products such as soybeans, vegetable oils, and sugar. For example, soybean imports today cover three quarters of domestic demand. Agricultural investments in Latin America and Eastern Europe (e.g., Bulgaria) try to grow these crops for export to China. See for instance Economic Observer (11 February 2012) and Council of Ministers (26 November 2013).
124 | Rui et al. (2010), 182.
125 | Jiang (2009), 589. Moran (2011), 64-71.

nies, resulting in less skill and technology transfer than had been hoped for by the political elite.[126] The current challenge is to avoid falling in the so-called "middle-income trap" that many emerging economies are confronted with. That is, China increasingly loses its competitive edge "against low-income countries at low wages;"[127] but, at the same time, the country has difficulties when trying to "compete with high-income countries on innovation and higher value production."[128]

Importantly, the changes in China's OFDI policy preferences and foreign policy regarding Africa have occurred in the context of these internal and external development challenges. Significant events in this process were the country becoming a net oil importer (1992); the collapse of export markets during the Asian crisis (1997); and the strong domestic competition that resulted from the IFDI-led development strategy, as well as the WTO accession, which negatively impacted indigenous enterprises due to their limited access to credit and world markets (2001). Moreover, the mounting socioeconomic and ecological pressures have pointed to the need to upgrade economic activity back home.

Regarding interests, these reforms are part of the political elite's continued pursuit of economic growth as a way to stabilize and legitimize the political system though economic success. Moreover, they reflect the interests of the country's resource intensive and export-dependent (state-owned) manufacturing industry, which functions as the country's economic backbone and plays an important role in the accumulation of foreign reserves. In addition, Chinese land-consuming OFDI also involves a number of actors which respond to these policy changes, such as workers that hope to improve their (family's) livelihoods; construction companies that establish themselves as independent contract bidders; and/or POEs or SOEs that seek to make their fortune overseas, evading political interference and/or crowding out effects of IFDI activities back home.

Summary

Land-consuming OFDI in SSA is part of China's resource and expansion diplomacy that has ensued since the late 1990s, picking up speed in 2000. Overseas investments by Chinese companies emerged as part of the toolbox available to the Chinese government to pursue certain interests and policy objectives. At the same time, the paths taken and choices made regarding the Chinese presence in African countries can only be fully grasped by revisiting the core

---

126 | Moran (2011), 64-71; Gaullier et al. (2005).
127 | Zhuang et al. (2012), 11.
128 | Zhuang et al. (2012), 11.

traits of the Chinese political economy, such as the rise of bureaucratic entrepreneurs, the marketization of power, and the emergence of a "neoliberal governmentality,"[129] all of which have been conducive to a promotional OFDI policy stance and guiding ideology.

The previous assessment of the home country context also demonstrates that China is not an isolated country; rather, the international context matters. The choice of instruments, as well as the guiding ideology characteristic of Chinese OFDI in SSA, reflects major traits of mainstream economic theory that are embedded in the international economic and aid governance architecture. Interestingly, the international context is crucial for understanding the Chinese foreign policy concept of "peaceful development" that aims to differentiate China's expansion overseas from the violent history of the North. Regarding the liberal international context within which Chinese expansion occurs, the "peaceful development" idea seems less 'innovative' than the Chinese government wants it to appear. Instead, China is profiting from an international economic system that allows countries and societies to expand their consumption and production patterns beyond their sovereign borders without waging war. In contrast to those of the late 19th century, contemporary overseas investments are rationalized within a "win-win" narrative and are part of a technical regime of international economic governance that regulates how they should take place but does not query their legitimacy, such as the WTO or BITs.[130]

Moreover, other features of the international context, such as the price volatility of international energy markets, their quasi-monopolistic structure, and/or the reluctance of Western governments and companies to integrate emerging Chinese companies into the international (energy) markets play a role in explaining why these investments occur.[131] These aspects have led the Chinese government to search for new partners—such as African countries—to facilitate the economic expansion and globalization process that land-consuming FDI is part of. At the same time, Chinese OFDI is not a unilateral undertaking: African governments play a crucial role in shaping which investments take place and how.

This section will conclude by looking at the question of whether, in fact, OFDI lives up to the rhetoric used for its legitimization. Can we say that land-consuming FDI activities in Sub-Saharan Africa are a success story from

---

129 | Feng (2009), 432.
130 | See Chapter 3 and Trentmann (2008), 7. Consequently, this raises the interesting question of what such a "peaceful development" approach would look like under a different international architecture which acknowledged zero-sum aspects of international social, ecological, and economic relations.
131 | Goldthau and Witte (2010).

a home country perspective, particularly given the empirical evidence which underlined that many of the stated goals attached to FDI projects in the recipient countries did not materialize? Again, it appears that the reality of these investments, as well as their utility, is rather complex.

From the official Chinese perspective, these investments are said to "deepen the development of international energy resources and [...] processing cooperation."[132] In international comparison, China is just catching up to international practices and standards of development that have a long tradition within OECD countries. Yet, there remains great skepticism among the Chinese public, which largely seems to oppose OFDI.[133] In particular, overseas investment projects that construct hospitals or schools have been commented on with rising sarcasm by Chinese netizens who point to the rural areas in China where such services and infrastructure are largely missing. In view of the high social costs of the Chinese development trajectory over the past three decades, characterized as it is by a dramatic increase in social wealth inequality, the denial of social rights, and very low wages, it seems to be widespread public opinion that these investments, grants, and social development measures should instead be put to work in the Western provinces and rural areas, which for the time being remain decoupled from the overall development process.[134] The aspect of high wealth inequality[135] is particularly interesting from a historical perspective. This usually curbs demand in home countries while also contributing to an unprecedentedly high level of capital to be exported. Accordingly, calling Chinese land-consuming OFDI a success story at this point does not capture the complexity associated with OFDI from the perspective of home country development.

6. Conclusion

Given the multifaceted dynamics at play, this chapter has not attempted to provide a monocausal explanation of how and why these investments take place as they do. As Marks has rightly noted, "[m]onocausal explanations are too simple to take account of the complexity of people, societies, and historical change."[136] However, the key argument that has been put forward in this case study is that these investments are part of several (interrelated) drivers, namely

---

132 | See National People's Congress (2011); and State Council (2012).
133 | Broadman (2010), 330.
134 | Broadman (2010), 330; Chinese Academy of Social Sciences and UNDP China (2013), 1-13.
135 | Chinese Academy of Social Sciences and UNDP China (2013), 1-13.
136 | Marks (2007), 13.

Chinese efforts to diversify the country's resource supply, open new markets, to internationalize production processes, and strengthen the "soft power" in international relations.

Moreover, the review of the home country context has highlighted that China has moved away from self-identifying as a planned economy aimed at a high degree of autarky, and transitioned towards a "socialist market economy"[137] that is increasingly integrated in the world economy. Responding to particular events in time, such as the growing external resource dependency, the collapse of its main export markets during the Asian crisis, the unfavorably tough competition between foreign investors and domestic industry, and the untenably high social and environmental costs of development, the government has adopted a promotional policy stance towards OFDI.

Since 2000, Chinese SOEs going overseas operate in an increasingly elaborate institutional framework, and they benefit directly or indirectly from the wide range of home country measures supporting overseas activities, such as commercial diplomacy, economic cooperation projects, and/or new forms of development finance. At the same time, substantial reforms of corporate governance have given SOEs more leeway from state control in their business operations. Importantly, these ideological shifts and the reform processes are part of profound political reforms that have occurred since the 1980s which have significantly changed the country's political economy. While the state remains the central actor, the rule of law and markets play a greater role in China's economic governance; regulatory procedures have been eased; a new actor group of bureaucratic entrepreneurs—i.e. officials who use their favorable political positions in the system to profit economically—has emerged; party structures have been opened to private sector actors; and competencies in particular policy fields have been decentralized, increasing the importance of sub-state actors (see brief summary in Table 5-4).

Together, these home country features explain the core empirical characteristics of Chinese land-consuming OFDI in SSA. Accordingly, the sectoral composition, with its focus on resources and manufacturing, reflects the home country economic setting, i.e. the manufacturing industry's interest in external resources and business opportunities to continue and/or expand its operations; and the political elites' focus on growth as a source of wealth and political stability. This also explains the minor share of agricultural investments in SSA, as these have not been a priority. Instead, SOE-run agricultural and construction projects often started at the request of African governments that wanted to reactivate the former friendship farms and build infrastructure in exchange for resources. From the Chinese perspective, these are part of a "soft power" strategy to build up a reputation as a peaceful emerging power that acts to the

---

137 | See, for instance, People's Daily (13 July 2005).

benefit of its partners. At the same time, the labor exports that are accompanying the increases in trade with and investment to SSA highlight the very low levels of worker welfare in the home country—the competitive edge of Chinese companies seemingly remains to be their low costs.

Chinese investments in SSA also reflect the increasingly elaborate home country measures. As a result of the newly established forms and forums of China-Africa economic cooperation, Chinese trade with, and OFDI in Africa has risen significantly. At the same time, the altered quality of China-Africa cooperation mirrors the profound political reforms and related changes in the ideological superstructure and economic governance that have taken place since the 1980s. As a consequence of the rise of bureaucratic entrepreneurs, the adoption of mainstream economic theory to guide foreign and industrial policy, and the reform of SOE corporate governance back home, Chinese companies that have been active in SSA for decades no longer act only as non-profit operators of aid projects. Using the new leeway at their disposal when doing business (for private or public gain), they have often become successful contract bidders (e.g., construction companies) and profitable transnational companies (e.g., agricultural companies). Even in the case of development finance and economic cooperation projects, SOEs apply a for-profit rationale in their operations. This also has implications for the role of land in these investment projects. In projects that use land as space for productive activities (e.g., manufacturing and construction), the main driver is clearly to profit from the productive activities rather than to secure land. However, even in the case of resource exploitation projects, products are often not intended for consumption back home, nor are they allocated outside of domestic, regional, or international markets. Instead, land consumption in almost all cases is related to the profit orientation of related operations.

Finally, this chapter has shown that Chinese OFDI is characterized by a diversity of actors, public and private, with divergent and often conflicting agendas. In particular, the rising importance of sub-state actors in the Chinese development context explains the significance of provincial actors in China's overseas activities. Sometimes the latter can even evolve to the extent of non-conformance with central state policy objectives (see summary of findings in Table 5-4). From a micro-perspective, the interests in these investments are many: on the part of the political elite they represent a welcome mechanism to ensure the continued pursuit of economic growth as a way to stabilize and legitimize the political system though economic success. Moreover, they reflect the interests of the country's resource-intensive and export-dependent (state-owned) manufacturing industry. They also involve a diverse range of actors that hope to improve their (family's) livelihoods; establish themselves as independent contract bidders; and/or seek alternatives to the political interference and/or crowding out effects back home.

In conclusion, the multiplicity of actors involved in the investments, as well as their entrenchment in mainstream economics, raises the question of what exactly makes these investments *Chinese*? The widely made distinction between state-backed and private investments, on the basis of which the difference between Chinese and non-Chinese investments is usually discussed, fails to answer this question in a meaningful way while oversimplifying state-market relations in the context of OFDI. Instead, the factors that make these land-consuming OFDI activities *Chinese* are to be found in the specific combination of industrial set-up, development trajectory, contingent events, ideology, and political economy that were outlined above.

More broadly, reflecting on the role of land-consuming OFDI in the context of the home country's development trajectory, these investments are part of a trend to "catch up" and establish an open economic system that can meet the resource and export interests of the manufacturing industry, which has become the backbone of economic development and foreign exchange accumulation since the 1990s. Looking beyond China's industrial set-up, the investments reflect the specificities of the country's current development context, and especially its challenges. For instance, the problem of social development, which is reflected in surplus labor and low wages, is tied to both increasing migration and the ability of Chinese companies to gain a competitive advantage. Other key challenges in the context of China's development include resource dependency, which is reflected in the expanding resource diplomacy that these investments are part of; unsustainable levels of pollution, which have led to a push toward offshore pollution processing segments; and heightened competitive pressures – following the IFDI-led development approach and WTO accession—that have led to the search for knowhow and technology abroad.

The consequences of this development for the broader development context of China remain to be seen. While the approach since 2000 (and up until 2016) has strengthened investment, trade, and aid relations with African countries, it is unclear how capital exports will improve worker welfare or productivity levels back home. While they might help to diversify resource supplies, establish trading hubs to access European markets, engage in economic opportunities on the African continent, stimulate exports of manufactured goods, and establish economies of scale, they also represent an outflow of capital that will no longer be available for investment back home. The capital outflow also portends a potential loss in domestic jobs and the danger that large companies might move permanently offshore. Though it might be too early to draw any strong conclusions, there is no evidence to suggest that we are witnessing the off-shoring of Chinese industry's polluting and energy-intensive operations to African countries (in 2016).

Table 5-4 – *Brief Review of the Home Country Context and Chinese OFDI in SSA*

Category	Home Country Context	Chinese OFDI in SSA
Development context	Since opening up in the 1980s, the country has focused on the growth of its resource-intensive manufacturing industry, resulting in rising resource dependency, overcapacity, and high social and environmental costs.	The resource-intensive manufacturing industry is reflected in the sectoral composition of Chinese investments, namely in the focus on the resources sector and manufacturing operations. The small share of agricultural projects is a result of economic cooperation and part of China's resource diplomacy.
Home Country Measures	Reform processes since the 1990s, and the "Go Out" OFDI framework since 2000, have led the country to catch up with international standards.	It is unclear how much support companies receive. However, OFDI in Africa could potentially profit from various measures, such as commercial diplomacy, regulatory reforms, and newly introduced forms of development finance.
Guiding Ideologies	The country has shifted away from a focus on self-sufficiency and adopted a growth agenda for development that follows mainstream economic theory in many respects.	The ideological shift is reflected in projects that have been operating for a long time in Africa and have recently moved from an aid to business management approach.
Investor Legacy	While China has only recently become an important source of investment, it shares a long history of aid and political cooperation with African countries.	China builds on relations established since the 1950s with African countries and the related capacities of companies, but it has also established diplomatic and economic relations with additional African countries.
Political Economy	China's political economy has changed significantly over the past decades. Key events include the rise of bureaucratic entrepreneurs, i.e. officials who use their favorable political positions to profit economically; corporate governance reforms that have provided SOEs with managerial leeway; the opening up of party structures to private sector actors; the decentralization of competencies in particular policy fields and the related rise of sub-state actors; and the formalization of regulatory procedures.	Changes in the political economy explain the diversity of actors and interests involved in land-consuming OFDI (e.g., provincial actors) and the profit orientation that even holds true for economic cooperation projects (e.g., agricultural development centers). The multiple actors come from different levels of government and some of act in conflict with the central government's foreign policy. The marketization of power has led to a profit focus.
Events	Becoming a net energy importer; Asian crisis; WTO accession influenced the OFDI policy framework, as well as the social and ecological costs of the development trajectory.	Core events influencing the development of a favorable OFDI policy framework since the country's opening up, as well as its turn to Africa have been several: the rising resources dependency, the Asian crisis, and the WTO accession.

Chapter 6: British Investments in Africa
"The Last Frontier to Find Alpha?"[1]

> We want to support African countries to seize the opportunities before them and are injecting new energy into partnerships to build growth. [...] this government believes global business—including British business—can make an absolutely vital contribution here and we will do all we can to foster further commercial ties, open up trade and deepen investment.
> (Henry Bellingham, Minister for Africa, 2011[2])

> The UK is well placed to benefit from the world of the future. The National Security Strategy of the United Kingdom is: to use all our national capabilities to build Britain's prosperity, extend our nation's influence in the world and strengthen our security. The networks we use to build our prosperity we will also use to build our security.
> (National Security Strategy (Whitepaper), 2010)

1. INTRODUCTION

Land-consuming FDI emerging from liberal economies is often portrayed as the rational choice of profit-seeking private actors in a context of resource scarcity and/or financial crisis. In the case of the UK, for instance, Susan Payne, CEO of the London-based Emergent Asset Management, has been repeatedly quoted as saying that her African Agricultural Land Fund focuses on Africa as "the last frontier for finding alpha"—that is, for finding above-average returns

---
1 | Quote by Susan Payne, CEO of Emergent Asset Management in Knaup and von Mittelstaedt (30 July 2009).
2 | Speech by Bellingham (2010).

on investments.³ In a similar vein, other British investors, particularly in the biofuel and financial sectors, have argued that above-average returns outweigh the risks attached to agricultural and land-consuming projects in Sub-Saharan Africa and other parts of the world. Indeed, investors commonly refer to mounting scarcity pressures, growing demand, commodity price rises, and/or (comparatively) cheap land prices to make these investments appear like safe bets while also emphasizing their positive contributions to greater food and energy security. Hence, land-consuming investments are seen not only to promise above-average returns but to be ethically sound.

In practice, however, the empirical evidence shows that this narrative oversimplifies the drivers and interests involved, while the related rhetoric of success and the promise of high returns rarely materialize.⁴ Projects fail, people are dispossessed in the process, and seemingly cheap land turns out to be very costly due to the upfront investments required to build roads and housing and undertake planting.⁵ Furthermore, the financial crisis also led to massive crashes in the share values of companies and/or contributed to the ultimate failure of projects. As this case study will show, this verdict applies to many of the British land-consuming investments made since 2000.

The core findings of this chapter accentuate the fact that the empirical characteristics of British land-consuming investments in Sub-Saharan Africa are more multi-layered than is commonly acknowledged. Many projects predate the 2007/2008 crises and they comprise investments in multiple sectors, from construction and mining to farming. They are distributed highly uneven across the continent, reflecting the British investor legacy. Biofuels composed the largest share of listed projects, and the general emphasis has been on the primary sector and related activities (food processing). Overall, the investments reflect a very diverse private sector: companies with a long presence on the African continent are involved, as are early stage companies that invest in biofuels, and/or alternative stock markets, and financial investors. In addition, several public institutions and multilateral organizations seem to be relevant, together with host country governments. Land is of primary importance in these investments. It is used as a resource and productive space, and, increasingly, as a strategic asset. The empirical evidence shows the exposure of British investment to financial volatility, the dependency on developments back home, such as the economic crisis, and the lack of realistic business models.

The chapter proceeds as follows: Section 2 presents the history of British-African relations. These relations go far back, but they have intensified significantly since 2000. Section 3 then discusses the details of how these invest-

---

3 | Knaup and von Mittelstaedt (30 July 2009).
4 | WB (2011), 51.
5 | Interview with CEO of Highbury Finance, London, (2013).

ments occur. In particular, it will focus on land-consuming FDI's sectoral composition and timelines, the role of land, the recipient context, key actors and institutions, and the issue of investment funds. The chapter will conclude by summarizing the key empirical findings about British land-consuming FDI in Sub-Saharan Africa.

2. BACKGROUND ON THE UK IN AFRICA

British relations with the African continent go far back, while the "Second Wave of European Imperialism"[6] in the 19th century seems to be most relevant for the assessment of contemporary relations. Importantly, the dominant presence of Britain on the continent continued after the empire's post-WWII disintegration.[7] As of 2011, British companies are still among the top five investors and trading partners in former dependencies, and on the political level, most former colonies are members in the Commonwealth of Nations, an intergovernmental organization that emerged out of the British Commonwealth.[8]

British engagement with the African continent has been characterized by several waves of intensifying and decreasing exchanges of capital, people, and goods, reflecting broad domestic and global restructuring processes, like, for instance, colonization and decolonization. Since 2000, British interest in the African continent has been growing again. This was first led by the private sector, but then the public sector followed the corporate trend. There seems to be a new "gold-rush mood" among British investors and trading companies as the following 2012 statement from the CEO of British-American Tobacco (BAT) highlights: "So the point really is not whether you should be doing business in Africa, but rather how."[9]

---

6 | Kegley and Raymond (2011), 110-112.

7 | See White (1999), 184-185. British decolonization was the function of multiple factors, including nationalist pressures and global economic trends (e.g., UK financial industry focused beyond formal and informal empire in its investments; decline in the worldwide rubber trade after innovative synthetic rubber introduction; improved balance of the payment position of Great Britain; new economic strategies pursued in the metropolis that focus on North America and Europe; and/or the declining meaning of the sterling area).

8 | See, for instance, the edited volume by Dumett (1999). It critically evaluates the influential publication by Cain and Hopkins on British imperialism published in 1993. The latter publication is referenced in the following as Cain and Hopkins (2001), which refers to the second edition of the 1993 publication. Also see Ernst & Young (2011a), 38-41.

9 | Ernst & Young (2012), 9.

The new focus on African economies by private and, increasingly, public actors is reflected in the intensifying trade and investment relations of the UK with the continent. From 2007 to 2011, UK FDI in Africa increased by 9 % per annum, and UK exports to Sub-Saharan Africa have risen faster than in other transitioning or developing countries.[10] According to the British Chambers of Commerce, currently "[m]ore Chamber member exporters currently export to the Middle East and Africa (57 %) than to North America (47 %) and Australasia (40 %)."[11] At the same time, UK-African relations are not a one-way street: imports from SSA to the UK have nearly tripled, climbing from USD 4 billion in 1990 to USD 11 billion in 2004. However, this trend was primarily linked to rising imports of a few products (primarily clothing, petroleum, and minerals) from a small number of countries, namely South Africa and Botswana.[12]

Similar to the case of China, the growing interest in Africa since 2000 has been accompanied by significant changes in the official rationalization of these relations. Moving away from the previous focus on humanitarianism and security/terrorism, more recent official statements stress the economic and social benefits of engagement with Africa for the actors involved.[13] At the same time, the budget deficit and fiscal conservatism of the Cameron government limited the extent to which this new interest of the UK government could be met by assigning resources to its promotion. In fact, "[r]esources allocated to Africa are [...] extremely stretched, and the British presence on the continent [which has never been a high priority] already consists of a network in which large regions are covered by as few as one or two diplomats in the field."[14] As of 2011, the UK's diplomatic presence (e.g., sovereign embassies) ranked tenth after that of the US, Russia, China, France, South Africa, Nigeria, Germany, Brazil, and Japan.[15]

Against this background of tight budgets, it is worth noting that the UK also benefits from membership in institutions of pooled sovereignty, such as the European Union (EU), which is an active and important investor and trading partner on the African continent.[16] However, domestic economic reces-

---

10 | Ernst & Young (2013), 34; Te Velde and Calì (2006), 9-10; Smallbusiness.co.uk (13 October 2011).
11 | Dhillon (3 February 2014).
12 | Simultaneously, EU and global imports from SSA have declined or risen only moderately, indicating that the intensification of trade relations between the UK and SSA is rather unique. See Te Velde and Calì (2006), 9-10.
13 | E.g. Bellingham (2010); and Cargill (2011). Also, see Chapter 7 on guiding ideology.
14 | Cargill (2011), 3.
15 | Cargill (2011), 3.
16 | Allen (8 October 2012), 9; Cargill (2011), 11. Note: This study has been carried out prior to Brexit. The implications of the latter for land-consuming OFDI from the UK are not yet clear or forseeable.

sion and the rise of the BRICS have begun to affect the UK's relative economic and political presence on the African continent. For instance, the UK's leading investor position, particularly in the extractive industries, which it historically shared with the US and France, is increasingly contested by newcomers such as China and India, the latter of which "edged out" the UK as leading investor in Ghana in 2005 (measured by the number of projects per annum since 2000).[17] Simultaneously, some African countries, like South Africa, have started to critically review the role of British companies in economic development—asking whether these are "viable investment partner[s]" or just a "remnant of the British Empire," compared to newcomer investors from the emerging powers.[18]

Despite the new attention directed towards UK-Africa relations, it is crucial to note that by both regional and historical comparison, the share of British FDI in Africa since 2000 has been marginal—at least from the investor country's point of view. The regional figures point to the issue of asymmetric significance mentioned previously.[19] In 2011, the African continent continued to rank lowest regarding the share of total UK FDI stock by region.[20] At the same time, UK overseas investment flows to the continent have been highly volatile: while in 2010, UK overseas investment flows to Africa (GBP 7,822 million) were astonishingly close to those to Europe (GBP 11,374 million) and higher than those to the Americas (GBP -13,814 million), the year 2011 was characterized by divestment (GBP -3,291 million).[21] Importantly, UK investment in SSA has remained highly concentrated in four countries, namely Kenya, Nigeria, Zimbabwe, and South Africa. This reflects legacies of very uneven regional and sectoral investment.[22]

3. KEY CHARACTERISTICS OF BRITISH LAND-CONSUMING OFDI IN SUB-SAHARAN AFRICA

The complex and evolving nature of economic and political relations between the UK and African countries has largely been ignored by common "free market" explanations. This section will summarize the key empirical characteristics, focusing on sector distribution, timelines, the role of land, stated goals in the recipient context, the phenomenon of investor funds involved in agriculture, and other key actors and institutions.

---

17 | AfDB/OECD/UNDP/UNECA (2011), 10; and Modern Ghana.com (23 January 2005).
18 | Osei (2011), 1.
19 | See Chapter 3.
20 | Allen and Dar (14 March 2013), 11-12.
21 | Allen and Dar (14 March 2013), 11-12; and Loots and Kabundi (2012), 134.
22 | Joint Nature Conservation Committee (2009), 14.

The major findings are as follows: firstly, the majority of "land grab" projects consist of biofuel projects which have been initiated since 2005. Secondly, land is of primary importance in most of these investments. It is accessed through mixed forms of direct lease and/or outgrower schemes. Thirdly, contrary to the "profit through scarcity" and "seeking alpha" rhetoric, most biofuel projects, as well as some investment funds, have failed, for multiple reasons. Fourthly, the respective host country government is a central actor in these investments. It often cooperates with British corporations, some of which have been invited to participate in host country policy-writing processes—for instance, regarding the national biofuel strategy. Fifthly and finally, from the UK perspective, a diverse private sector, and, increasingly, public institutions are at work.

Sector

A breakdown of investments by industry highlights both the UK's colonial investor legacy on the continent, with its focus on natural resources, and the processes of diversification that have occurred since decolonization.[23] While detailed data was very difficult to obtain, an itemization of FDI projects by industry for the year 2008, which was received upon request from the Office for National Statistics (ONS), shows that the bulk of UK FDI went into mining and quarrying (42.5 %) and financial services (43.5 %), followed by real estate and business services (3.9 %) and food production (2.5 %).[24] Not a single project was recorded for the agricultural sector during that particular year (see Figure 61).[25] 2006 data on British FDI projects by industry and target country also emphasizes the aforementioned uneven sectoral and capital stock distribution across the continent.[26] Regarding sectoral distribution, 74 % of investments in South Africa went into financial services (most of which did not have any relation to natural resources), while FDI in Kenya was largely geared towards food production, and investments in Eastern Africa primarily directed towards

---

23 | In 1999, 40 % of UK OFDI in Africa still went to the mining and quarrying industry (compared to 20 % worldwide), and two thirds of US OFDI stock was in the petroleum sector. In addition, UK OFDI undertakings in African countries have an extraordinary high degree of profit repatriation: about 75 cents of every dollar invested went back to the parent company (compared to a UK average of 37 cents in other countries). See Te Velde (2002), 4.

24 | Data obtained from Office for National Statistics (UK) via email request in June 2012.

25 | Data obtained from Office for National Statistics (UK) via email request in June 2012.

26 | Joint Nature Conservation Committee (2009), 14.

biofuel production.[27] At the same time, British FDI stock was primarily located in South Africa.[28]

The investments that this research project has investigated, as well as newly established databases (such as Land Matrix), show that British land-consuming OFDI covers the full range of sectors from food and biofuel production, livestock farming, and forestry for wood to tourism and mineral extraction (including petroleum).[29] In more detail, the projects grow, process and trade Jatropha, sugar cane, palm oil, cassava, and sweet sorghum; cultivate rice, livestock(e.g., beef), and horticulture (e.g., paprika, chilies, maize, and cocoa); exploit uranium; or are involved in construction (e.g. infrastructure) and the provision of agribusiness support services (e.g., agriculture machinery showcase).

While the sectoral composition of British land-consuming OFDI is important for a better understanding of what is happening, it is equally essential to be aware that on the project level, this sectoral differentiation might not fully capture the nature of activities on the ground in cases where land-consuming OFDI is part of processes of integration or conglomeration of the companies involved. In fact, several investor companies are involved in multiple sectors that together make up one project. Take, for example, the biofuel projects, in which companies integrate the whole supply chain from farming to refining to trading activities. In other cases, a single company engages in multiple unrelated industries, such as the Avana Group in Madagascar, which exploits minerals while also being involved in biofuel production, at least temporarily.[30] Finally, some companies have switched their operations from one sector to another. One example is Agriterra Ltd., which was active in the petroleum sector prior to moving into farming with the goal to "build itself into a multi-commodity African focused agricultural business."[31]

From a broader perspective, the rising number of early-stage companies involved in the agricultural sector mirrors the widespread belief in its potential as a future growth market, as stated by Agriterra Ltd.: "We believe that the agricultural sector in Africa is an area of activity which has the potential to be particularly resilient to the current global economic climate."[32] At the same time,

---

27 | Joint Nature Conservation Committee (2009), 14.
28 | Wei and Balasubramanyam (2004), 177-178; and Schenk (2005), 463-481.
29 | TradeInvestNigeria.com (10 October 2009); and TradeInvestNigeria (19 November 2009).
30 | It seems that Avana dropped its biofuel activities and is now focusing on mining again; no information is available on the former plans to plant Jatropha on 10.000 ha. See, for instance, GEXSI LLP (2008), Slide 58; Energy-profile (2009), 53; Matthews (2010), 117-119.
31 | Agriterra Ltd. (29 February 2012).
32 | Agriterra Ltd (6 January 2009).

the British government remains indeterminate on the matter of agricultural OFDI in Africa. On the one hand, statements by the former Minister for Africa (2010-2012), Henry Bellingham, clearly reveal the established bias towards the extractive sector.[33] On the other hand, the CDC Group, the UK's development finance institution, has begun to step up its private equity activities in African agriculture, and British industrial policy promotes farmland-consuming "clean tech" investments like those in biofuels.

Figure 6-1 – UK OFDI in Africa by Industry, 2008 (in USD millions, ONS 2008)[34]

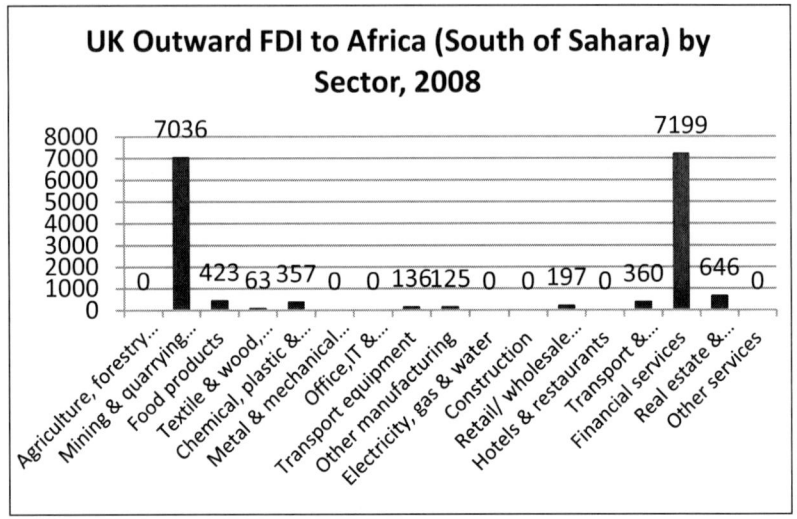

Timelines

In stark contrast to the case of China, British "land grab" projects have largely occurred after the year 2000.[35] A closer look at the timelines of British land-consuming FDI in SSA shows three investment trends—characterized by investment focus and investor type—since 2000. Firstly, around the year 2000, land-consuming investments were largely conducted by British compa-

---

33 | Aigaforum (9 June 2011).
34 | Data obtained from the Office for National Statistics upon email request in June 2012.
35 | It remains unclear whether this is simply owing to the problem of data collection through the method of crowdsourcing or if it also reflects the problem of biased attention towards some industries (e.g., biofuels campaigns by NGOs) and countries (e.g., China) compared to others.

nies already present on the continent, and they were related to legal and institutional reforms in the recipient country. A good example is Unilever Ghana, which acquired plantations in Ghana in 1999 by taking advantage of the opportunities presented to it by the host government's divestiture program.[36]

Secondly, from 2005/2006, another investment trend can be observed. Around that time, a large share of projects was seemingly related to the international climate negotiations and, more specifically, the emerging British and European policy framework promoting renewable energy. The predominant investor types were newly founded companies, many of which floated their shares on the AIM Stock Exchange in London,[37] and financial investors. Both actor groups tried to profit from the policy-induced (new) biofuel market and related support structures at the domestic, regional (EU), and international levels (UN FCCC). Importantly, "old investors" with a long presence on the continent were hardly involved in this trend. For instance, British Petroleum (BP) engaged in biofuel production through a joint venture ("D1-BP Fuel Crops") with D1 Oils Plc., one of the doyens of the crude Jatropha oil industry. However, this cooperation remained rather short-lived, and BP exited the project in 2009.[38] Similar divestments happened in other sectors, such as the aviation industry. Lufthansa, for example, originally participated in biofuel investments in the form of offtake agreements[39] with the British biofuel producer Sun Biofuels, but later decided to end the cooperation in response to protests regarding the potentially unsustainable production of biofuels and the resulting land use competition and food insecurity.

Finally, a significant share of investments started in 2008/2009. These investors—investment banks and private equity funds (public and private)—are seeking "alpha." That is to say, they are aiming to achieve extraordinary returns on their investments in spite of the financial crisis. In practice, they are making land-consuming investments in agriculture or trying to cash in on opportunities offered by international climate finance, like, for instance, the Clean Development Mechanism (CDM).[40] As a consequence, this group of actors is increasingly involved, primarily as shareholders, in the business

---

36 | Ntsiful (2010), 129-137.
37 | AIM stands for Alternative Investment Market, a sub-market of the London Stock Exchange where small firms can float their shares under less restrictive regulations than in the London Stock Exchange.
38 | Bloomberg News (17 July 2009).
39 | An offtake agreement is an agreement between a producer and a buyer to acquire a certain amount of the anticipated production. It is very common in the natural resources sector.
40 | For more information on the CDM, see the website of the United Nations Framework Convention on Climate Change (UNFCCC) (http://cdm.unfccc.int/).

operations of the early-stage companies that began investing in 2006. Some, however, have also taken over the existing operations, such as Highbury Finance Ltd. in the case of Sun Biofuels Mozambique.[41] While financial investors involved in agricultural projects are often framed as pioneers in the sector, this perception is only partially true. Instead, they follow in the footsteps of UK development finance, such as the CDC Group and Department for International Development (DFID). Investments in agribusiness have been a major part of the CDC's operations since 1948, allegedly producing high returns of "up to 40 percent."[42] Moreover, recent private equity investments by the CDC Group were also explicitly intended to motivate financial investors to operate in African agriculture projects.[43]

A look at these timelines reveals general investment trends, and an assessment of detailed project life cycles shows what is actually happening on the ground. In this regard, the empirical evidence reveals that many projects do not merit comparison with their rhetoric of success and promise of high returns. Instead, they are often rather short-lived, for numerous reasons. For example, the case of Sun Biofuels (SBF) shows that a company's performance can suffer from inexperience, false assumptions, lack of funding, and/or the financial crisis. In 2005, the company began to grow Jatropha in Ethiopia on land with poor soil, which together with drought conditions made the 1.000 ha planted trial area economically unviable.[44] In the words of the SBF Business Development Director, Harry Stourton: "The idea that jatropha can be grown on marginal land is a red herring."[45] Consequently, SBF moved its biofuel operations to Mozambique and Tanzania in 2006. In these countries it acquired a total of 4,854 ha and 8.000 ha of prime land, respectively, with long-term plans to expand the operations to cover 20.000 ha in total. Yet, the company's operations continued to face difficulties in the form of a dramatic decline in share value (see Figure 62) due to the financial crisis and a constant lack of funding. Finally, in 2011, SBF went into administration after its majority shareholder, Trading Emissions Plc., decided to divest. As a consequence, SBF's Tanzania- and Mozambique-located subsidiary companies were sold to financial investors and some plots were discontinued. Data is lacking on the latest status of these projects (as of 2014).[46]

---

41 | Highbury Finance (2013).
42 | AltAssets.net (26 April 2006).
43 | AltAssets.net (26 April 2006). CDC (8 November 2013).
44 | Wendimu (2013), 12.
45 | Reppert-Bismarck (21 January 2011); and see Pohl (2010) on Jatropha.
46 | Subsequently, SBF's subsidiary companies in Tanzania and Mozambique were sold to two financial investors in 2011, namely the London based merchant bank Lion's Head Global Partners, operated by former Goldman Sachs employees, and Highbury Finance,

A similar story of failed potential emerges from the investigation of most biofuel projects. Take, for example, D1 Oils, a UK-based share company founded in 2005. It was one of the first companies worldwide to focus on value-added operations of Jatropha biofuel production; and it experienced a crash in share value from 2007 to 2012 (Figure 62). Throughout its existence, it has been struggling with the economic viability of its operations, and up to this day it has not paid any dividends to its shareholders. By 2012, D1 Oils' operational losses amounted to more than GBP 1 million.[47] In order to demonstrate its commitment to a fresh start, the company changed its name to NEOS Resources in 2010, shifted its focus to India, and announced a diversification away from Jatropha production in African countries.[48] However, this strategy was not successful either, as the latest update from NEOS in 2014 highlights. A corporate notice from 30 January 2014 states that the company is in the process of selling off the assets from its Indian and other ventures: "it will not be possible to reach sustainable profitable volumes in the near future and therefore plans to develop the trade have been put on hold and all revenue generating activities within the Group have effectively ceased with effect from January 2014."[49] Short of funding and running the risk of losing its AIM London Stock Exchange listing, the company's board and key shareholders have begun to negotiate "the future direction of the Group and its funding requirements for the next 12 months."[50]

Another example of the difficulties encountered by these projects is GEM Biofuels. The company was founded in 2004, and it has been AIM-listed since 2007. Focusing on Jatropha production, the company has managed to secure over 495.000 ha in Madagascar since 2005.[51] Yet, its planting operations came to a halt in 2009, when tied-up capital markets and bad plantation management forced it to focus on maintaining existing plantations rather than (re)

---

a project development and investment advisory firm, founded in 2004 with a specialization in "alternative investment opportunities." In both cases, the new owners have only conducted maintenance work on the former SBF plantations, which means that large parts of the acquired land lie fallow. Moreover, LGHP only employs 50 of the former 700 workers while also falling short of clarifying the problem of outstanding compensation payments. See Lion's Head Global Partners (2013); Highbury Finance (2013); Bergius (September 2012); and Bergius (5 July 2013).
47 | StockMarketWire.com (13 March 2012); Hawkins and Chen (2011), 21-23; Mitchell (2010), 118-125.
48 | NEOS Resources Plc (12 October 2011); NEOS Resources Plc (15 November 2011); NEOS Resources Plc (15 March 2012).
49 | Investigate.co.uk (30 January 2014).
50 | Investegate.co.uk (30 January 2014).
51 | GEMBioFuels (28 September 2011).

investing in their planned expansion.[52] Thus, during 2011, GEM concentrated on letting the plantations mature, and did not engage in any further planting while reducing the number of staff. By the end of 2011, it had planted Jatropha on a total of 55,737 hectares.[53] Still, the share value did not recover, nor did the company manage to attract additional funding during 2012.[54] Unable to profit from its land bank, the company changed its name to Hunter Resources PLC in January 2013 to indicate its new investing policy and board changes.[55] The latest corporate notice from December 2013 stated that the company's share trading had been suspended as it did not become an investment company in time to meet AIM London Stock Exchange requirements. The same notice announced that the management was in negotiations to become active in Peruvian mining projects which are 563km from the city of Lima in an area where eight exploration concessions (a total of 3,500 ha) are located.[56] What has happened to the Jatropha production remains unclear.

Figure 6-2 – Three Examples of Crashes in Share Value, 2008-2012 (www.iii.co.uk.uk)

Agriterra Ltd, 2008-2012	GEM Biofuels, 2010-2012	D1Oils Plc, 2008-2012

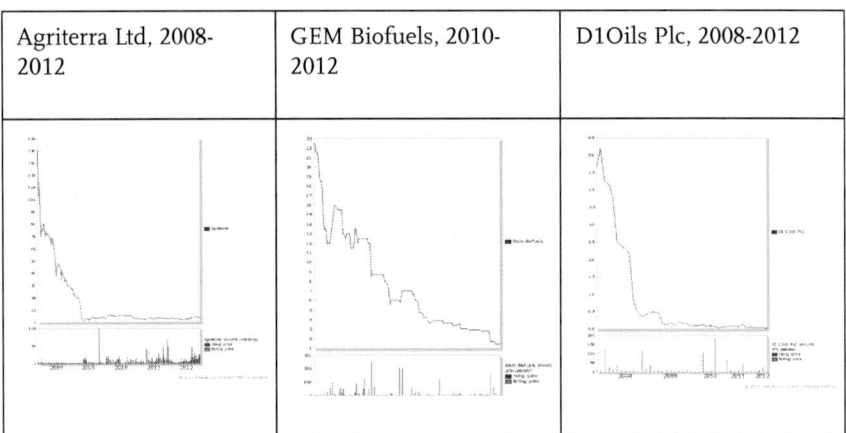

Together, these project timelines emphasize that those explanations which identify the financial crisis as a primary driver of land-consuming FDI fall short of comprehending the complexity at play. On the one hand, many land-consuming projects were started prior to the crisis and seem to be related to other

---

52 | Hawkins and Chen (2011), 3, 24-25.
53 | OnVista.de (2014); and GEM Biofuels (12 April 2012).
54 | GEM Biofuels (5 December 2012).
55 | ADVFN.com (1 August 2013); and Hunter Resources Plc (30 December 2013).
56 | Hunter Resources Plc (30 December 2013).

events in the home and host countries, such as the climate regulations or divestiture programs. On the other hand, the financial crisis also resulted in massive crashes in the share values of companies and contributed to the failure of investors in search of profitable investments during a time of economic crisis.

Moreover, these timelines provide interesting clues about the multiple individual and systemic difficulties encountered by different actors during a project's life cycle. For example, the financial situation has been aggravated by a systemic conflict of interest between the different actors involved in these projects: while companies "on the ground" focus on long-term value creation, financial investors "off the ground" are interested primarily in short-term profit. In this regard, the operational problems and long maturation timelines of agricultural projects "on the ground" (for instance, five years for Jatropha) led to constant struggles for early-stage companies that also negatively impacted the respective company's majority shareholder, usually a financial company promising high returns to its investors and under pressure to deliver. In the case of SBF and its majority shareholder Trading Emissions Plc, a board decision was reached in 2010 to deny SBF additional funds, because the "value creation in this business was a long-term project."[57]

In other cases, data shows that financial investors made unrealistic earnings forecasts, sometimes in combination with allegedly fraudulent business practices. Cru Investment Management and its Africa Invest Fund, for instance, did not live up to predicted earnings of 30 % for 2009 to 2010. Instead, Cru and Africa Invest were facing fraud investigations for misuse of funds in 2010, as money invested in other funds managed by Cru had been transferred to Africa Invest as loans, without notification of the respective shareholders. At the same time, the CEO Jon Maguire was accused of having withdrawn money without proper documentation.[58] In 2010, Africa Invest was sold for GBP 175.000. This was hardly sufficient to cover fees and liabilities, and investors were unable to recover their investments.[59] An audit by PricewaterhouseCoopers revealed that Cru's asset base was overvalued, and this aggravated liquidity problems in 2011, when the company was unable to sell the (illiquid) holdings of land fast enough to respond to the massive withdrawal of investors.[60]

In summary, the empirical evidence on project timelines illustrates that investment projects are characterized by constant changes in focus and details over time, including projects that do not end in failure. A good example is the aforementioned Unilever Ghana. It operated plantations in Ghana that it had

---

57 | Trading Emissions Plc (2011), 7.
58 | Merrett (29 November 2013); BBC (6 February 2010); and Miller (7 July 2011).
59 | Grote (16 March 2010).
60 | Miller (7 July 2011).

acquired in 1999 through the host government's divestiture program.[61] Eight years later, in 2010, Unilever sold its majority share in the 7,200 ha Benso Oil Plantation Ltd, which is listed on the Ghana Stock Exchange and on which more than 9.000 people's livelihoods depend, to Wilmar Africa.[62] This was the result of a headquarter decision to concentrate on the company's core business of manufacturing, marketing, and distribution.[63] Moreover, the empirical evidence highlights the exposure of British land-consuming FDI to financial volatility; the dependency on developments in the home country, such as the economic crisis; or the inadequacy of business models to factor in the reality on the ground in the form of insufficient markets, limited economies of scale in agriculture, or bad plantation management. Together, these facts illuminate the discrepancy between the 'profit from scarcity' rhetoric and the actual performance of the respective companies, even in areas, such as biofuels, that are supported by governments worldwide.

Land: Its Role and Use in These Investments

The previous sections showed that British land-consuming FDI takes place in multiple sectors and engages multiple actors. At the same time, their assessment has pointed to fundamental challenges that several investment projects are facing, sometimes even leading to their ultimate failure. The following section will assess more closely the role of land used in these investments, major approaches used to access land, as well as relevant features of its governance. It can be noted that the Chinese cases do not differ in any significant way on these issues from the UK projects.

Extent

The scale of British land-consuming investments varies enormously, with projects ranging in size from a 100 ha pilot farm to a total investment of 495.000 ha (e.g., GEM Biofuels). While this range indicates the great diversity of investment projects falling under the label of land-consuming FDI, these numbers also show that compared to Chinese investments in SSA, the majority of which

---

61 | Ntsiful (2010), 129-137.
62 | Wilmar Africa, a wholly owned subsidiary of the Singapore-headquartered Wilmar International Ltd, which was "founded in 1991 as a palm oil trading company," and "is today amongst the largest listed companies by market capitalisation on the Singapore Exchange and one of Asia's leading agribusiness groups." See Wilmar International Limited (7 February 2011), 3.
63 | Ntsiful (2010), 129-137. With regard to Unilevers' standpoint on plantations over time, see Jones (2005b), 185-214. Also see statement by Wilmar International Limited (7 February 2011), 2.

use less than 10.000 ha, British investments are fairly large, particularly in the biofuel sector. To provide some examples: the Equatorial Palm Oil Company (EPO) acquired a total landholding of 169.000 ha-182.000 ha in Liberia;[64] D1 Oils held 155.000 ha in Zambia;[65] CAMS Agri-Energy acquired 45.000 ha in Tanzania;[66] and VEPOWER Ltd, a bioenergy company focusing on fuel production and power generation, teamed up with Jatropha Africa, a biofuel feedstock company, and signed a feedstock acquisition agreement regarding the produce from the 50.000 ha leased land area in Ghana.[67] However, UK investment projects also tend to be large in other sectors, such as timber: the Equatoria Teak Company owned by the CDC and FinnFund was managing an 18,640 ha forest reserve in South Sudan;[68] and livestock farming: Madabeef, a company active in Madagascar, seems to be operating ranching activities on 200.000 ha.[69] In many cases, companies (e.g., D1Oils, SBF, Agriterra Ltd.) have or had enormous land banks in multiple countries located in SSA, making the total land at their disposal even larger.

However, it has already been highlighted above that a large land bank does not necessarily result in great returns or necessarily represent high asset values for the company in case of a need to sell company assets due to project failure. Still, these figures are impressive, at least at first sight and in view of the local repercussions in the form of land tenure. In practice, a closer assessment of the timelines and details of many projects reveals a huge discrepancy between announced, acquired, and actually planted land area (see Table 6-1). For instance, Sun Biofuels' (failed) business model envisioned 20.000 ha. However, the company 'only' managed to secure a total of approximately 12,854 ha-13,854 ha. And of this land area, which spread across three countries, it had only planted a total of (approximately) 4,310 ha prior to its failure.[70] Similarly,

---

64 | Global Witness (20 December 2013); Equatorial Palm Oil (2011); Equatorial Palm Oil (2013); and The Rights and Resources Group (2013), 267.
65 | Investigate.co.uk (14 June 2006). There is diverging data on how much land has been secured and how much has been planted. See Table 6-1 for competing sources.
66 | Obulutsa (19 September 2008).; Oakland Institute (2011b), 4, 18-19, 30.
67 | BioZio (2011), 110, 127.
68 | In 2010, the CDC and FinnFund divested and sold the companies to unknown investors following controversies that resulted from protests by local communities and an inability to make the forest plantation economically viable in a sustainable way. However, as of 2014, the company and the acquired area, which was leased for 32 years, continue to exist. It is now managed by Maris Capital, a London based venture capital group. See corporate website under Equatoria Teak Company (2014). Also see Concession Agreement (28 June 2006), 11, 15; Deng and Mittal (2011), 2, 11, 28-29.
69 | Üllenberg (2008); Hamelinck (2013), 87.
70 | See Table 6-1 for details.

as of 2011, (then) D1 Oils had only managed to plant a minor part of the total of 174.000 ha it had negotiated in Zambia in 2006 (see Table 6-1).

These enormous gaps between announced, negotiated, and planted land areas under management point to the challenges that these projects face on the ground, some of which were already alluded to in the previous section, such as expansion difficulties, unprofessional plantation management (GEM), inexperience and/or natural events (SBF), land disputes (Equatorial Palm Oil), competition over scarce input seeds, lack of funding and/or marginally viable business models, and administrative challenges.[71] More broadly, these discrepancies between the secured and planted areas over time provide useful data for a grounded discussion about the benefits of large-scale agricultural production in view of rural development or food security, since most large-scale projects have not managed to fully operationalize their business models.

Use and Purpose

Land in British land-consuming FDI projects fulfills three functions, namely land as natural resource, as strategic asset, and as productive space for industrial purposes and/or modernization projects. Lonrho, a formerly UK-listed company with an ambiguous reputation and operations in agriculture, infrastructure, transport, and support services in SSA dating back to 1909, was taken over by a Swiss investor in 2013. Two years before that takeover it described the attractiveness of investments in land and agriculture in Africa as a composite of the following factors: 60 % of the world's arable land, of which only 10 % is cultivated;[72] a major continent for oil and gas reserves; a primary source for minerals; and the relatively low external debt levels of African countries.[73]

---

71 | D1 Oils (2011), 30; and Hawkins and Chen (2011).
72 | These figures are false. They are a modified version of a dominant narrative promoting agribusiness in Africa. The origin is a report by McKinsey (2010, 7-8, 42-44) which states that "Africa's agriculture holds enormous potential for companies across the value chain. With 60 percent of the world's uncultivated arable land and low crop yields, Africa is ripe for a "green revolution" like the ones that have transformed agriculture in Asia and Brazil." Since then, this storyline has been taken up by international organizations (e.g., United Nations Economic Commission for Africa (UNECA)) and businesses, often with a significant change in wording: uncultivated (with crops) land has become "unused," resembling the idea of a "terra nullius." Take the example of an article by UNECA, which argues that the "world's largest reservoir of unused arable land, about 60 %," is located in Africa. See Lopes (2014).
73 | See *The African Business Journal* (May 2013); Bloomberg News (20 July 2011); and Lonrho (2012), 1-5.

Table 6-1 – *Discrepancies between Announced, Acquired, and Planted Land Areas in Selected Projects*[74]

Project	Country	Hectares announced/ acquired	Hectares acquired	Hectares planted
Sun Biofuels (SBF)	Ethiopia[75]	Business model aimed at 20.000 ha, but company only managed to acquire 13.000 ha	5.000 ha since 2005	1.000 ha
	Tanzania[76]		8-9.000 ha since 2006	Approx. 2.000 ha by 2010
	Mozambique[77]		4,854 ha since 2006 plus two farms of 607 ha and additional 3.000 ha under negotiation	2,310 ha
D1Oils[78]	Zambia	155.000-174.000 ha (including outgrower schemes) allocated by Zambian government in 2006	155.000 ha	In 2007: 2,411 ha; and 20,760 ha through contract farming
GEM Biofuels[79]	Madagascar	Secured 495,500 ha; plan: 200.000 ha planted area by 2010	Exclusive rights over more than 495.000 ha	55,700 ha (in 2010), plus access to 40.000 ha forest area

---

74 | Adopted from Hawkins and Chen (2011), 29-30.
75 | Hawkins and Chen (2011), 29-30.
76 | Bergius (September 2012), 3; Hawkins and Chen (2011), 29-30.
77 | Highbury Finance (2013); Hawkins and Chen (2011), 29-30.
78 | Data remains unclear. According to GEXSI LLP (2008, 50, 55), the company had 7,386 ha in South Africa and 25,525 ha in Zambia under operation in 2008. Other reports state that D1Oils had been allocated 155.000 ha of land by the Zambian government in 2005 for Jatropha planting (e.g., Investigate.co.uk (14 June 2006)), amounting to a total of 174.000 ha when including the company's contract farming relations (e.g., Reuk.co.uk (15 January 2007)). The Home and Mittal (2011, 28) country report confirms that the company was using 2,411 ha of managed plantations and 20,760 ha of outgrower schemes by 2007. The 2010 annual report by D1 Oils shows that the company has subsidiaries in multiple African countries (Malawi, Ghana, South Africa, Zambia, and Swaziland), all of which focus on biofuels. See D1 Oils (2010), 50. However, no data is provided regarding the total land bank or planted area.
79 | Data from 2010; see Gasparatos and Stromberg (2012), 296; Hawkins and Chen (2011), 21, 23-24; GEM Biofuels (2010); Biofuelsdigest.com (1 July 2010); Biofuelsdigest.com (25 June 2010); Cleantech Investor (May 2008); Proactiveinvestors.co.uk (25 November 2009); and GEM Biofuels (28 September 2011).

Equa-torial Palm Oil[80]	Liberia	169.000 ha; plans to develop 50.000 ha within first 10 years, and 100.000 ha within 20 years	169.000-182.000 ha since 2008 in the form of three concessions	Unclear, but due to financial problems and social resistance the planted area is limited (est. 3,200 ha in 2012 according to RRI 2013).

While use of land as a natural resource or productive space for industrial purposes has been a common trait of British land-consuming OFDI in African countries, use of land as a strategic asset in overseas investments is relatively new, though not unprecedented. In fact, land's asset function was already a component of business models of chartered companies granting land titles, and of investment portfolios during late 19th century globalization.[81] However, historical evidence on land acquisitions by businesses also highlights that land constituted only a minor share of personal wealth. Instead, it was largely a reflection thereof, and land holding was a status symbol rather than a standalone promise of extraordinary returns.[82] In this context, and against the background of the high failure rate of land-consuming investments by funds (presented in Section 5), this chapter argues for the need to critically revise contemporary claims that land is an asset class which withstands the wealth destruction witnessed in equity investments during times of financial crisis.[83] Clearly, the aforementioned summary of project timelines highlighted problems related to the overvaluation of assets and the limited economies of scale that can be gained through large-scale land holding. Moreover, the illiquidity of land turns out to be disadvantageous once a project runs into financial problems.

The quality of land is equally important for assessing the meaning and impact of British investment projects. Project details show that food and biofuel investments occur on prime land, which is defined by fertile soils, moderate climatic conditions, and proximity to important infrastructure and cities. Agriterra Ltd., for instance, leased 45.000 ha of brownfield agricultural land in Sierra Leone, close to the Liberian border, to produce palm oil in an area with high levels of rainfall.[84] And the Equatorial Palm Oil Company has been granted concessions for three palm oil plantations in Liberia, all of which are located in a favorable climatic zone, close to cities, and in proximity to ports

---

80 | Global Witness (20 December 2013); Equatorial Palm Oil (2011); Equatorial Palm Oil (2013); and The Rights and Resources Group (2013), 267.
81 | See Chapter 3.
82 | Nicholas (1999).
83 | Collinson (24 July 2010).
84 | Agritrade (6 February 2012); Agriterra (29 February 2012).

with facilities that can accommodate export operations.[85] Similarly, the plots that SBF negotiated for biofuel production in Tanzania and Mozambique were prime land, following the project failure in Ethiopia due to poor soils.[86]

In most cases, it remains difficult to judge the environmental impact of land acquisitions due to the limited data available on the prior use of the lands. The few cases where such data is available show that land deals resulted in land-use rehabilitation[87] as well as land-use change. Particularly in the latter case of land-use change, several projects reveal ways in which these investments might negatively affect local and regional livelihoods, climates, and landscapes (e.g., water security, wildlife habitat, or microclimate). For instance, SBF's operations in Tanzania took place on land formerly used by charcoal makers, including a swamp area that was important for local water security.[88] In some cases, a given company has stalled its operations due to international pressure over the environmental implications. This was the case with G4 Industries Ltd, which abandoned its 28.000 ha biofuel project in Kenya before operations had begun in response to pressure from NGOs over the potential negative impact on wildlife in the wetlands of the Tana River Delta.[89]

Moreover, the question remains of whether the land is intended to produce for overseas consumption, as is widely assumed in the "land grab" literature (see Chapter 2). In the case of British land acquisitions, most projects were indeed originally intended for international markets, and several had clear export infrastructure in place (e.g., Equatorial Palm Oil). In this context, it appears that host governments have been largely reluctant to ensure that a certain percentage of the harvest is available for domestic consumption and/or value-added operations (e.g., refining).[90] However, in practice, the exports often did not materialize. To provide several examples: the Equatoria Teak Company only managed to sell a few consignments (of timber) from its forest reserves in South Sudan due to local protests. Consequently, the CDC Group and FinnFund sold the concessions in 2010, after three years of operations.[91] Also SBF (in Mozambique and Tanzania) had only managed to sell and export one consignment of 30 tons of biofuel (Jatropha) by 2011. Thereafter, the company went

---

85 | Global Witness (20 December 2013); Equatorial Palm Oil (2011); Equatorial Palm Oil (2013); and The Rights and Resources Group (2013), 267.
86 | Hawkins and Chen (2011), 29-30.
87 | For instance, SBF's operations in Mozambique involved land that had formerly been used as a tobacco plantation, and Equatorial Palm Oil (Liberia) engages both in the rehabilitation of old plantations and the creation of new ones. Hawkins and Chen (2011).
88 | WWF Tanzania (2009), 84-86.
89 | Cernansky (26 October 2011).
90 | Zagema (2011); and Cotula (2011).
91 | Burnett (7 April 2014).

into administration and its subsidiaries were sold to new owners who focus on plantation maintenance (rather than expansion). Meanwhile, Lufthansa, which had a biofuel offtake agreement with SBF, withdrew from this form of cooperation due to European protests over unsustainable biofuel production practices.[92] Similarly, D1 Oils, active in Malawi and Zambia, ended up selling locally prior to its closure. The small scale of its operations—largely a function of limited availability of input seeds—made the pricing difficult. Marketing locally had the advantages of low transport costs and local offtake agreements, both of which allowed for agreement on market value.[93] In other cases, such as Cru Investment Management's Africa Invest fund, the project had simply collapsed by the time of the first harvest. Regarding the question of how much of the biofuel produced in Africa has actually ended up in British transport fuel, it is interesting to note that, according to the UK Renewable Fuel Agency, no Africa-produced biofuel was used in 2010-2011, even though 78 % of biofuels had been imported.[94] This information correlates with the empirical findings of this research project, according to which most British biofuel producers ended up selling locally or closing operations altogether.[95]

To better understand the utility derived from overseas land acquisitions, it is important to look beyond the question of exports. In addition to land, these projects employ multiple factors of production, including labor, while also creating new markets for British input services and thus potentially creating jobs back home. Moreover, they are reflective of profitable policy frameworks, such as climate finance and related carbon credits, for which at least two biofuel companies, D1 Oils and the SBF, applied. At the same time, the government operates on the assumption that these projects will generate state revenues derived from overseas investment earnings, and the early-stage companies' projects represent profitable business streams for London banks issuing Initial Public Offerings.

Strategies of Access

Land is accessed through lease agreements, public-private partnership programs, the granting of concessions, joint ventures, outgrower schemes, Memoranda of Understanding (MoU) with county districts and tribal communities, and/or the purchasing of shares in listed plantations. In many cases, mixed access strate-

---

92 | Insight Group Plc (26 October 2011); Dahlbeck (2012), 21; Lufthansa (2014); Greenaironline.com (23 January 2012).
93 | Mitchell (2010), 124-125.
94 | See UK Trade and Investment (2012), 17.
95 | Instead, land used for UK biofuels has been located in Europe (e.g., France, Germany, Ukraine, UK, Belgium), Latin America (e.g., Argentina, Brazil), and Asia (e.g., Malaysia, Indonesia), with a focus on oilseeds, rapeseed, palm oil, soy, corn, sugar beet, sugar cane, and wheat as input factors. Renewable Fuels Agency (2011), 50.

gies are applied, such as plantation production plus outgrower schemes, or the purchase of a trading company (e.g., Agriterra Ltd. in Sierra Leone) that has preferential supply agreements with a sufficiently large farmer base.[96] Moreover, several companies rely on additional land-intensive inputs from third parties, such as Jatropha seedlings grown by the supplier Diligent Tanzania Ltd. on 3,500 ha.[97] In some cases, the privatization of public plantations provided investors with access options. For instance, the two plantations acquired by Unilever in 1999 and 2004 (through shareholding) both trace back to 1976.[98]

Aspects of Governance

Since the land that is leased is often owned by the state, key ministries and government agencies are involved in the land deals, as are parliaments.[99] At the same time, several British biofuel companies have been part of committees established by host governments to develop governance structures in their particular sector. Jatropha Africa participated in the biofuel committee that supported the Ghanaian Ministry of Energy during deliberations on a renewable energy policy;[100] D1Oils took part in a task force committee on renewable energy that framed biodiesel regulations in Zambia;[101] and G4 International West contributed to West Africa's biofuel strategy under UEMOA.[102]

Most of the deals seem to be fully embraced and promoted by the respective recipient government.[103] For instance, the Equatorial Palm Oil Company's

---

96 | Agriterra (29 February 2012).
97 | Chaponniere et al. (2010), 10. From a historical perspective, these strategies of indirect land (function) access are not new. During British colonial administration, smallholder schemes were often favored over plantations out of concern over social tensions and because they were seen to be more efficient. Also see the summary on "Oil Palm in Ghana" by the World Rainforest Movement (6 August 2010); and Gyasi (1996).
98 | Ntsiful (2010), 129-137.
99 | Cotula (2011), 16; Lahiff (2012).
100 | Jatropha Africa (22 August 2010). However, due to the unclear policy environment and lack of funding, a policy overview by Antwi-Bediako (31 October 2013) mentions that Jatropha Africa went into administration.
101 | See Investigate.co.uk (14 June 2006).
102 | See ESG/ICTSD/LeHub/UEMOA/UN Foundation (2008), vii.
103 | In most cases, the terms seem very favorable to foreign investors. In Sierra Leone, for example, investors often seem to be exempt from taxation and they are allowed to lease land for up to 71 years (for USD 20-30 per ha per year) while profiting from low labor costs, which range between two and three dollars per day. See Caulker (2010), 12. A similar case is Liberia, which is currently extending and rehabilitating its plantations by granting concessions to foreign investors such as the Equatorial Oil Palm Company. That this company's investments are fully embraced by Liberian President

169.000 ha holding, of which 89.000 ha are concessions granted by the government and 80.000 ha are part of an MoU with the county district and tribal communities, is embedded in a plan by the Liberian government to re-establish export-oriented plantations as a growth sector and foreign exchange earner. On a similar note, Agriterra Ltd.'s lease of over 45.000 ha of brownfield agricultural land has been promoted by the Sierra Leone Investment and Export Promotion Agency (SLIEPA) in line with the government agenda to use "oil palm as a priority growth sector."[104] SLIEPA, in cooperation with the District Councils and the Ministries of Land and Agriculture, has been "earmarking and preparing a number of suitable sites for 10.000+ hectare palm plantations."[105] Also, several companies cooperate with state agencies, such as D1 Oils, which co-manages a 600 ha farm with the Zambian Ministry of Agriculture, and CAMS Agri-Energy Tanzania, which collaborates with a Tanzanian seed authority and Indian NGO to reach out to farmers.[106] Also, the terms of the agreements seem highly favorable to the investor side, as land leases range between 32 (Equatorial Teak Company) and 50 years,[107] the costs of compensation schemes appear to be extremely low, while governance structures in the host countries are rather weak, and labor costs are very low.[108]

Aside from governance schemes at the domestic level, some investments are also part of international governance arrangements. Jatropha Africa, for instance, is an industry partner of an EU-funded interregional cooperation program (EU-ACP) on "Capacity Building in South Africa, Namibia and Ghana to create Sustainable, Non-Food Bio-Oil Supply Chains."[109]

Actors and Institutions

The empirical evidence on the governance of land has highlighted that, as in the Chinese case study, the presence of African governments in these investments is obvious in the form of ministerial and parliamentary involvement,

---

Sirleaf is highlighted by the fact that she took part in the 2011 inauguration ceremony of the company's newly established mill. Moreover, the concessions over 50 years were enacted by the Parliament of Liberia. Equatorial Palm Oil 2011; Equatorial Palm Oil (23 February 2010), 6-8; Carrere (2013), 15, 55-56.
104 | Bangura (2011); World Rainforest Movement (9 August 2011).
105 | Caulker (2010), 29.
106 | Obulutsa (19 September 2008).; and WWF (2009), 14-15, 23, 26, 29-36.
107 | One of the largest investments by land area, the 495.000 ha GEM Biofuels project in Madagascar, is granted for over 50 years and made up of parcels which range between 2,500 and 50.000 ha. Included are the rights to a 40.000 ha natural forest.
108 | Caulker (2010), 12.
109 | Jatropha Africa (n.d.).

investment promotion centers, and/or legislation. At the same time, civil society groups and local community members seem to remain largely on the sidelines during the negotiations, and investor promises made to these groups, such as the building of health services and schools or the provision of sufficient jobs for the community, are often the first to be broken when a project fails and/or is taken over by new investors—as, for instance, in the case of the projects of SBF in Tanzania and Mozambique.

From the British side, public agencies and government officials from different levels, as well as private actors and institutions, are involved. In addition to the prominent roles played by early stage companies, alternative stock markets, and financial investors, several public institutions seem to be relevant. One such institution is the CDC Group, the UK's public development finance institution that has begun to enhance its efforts with regard to land-consuming (private equity) investments in Africa, focusing on infrastructure, real estate, and, increasingly, agriculture. Moreover, new political institutions and reforms, such as bilateral investment forums or aid programs, have been introduced by the acting government as part of a broader attempt to step up commercial diplomacy with African countries.

Also, several financial institutions, such as the Standard Chartered Bank, a UK merchant bank with a long presence in African economies, and/or investment funds, and the AIM London Stock Exchange play an important role, as the majority of companies rely on their financial services for funding. At the same time, the UK government proactively calls on entrepreneurs to make use of aid-funded business opportunities in the form of public-private-partnerships. Some companies have also accessed aid funding through institutions of pooled sovereignty, such as the EU.[110]

On a (inter)national and regional level, there are a number of interlinked (non-) financial institutions at work, especially in the biofuel sector. These include domestic obligatory blending mandates, European and UK directives on carbon dioxide (CO_2) emissions reduction, the EU Emissions Trading Scheme, and/or UNFCCC-related mechanisms, all of which promote a renewable energy market. Also, the newly launched G8 Alliance for Food Security, which was established in 2012 and "gathers together donors, partner countries and the private sector" to "promote private sector investments in agriculture by improving the business environment and explore ways to reduce risk through providing better legal and administrative conditions for investors," has British companies among its members.[111] In the G8 Alliance program for Tanzania, for instance, the UK is expected to contribute GBP 63 million from 2012 to 2015. Several British companies submitted a letter of intent to participate in the

---

110 | P. Harvey (2010).
111 | European Commission (18 May 2012).

program, namely Syngenta, Unilever, and Vodafone, which basically implies expanding their business activities in multiple African countries.[112]

A significant share of the actors and institutions active in these investments also reflects the existence of a transnational or even global business culture that is characterized by personal linkages; registration in the same locations, namely the tax havens of Mauritius and Guernsey; the involvement of multiple investors from different countries in one project; and the reappearance of the same actors in different institutions.[113] At the same time, the network does not consist entirely of private actors but also includes UN agencies (UNECA; UN FCCC; WB) and other public agencies on the international (AfDB), regional (European Investment Bank), and domestic levels (see Table 6-2).

Table 6-2 – The UK in Africa: Actors involved in Land-Consuming OFDI (selected)

Actors Involved at Different Levels of Governance		Public	Private	Hybrid
INTERNATIONAL	International agents	• United Nations Industrial Development Organization (UNIDO) • UNFCCC Clean Development Executive Board • UNECA • European Commission Biofuel Directive • African Union • NEPAD Cassava Initiative • EU-ACP • AU (biofuel promise)	• Jatropha Alliance • Lufthansa • UoP Houston • Refining company in Helsinki • Africa Invest (Channel Island-listed)	• African Biofuel Board • G-8 New Alliance for Food and Nutrition Security • Jatropha Africa in cooperation with EU-ACP

---

112 | See New Alliance for Food Security and Nutrition (http://new-alliance.org/). For a critical discussion of the G8 Alliance in the context of commercial pressure on land, concentration of land ownership, and crowding out effects, see Hall and Sulle (2013).
113 | For instance, SilverStreet advised GAVI alliance, and CAMEC and Agriterra had the same board members before CAMEC was sold to a Kazakh firm.

UK	National	• The CDC Group Plc • UK Renewable Fuels Agency (closed 2011) • UK Department of Trade and Investment (UK TI)	• British Airways • G4 Industries ltd • GEM Biofuels • CAMS Agri-Energy Tanzania • Schroders Investment Management • Vepower Ltd • Cru Investment Management • Virgin Train • Biodiesel Plants • Sun Biofuels Ltd • Trading Emissions Plc • ReSolve group • D1Oils (called NEOS -Resources Plc since 2012) • BP International (exited 2009) • Lion's Head Global Partners (run by former Goldman Sachs employees) • Highbury Finance • Principle Capital Investments • Saner Plc • Avana Group • Funds	• Private Equity Funds
	Subnational	• Regional investors (Wales)		• Investment Forums (e.g. UK-Nigeria Investment Forum 2012)
RECIPIENT COUNTRY	National	• Ministries • Parliament of Liberia • President of Liberia • President of Sierra Leone • Sierra Leone Investment and Export Promotion Agency	• Jatropha Africa (Ghana)	
	Subnational	• Government agencies • Communities • Farmers	• Contract farmers • Diligent Tanzania Ltd (Seed company)	

4. THE INVESTMENTS IN THE RECIPIENT CONTEXT: STATED GOALS AND MULTIFACETED REALITY

British FDI projects are embedded (as described above) in national and regional development frameworks which are characterized by their rhetoric of rural development, energy/food security, and economic growth with its alleged promise of jobs, better livelihoods, and state revenues. The Tanzanian government, for instance, has leased 600.000 ha to foreign investors since 2006 in the context of a national development program that prioritizes biofuel production.¹¹⁴ Similarly, the Ghanaian government promotes biofuel investments in the context of its national energy policy.¹¹⁵

Many host countries' national development programs aim to ease the administrative process that affects land-consuming FDI. At the core of such IFDI-attraction strategies is the perception that the host countries have to reduce barriers to investment "and tap their potential and comparative advantages to develop the biofuels sector and benefit from globalization through CDM [Clean Development Mechanism] and the global carbon market"¹¹⁶ while boosting their agricultural sectors. This is expected to improve negative terms of trade and earn foreign exchange through export growth, but also to contribute to greater self-sufficiency in food and energy within the context of global market failure, namely the failure of the global market to ensure reliable access to cheap resources. Also, on a regional level, these investments are embedded in development frameworks. For instance, West African countries agreed on a "blueprint for bioenergy, agriculture and rural development" for 2009-2011. This so-called UEMOA strategy was facilitated by UN agencies.¹¹⁷

In line with the official rhetoric, most companies identify their projects as impact investments that combine profits with development objectives. Notably, there is a difference between "on the ground" and "off the ground" investors. "On the ground" companies tend to highlight the benefits of their programs, which allegedly contribute to rural development through jobs, housing, or health services. "Off the ground" actors, such as the financial companies that are majority shareholders in "on the ground" companies, seem to focus more on goals related to the context in which their headquarters operate, such as the UK and the EU. Trading Emissions Plc., for instance, stated its intent to profit from climate change mitigation policy by producing "clean" and renewable energy. Moreover, the scarcity rhetoric pursued by most agricultural funds appears to be more targeted towards capital from rich investor countries than poor ones, as in the latter case scarcity might be associated more with poverty than profit.

Whether the choice made by African governments to realize their development plans with foreign capital will be sustainable remains to be seen. In contrast to contemporary mainstream economics, with its focus on capital location, the above highlights that capital ownership and home country context could be equally important for a country's sustainable development. Take, for example, those biofuel investments that struggled to gain funding in the UK

---

114 | See, for instance, Veit (2010).
115 | Dietrich-O'Connor (2011); and Ministry of Energy, Republic of Ghana (2010), 20.
116 | UNECA (2008), 30.
117 | ESG/ICTSD/LeHub/UEMOA/UN Foundation (2008), 3-26, 110-118.

due to conflicting interests between headquarters and the subsidiary regarding timelines, or other events in the home country that affected the realization of development plans in the host country, such as the economic recession. Another factor to consider is the historically low rate of reinvestment regarding the profits made. At the same time, host governments have made unfortunate choices, such as providing support without accounting for the specific planting season of a crop.[118]

The discrepancy between planned and actually planted areas of land over time, the frequent change of owners, and the high degree of project failure all highlight the challenges of realizing domestic development plans through private foreign capital. For instance, the company SBF had not resolved its compensation problems by the time the company was resold, and the new investor was not interested in acting on the matter either. In many cases, new investors taking over failed projects do not make necessary investments while only reemploying a minor share of the previous workers. In addition, the above-average remittance rate that has characterized some British subsidiaries in Africa for a long time—with 75 cents of every dollar of profit being repatriated to the home country[119]—appears worrisome, as this means that only a minor share of the realized profits might actually be reinvested in host country operations. The ambiguous developmental impact of these investments also holds true in view of the underpinning business models. Many of these foresee the reduction of labor over time while relying on constantly low wages and minimum environmental standards to stay economically viable (e.g., Jatropha).[120]

Consequently, there remains sufficient room for doubt about whether these investments, and the extended commercial presence of British companies and actors in the form of aid and trade, will be "Delivering Prosperity Together"[121] as claimed. On a national scale, many host countries' overall governance performance has improved over the last decade.[122] At the same time, governance areas that are relevant in order for land-consuming OFDI to be beneficial for host country development, such as the rule of law, have deteriorated in many countries, including those that are considered to be the continent's economic powerhouses (Nigeria, South Africa).[123] Also, from a broader perspective, it is debatable whether export-oriented biofuel investments are a good way to

---

118 | Mitchell (2010), 124-125.
119 | Te Velde (2002), 4.
120 | See, for instance, the case of D1 Oils in Mitchell (2010), 124-125.
121 | Bellingham (2010).
122 | *The Africa Report* (29 September 2014).
123 | See, for instance, WB Governance Indicators (http://info.worldbank.org/governance/wgi/index.aspx#countryReports); and findings of the 2014 Ibrahim Index of African Governance survey (http://www.moibrahimfoundation.org/interact/9).

achieve greater food and energy self-sufficiency, as assumed by many national development programs. In fact, many African countries seem to be already over-extracting locally produced biomass, and this is a challenge that is likely to escalate in view of anticipated population growth, negative effects of climate change on land and soils, and/or general land-use conflicts (food vs. fuel vs. urbanization/modernization).[124] Many governments do not seem to attach any export restrictions or local content requirements to land-consuming investment projects, or to demand the development of domestic refining capacities to diversify their countries' economies.

5. INVESTMENT FUNDS FOR AGRICULTURE

Similar to the issue of labor in the Chinese case, one particular aspect of British land-consuming FDI has gained widespread international attention: the rise of new actors in the form of investment funds that engage in agricultural projects. For a better understanding of what is actually happening, the following paragraphs outline the key characteristics of these projects. The goal is to capture the reality of this investor type, which is responsible for, or at least involved in, a significant number of British land-consuming FDI projects (see Table 6-3).

A first challenge towards the assessment of these funds is their complex and evolving nature and opaque structures. Accordingly, the crucial question is who is actually investing. Take, for example, the self-proclaimed "largest agricultural fund in Africa," African AgriLandFund, which has been launched by the British hedge fund Emergent Asset Management. It is based on a capital transfer made by a US pension fund with the stated intent to make private equity investments in African agriculture.[125] Running from 2009 to 2011 under the management of EmVest, an operating company under the control of Emergent Asset Management, the fund was spun out of the Asset Management investment portfolio in 2011. These constant changes in management and shareholding are key characteristics of these funds, which makes it difficult to capture what is occurring.

Judging from the rhetoric of a range of fund managers, the focus on SSA is explained by the region's favorable conditions for food production. In the words of the African AgriLandFund: "because of its series of microclimates, its highlands, its agricultural diversity and good logistics, South Africa and Sub-Saharan Africa can deliver an enormous amount of food."[126] At the same time, most funds use the same overarching theme to explain their business interest

---

124 | Mushi (18 May 2012).
125 | EdificeCapital.com (2014); and McNellis (2009), 11.
126 | McNellis (2009), 13.

in farmland and agriculture: they apply a resource scarcity framing. Accordingly, in a world with a growing population, a rising middle class, a declining arable land per capita ratio, climate pressures, high commodity prices, and competing claims over (farm)land, investments in agriculture promise high returns at a time of otherwise meager investment prospects as a result of the financial crisis.[127]

In practice, however, the connection to farmland and food production is in many cases less obvious than it first appears. While empirical evidence does highlight a variety of farmland- and food-related activities, it primarily reveals funds investing in the private equity of agricultural companies (e.g., Cru Investment Management) or going into related sectors, such as real estate, trading, shipping. So far, only a few funds have invested in land itself. For instance, Schroders Investment Management's "Agricultural Land Fund," which was launched in 2008 when commodity prices peaked, pursues a mixed strategy by investing "in companies and funds which 'will generate capital and income from the efficient management of land,' as well as holding direct stakes in agricultural land."[128]

Moreover, alongside this new trend of investment funds framing agriculture and land as an asset class, there are critical voices as well. Take, for example, David Bryant, Managing Director of Rural Fund Management (Australia), who warns that the rise of investments in natural assets, such as agricultural land, hints at the formation of a new bubble that is likely to burst in the future.[129] According to Bryant, the rosy predictions of a continuous appreciation in farmland value are by no means certain. Instead, the correlation of high commodity prices and land value raises serious doubts about the long-term profitability of such undertakings. From a historical perspective, total returns from agriculture, of which land values are a key component, "rose in line with [commodity] prices, but were driven back again by economic events," most of which were outside the control of individual companies, such as the Asian crisis. In reality, the "property component of agricultural businesses is that these assets are natural resources;" and the "dynamic of agricultural property business is that the ability to yield, combined with the price of the commodity it produces" defines the profitability of the operation and the value of agricultural land.

Returns from large-scale agricultural projects are also severely challenged by other factors, such as the price volatility of agricultural markets, and/or the risks of currency appreciation, extreme weather events, and pests; the fact that "economies of scale in agriculture tend to approach an optimum at relatively

---
127 | Schroder (August 2008).
128 | McNellis (2009), 16.
129 | Bryant (2011), 16-18.

low levels of scale"—due to the relative increase of overhead costs compared to returns; and the difficulty of establishing adequate corporate structures which respond to the volatile and dynamic farming realities on the ground.[130] In practice, and similar to the biofuel projects discussed before, the investment fund sector has already witnessed cases of dramatic value destruction and allegedly fraudulent behavior, as the case of Cru Investment Management (Africa Invest) highlighted.[131] Moreover, the illiquidity problem experienced by Cru Investment shows that holding land as a strategic asset also poses a challenge in the case of project failure.

Together, these factors indicate that it is not surprising that the business rationale of agricultural investment funds often turns out to be less successful than it first appears, particularly with regard to the claim of above average returns in the medium term (see below). They also suggest that a business rationale which assumes appreciation in land and commodity values in its profitability calculations could become troublesome in view of global food security. The inherent problem for food security becomes obvious in a 2002 presentation about falling wheat prices by Silver Street Capital, "an investment management firm focusing on investing in two major areas: Africa and the agricultural sector."[132] The presentation starts out with a "problem definition" centered on the fact that the front month futures prices for wheat were "still around 40 % off the 2008 peak."[133] Ascribing declining world wheat inventories to extreme weather events since 2008, the presentation comes to a 'positive' outlook of re-rising wheat prices:[134] "Global inventories are now near balance once the Black sea shortfall [i.e. reduced production due to drought conditions] is replaced [i.e. once US farmers have sold surplus inventories] so any further negative surprises in wheat harvests will lead to price rises."[135] While expected price increases are clearly bad news for people depending on markets to access their food supplies, they are good news for the investor.

Against this background, a growing body of literature has been emerging since 2008 that discusses the disconcerting implications of this financialization of the food sector, i.e. the increasing role of financial actors, instruments, and rationalizations in the food and agriculture sector.[136] It seems particularly worrisome to see financial actors gaining equity related control over various

---

130 | Bryant (2011), 16-18.
131 | See Chapter 6 (Section 3).
132 | Silver Street Capital (12 March 2015).
133 | Silver Street Capital (9 August 2010), 10.
134 | Silver Street Capital (9 August 2010), 10.
135 | Silver Street Capital (9 August 2010), 10.
136 | For a detailed discussion of the political implications of the financialization of the food sector in the form of distancing and private accumulation, see Clapp (2013).

activities in the global food-supply-chain.[137] This could bestow investors with the power to induce scarcity in the medium term in order to increase profits,— for instance, by withholding crops in storage or not planting anything. It also reflects the broader trend of the concentration of land ownership in the hands of a few. In this case, the owned land is then leased to farmers or directly operated by the investment fund.[138] At a minimum, examples from other sectors characterized by similar processes of ownership concentration and control over supply chains—from production to storage and distribution—serve as a warning about the potential repercussions. Take, for example, the manipulative control of a physical commodity market in the form of price rigging through hoarding—an accusation that Goldman Sachs was confronted with in 2013, when the stockpiling of tons of aluminum allegedly drove up prices.[139]

For the time being, the empirical evidence on UK financial companies investing in African land and agriculture (presented below in Table 6-3), highlights that reality is starkly different than the assertion that scarcity pressures and rising demand will ensure the success of these undertakings, which in turn will contribute to food security and reduce import dependency in host countries. Instead, Cru Investment Management's Africa Invest turned out to be fraudulent in its use of financial resources and, Susan Payne's widely mentioned African Agricultural Land Fund came under new management in 2011, though it did attract an impact investment of USD 500 million from another financial investor. At the same time, Actis' Africa Agribusiness Fund's monopoly in grain handling allegedly led to food price increases in Kenya, highlighting the dangers associated with excessive market power. And Schroders' Agricultural Land Fund did not generate the alpha returns promised; in fact, it mostly performed under the benchmark level from 2006 to 2013, showed great volatility over time, and invested largely in futures rather than equity.

This empirical evidence, then, raises a very different question: How is it that this rhetoric of success and profit continues to be so powerful (and go unchallenged) in the media and government policies, even though the counter-examples are so numerous? Additional and more detailed assessments of these investment projects are needed in order to trace the path of the millions of US dollars associated with cases of fund failure. This would help to clarify the underpinning interest formations that are characteristic of a significant share of these investments.

---

137 | Also see Patel (2012); and Clapp (2013).
138 | Wilson (28 July 2013).
139 | Wilson (28 July 2013); United States Senate Committee on Banking, Housing and Urban Affairs (23 July 2013); and *The New York Times* (26 July 2013).

Table 6-3 – Examples of UK Financial Companies Investing in Africa (Merian Research and CRBM 2010)[140]

Name	Time	Vehicle & Activity	Projects	Additional Information
Cru Investment Management	Unclear start (2008?); suspended in 2009	Africa Invest Management Ltd. London Activity: Invest in agriculture for food production (e.g., paprika, chilies, potatoes) and profit from rising global food demand	Private equity investments in five to seven farms in Malawi (conflicting information) Approx. 6.000 ha and additional outgrower schemes	The fund was suspended in 2009, farms were sold to a Malawi farming company, and CEO Jon Maguire was accused of misuse of financial resources for personal profit.[141] Just before its closure, Africa Invest was awarded the European Market Research Centre award at a UN FAO conference, as well as the "Best SME in Africa" Award at the "Commonwealth Business Council—African Business Awards Ceremony" held in London in 2008.[142]
Actis Capital LLP London	Actis was established in 2004. Until then, it had been part of the CDC, the UK's development arm, which was founded in 1948 to invest in the Commonwealth.[143]	Actis Africa Agribusiness Fund Activity: tea and coffee processing, aquaculture, horticulture, forestry, and bio-power.[144]	Private equity investments	Actis was previously part of the CDC, which still holds 40%.[145] Grain Bulk Handlers Ltd., in which Actis is invested, has established a monopoly in grain handling in Kenya which has driven up food prices.[146] In 2009, Actis was voted Africa real estate firm of the year, highlighting that most of its investments are in effect not flowing into agricultural projects.[147] Instead, the Fund focuses on mining, gas and oil, financial services, and/or real estate rather than agriculture.[148]

140 | The table is based on Merian Research and CRBM (2010), as well as information from corporate websites.
141 | Merian Research and CRBM (2010), 28.
142 | Merian Research and CRBM (2010), 28.
143 | Actis (2014a).
144 | AltAssets (26 April 2006).
145 | AltAssets (26 April 2006). Accordingly, "[a]gribusiness has been a core part of CDC's investments in Africa over the past 50 years and realizations have generated returns of up to 40 per cent, according to CDC. All of CDC's portfolio companies need to comply with CDC's business principles, including health and safety, business integrity and social policies."
146 | Merian Research and CRBM (2010), 9.
147 | Actis (2014a).
148 | Actis (2014b).

Emergent Asset Management Ltd. London[149]	2008 until 2011	African Agricultural Land Fund, London[150] *Activity*: biofuel, livestock, game farming, and timber	Private equity fund investing in multiple projects 150.000 ha of land under management in 15 African countries (in 2008)	Opened by former employees of Goldman Sachs and JP Morgan, Susan Payne and David Murran. Susan Payne also has microfinance projects in Africa. When Susan Payne left Emergent Asset Management Ltd. in 2011 the fund was spun out as well. As of 2012, the fund had received a USD 500 million investment from Truestone Impact Investment Management.[151]
Schroders Investment Management	2008	Schroders Agricultural Land Fund	Hybrid fund involved in real estate, private equity, and equity markets[152] Follows investment theory that 44 % growth in population over next 40 years will be highly profitable in these areas. Total fund size is USD 200.8 million.	The fund shall deliver 10-15 % to institutional investors per year over 5 years by investing 25 % in agricultural land related equities and commodities—to get returns on land holding and land management.[153] De facto, it had primarily invested in futures of agricultural commodities by 2013, and it did not generate alpha (above-average returns) but rather stayed largely below the benchmark value while reflecting great volatility.[154]

6. Conclusion

This chapter has presented the main empirical characteristics of what has happened regarding British land-consuming OFDI since 2000. The key empirical characteristics of British land-consuming FDI in African countries highlight the necessity to critically investigate investor claims. Instead of representing cases of scarcity-induced success, many projects have failed and/or never lived up to their promise of high returns and developmental impact. This holds even in areas, such as the biofuel sector, where government policies and international frameworks are highly supportive of related entrepreneurial activities. In some cases, the resulting market concentration even led to price

---

149 | McNellis (2009), 11, 13.
150 | Murrin (2009); and Private Equity (10 February 2012).
151 | See Private Equity (10 February 2012); and corporate website Truestone Impact Investment Management (n.d.).
152 | Also see De Schutter (2011b).
153 | Schroders (2008).
154 | Schroders (2014).

rises, pointing to the challenges associated with massive capital inflows in developing countries.

The predominant actors in British land-consuming FDI in SSA are large corporations with a long presence on the continent, early-stage companies, and financial investors. More recently, British government officials have also become involved in promoting OFDI, and the CDC, the development finance institution, has expanded the range of its activities in SSA. It promotes trade and investment and also acts as both an indirect and direct investor in land-consuming OFDI projects. Important institutions that influence investor rationales and/or open business opportunities are the international and domestic climate regime, host country privatization policies, the London Stock Exchange, and multilateral aid projects.

The UK's long investor history is obvious in the activities of "old" companies in the recipient countries, but also in the responsiveness of new actors to international/transnational incentive structures. At the same time, it is surprising that the majority of investments are undertaken by newly founded companies, or by actors (e.g., funds) that engage in new operations (e.g., agriculture). Thus far, the majority of investments have used land as a natural resource, with the focus on export to world markets. However, the reliance on stock markets for industry finance often leads to the problem of crashing share values and a lack of patient capital, particularly in agricultural projects with medium-term maturation timelines.

The previous assessment devoted a section on the nature and implications of new actors that have attracted a lot of attention in the contemporary debate, namely financial funds investing in the physical commodities of food and land. The overview highlighted that their business rationale is less self-explanatory than it might appear at first sight. Indeed, their business models might come at a high price in cases where this yields market power concentration and wealth destruction. Even though their access to large sums of capital puts these investors at an advantage over competitors that are only active in the productive or farming sector, the poor performances of the various funds raises doubt about their business rationale and developmental impact. Moreover, and similar to the Chinese case study, the agency in host countries featured prominently in these investment projects: not only did the respective governments try to attract British land-consuming FDI, but British companies also participated in regulatory initiatives of host countries.

In conclusion, several tendencies of British land-consuming OFDI seem notable and demand a more detailed assessment in the home country context. In particular, the British investment projects in SSA reflect a very diverse private sector that seems to have distinct business interests that relate to host country reforms, biofuels legislation, and/or the search for alternative investment outlets at a time of financial crisis. In this context, the findings also show the predominant use of alternative stock markets to access funding and the related lack of patient capital has led many projects 'on the ground' to ultimately fail—highlighting a potential dysfunctionality of the UK's political economy. More recently, public actors and institutions have begun to engage in British land-consuming FDI activities, as investors and/or agents that pro-actively support the private sector through commercial diplomacy. Importantly, these investments seem to respond to home country policies and/or crises that influence investor choices, and the government promotes them as a part of its development agenda and foreign policy—indicating that they do not take place in a "free market" vacuum.

Table 6-4 – Brief Review of the Empirical Characteristics of UK OFDI[155]

Category	Core Empirical Characteristic
Actors	Three types of actors are predominantly involved: corporations with a long presence on the continent, early-stage companies, and financial investors. Recently, the British development finance institution, the CDC, has become involved as investor.
Institutions	Important institutions include the international and domestic climate regime (e.g., the CDM), host country privatization policies, the London Stock Exchange, and multilateral aid projects (e.g., the G8 Alliance). Increasingly, commercial diplomacy institutions (e.g., bilateral investment forums) and British development finance (the CDC Group) are involved.
Sectors	While official data shows that British OFDI in SSA goes largely into mining projects and financial services, "land grab" databases largely list projects in agriculture for food and energy (biofuel) purposes.
Timelines	Most investments started around 2000 or later. Three major timelines can be identified: around 2000, from 2005 onwards, and post-2007.
Role of land	Land is used as a natural resource, as a space where profitable business opportunities open up (e.g., construction), and as an asset. Investments often intend to produce for export; however, they often end up selling locally.
Recipient context	British investments are part of national development plans in host countries which try to attract IFDI. In the case of biofuels, British companies were invited by several host governments to participate in the development of sectoral regulations.

---

155 | This table intends to reduce complexity and orientate the reader. In doing so, it leaves out some findings presented in this chapter that though important, do not form the core of British OFDI in SSA.

Chapter 7: The British Context
Investments from a Home Country Perspective

1. INTRODUCTION

The empirical evidence highlights that British land-consuming FDI in African countries comprises several sectors, and reflects distinct motivations, as well as a wide range of operations. The evidence also shows a complex actor constellation: in addition to the highly diverse private sector, increasingly, agents of the public sector are involved. A significant share of these investments clearly pre-dates the 2008 crises. The production of food does not seem of primary importance in these investments, while biofuels investments have featured quite prominently—producing largely for international markets. Together with the important role of the financial sector, also the use of land as a strategic asset has been increasing.

This chapter assesses how and why British land-consuming OFDI activities happen against the background of the investor country. In particular, it will discuss these activities in view of the country's OFDI policy (Section 2), the guiding ideology of UK-Africa relations (Section 3), and, finally, against the backdrop of the country's political economy (Section 4) and development trajectory (Section 5). The multiple threads emerging from this discussion will be summarized in the conclusion (Section 6), which will be guided by the question of why these investments occur as they do in and over time. In addition to domestic dynamics and international contexts, this section will also briefly assess the investments' likely welfare implications.

It is argued that the following features of the home country context are significant in explaining British land-consuming OFDI from a home country perspective: (1) The investments are embedded in a long-established OFDI framework; however, this framework has undergone some changes in the past decade, such as the new "official" focus on Africa and the introduction of novel financial instruments. (2) Many investments are part of a foreign policy ideology tailored to domestic development ambitions captured under the acting government's "prosperity agenda," while some relate to (inter)national climate policies. (3) The actors and institutions involved reflect the dominance of the financial industry in an era of deregulated capital markets while highlighting the challenge of attracting patient capital for agricultural investments through the stock exchange (AIM) mechanism. At the same time, (4) the detrimental impact of the financialization-led growth model pursued over the last decades has led the acting government to support land-consuming FDI in African countries as a way to reindustrialize and "rebalance the economy"—after the financial crisis hit.

More broadly, four drivers explain why British land-consuming FDI in SSA happens from the home country perspective. Accordingly, British land-consuming FDI projects are part of multiple strategies to profit from the economic reforms and rapidly growing consumer markets in the host countries; to abide by the international climate regulations and use domestic energy and climate policies to encourage investments in 'clean' biofuels; and/or to "seek alpha" through alternative investments in the primary sector in African countries at a time of the financial crisis, Eurozone crisis, and economic stagnation back home. Increasingly, land-consuming FDI projects are also part of a (long-term) political strategy to economic recovery and international political power through rising exports and industrial activity.

2. Home Country Measures

> Britain has benefited from that global system over a long period of time. But we cannot afford to rely on history or sentiment if we are to earn our living. We cannot take it for granted that markets will remain open to our business, or that our businesses will always be able to take full advantage of the opportunities that exist.
> (Department for Business, Innovation and Skills, 2011[1])

British land-consuming investments in Africa are embedded in a fully developed framework of home country measures that has evolved over time. Some of its elements trace back to the late 19th century, such as the Foreign and Commonwealth Office that emerged out of the Colonial Office (est.1854) and the Dominions Office (est.1925). Historically, the adoption of home country measures underwent several stages, from a pre-WWI *laissez-faire* approach to a more guided course since WWI, and an increasingly promotional stance

---

1 | BIS (2011a), 3.

since the mid-1970s.[2] The introduction of explicitly promotional OFDI policies occurred in the UK in 1974.[3]

The shifting OFDI policy stances of the various UK governments reflect specific domestic development concerns and international events in time. For instance, Treasury instructions in 1919 to tighten OFDI regulations reveal the intention to protect foreign exchange and ensure the availability of capital for domestic development, like housing, following WWI. Also, more recently, the promotion of overseas FDI by the UK government seems to be related to the prevailing perception that OFDI is an important component of the UK's ability to "punch above its weight" and maintain "prosperity" at home in a changing world order characterized by the rise of the BRICS, that is, to play an extraordinarily influential role in international political and economic relations given the country's actual size.[4] At the same time, UK OFDI has remained astonishingly stable, at about 2% of GDP, since the end of WWII while the British share in world stock of FDI has mostly ranged between 14% and 15%.[5]

OFDI: Development, Context, Objectives

A closer look at the historical evidence shows the nature and sequence of events and development objectives that made various governments (under their respective political economies and development strategies) reach conclusions about the usefulness (or ineffectiveness) of overseas investments to address internal or external challenges or realize certain development ambitions. As has been mentioned before, the UK moved through several stages in this respect, namely a laissez-faire approach during the 19th century, when it was a significant capital-exporting country; a permissive approach in the late 19th century "when it was rapidly losing its industrial supremacy;"[6] a slightly more regulated phase post-WWII, when the country was focusing on recovering its industry and infrastructure; and an increasingly promotional stance since the mid-1970s, following EU accession and the oil crisis, when OFDI was seen as a way to help the tarnished manufacturing industry to access European markets.

---

2 | Atkin (1970), 324-335; and De Beule and Van den Bulcke (2010), 296-297.
3 | De Beule and Van den Bulcke (2010), 296-297.
4 | Atkin (1970), 325; M.Harvey (2011).
5 | While OFDI flows briefly spiked to nearly 15% during 1996-2000, due to an increase in mergers and acquisitions of British firms overseas (e.g., Unilever), the percentage of overseas FDI as a portion of GDP had dropped again to 2.5% by 2002. However, the interim spike had the long-term effect of raising "the stock of UK FDI" to 1980s levels of approximately "14.5 per cent of world stock of FDI." See Schenk (2005), 474.
6 | Chang (2004), 695-697.

Over time, government rhetoric suggested that OFDI would facilitate the acquisition of natural resources, technology, and know-how for domestic industry, promote exports, mitigate market failure, and, to a rising degree, create new markets and strengthen UK industry through globalized production processes that allow companies to internalize locational advantages. At the same time, OFDI has increasingly been perceived as an income earner able to moderate the negative post-1947 UK trade accounts. This holds particularly true since the Thatcherite era in the 1980s, when the terms of trade deteriorated as a result of multiple factors, such as structural changes within the economy in the form of deindustrialization, financialization, and deregulation; high commodity prices during the oil crisis in the 1970s; and a changing international context, in which many countries had begun to catch up with regard to industrialization, and British companies were losing their competitive edge.[7]

Through the aforementioned periods, the framing and administration of OFDI changed significantly: while the 19th century was characterized by a political perception of OFDI that reflected mercantilist thought and great power struggles over resources, markets, strategic locations, and spheres of influence, increasingly, an economic-technical framing of OFDI gained influence in public debates and international economic governance. However, more recently, under the trade and investment agenda of the acting government (since 2011), OFDI has been loosely yet explicitly (re)linked to the UK's national interests.

In practice, official documentation shows that in the years after the British Empire's disintegration, particularly during the 1970s, 1980s, and 1990s, the UK focused on resource security and negotiated bilateral investment treaties (BITs). The UK governments were concerned over expropriations in the former dependencies, where the colonial investor legacy, the call for a New International Economic Order (1974), and the popularity of dependencia theories (early 1980s) had led to a hostile attitude among host countries towards British FDI.[8] At that time, OFDI policy was still strongly guided by the UK's foreign policy agency, the Foreign and Commonwealth Office (FCO), which was in charge of the negotiations. Once British officials and business reoriented their focus towards market access as well as investment and export promotion, competencies were transferred to the UK Trade and Investment Department.[9]

As of 2012, proactive OFDI promotion is part of a larger package of industrial policy that focuses primarily on export promotion and IFDI attraction while being embedded in a reindustrialization program designed to "rebalance the

---

7 | Carnell (1996).
8 | For information on the history of UK bilateral investment treaties, see Walter (2000), 9-11, 23-26.
9 | Walter (2000), 9-11, 23-26.

economy."[10] The reindustrialization program aims to promote "the growth of high-tech industry, small firms, and service providers (tertiary sector)."[11] In this context, OFDI promotion is framed as helping British business to "go global," thereby opening markets for specific industries that the government perceives to be the UK's comparative advantage (e.g., pharmaceutical, biotech sector, food manufacture), encouraging trade, securing access to resources (oil, minerals), enhancing competitiveness, and profiting from growth markets overseas and from contract work opportunities that might help to secure jobs back home (e.g., construction projects).[12] While the geographical focus rests on Asia, the Gulf, and Latin America, there has been a growing interest in Africa as well. For instance, the Foreign Secretary has established a Commercial Taskforce "to increase the presence of British companies across Africa."[13] Correlating with the intensified commercial diplomacy, exports to African countries, as well as investments, increased significantly. However, the case of Angola, a major crude oil exporting country with little refining capacity where British companies have managed to significantly increase their exports (of refined oil) since 2012, highlights that in many cases, the established trade and investment legacies of the UK continue to play out as they have done in the past.[14]

Jumping on the Corporate Bandwagon and "Rebalancing the Economy"[15]

As of 2014, the UK is categorized as a country with a low degree of OFDI control and a high degree of OFDI promotion.[16] In comparison, China has been characterized as a country with a high degree of control and promotion of OFDI flows. The UK's set of home country measures involves multiple policy areas. It is composed of encouragement policies, simplified approval processes, and regularized supervision. While some features were disbanded at a certain point, such as the energy attachés, and/or taken over by diplomatic staff, others persist, such as the net food-importing country's agricultural attachés, though their locations and numbers have changed, particularly after the UK's accession to the European Economic Community in 1973.[17] Several agencies were

---

10 | BIS (2011a).
11 | Nagle (2000), 304.
12 | BIS (2011b); BIS (2011a), 1-25; and HM Treasury and BIS (2011), 3-4; FCO (2011b).
13 | Bellingham (2010).
14 | Soque (30 June 2014); KPMG (2014).
15 | See HM Treasury and Osborne (9 July 2013); and Cargill (2011), 13.
16 | De Beule and Van den Bulcke (2010), 299.
17 | The National Archives (2005), 21-22.

transformed into hybrid organizations that now comprise private and public actors. Take, for example, the FCO/Department of Trade and Industry (DTI) Joint Export Directorate that became the UK Department of Trade and Investment (UKTI), a government agency that works closely with industry partners and associations. In addition, British investors have increasingly profited from the pooled sovereignty of the EU, as well as from multilateral institutions and related political and financial support mechanisms. At the same time, it has to be noted that the OFDI policy framework should not be overestimated in view of effectiveness. In practice, the government budget is tight, and the multilevel home country measures' framework lacks coherence. For instance, the UK's BITs can be in disaccord with EU standards, as many have been negotiated prior to the UK's accession to the European Economic Community (now European Union).[18] Also, the government does not have a long-term vision for its engagement with the African continent.[19]

The home country measures (HCMs) that apply particularly to investment projects in African countries have often been in place for several decades. As mentioned above, the BITs were negotiated in the 1980s and 1990s, and the Export Credits Guarantee Department (ECGD), the UK's export finance and credit agency, has been offering political risk insurance for overseas investments since 1970, in the form of loans to finance purchases, sharing credit risks with banks, and insuring UK overseas investors.[20] However, the case of the UK's political risk insurance also highlights the degree to which the utilization of home country measure services has amplified: investor insurance liability increased by 58% between 1998 and 2001, covering GBP 1 billion.[21] With regard to regional distribution, however, Africa ranks rather low in HCM services. In 2007, only 6% of ECGD services went to projects in Africa.[22]

Key institutional reforms and program re-conceptualizations linked to these long-standing policy frameworks took place under the Labour (1997-2010) and Conservative governments (since 2010). These reforms and re-conceptualizations have proven important for British land-consuming investments in SSA. Already in the late 1990s, UK development assistance began to focus on Africa while embracing the concept of poverty alleviation through private-sector-led growth. In 2010, the Conservative government re-aligned the DFID programs with FCO interests, echoing the credo of the 1980s to "give greater weight in the allocation of our aid to political, industrial, and commercial objectives along-

---

18 | Harrison (2010) and (2013).
19 | Chafer (2010).
20 | For an assessment of the UK's export promotion agencies, see Hauswirth (2006), 96-102.
21 | TeVelde (2007), 97.
22 | Te Velde (2007), 97.

side our basic development objectives" (Neil Marten, Minister for Overseas Development, 1980).²³

In practice, this has meant that investment-related bilateral aid, which research shows to positively correlate with OFDI flows, has increased from 18% in the 1970s to 30% in 2002 (as a share of total UK aid).²⁴ Major emphasis lies on improving the investment environments of host countries through programs that focus on infrastructure, human resource development, macroeconomic stability, legal rules, or private sector support.²⁵ For example, the Investment Climate Facility for Africa finances policy and regulatory work "to improve the investment conditions in Africa," while providing a platform "for the private sector to work in partnership with governments and donors."²⁶

Moreover, the UK's development finance institution, the CDC, strengthened its geographical focus on Africa (and South Asia) in 2011, and it has transformed its operational strategy from being a "fund of funds" (i.e., intermediary equity investments) to becoming an investor engaged in direct private equity operations. This move is important as it will result in more equity investment geared towards improving the economic fundamentals of recipient countries—to the benefit of British investors—while reducing the risk potential. By 2011, the CDC had invested in several funds that were engaged in land-consuming investments in SSA: it transferred USD 20 million to the previously-mentioned SilverLandsFund of London-based Silver Street Capital LLP, which concentrates on agribusiness operations in Central and Southern Africa. It also invested in the Global Environmental Fund (GEF), a firm focusing on clean tech operations which currently manages 468,860 ha of forestry land in Ghana, Mozambique, Tanzania, Swaziland, and South Africa (in 2014).²⁷ It also made a USD 15 million investment (i.e., 15% of the total target of USD 100 million) in Schulze Global Ethiopia Growth and Transformation Fund I, a private equity investment fund involved in agriculture and food production in Ethiopia.²⁸

In the words of Andrew Mitchell, former Secretary of State (2010-2012) for DFID, the sole CDC shareholder, these investment activities, particularly the investment in Schulze Ethiopia Growth, are living proof of the marked shift in geographical and strategic focus that the CDC Group has experienced: "For the first time, CDC is directing its much needed capital to help promising entrepreneurs and businesses in Ethiopia to transform agriculture and food

---

23 | Barder (2005), 7, 10.
24 | Te Velde (2006), 24.
25 | Te Velde (2006), 24; and Te Velde (2007), 96.
26 | Department for International Development (25 March 2013).
27 | Data calculated from data provided by GEF (http://www.globalenvironmentalfund.com/).
28 | Department for International Development (9 May 2012).

production."²⁹ At the same time, the CDC has begun to invest in service industries catering to the interests of these agribusiness investments. For instance, it is involved in the Progression Eastern African Microfinance Equity Fund (2012) that provides microfinance in Kenya Tanzania, Rwanda, Zambia, and Uganda.³⁰ This is particularly interesting against the background of the outgrower schemes that are applied by many investor companies. These schemes, as described above, rely on farmers who are able to pay for inputs; as a result, microfinance has repeatedly been recommended by industry representatives to support rural development and private-sector-led growth.

In the bilateral political realm, the Cameron government in the UK has begun to step up its commercial diplomacy in the form of high level visits and the launch of bilateral investment forums. These resemble similar Chinese and French platforms, though they are undertaken in a more ad hoc fashion. In this context, the then Minister for Africa, Henry Bellingham (2010-2012), stated in 2010 that he was "on track to visit all 53 states in Africa by our next general election in 2015."³¹ The key actors in this commercial diplomacy spree are the FCO, DFID, and UKTI, which are frequently located in the same offices in African countries due to the previously mentioned budget cuts that have impacted diplomatic infrastructures.³²

In addition to these domestic home country measures, the previous chapter has highlighted that companies from liberal economies which are well-integrated in the global economy, such as the UK, also have access to regional institutions that belong to the wider set of HCMs. Take, for example, the ACP Investment Facility (IF) under the management of the European Investment Bank (EIB). Set up in 2003 to "[p]rovide long term lending to promote European objectives,"³³ the IF is a "EUR 3.137bn risk-bearing revolving fund [...] [that] was established to support investment in private businesses and commercially-run public sector companies (including revenue-generating infrastructure)" in African, Caribbean, and Pacific countries.³⁴ The IF provides risk capital through equity participation, quasi capital, and guarantees, as well as ordinary loans (non-concessional and concessional).³⁵ Moreover, other regional and international institutions are important, such as the EU-Africa strategic

---

29 | CDC (9 May 2012).
30 | Manson (8 March 2012).
31 | Bellingham (2010).
32 | Bellingham (2010).
33 | See, for instance, Sakellaris (4 October 2010).
34 | European Investment Bank (9 December 2010).
35 | Analysis for Economic Decisions (2010), 4-10.

partnership and related summits and action plans since 2007;[36] the Lomé and, now, Cotonou agreement between the EU and ACP countries;[37] the UNFCCC's Clean Development Mechanism; and the G8's "New Alliance to improve Food and Nutrition Security."[38]

This means that (inter)national regulatory frameworks and support structures that go beyond the traditional understanding of home country measures play a significant role in British land-consuming investments. They impact investor choices, and match the self-description of the UK as a cosmopolitan economy. The following paragraphs will briefly outline the key features of the frameworks that are most important with respect to British land-consuming FDI in SSA, the setting of incentive structures at different levels of governance, and the creation of new markets: climate finance and biofuels regulations.

Empirical evidence presented in Chapter 6 pointed to the importance of international climate negotiations for overseas biofuel investments. In particular, the Kyoto Protocol (1997), an agreement related to the 1992 United Nations Framework Convention on Climate Change, has been influential because it established legally binding greenhouse gases emissions reductions which feature prominently in biofuel industry statements, particularly with regards to the Clean Development Mechanism (CDM) and the tradable Carbon Emission Reduction (CER) mechanism. For example, Trading Emissions Plc., the investment company that bought a majority share of SBF (2008-2011), stated at the time that it was "paying close regard to the growth and development of these businesses and their market position vis-à-vis domestic and international climate and renewable energy policy."[39]

Related developments on the European level were equally important in the creation of the biofuel market. In 1997, the European Commission (EC) published the first white paper which set the target for renewable energy in Europe's energy mix at 12% by 2010.[40] The white paper was a response to the climate negotiations and related concerns over the potential socioeconomic implications of emissions reductions for European growth. Renewable energy sources were framed as low-carbon energy sources that would allow the European Union Member States to meet the legally binding reduction targets

---

36 | See European Union, External Action (2014b); European Union, External Action (2014a); and Rodt (2012), 1-6.
37 | See Te Velde and Bilal (2003).
38 | European Commission (18 May 2012). For a critical discussion of the G8 initiative as industrial policy to strengthen UK agribusiness, see Haigh (2014).
39 | Trading Emissions Plc (2010), 9, 32.
40 | European Commission (1997).

(amongst other measures, such as energy efficiency), without threatening the overall growth strategy regarding trade and transport activities.[41]

Consequently, renewable energy has been deemed to improve energy (supply) security, foster industrial innovation, provide low-carbon energy, and promote rural development—a rhetoric that remains central in European development strategies as of 2014. Subsequent EC directives followed this line of reasoning while advancing the details: Directive 2003/30/EC established a 5.75% share of renewable energy in the transport sector, to be reached by 2010. In 2009, Directive 3009/28/EC raised the renewable energy target to 10% in all Member States by 2020, and it introduced sustainability criteria to counter rising criticism of biofuels, particularly regarding their negative impact on food security.[42] In addition to the introduction of targets and the framing of renewable energy as low-carbon energy, the EU established a European Emissions Trading Scheme.[43] As aviation emissions have been included in the scheme since 2012, the aviation sector has taken great interest in the biofuel industry. In the case of British investments in SSA, Lufthansa had signed offtake

---

41 | See, for instance, the guidance note from the Department for Transport (5 November 2012). It discusses the renewable transport fuels obligations (RTFO) and applies this narrative.

42 | The European Commission introduced sustainability criteria in 2009 (European Directive 2009/28/EC, articles 17, 18 and 19). These relate to greenhouse gas (GHG) reductions, biodiversity, high-carbon stock land, and agro-environmental practices. The sustainability scheme is based on two tools: firstly, voluntary schemes (to be assessed and recognized) and multilateral and bilateral agreements that promote "sustainable production of agricultural raw materials"; and, secondly, a review of "default values" in the context of CO_2 accounting. While these sustainability criteria focus solely on the environmental aspect of biofuel investments, social sustainability criteria (e.g., land rights, wages) were deliberately left unacknowledged, as these conflict with WTO rules on trade barriers (Directive 2009/28/EC, articles 17, 18 and 19). Moreover, they ignore the problem of direct and indirect land use changes as a result of biofuels production, which would significantly change the CO_2 calculation—to the extent that biofuels are more CO_2 intensive than fossil fuels, while their land take creates a wide range of new problems. In the policy world, the view that renewable resources provide low-carbon energy, persists. See, for instance, UK Trade and Investment (2012, 16): "Reducing carbon emissions of the transport sector is vital if the UK is to meet its 2020 targets; the replacement of fossil fuels in vehicles by biofuels has been identified as one of the key mechanisms." A more detailed analysis of assumptions and critical interrogation of framings in the European biofuels debate is provided by Franco et al. (2010).

43 | European Directive 2003/87/EC. This cap and trade scheme uses market mechanisms to limit emissions from intensive industry while rewarding companies with low emissions. See Cleveland and Tietenberg (29 August 2009).

agreements with SBF, and it conducted trial flights with biofuels.[44] While the company backed out of that agreement in the face of mounting protest in the home country, it continues to consider Jatropha and its resourcing via offtake agreements as a viable option to meet its CO_2 emission reduction requirements in the near future.[45]

The international and European agreements have also had relevant repercussions at the domestic level. While the UK government introduced its first biofuel regulations in 2000 as a response to the Kyoto Protocol obligations, it raised the targets in 2003 to 20% CO_2 savings by 2050 (compared to 1990 levels). The 2003 Energy White Paper stated that the "increased use of biofuels is considered a way to contribute to the achievement of these targets."[46] In 2007, the Renewable Transport Fuel Obligation (RTFO) was legally enacted by the government. It required major transport fuel suppliers "to ensure that a percentage of their sales were from a renewable source, intended to deliver carbon savings in the transport sector and provide a sound platform for private sector investment in renewable fuels infrastructure and technology."[47] From 2008 to 2011, the Renewable Fuel Agency, a non-departmental public body, administered the implementation of the RFTO.[48] Moreover, the Climate Change Act was published, establishing a framework to cut between 26% and 32% of the UK's carbon emissions by 2020, and 80% by 2050 (compared to 1990 levels).[49] With regard to the socioeconomic outlook, the "clean tech" industry has been reframed as a future industrial growth sector under the reindustrialization program, and has also been at the core of the traditional HCM framework (see above). For instance, the 2009 UK Low Carbon Transition Plan foresees the medium-term creation of 1.2 million green jobs.

It is usually difficult to evaluate the effectiveness of such frameworks in achieving their objectives of CO_2 reduction and reindustrialization. However, the empirical assessment of biofuel projects in Chapter 6 has provided valuable insights in this regard, and they will be presented in the remainder of this section. Operators of British land-consuming FDI in the biofuel industry, as well as financial investors in London, constantly refer to these political frameworks, if only to use the related rhetoric in their promotional materials. Biofuel investments appear as a 'safe bet' in view of the (predicted) growth in demand

---

44 | See UK Trade and Investment (2012), 26-27.
45 | Personal communication with Lufthansa staff, November 2014.
46 | MRL Public Sector Consultants (2014); Department of Trade and Industry (2003).
47 | See MRL Public Sector Consultants (2014).
48 | The Renewable Transport Fuel Obligation applies to fuel suppliers. These have to prove that a certain percentage of fuel consists of renewable energy sources. See Department for Transport (5 November 2012).
49 | UK Climate Change Act (2008).

for bioenergy in the future, which is based on the assumption that biofuels will become an alternative to oil. Moreover, the framing of biofuels as an alternative energy source that provides "clean" energy and contributes to "green growth" through multiplier effects in the form of jobs and energy security in the host, as well as the home country, bestowed these investments initially with a positive image.[50] By 2004, so-called "clean tech" companies made up 6% of the AIM London Stock Exchange's initial public offerings (IPOs).[51]

However, contrary to the extremely ambitious sector goals embedded in the policy framework and/or business plans of companies involved in biofuel projects that aim at becoming a "clean energy leader," and in spite of the largely positive outlook of companies and sector analysts alike, the empirical data presented in Chapter 6 showed that most biofuel projects experienced dramatic wealth destruction. Aside from operational challenges, alternative energy (i.e. first generation biofuels) has not lived up to its socioeconomic and environmental promises, and the business models rely on minimum social and environmental standards to be economically viable.[52] In the UK context, the Gallagher Review (Renewable Fuels Agency 2008), commissioned by the Secretary of State for Transport to study the "indirect effects of biofuels production,"[53] came to the conclusion that biofuels contributed to rising food prices and deforestation while failing to reduce CO_2 emissions. Subsequently, the report called for a moratorium on biofuel investments until government could ensure that only idle and marginal lands were used for biofuel production—if they do exist.[54]

---

50 | This framing and rhetoric is directly taken from the official frameworks, such as European Directive 2009/28/EC, which explicitly argues as follows: "The control of European energy consumption and the increased use of energy from renewable sources, together with energy savings and increased energy efficiency, constitute important parts of the package of measures needed to reduce greenhouse gas emissions and comply with the Kyoto Protocol to the United Nations Framework Convention on Climate Change, and with further Community and international greenhouse gas emission reduction commitments beyond 2012. Those factors also have an important part to play in promoting the security of energy supply, promoting technological development and innovation and providing opportunities for employment and regional development, especially in rural and isolated areas." For a discussion of the evolving bioenergy directives, see Ismail and Rossi (2010).
51 | Cleantech Investor (March 2007).
52 | This finding is not unique to the British case. See Hunsberger et al. (2017) and Goetz et al. (2018).
53 | Renewable Fuels Agency (2008).
54 | The UK Renewable Fuels Agency (RFA), the first organization globally with an independent board intended to assist in the implementation of the Renewable Fuel Trans-

In summary, the multi-level regulatory climate regime that biofuels are embedded in and supported by highlights a key problem, namely that such frameworks and measures might have significant undesirable repercussions. It is ironic that it was the growing awareness of the negative feedback loops between food and energy production that led many investors to focus on Jatropha-based biofuel projects, assuming that such projects could flourish on marginal land. In practice, however, the empirical evidence presented, such as the SBF trial plots in Ethiopia, has revealed that Jatropha is not economically viable under harsh conditions. Moreover, its prevalence on prime land clearly intensifies the negative feedback between food and energy production under conditions of insufficient governance while hardly resulting in economically viable undertakings conducive to rural development.

Summary

Four observations follow from the interrelation of UK HCMs and British land-consuming investments in SSA. First, OFDI promotion continues to be a by-element of the UK's broader trade and investment strategy, which puts primary emphasis on export promotion, market access, and the attraction of IFDI.[55] This is highlighted by white papers and strategy papers published since 2000.[56] At the same time, the OFDI approach to SSA has become more planned as a consequence of institutional reform, changing strategies, and geographical program adjustment.

Second, from a broader perspective, the proactive government approach and the cooperation of public and private actors in the area of OFDI reflect the newly adopted "grand strategy" of the current UK government.[57] It tries to encourage the close cooperation of government agencies in support of British trade and

---

port Obligation (RFTO) from 2008-2011. It identified additional problems preventing sustainable biofuels production: First, "under a largely voluntary system, obligated suppliers are able to buy un-certified biofuels on the spot market, avoiding the need to establish supply contracts that are longer term;" second, the lack of a "price premium for feedstock with assured Carbon and Sustainability provenance" discouraged producers; and, third, the sustainability criteria under the European Renewable Energy Directive "focused on avoiding the worst practices rather than promoting the best"—setting only very broad sustainability standards in view of land use, which were related to biodiversity and carbon stocks. See Renewable Fuels Agency (2008), 6-8; and Renewable Fuels Agency (2011), 6.

55 | See, for instance, BIS (2011a); and HM Treasury and BIS (2011).
56 | BIS (2011a); UK Trade and Investment (2006); BIS (2011b); UK Trade and Investment (2011).
57 | E.g., BIS (2011a); or Allen (8 October 2012).

investment activities (e.g., cooperation by UK DTI, DFID, the FCO, and BIS[58]), and reflects the government's decision to revive the economy by jumping on the rising corporate interest in the African continent as a new growth region. In particular, the rise in investment-related aid, a significant part of which is going to SSA, will have a positive impact on British investment flows to the region. For instance, the CDC Group and DFID have expanded their operational activities and shifted their focus (at least part of it) towards SSA.[59] At the same time, aid-funded business opportunities are promoted by the FCO and UK DTI and facilitated by DFID. New trade policy initiatives, such as the Africa Free Trade initiative (AFTi) promoted by UK DTI, are also explicitly geared towards securing market access in SSA. Overall, however, it is important to remember that it was the private sector that led the way and invested in African economies, and that the government largely followed suit, matching public finance programs with private sector interests.

Third, despite the growing interest in SSA-directed OFDI, recent budget cuts and the dramatic indebtedness of the UK government limit the prospects of the ambitious grand strategy approach. This problem is multiplied by the fact that the UK does not have a coherent and long-term vision for its political and economic relations with African countries.[60] However, the access to EU support structures mitigates the budget constraint problem.

Fourth, the importance of UK-Africa relations is highlighted by the impressive quantitative increase in UK OFDI in Africa during the last decade. This is remarkable, considering that it is happening at a time when UK OFDI flows worldwide have been falling dramatically, from USD 233,371 million in 2000 to USD 11,020 million (sic!) in 2010.[61] While the dramatic fall of OFDI flows is related to the financial crash and the Eurozone crisis, the intensified trade and investment with African economies correlates with UK interests of the private (and, more recently, public) sector to participate in and profit from the conti-

---

58 | This acronym stands for the UK Department for Business, Innovation & Skills.
59 | E.g., the CDC shifted from intermediary equity to direct equity and debt investments, and DFID established Challenge Funds to support UK companies overseas.
60 | Chafer (2010, 1) has argued that "[...] policy relating to Africa is often short-termist and preoccupied with meeting, often annual, targets, with the result that a long-term view of the strategic importance of Africa is not taken and that the resources deployed in support of UK Africa policy by the FCO/MoD/DFID are not deployed in a strategic way (e.g., initiatives launched one year and then abandoned a year or two years later, leading to waste of effort and resources). On Africa policy, both London and Paris are confronted by what one might describe as the „ends vs. means" dilemma: in other words, both the UK and France wish to remain key players in Africa but increasingly do not have the means (financial and personnel) of their ambitions."
61 | See Annex 1 of Allen and Dar (14 March 2013).

nent's growth dynamics. It strongly mirrors an international trend, namely the shifting perception within the capital markets of the African continent.[62] For instance, the British Standard Chartered Bank estimates that the region will grow at a rate of 7% per annum, faster than China.[63] In practice, data from 2001, 2002, and 2003 highlights that UK OFDI has generated "profit rates that are two to three times higher in Africa than worldwide."[64] However, this is a finding that hardly matches the empirical evidence about land-consuming FDI presented in this book.

3. GUIDING IDEOLOGY

The rhetoric running through the key documents of the political and financial mechanisms introduced above highlights that British land-consuming investments are embedded in a guiding ideology (in the form of several sets of ideas that perform ideological functions) about national development and international grandeur that has emerged over the last decade from significant government speeches, reports, and white papers across several policy sectors. While some elements of this ideological schema are clearly about framing development challenges and pathways of the UK regarding economic recovery, others serve to legitimate the measures taken, by underlining that they help to mitigate environmental challenges, or that they are tailored to host countries' interests while ensuring domestic security and prosperity back home, creating jobs, ensuring international influence, strengthening energy security, and meeting climate obligations. In summary, the argumentative structure of the guiding ideology flowing through relevant government documents connects growth, prosperity, and security, and takes the form of a hypothetical syllogism along the following lines: when there is private-sector-led growth there is prosperity,[65] and when there is prosperity, there is security (and vice versa);[66] therefore, when there is private-sector-led growth, there will be both prosperity and security.[67]

---

62 | See Ernst & Young (2012). Accordingly, between 2003 and 2011, the number of FDI projects increased by 253%, from 339 (2003) to 857 (2011), and—as the diverse sector distribution in the China case indicated—this growth in the number of projects was associated with an increasing share in the non-extractive industry sectors, such as manufacturing or business services.
63 | Ernst & Young (2012), 18.
64 | Te Velde and Calì (2006), 12.
65 | BIS (2011a).
66 | HM Government (2010).
67 | HM Treasury and BIS (2011); and BIS (2011a).

In more detail, the discourse surrounding British investments in Africa reflects the fundamental transformations that have taken place in view of domestic and international economic relations. On the one hand, a shift in UK industrial policy is detectable. After decades of an arm's length approach and relative neglect of this sector, the current UK government openly embraces a closer linkage of business and state actors, domestically, as well as with regards to overseas business opportunities;[68] and it favors reindustrialization as a way to promote domestic economic recovery.[69] On the other hand, the tone in bilateral relations has begun to shift from an asymmetric top-down rhetoric that highlighted the challenges of African economies to one that praises the opportunities African economies have to offer. In this context, the public statement by BIS that national economic interests are a key driver behind the intensified relations with African countries constitutes a major change in the UK's more recent development policy.[70] In fact, following the empire's post-WWII disintegration, international development narratives concentrated strongly on topics of humanitarianism and security, and national interests were considered by many (politicians and public) to be a rhetorical taboo in relation to Africa.[71] Additionally, the outlook on international economic relations has changed. Since the failure of the OECD initiative to promote a multilateral investment regime in the 1990s—during which time bilateralism was framed as a step away from multilateralism—the UK now officially embraces bilateralism as a stepping stone towards multilateral economic institutions.[72]

---

68 | This "grand strategy" is envisioned in multiple government white papers and publications, such as the "Trade and Investment" Whitepaper (BIS (2011a)) and the FCO's Five Year Plan (FCO (2011a)). It is also mentioned in government speeches (Hague 2010). Accordingly, "British Ministers" can be "a valuable asset when it comes to persuading other countries to work with us or adopt our objectives as their own"; and "joint initiatives between businesses" can be influential in "changing attitudes" in different governance forums as well. See Hague (2010); HM Treasury and BIS (2011); BIS (2011a), 55-59.
69 | Hague (2010).
70 | BIS (2011a).
71 | Cargill (2011).
72 | The Multilateral Agreement on Investment (MAI) was an initiative in the mid-1990s (1995-1997) by the US and other OECD countries to negotiate universal investment rules, similar to those for trade under the WTO. For more information, see the collection of articles at the Global Policy Forum (2014).

A British Africa Policy?

As mentioned above, British land-consuming overseas investments in SSA are part of development rhetoric about coming to terms with international challenges and changes and about "rebalancing the economy" through trade, investment, and reindustrialization in particular areas, such as "advanced manufacturing, life sciences, creative industries, green energy and non-financial business services."[73] In this context, OFDI is seen as a way to secure overseas business opportunities and "allow [...] businesses to grow and diversify."[74] However, the lack of a coherent long-term vision means that there is no visionary 'Africa policy' in place.

To counter concerns about the fact that trade and investment has become a topic of British foreign policy, all relevant official documentation (see Table 7-1) applies the rhetoric of mutual benefit, using mainstream economic arguments ("win-win") while also embracing an image of the UK as a country characterized by "enlightened national interest."[75] As the "Trade and Investment for Growth" white paper puts it:

[...] as we work to rebuild our economy, we must redouble our efforts to enable developing countries to build their own paths to growth through trade and investment, and to help them develop the capacity to do so, especially in Africa. This is the right thing to do both on moral grounds and for Britain's national interest.[76]

In the words of the former Minister for Africa, MP Henry Bellingham (2010-2012), the UK pursues "a foreign policy in which the promotion and protection of human rights around the world is indivisible from our efforts to bring security and prosperity to Britain, and, of course, in Africa as well."[77] On the project level, the mutual benefit rhetoric is taken up by framing many investment projects as impact investments that contribute to the host country's development while generating above-average returns. Yet, in spite of this mutual benefit rhetoric, the African continent continues to be portrayed largely as a source of primary commodities, i.e. as possessing "relatively abundant reserves" to meet the "global demand for oil, minerals, natural gas, food and agriculture and other natural resources."[78]

---

73 | HM Treasury and BIS (2011), 4.
74 | BIS (2011a), 4; also BIS/FCO/UK Trade and Investment (2012).
75 | FCO (2011a), 1-2.
76 | BIS (2011a), 4.
77 | Bellingham (2010).
78 | BIS (2011a), 41.

In his speech "UK and Africa: Delivering Prosperity Together," Bellingham lists three aspects of how this mutual development agenda is being operationalized. Firstly, cooperation with governments and enterprises has been intensified in order to profit from "the trade and investment opportunities on offer."[79] Secondly, enhanced intra-African trade has been supported by the UK government. And, thirdly, the "removing of barriers to Africa's goods in global markets" is being promoted.[80] In practice, the discourse supports several measures that were introduced to operationalize the new interest in African resources and growth markets, such as the Africa Free Trade initiative (AFTi[81]), the proactively pursued commercial diplomacy in the form of high level forums and visits, the channeling of aid funding through the Foreign Office (FCO), the alignment of DFID programs with FCO trade and investment objectives using, for instance, global challenge funds, and the generally close cooperation between the government and private sector.

Table 7-1 – Key Documents Outlining the UK's Development in Relation to UK in Africa (selected)[82]

Speeches
2010 – "Britain's Foreign Policy in a Networked World," William Hague (FCO)
2010 – "UK and Africa: Delivering Prosperity Together," Henry Bellingham (Minister for Africa)
2011 – "The UK Prosperity Agenda—growth, open markets and good governance," Henry Bellingham
Government (White) Papers
1997 – White paper, "Eliminating World Poverty: A Challenge for the 21st Century," DFID
2000 – White paper, "Eliminating World Poverty: Making Globalisation Work for the Poor," DFID

---

79 | Bellingham (2010).
80 | Bellingham (2010).
81 | BIS (2012), 8.
82 | The references for the documents listed are as follows: Hague (2010); Bellingham (2010); Bellingham (2011); BIS (2011a); FCO (2011b); HM Treasury and BIS (2011); UK Department of Trade and Investment (UKTI) (2011); DTI (2004); UK Department of Energy & Climate Change (DECC) (2007); DFID (2000); DFID (1997); HM Government (2010); FCO (2011a); BIS (2011c); RFA (2008); DECC (2006); Department for Environment, Food and Rural Affairs (DEFRA) (2008); RTFO (2007); Commission for Africa (2005); Commission for Africa (2010).

2004 – White paper, "Making Globalization a Force for Good," DTI
2007 – White paper, "Meeting the Energy Challenge," DECC
2010 – Strategy paper, "A Strong Britain in an age of Uncertainty: The National Security Strategy," HM Government
2011 – White paper "Trade and Investment for Growth," BIS
2011 – Strategy paper, "A Charter for Business," FCO
2011 – Strategy paper, "The Plan for Growth," HM Treasury and BIS
2011 – Strategy paper, "Britain open for business," UKTI
2011 – Strategy paper, "FCO: Business Plan 2011-2015," FCO

Reports and policy

2011 – Report, "International Trade & Investment: The Economic Rationale for Government Support," BIS
2008 – Report, "Ensuring the UK's Food Security in a Changing World," DEFRA
2008 – Policy, "Climate Change Act 2008, Charter 27"
2008 – Report, "The Gallagher Review of the indirect effects of biofuels production," RFA
2007 – Legislation, "The Renewable Transport Fuel Obligation Order (RTFO) 2007"
2006 – Report, "The Energy Challenge: Energy Review Report 2006," DECC

International Policy

1997 – International Agreement, "Kyoto Protocol," UNFCCC
2003, 2007, 2009 – Policy, EU Renewable Energy Directives
2005 – Report, "Our Common Interest," Commission for Africa
2010 – Report, " Still Our Common Interest," Commission for Africa

Summary

The UK's changing development rhetoric, which has moved from humanitarianism to mutual development, as well as its renewed interest in the African continent, correlates with the contemporary challenges that the country is facing. These include prolonged economic recession, the financial crisis, and the failure of the financialization-led growth model—embraced by British governments since the Thatcher era—to generate sufficient jobs, growth, and revenues (for more details, see also Section 4 on political economy). Most striking is the similarity of the Chinese and British guiding ideologies—the mutual development rhetoric applied in British policy documents might have been influenced by the rise of the BRICS and the popular discourse characteristic of South-South Cooperation.[83]

---

83 | Goetz (2018) (forthcoming).

At the same time, the empirical evidence on the timelines of British land-consuming FDI projects emphasizes that the framing of UK-Africa relations as mutual development opportunity and national security measure is the result of the government jumping on the corporate trend of investing in African economies, a trend that has been gaining momentum since 2000. Therefore, the relatively recent promotion of British land-consuming FDI in SSA by the UK government has to be seen in the broader effort to address the economic recession that the country has been suffering from since 2007/2008. Many investors who saw Africa as a new growth region where novel markets could be won, and extraordinary profits and returns on investments earned, moved their business focus towards African economies long before the 2008 crisis became an additional driver to look for profitable options overseas. However, the crisis does seem to have instigated actors from the public sector to redirect development finance, expand commercial diplomacy, and introduce a range of mechanisms to support this trend as part of a national recovery approach.

Importantly, the change in UK-Africa relations that is reflected in the application of a "grand strategy" of business-government cooperation for economic development and the strengthening of explicitly identified British stronghold industries (in the form of advanced manufacturing, life sciences, creative industries, green energy, and non-financial business services) does not only apply to international economic relations.[84] Instead, the core characteristic of the close cooperation and coordination between public and private actors is a reflection of the fundamental domestic reforms that have been occurring over the past two decades. These are characterized by the ongoing privatization of public services, which has led to the state funded operation of public services by private actors—under the assumption that this will promote private sector growth while enhancing efficiency.

---

84 | HM Treasury and BIS (2011), 4.

4. POLITICAL ECONOMY

> As a country that has a proud and successful history of trading and benefiting from investment and that sees these factors vital to our prospects for growth, the UK offers a good case for how, in practice, trade and investment drive growth.
> (Department for Business, Innovation and Skills 2011[85])

While the UK continues to be portrayed as having the ideal type of liberal economy,[86] particularly against the European background of so-called coordinated continental economies, this simplified typology ignores the changes that have taken place since the 1980s, such as the increase in public regulation during the New Public Management era in the 1990s,[87] the adoption of a "grand strategy" approach towards trade and investment under Conservative rule (since 2011), and the changing quality of (foreign) economic policy and state-market relations.

This section will focus on two aspects of British political economy, namely state-market relations in the context of financialization[88] and the transformation of the political economic paradigm. It will show that both are relevant for a meaningful understanding of what is occurring with regard to land-consuming FDI. The major arguments emerging from the findings are as follows: firstly, even though the financial sector (aka "the City") features prominently in overseas investments, it would be wrong to argue that these investments are primarily driven by it. Instead, there is an overlap of interests and "intellectual capture" across different actor groups in the public and private sectors. Secondly, these investments are embedded in broader economic restructuring endeavors, such as reforms that aim at the delivery of public services by private actors and foreign economic policies that focus on strengthening the capacity of British producers to retain influence in international political and economic governance while rebalancing the economy. However, in the meantime, thirdly, the economy remains highly dysfunctional in view of industry finance, as has been highlighted by biofuel investments in SSA.

---

85 | BIS (2011a), 17.
86 | Hall and Soskice (2001).
87 | Hood et al. (1999).
88 | This term refers to a shift of power from industry capitalism to finance capitalism.

The City, Once Again?—State-Market Relations in the Context of Financialization

The empirical evidence on industrial finance (presented in the previous chapter), together with the rising number of investment funds "seeking alpha," has highlighted the prominent role of the financial sector in British land-consuming investments in SSA. Based on this evidence and the liberal characterization of the UK economy, it would be rather easy to conclude that, similar to claims about the British Empire and 'gentlemanly' capitalism in the 19th century, the financial sector in London is once again—under "free market" conditions—the primary driver of these investments. However, state-market relations in general, and issues pertaining to finance and industrial development in particular, are far more complex than the liberal characterization would suggest—even under conditions of financialization. Also, the national context continues to influence the perceptions of and options available to financial investors, as in those cases where the capital that is exported via London to Sub-Saharan countries has its origins outside of the UK.

In fact, the empirical evidence about British investments in SSA has emphasized that there are multiple actors and mechanisms at play, extending beyond stock markets and private enterprises, such as public policy-induced markets in the renewables sector, public finance through the CDC Group, and/or investment-related aid programs. Moreover, the old narrative, according to which the financial sector (alias "the City") was the sole driver behind the colonial expansion, has long been undermined by subsequent historical research.[89] Next, I will highlight relevant developments that have occurred in the financial and state sectors since the 1980s, both with regard to actor constitution and economic orientation, and in view of related changes in state-market relations.

While the financial sector plays a key role in the British economy, it is important to note that the City's actor composition and business culture has been altered significantly since the "Big Bang" stock exchange reforms in the mid-1980s—in the sense that it has been globalized. These reforms have opened the investment banking sector to foreign competitors, resulting in the

---

89 | Great Britain's political economy of decision making was fairly complex at the end of the 19th century, when "fractions between free marketers and interventionists ran across business and political actors," and the bias towards financial interests in public policy was the outcome of many factors, such as personal ties, profit seeking, and/or regime stability. In the medium term, overseas expansion facilitated the continuation of elite strata and the maintenance of a high degree of social inequality (characterized by low domestic demand), in spite of the profound changes in the economic and political systems that emerged as a consequence of the first Industrial Revolution. Cain and Hopkins (1987), 199-200; and Halperin (2005).

dramatic decline of investment banks under British ownership and the related "death of gentlemanly capitalism."[90] The latter has been described by Augar as the demise of a business culture characterized by strong relational ties and aristocratic cultural traits.[91] In its place, a global financial business elite has emerged.[92] The corresponding internationalization of London's financial sector is well reflected in the British biofuel investments in SSA, where lead actors have personal linkages with US investment banks, sometimes being former high level employees. For example, Susan Payne and David Murrin, who launched the Emergent Asset Fund in 1997, had worked as traders at JP Morgan and Goldman Sachs.[93] Also, Bim Hundal, founder of Lion's Head Global Partners, a London-based investment banking group which took over the operations of Sun Biofuels in Tanzania in 2011, previously worked for over 17 years at Goldman Sachs, running the capital markets business for Central Europe, Russia, the Middle East, and Africa.[94]

At the same time, the state and its political economy paradigm have transformed considerably, moving from "embedded liberalism" to an "embedded financial orthodoxy"[95] and "free market" ideology during the Thatcher era in the 1980s. This shift has been characterized by deregulation, a hands-off approach, and an arm's length industrial policy. In practice, this paradigm modification has had far-reaching consequences for the state's relations with the financial sector and the society, as well as with regard to industry development. Since these developments partially explain how British land-consuming FDI occurs, the following paragraphs will introduce them by focusing on three aspects, namely transformations of the state, industrial development, and societal implications.

Firstly, the state has grown ever more dependent on the City's overseas earnings as a result of this paradigmatic shift.[96] In fact, financial sector OFDI

---

90 | See Augar (2001) for a description of the demise of the *British* banking system since the late 1980s.
91 | Augar (2001), 6.
92 | Augar (2001), 6-7. Accordingly, the reasons for this failure were multiple: British banks did not have the level of experience and scale of their US counterparts; the hands-off approach under Thatcher led to "the existence of a vacuum where the authorities should have been;" and the business culture itself that had largely remained unchanged since the 1950s and revealed traits of new aristocracy that "inhibited good management." Augar (2001), 320.
93 | Oakland Institute (2011a).
94 | Lion's Head Global Partners (n.d.).
95 | Cerny and Evans (2004), 53.
96 | Augar (2006), 181.

earnings "kept the trade account in reasonable balance."[97] While the trade in the goods account had deteriorated over time, its last net surplus being recorded in 1980-1982, the UK's trade in (financial) services has largely been in surplus since the mid-1960s.[98] Contributing factors for this growing dependency of the state on the financial sector are structural and personal, comprising, for instance, rising public debt due to the tax cuts during the Thatcher era; personal ties and "intellectual capture";[99] the need for electoral funding of political parties and the fact that the financial sector has made significant contributions to the acting government's Conservative party; and the phenomenon of revolving doors.[100]

Secondly, the financialization of the British political economy since the 1980s has impacted the country's industrial development, especially by aggravating the negative deindustrialization path[101] that had set in post-WWII.[102] While the collapse of the manufacturing sector during the late 1970s was strongly related to the oil crisis, the financialization of the economy and the adoption of the "free-market ideal based on neo-classical political economy" slowed reinvestments by the private sector necessary to modernize the UK's industrial base.[103] Specifically, four aspects contributed to this effect, which is best described by the rise of market control over organizational control. On the one hand, British companies had hardly established organizational control models at the time of liberalization. On the other hand, the accounting practices and corporate law made it more unlikely for organizational reforms to occur, as they treated investments in labor, as well as returns on labor, as expenses, making it—from a market control perspective—undesirable to invest in these factors of production and thereby enhance productivity and foster innovation. In addition, the framing of market control as "shareholder value" prevented

---

97 | BIS (2010), 15.

98 | BIS (2010), 15.

99 | The degree to which governments embraced the financial sector as source of prosperity is reflected by a speech made by (then) chancellor Gordon Brown at the annual Mansion House Dinner in 2004, in which he praised the City's innovative capacity to adopt to changes in the international economy (e.g., derivatives), and referred to it as a role model for British industry at a time of globalization. See Brown (2004).

100 | See Augar (2006), 180-186.

101 | Negative deindustrialization means that the decline in industry production was not the result of upgrading of economic production or economic re-orientation, but primarily the result of companies going into administration.

102 | Specifically, the traditional separation of finance and industry in the UK accelerated the decline of the industrial sector. See Lazonick and O'Sullivan (1997). Also see HM Treasury and BIS (2011) for a critical assessment of this development path.

103 | The New Political Economy Network (2010), 14, 11, 12.

changes towards greater organizational control within the company structures, as these would negatively impact the "principal."[104] Finally, the generous (financial) rewards received by the top managers of industrial companies applying market control strategies advanced the adoption of market control strategies.[105] In view of British land-consuming FDI in SSA, biofuel projects, such as the SBF, highlight a key difficulty presented by this political economy, namely the absence of patient capital and lagging reinvestment.

Thirdly, the process of financialization has also produced multiple long-term effects with regard to state-society relations, both domestically and internationally. As a result of an ongoing domestic reform process, public services under the new public management approach became increasingly commodified and framed as commercial contracts.[106] This process led to a high degree of interconnectedness between private and public actors in the provision of public services that is characteristic of the UK's political economy today. In the context of British land-consuming FDI, this trend is highlighted by the shift of public development finance and diplomacy to match corporate interest in the African continent.

At the same time, this process of publicly-funded privatization also led to the gradual integration of citizens into financial markets with their volatile pressures, increasingly linking the realization of British workers' social security rights with the livelihoods of people in other countries. In fact, the history of pension funds depicts the ensuing connection of workers and people through financial markets, where the prosperity of some might be founded on the impoverishment of others through land-consuming investments that result in forced disappropriation and/or low workers' welfare. Pension funds and other institutional investors began to divest from fixed-interest securities, searching instead for more profitable investments. Some have started to explore investments in commodities and farmland, though not necessarily in SSA. For

---

104 | Lazonick and O'Sullivan (1997, 29) have highlighted the importance of this "shareholder" ideology in preventing change: "The ideology that the 'shareholder' is the 'principal' of the industrial corporation helps to ensure that such organizational transformations will not take place. This ideology places a premium on economic performance that reaps the benefits of prior investments in productive capabilities while ignoring the new investments in organizational learning that can potentially generate greater returns for more people in the future."
105 | Lazonick and O'Sullivan (1997), 27.
106 | The New Political Economy Network (2010), 13-14. Accordingly, "[p]ublic services were turned into quasi-markets governed by cost efficiency and targets. Commercial values all but supplanted the ethos of public service. [...] A new kind of consumer compact between individual and the market began to replace the old social welfare contract."

instance, BT Pension Scheme, a large UK pension fund, stated its intent in 2012 to replace its commodity future investments with farmland investments in the near future.[107] These actors have prominent supporters, such as Sir Bob Geldof, who allegedly "warn[s] UK pension funds they are missing out on the 'last great investment opportunity left' by not placing money in Africa."[108]

The Transformation of the Political Economy Paradigm

The resulting dominance of the financial sector within the UK economy is highlighted by the sectoral distribution of British OFDI in SSA (see introduction).[109] At the height of the "embedded financial orthodoxy," Gordon Brown praised the achievements of the financial sector as an extraordinary contribution to the UK's prosperity and economic position in the globalized world. Accordingly, the fact that over 40% of the world's foreign equities are transacted in London was perceived as proof of the rise of "an era that history will record as the beginning of a new golden age for the City of London" and that will benefit the UK at large.[110]

However, these hopes for a financialization- and service-led solution to the economic development challenges posed to the UK by deindustrialization and a globalized economy were unrealistic—and soon to be shattered. Instead, the financial crisis and the ensuing Eurozone crisis aggravated problems that had been accumulating. Key examples are the rising unemployment (over 8% till 2009),[111] unsustainable and rising wealth inequality,[112] and mounting private sector debt.[113] Regarding the latter, it is important to note that part of the rising private sector debt was escalating personal debt whose share of disposable income increased from 45 per cent to 160 per cent between the 1980s and 2007.[114] While other European countries managed to recover from the financial crash, at least partially, Britain, with its reliance on the financial sector experienced a prolonged economic recession up until 2014. At the same time, growing public debt and fear over international marginalization made the development approach seem unsustainable.

---

107 | Bow (13 March 2012). It remains unclear whether this actually happened—according to the latest BT Pension Scheme report (2013), it did not.
108 | Silver Street Capital (20 June 2010), quoting an article in the *Financial Times*.
109 | US Central Intelligence Agency (2014).
110 | See Brown (2002).
111 | TradingEconomics.com (2014).
112 | See Hills et al. (2010); and The Equality Trust (2012).
113 | The New Political Economy Network (2010), 10.
114 | The New Political Economy Network (2010), 25.

Consequently, the detrimental impact of the financialization-led growth model pursued over the last decades has been identified in the then acting government's Plan for Growth (2011-2015):

This Plan for Growth is an urgent call for action.

Britain has lost ground in the world's economy, and needs to catch up.

If we do not act now, jobs will be lost, our country will become poorer and we will find it difficult to afford the public services we all want. If we do not wake up to the world around us, our standard of living will fall, not rise. In the last decade other nations have worked hard to make their economies more competitive. They have reduced their business tax rates, removed barriers to enterprise, invested in their infrastructure, improved their education systems, reformed welfare and increased their exports.

Sadly the reverse has happened in Britain over the last ten years. The UK economy stopped saving, investing and exporting and instead turned to a model of growth that failed. It resulted in rising levels of debt, over-leveraged banks, an unsustainable property boom, and a budget deficit that was forecast to be the largest of any of the world's twenty leading economies. Continuously rising but unaffordable government spending disguised the fact that it was an unsustainable economic boom, with the economy becoming steadily more unbalanced, less competitive and less prepared to meet the challenges of the future.[115]

The ongoing transition towards a new political economy paradigm has been promoted under the heading of "rebalancing the economy"[116] and guided by the FCO. The current Conservative government aims to address the legacy of deindustrialization through reindustrialization in the form of advanced manufacturing projects:

We want to remain the world's leading centre for financial services, yes; but we should determine to become a world-leader in, for example, advanced manufacturing, life sciences, creative industries, green energy and non-financial business services.[117]

Aside from financial services, telecommunications technology, clean tech and low-carbon goods and services, business to business services (excluding finance), biotech and pharma, energy and utilities, retail, oil, and gas are among the key sectors that have been identified as contributors to UK economic

---

115 | HM Treasury and BIS (2011), 3.
116 | BIS, FCO, UK Trade and Investment (2012).
117 | HM Treasury and BIS (2011), 3.

growth.[118] In practice, this new development approach, implemented under the current government's "Plan for Growth" (2011-2015), focuses on private sector growth through export promotion, access to growth markets, high-quality IFDI attraction, and OFDI advancement. For its operationalization, the FCO and UK TI have begun to cooperate across government agencies and work closely with industry, the government has stepped up its commercial diplomacy in Africa, and new aid programs have been created that call for public-private partnerships in their realization, thereby opening up publicly-funded business opportunities for British companies overseas.

The relatively open economy, with a deregulated capital market and a great dependency on foreign inputs, leaves the government with only limited options at its disposal to moderate the negative side effects of its economy's global exposure and financialization. In this regard, reindustrialization as an approach to rebuilding the economy seems to be among the few measures remaining that would not prompt fears of retaliatory action from countries and actors that the UK has come to rely on.

Summary

The assessment of state-market relations highlights that simply pointing to the financial sector to explain why land-consuming investments occur does not tell the whole story. One must also take into account the "embedded financial orthodoxy" that has informed British economic policies and trajectories since the 1980s; the intellectual capture of the public sector agents who have prepared the ground for the dominance of "the City" and the neglect of the industrial sector; the increasing dependence of public and private sector actors on financial markets in their operations; and, more recently, the adoption of a strategy to strengthen industry through better coordination of government agencies and their cooperation with the private sector.

Core traits of the British political economy explain certain characteristics of land-consuming OFDI in SSA. Firstly, the great number of financial investors involved in these investments has been highlighted. The material presented above shows that this situation has developed for multiple reasons. Clearly, some investors have begun investing in African economies and agricultural projects as part of their strategy to "seek alpha" at a time of financial crisis back home. Others, however, are involved primarily as providers of industry finance. In fact, most of the early-stage companies that invested in biofuel projects had to turn to the AIM stock exchange for funding. In this context, the short-term focus of the financial investors who are financing such operations reflects the dysfunctional nature of the existing structures for industry finance, specifically

---

118 | Ernst & Young (2011b), 18 (Graph 19).

the lack of patient capital. For example, the case of the SBF highlights that financial investors withdraw their investments after a period of time that does not match the long maturation time of Jatropha plantations, contributing to the failure of the project.

Secondly, following the financial crisis, British land-consuming OFDI has taken place in the context of a rise in commercial diplomacy and a reorientation of existing UK development finance programs. Take, for example, the strategic modification that occurred in the CDC Group's investment strategy. The increasing presence of public actors and institutions in private British OFDI projects in SSA is related to the government's renewed interest in industrial policy and the rebalancing of the UK's economy.

5. Development Context

The current government promotes OFDI as a way to "rebalance the economy"[119] and maintain the UK's influential international status as a major investor and trading country. At the same time, the UK has a long investor legacy, and a promotional OFDI policy stance has been evident since the 1970s. Therefore, it is not surprising that in the case of British land-consuming FDI projects in African countries, national and foreign factors have played crucial roles in the interest formation of investors, such as the IFDI attraction programs of recipient countries; the international and European climate regime and the related creation of a market for biofuels; and the Eurozone crisis that led to a search for new growth markets. Importantly, though, it was the private sector that pioneered the UK's reorientation towards the African continent. Due to the liberal economic context of the home country, global markets and overseas developments are key parameters shaping corporate portfolios. In the context of British OFDI in Africa, it is the perception of the continent as a new growth region that has been influential.

From the perspective of the home country's development context, the empirical evidence that emerges from official documentation, policies, and speeches suggests that overseas investments in SSA are explicitly linked to particular national interests and development ambitions of individual or collective actors. In addition to concerns about the home country's energy security and CO_2 emission targets, as well as related policy regimes that explain the high number of biofuel investments by early-stage companies, these investments are also part of the search for (more) profitable investment outlets by the financial sector. More recently, these investments have become part of the proactive trade and investment agenda of the current UK government (since 2011)—a

---

119 | See, for instance, BIS/FCO/UK Trade and Investment (2012).

development that contrasts starkly with the "embedded financial orthodoxy," "free market" ideology, and related development strategies pursued since the 1980s. It seems remarkable that OFDI in Africa today is part of a larger development ambition to both rehabilitate the country's crisis-stricken state budget and economy through reindustrialization and secure its international position by promoting investment in productive assets and related operations, such as export promotion and overseas expansion. Yet, the financial sector clearly remains an important component of the British economy, and the focus on reindustrialization is seen as a necessary complement to address the development challenges yielded by the financialization-led growth model over time.

In fact, the development model that has been pursued since the 1980s, with its focus on the financial sector and "free market" ideology, has come at a high cost in view of economic and social development, and since the financial crisis in 2008, the volatility of state revenues and incidents of social unrest have provided an additional incentive to modify the emphasis of the existing development model.[120] Among the most pressing problems of the service-oriented development trajectory is the neglect of productive industry. For decades, the productive sector only contributed a small share of the country's GDP, and the UK's share in the international trade of manufactured goods has been declining. Since 2000, the rise of, and heightened competition from, emerging countries has aggravated the problems confronting the British manufacturing industry and the government.

On a national level, this non-productive development trajectory has resulted in a vicious cycle of lagging investment in the industrial base at home, declining exports and increasing imports (machinery and transport equipment), deteriorating terms of trade, and a growing dependence on the financial sector for jobs, growth, and revenues.[121] This situation is further aggravated by the country's increasing dependence on external resources (energy and food), which is unsustainable, especially during times of high and/or very volatile commodity prices.[122] Socially, the country has recently faced rising unemployment—repeatedly over 8% between 2009 and 2012;[123] rising wealth and economic opportu-

---

120 | For a discussion of the UK's financialization-driven development trajectory, also see Lapavitsas (2014).
121 | Te Velde and Calì (2006), 8.
122 | In 2005, the UK, the EU's largest energy producer and exporter (e.g., natural gas and oil), became a net importer of energy due to its declining oil and natural gas reserves. See US Energy Information Administration (2013) and Kuzemko (2010). The UK is also a net food-importing country, raising concerns during the food price crisis in 2007/2008. In 2008, the UK imported 40% of its food needs. See Cabinet Office (2008), i-x.
123 | TradingEconomics.com (2014).

nity inequality, which was identified as a core driver of the 2011 London riots;[124] and mounting private sector debt, partly due to a personal debt load whose share of the disposable income rose to 160% in 2007 (compared to 45% in 1980).[125] The global economic slowdown also aggravated the mounting public debt. Since the financial recession began, the national debt has risen to 76.6% of GDP (January 2014), without accounting for the financial sector interventions.[126]

Summary

British land-consuming FDI has become part of the transformation of industrial policy towards reindustrialization. This is an official strategy to moderate unemployment; provide decent wages; ease social tensions; and increase state revenue while improving international accounts through the increased export of advanced manufacturing goods, thereby retaining the country's international economic standing. In the context of the financial crisis, the strengthening of high-tech manufacturing in particular sectors is supposed to provide the UK with the competitive advantage needed to successfully participate and compete in international markets.

However, tight government budgets and a dysfunctional industry finance system pose serious hurdles to operationalizing the then acting (Cameron) government's attempt to strengthen the secondary sector.[127] Moreover, it would be unrealistic to assume that the core traits of the country's political economy have changed since the crisis. Although the government has begun to promote reindustrialization, the key characteristics that run across all of the UK government parties, such as the credo of marketization and privatization, continue to prevail. Instead, the "grand strategy" approach towards OFDI promotion and reindustrialization shall mitigate the high costs of the "cosmopolitan economy," which include unemployment, private debt, rising wealth inequality and increasing import dependency, and declining state revenues. Also, the strategy is said to ensure the favorable position of the UK in world politics—allowing the country to "punch above its weight" despite changes in the international political and economic landscape.[128]

---

124 | The Equality Trust (2012). In 2010, a national survey on inequality revealed that the UK suffers from high levels of systematic inequality (within and across social groups) of income and opportunity. See Hills et al. (2010), 386.
125 | The New Political Economy Network (2010), 25, 10.
126 | Watt (7 June 2010).
127 | Theodora.com (31 January 2014).
128 | For a detailed discussion of the UK's attempts to position itself in a changing world, see M. Harvey (2011).

At the same time, international incentives have played a strong role in spurring contemporary land-consuming FDI. It is important to recall that the current government jumped on the corporate bandwagon rather late. In fact, British-African trade and investment relations have increased since 2000, when Africa was increasingly framed as a new growth region by the British private sector. Only after the financial crisis in 2007/2008 did the government adopt this perception as a way to address the country's prolonged economic recession. Significant events that influenced private decision making regarding the utility of land-consuming OFDI in SSA include economic reforms in the host countries (e.g., divestiture programs) and the emergence of a climate regime after Kyoto (1997).

Whether the foreign economic policy approach will be successful remains to be seen. However, at this point in time (2016), there is reason for doubt. On the one hand, a quote by the former Minister for Africa, Henry Bellingham, reflects the assumption that British relations with African economies will continue to be characterized by their asymmetry, sustaining prosperity on the one side while mitigating "abject poverty" on the other: "[o]pen markets offer the only realistic hope of pulling billions of people in developing countries out of abject poverty, while sustaining prosperity in the industrialized world."[129] This would be disadvantageous for the host countries.

At the same time, the empirical evidence reveals the reality that many projects, particularly in the 'clean' energy sector, witnessed dramatic wealth destruction over time and never actually realized their business goals. Even putting these operational challenges aside, alternative energy (i.e. first-generation biofuels) did not live up to its socioeconomic and environmental promises.[130] Moreover, the short-term focus on value creation by financial investors collided with the long-term maturation timelines of the projects "on the ground." Further investigation would be needed to identify the extent to which capital exports made during the Eurozone and financial crises are, in effect, manifestations of capital flight. According to one interview from a British corporate actor, the case of Cyprus, where savings above Euro 100.000 were taxed by a compulsory capital levy to moderate state debts, has led to capital owners deliberating on relocating their savings out of fear that something similar might take place in other European countries in the medium term. In this case, then, capital exports would aggravate the UK's domestic problems, such as lagging investments, rather than addressing them. Finally, historical evidence on the implications of OFDI for home country development underlines the high cost that such a capital export strategy might entail due to the

---

129 | Bellingham (2010).
130 | Renewable Fuels Agency (2008), 8.

often-inverse relationship of capital exports and domestic job creation; and/or lagging reinvestment in industry back home.

6. Conclusion

Overall, this case study has highlighted a great variety of factors at play in British land-consuming OFDI (from 2000 until 2015). The key argument that has been put forward is that these investments are part of multiple strategies to profit from the economic reforms and rapidly growing consumer markets in the host countries, to advance biofuels investments in the context of international and domestic energy and climate policies, and/or to "seek alpha" through alternative investments in the primary sector in Africa at a time of the financial crisis and economic stagnation back home. Increasingly, land-consuming OFDI to Sub-Saharan Africa is also part of a (long-term) political strategy to economic recovery and international political power through rising exports and industrial activity. Importantly, the private sector perceived Africa as a new growth region as early as 2000. Only later did the government jump on the corporate trend in an attempt to revive the economy.

Specifically, British OFDI in SSA is reflective both of the country's long investor legacy and the government's promotional policy stance towards OFDI since the 1970s; as well as the domestic challenges the country has been facing recently, such as the rising energy insecurity and the socioeconomic costs of the non-productive development model. British companies are experienced at factoring international incentive structures into their business operations; in contrast, Chinese companies are just beginning to globalize their operations. This is clearly reflected by the fact that host country and international reforms played an important role in corporate decision making, in addition to home country developments. More recently, the Conservative government (under David Cameron) in the UK explicitly (re)aligned OFDI in Africa with its foreign policy interests, namely by sustaining the country's favorable international economic and political presence at a time of domestic crises and global re-ordering. As a result, OFDI in Africa has become part of ODA-funded business opportunities; has been backed by commercial diplomacy; and has been promoted by a rhetoric that no longer frames the continent as a place ridden by humanitarian crises, but as a region of great opportunity and hope.

Consequently, these investments happen in the context of multiple country-specific developments that can be divided between pre-crisis and post-crisis dynamics. Pre-crisis dynamics include, for instance, economic liberalization in host and investor countries since the 1980s, as well as the introduction of domestic targets for biofuels to meet CO_2 emission targets and strengthen energy security. Post-crisis dynamics include the increasing severity of socioeconomic problems in the financial-sector-dependent domestic economy; the changing landscape at the international level, where the rise of new economic powers has led to increasing competition over political influence, economic opportunities, and access to resources; and the development of a fear among the British political elite which recognizes that the UK has an exceptional position in world politics relative to its actual geographical size, and that, accordingly, the country might lose its status as a great power in the future. At the same time, financial actors in the UK's deregulated capital markets have been drawn to African growth economies and the "real asset" sector at a time of economic crisis, when private equity investments are no longer profitable and growth at home is stagnant. In addition, the growing availability of multilateral finance mechanisms and development programs—particularly in the area of renewable energy, food security, and carbon credits—seems to have impacted investor choices.

These findings on how British land-consuming FDI occurs underline the broader argument that as in the case of liberal economies, these investments are not the outcome of so-called "free markets," but that the country's legacy, development trajectory and ambitions, political economy, guiding ideology, and international context matter. The investments around the year 2000 were related to host country reforms, largely conducted by investors with long histories in the host economies, often dating back to the late 19th century. Another cluster of investments reflects the emerging climate regulations and has involved a high number of early stage companies trying to profit from the newly created markets. Once the financial crisis hit, financial investors in search of extraordinary returns at a time of economic recession became involved in the investment projects. At the same time, the then acting government in the UK adopted a proactive approach, intensifying commercial diplomacy with African countries and introducing bilateral investment forums in the French and Chinese model, though on an ad hoc basis. Still, ODA programs have been aligned with foreign policy goals, and they place special emphasis on supporting private companies investing overseas. In this context, the official rhetoric with regards to African countries has changed significantly—they are now described as markets of opportunity rather than areas in need of humanitarian intervention.

Moreover, it has become clear that the importance of financial actors and the AIM stock exchange in these operations does not verify the assumption that these investments are largely driven by the financial sector. Instead, it reflects the intellectual capture and overlap of public and private-sector actors characteristic of the UK's political economy, and refers back to the financialization-led development trajectory pursued since the 1980s. Consequently, and promoted by public policy, financial actors play a major role in the British economy and land-consuming OFDI, both as direct investors as well as the main source of industry finance. The problems associated with this constellation have been visible in British OFDI projects, namely in the difficulty of identifying who is actually involved in a project due to the constant changes in shareholding and the lack of patient capital. The latter is something that institutional development finance (the CDC) and DFID-directed aid programs are intended to address. Similarly, the sectoral composition of British land-consuming OFDI reflects the country's investor legacy. The investments are directed to a few countries, and they primarily head towards the resources and services sectors. Perhaps unsurprisingly, this sectoral composition resembles the economic constitution of the home country, which is characterized by high external resource dependency and a strong services sector.

Finally, this case study has shown that British OFDI involves a wide range of interests from the very diverse private sector. Many of these actors share the perception of Africa as a new growth region. Consequently, we see investment funds from the public and private sector that try to profit from this growth dynamic at a time of economic recession back home. Others respond to public policy-induced markets. Early-stage companies, for instance, invest in the production of biofuels in African countries, which continue to be framed as "land-abundant," in spite of the ongoing land crisis. At the same time, related industries support these investments, such as actors from the aviation sector that seek access to cheap fossil fuel alternatives, and try to cooperate with biofuels companies through offtake agreements. What is surprising is the large numbers of inexperienced investors that engage in land-consuming OFDI, often with very unrealistic expectations and/or business models in place – a fact that also explains the high number of failed projects. From an official perspective, these investments are promoted as a way to strengthen economic recovery through increases in exports and sustained access to cheap resources. Moreover, geopolitical considerations have entered the debate, reflecting realist assumptions. Accordingly, an intensified economic presence is useful to sustain the country's influence at the international level at a time of global restructuring.

Similar to the Chinese case, and against the background of the diverse range of actors and interests at play, this book's description of British OFDI shows that what makes these investments *British* is the specific combination of industrial set-up, development trajectory, contingent events, ideology, and political economy in and over time.

More broadly, reflecting on the role of land-consuming OFDI from a home country perspective, the previous assessment stresses that these investments are part of a trend among private sector actors that has gained speed in the context of financial crises in the UK and the Eurozone, namely to profit from overseas growth markets and/or to respond to incentives provided by host country reforms or the domestic/international climate regime. More recently, the investments have become part of the government's attempt to support these corporate interests. The deeper context is the failure of the UK's financialization-led development path to deliver sufficient jobs, revenue, and other aspects of economic development. Against this background, the renewed expansion of the productive industry at home and abroad is part of a broader strategy and "prosperity agenda" that promises to deliver security while advancing domestic prosperity and growth:

The National Security Strategy of the United Kingdom is: to use all our national capabilities to build Britain's prosperity, extend our nation's influence in the world and strengthen our security. The networks we use to build our prosperity we will also use to build our security.[131]

The success of British land-consuming investment projects and the new foreign policy they are part of is not at all clear, however. The high project failure rate, regular involvement of fraudulent actors, and danger of capital flight all point at the challenges confronting these investments. Moreover, government efforts have so far not addressed the dysfunctional features of the home country political economy, such as the lack of patient capital or the effects of financialization on the state and society (as of 2016).

---

131 | HM Government (2010), 9.

Table 7-2 – Brief Review of the Home Country Context and British OFDI in SSA

Category	Home country Context	UK OFDI in SSA
Development context	Since the 1980s, the country has pursued a financialization-led development trajectory and neglected its productive sector, resulting in deteriorating terms of trade, a decline in British manufacturing, and high social and economic costs, particularly at a time of financial crisis, and in the context of heightened international competition (e.g., BRICS). Also, the country is a net importer of food and energy and confronted with the challenge of meeting its CO2 emission targets under the climate regime.	The unsustainable development trajectory has resulted in attempts to address related problems and reindustrialize. As a consequence, the British government has been proactively involved in land-consuming OFDI in SSA since 2010/2011. The outcomes of this involvement have to been seen yet. Moreover, the development trajectory, with its neglect of the industrial sector, and the investor legacy, with its focus on resources, explain the predominance of investments in resources and (financial) services (and fewer investments in manufacturing) characteristic of UK OFDI in SSA. At the same time, new actors (e.g., funds, early-stage companies) are investing in land for agricultural production.
Home Country Measures	The UK as a long-term liberal economy has had a promotional policy stance towards OFDI since its accession to the EU in the 1970s, as well as an elaborate HCM framework. Recently, OFDI has become a part of the country's foreign policy.	OFDI and trade to Africa as a new growth region is proactively promoted by newly introduced instruments, such as aid-funded business opportunities facilitated by DFID; new trade policy initiatives; and commercial diplomacy.
Guiding Ideologies	OFDI is embedded in a rhetoric which argues that related private sector-led growth is important for prosperity and national security and necessary for "rebalancing the economy."	In the particular case of Africa, the guiding ideology has shifted. It now links OFDI in Africa with national economic interests, formerly a taboo (after decolonization); rhetoric of mutual benefit has been adopted.

Investor Legacy	As a former empire and long-term investor in African economies, the UK is still a dominant investor country today.	This investor legacy is also highlighted by the uneven investment structure in terms of sectors (e.g., resources, financial services) and countries.
Political Economy	Since the 1980s, the political economy has been characterized by an "embedded financial orthodoxy" that only now is being challenged. Core traits are the overlap of public sector and financial sector interests through intellectual capture and personal affinity and the financialization of society.	The dominance of the financial sector in the British political economy is reflected in the prominent role of financial actors in the investments (in the form of finance provision and direct investments). More recently, public actors have become involved (e.g., the CDC), jumping on the corporate bandwagon. Most remarkable is the high number of early-stage companies responding to energy and climate policies.
Events	Several incentives have influenced investor choices: host country reforms; climate regime and energy policies; and the financial crisis.	These events explain different actors involved in land-consuming OFDI, namely old companies exploiting opportunities in host countries; new companies trying to profit from the novel climate and energy regime; and financial actors in a post-crisis search for "alpha."

Chapter 8: Land Grabbing and Home Country Development
Conclusion and Outlook

This project has sought to provide a more accurate version of the reasons for and the impact of "land grabbing" from a home country perspective. Consequently, it has assessed the empirical characteristics of Chinese and British land-consuming OFDI in SSA since 2000 (until 2015) in the home country settings, linking project-level data with the home countries' institutional frameworks, political economies, ideologies, and development trajectories. The comparative study of two major investor countries in SSA that are at different junctures of their economic development and have very dissimilar political economies was well-suited to identify the main country-specific and cross-country factors at play.

The book has shown that both countries' investments cover a range of different sectors, from agriculture to mining. Moreover, it has argued that diverse purposeful agents partake in land-consuming OFDI for distinct reasons. In fact, Chinese and British investments involve actors that are part of both the powerful and the marginalized groups in the home country's political economy. Some actors simply respond to the opportunities open to them—expecting higher returns, competitive advantages, and/or growing markets.[1] Others pursue these enterprises to 'fight the limits' they are confronted with back home—in the form of limited political influence, ecological boundaries, political interference, low social mobility and welfare, crowding out effects, limited markets, and/or (comparatively) low returns on investments made. Often, the fairly low opportunity costs reflected in the related rationalizations and expectations of the different actors explain why these investments occur, despite the high risks attached and the mixed record of economic success. Ulti-

---

[1] | In this context, it is also important to note that even though a company is unprofitable and accumulates huge losses, the chief executive staff still receives above-average annual salaries. See, for instance, Equatorial Palm Oil (2014).

mately, land-consuming OFDI projects are a function of geopolitical considerations, embedded in country-specific guiding ideologies, influenced by the social, economic, and ecological dimensions of domestic development, related to country-specific events, and supported by institutional frameworks—rather than being the outcome of any single master plan or mind. Therefore, their explanation from a home country perspective goes beyond the focus on resource security and/or the search for profitable investments.

Overall, this project makes three contributions to the contemporary research on "land grabbing" that will be summarized in the following sections in greater detail. First, it provides actual empirical evidence on Chinese and British investment activities and explains these from a home country perspective. The findings of the two case studies will be revised in Section 1 and 2, respectively. Second, the comparative research design identifies the differences, as well as the similarities, that are characteristic of both countries' overseas investments, in and over time. The review of the comparative findings of the contemporary and historical assessment will take place in Sections 3 and 4, respectively. The conclusion of the chapter considers the role(s) of land-consuming OFDI for home country development (Section 5).

1. CHINA IN AFRICA: RESOURCES, ALLIANCES, MARKETS, AND GLOBALIZATION

From an official perspective, Chinese land-consuming FDI projects in SSA, as this book has argued, are part of multiple strategies to diversify supply and access to resources (mineral products), foster political alliances and expand the country's soft power in international relations, develop and open new markets, and internationalize and upgrade China's industry in response to the competitive pressures as well as the ecological and social challenges back home. In this regard, these projects are part of the country's political transformation and the broader economic liberalization and globalization process, and reflective of its political economy.

From a project-level (agency) perspective, Chinese land-consuming investments comprise a very diverse range of actors and interests that often reflect the country's social and economic conditions. In practice, the projects include workers that hope to improve their families' standard of living; state-owned and private-owned companies searching for lucrative business opportunities; and central state officials that support and use the increasing levels of trade and investment in their diplomatic strategy to build political alliances. Chinese land-consuming investments also involve state-owned and foreign manufacturing companies in China that are interested in the access to cheap resources and new markets; sub-state government officials and representatives of China's financial institutions that promote the export of labor and pursue intergovernmental economic cooperation to facilitate growth and moderate the social tensions of their administrations' development plans; Chinese companies that have been crowded out by inward FDI and thus have tried to find new business opportunities overseas; and/or national oil companies interested in diversifying their portfolio in the face of declining reserves-to-production ratios (R/P ratio)[2] of Chinese oil fields and rising demand. Moreover, the investments comprise Chinese state-owned agribusiness companies delivering economic cooperation projects; as well as infrastructure companies that use changes in corporate law to act as contract bidders, in addition to implementing China-Africa cooperation programs.

In the following paragraphs, the core empirical elements of Chinese land-consuming FDI in SSA will be reviewed in the context of the social, ecological, and economic dimensions of China's development trajectory, as well as in view of the country's political economy, institutional frameworks, and ideological context.

The empirical findings have shown that these investment projects take place in a wide range of sectors, from farming and mining to infrastructure construction. They mostly pre-date the 2007/2008 crises, with some projects even tracing back to before the year 2000. Most projects involve multiple agencies from the private and public sectors, home and recipient countries (including key ministries and host country parliaments), and multilateral agencies. They are also embedded in the national development strategies of the home and host countries, and often rely on funding from third parties. Surprisingly, the Chinese government's official data suggests that investments in agriculture, the central focus of the "land grabbing" debate, only make up a minor share of total Chinese FDI (measured by value) in Sub-Saharan Africa. Also, the role of land in these investments is multifaceted. A significant share of projects uses land as a resource for mining or farming. However, other equally important projects use it as a productive space in which infrastructure projects are realized, Special Economic Zones constructed, or processing plants operated. On the operational level, most projects extract and produce primary commodities for domestic, regional, or international markets, rather than for export back to China. Moreover, the projects function on the basis of market principles and mainstream economic theory, and they are profit-oriented. The latter also applies to economic cooperation projects, including Chinese development finance.

Home-country-specific structures, agencies, ideologies, and events provide for a better understanding of why these investments occur, while also explicating their extent and the forms they take. Since the early 1990s, China's

---

2 | Jiang and Sinton (2011), 1-14.

government has opted for an IFDI-led, export-oriented economic development path. While the country has experienced tremendous quantitative economic growth during this period, specific events at different points in time have highlighted the shortfalls of this development trajectory. Insofar as they have presented a threat to the political and economic elite and/or led to relevant changes in the country's actor constellation, structural setting, or ideological superstructure, these events have been significant for Chinese OFDI policy and regulation. In particular, four successive events stand out: the economic expansion beyond the carrying and provisioning capacity of the country's resource base in the mid-1990s, the Asian crisis in the late 1990s, the WTO accession in 2001, and subsequently, rising civil discontent with the socioeconomic and ecological implications of the development pathway In the home country context, these events have stressed China's growing external dependency on resources, ecologies, markets, and political cooperation. They have also demonstrated the necessity of upgrading the country's domestic processing operations to improve the ecological and social conditions, and to reduce the crowding out effects of WTO accession on Chinese industry. In response to these events—and the underlying challenges for Chinese actors (individuals, firms, government) that have made them meaningful—the Chinese government has adopted an increasingly promotional policy stance towards OFDI (of which land-consuming FDI in Sub-Saharan Africa forms a part).

As a result, China, formerly a country with close to zero overseas investments, has become a major global capital exporter by 2009. While African economies still receive the smallest share of total Chinese OFDI, the continent's overall share has been rising significantly since 1991 (1991: 0.2%; 2007: 5.9%).[3] The home country's development trajectory also explains the sectoral composition of Chinese land-consuming FDI in African countries, namely the strong focus on resources for energy and industrial purposes, as well as the importance assigned to manufacturing activities and overseas markets. In addition, the infrastructure projects have improved the operating space of (Chinese) companies in African countries, and/or have strengthened the diplomatic relations by demonstrating the government's commitment to host country requests.

At the same time, it is this official emphasis on resources and commercial activities that sheds light on the surprisingly small share of agricultural investments in total OFDI since 2000. African governments have repeatedly asked the Chinese government to engage in the rehabilitation of the so-called Friendship Farms as part of the mutual benefit approach that allegedly characterizes China-Africa cooperation. In response, the Chinese government has agreed to build 30 agricultural demonstration centers across Africa, and it has

---

3 | TopForeignStocks.com (13 June 2009); and Renard (2011), 18.

become involved in other food security activities in the partnering countries through capacity building measures, donations to multilateral programs, and/or the establishment of a special fund (China-Africa Development Fund) that supports agricultural operations overseas. Largely, these activities relate to the reputational concerns of the Chinese government, which has to rely on soft power to advance its economic and political interests in its relationships with African countries. Thus, investments in the agricultural sector, particularly by SOEs, have been driven by the desire to demonstrate a different approach than the major resource importers from the North, with their violent histories of expansion and exploitation. At the same time, these activities have enabled Chinese actors, such as the Chinese agribusinesses which run the Friendship Farms on the basis of mainstream managerial economics, to internationalize their operations and gather first-hand managerial experience as transnational companies.

Moreover, the home country's particular actor constellations and ideological context are important factors in understanding Chinese land-consuming OFDI from a home country perspective. They constitute important "mechanisms of selection"[4] with regard to the responses to the particular events described above, while also explaining the form of these land-consuming investments. In particular, the victory of the economically liberal faction within the Chinese Communist Party (CCP) in the 1990s has led to the adoption of an expansionist guiding ideology of development. Importantly, (GDP) growth is perceived by the political elite as a way to identify whether development plans and strategies for economic governance are achieving success. It has thus come to determine political career paths within the CCP. In addition, the cluster of expansionist ideas (alias: guiding ideology) frames growth as a means to ensure the stability of the political regime by offering jobs and opportunities to the Chinese population. In this regard, the adoption of the set of ideas about growth performs ideological functions—it legitimizes, rationalizes, and promotes what is happening. It also drives overseas investment of which land-consuming OFDI forms a part.

Concurrently, political reforms since the 1990s have resulted in the growing importance of sub-state actors in the home country's domestic politics and international relations; the rising degree of "rule by regulation;"[5] the modification of Chinese corporate law so that it bestows SOEs with discretionary managerial power in their enterprises; and the shifting mindset of political agents who act as "bureaucratic entrepreneurs" and are interested in profitable business.[6] Together, these home country features explain why multiple actors with diverse

---

4 | Hein (2001), 16.
5 | Feng (2009), 432; and Yu (2008), 23.
6 | Cheng (2001), 241.

interests are involved in the initiation, implementation, and operationalization of Chinese land-consuming OFDI projects in Sub-Saharan Africa.

Regarding Chinese land-consuming FDI in SSA, this politico-economic and ideological transformation process explains the shifting nature of China-Africa cooperation visible on policy and project levels. Powerful interests of the country's altered political and economic elite, particularly the manufacturing industry and bureaucratic entrepreneurs at different levels of government, in economic expansion, resource security, and profitable business opportunities have shaped OFDI-related policies. Official documentation, significant speeches, and white papers published since 2000 showcase the government's move away from the historical framing of self-reliance and autarky as the ultimate (foreign) policy goal informing China-Africa relations. Instead, mainstream economic ideas have become the core framing and *modus operandi* of economic cooperation. This has resulted in the profound modification of how projects are run by Chinese actors. For instance, construction companies that were previously aid-funded have become successful entrepreneurs and contract bidders on the African continent, and even aid projects have adopted a for-profit rationale in their operations.

It remains unclear how successful the promotion of land-consuming OFDI will be in securing resources, opening markets, strengthen political partnerships, and/or internationalizing China's industrial base. Clearly, China-Africa trade and investment activities have intensified significantly. At the same time, the trade and investment patterns strongly take after traditional asymmetries of North-South relations, with the focus on resources and the export of machinery.[7] Regarding the official framing of China-Africa cooperation as "mutually beneficial," the effect could be very different for China and African countries. From a home country perspective, manifold evidence from other countries' globalization experiences emphasizes that the impact of overseas expansion on home country development is ambiguous and might entail the export of jobs and the hollowing out of the productive sector, amongst other problems. From a host country perspective, the outcome depends on whether the governments steer these activities to support the genuine development and diversification of their economies.

Overall, the varied assemblage of interests that range from geopolitical considerations, crowding out effects, individual hopes for a better life, and/or the specific characteristics of the Chinese political economy explains why the increase in land-consuming OFDI is likely to continue, even though many projects might fail and associated risks remain high.

---

7 | See for instance State Council (2013).

2. UK in Africa: Growth Regions, Climate and Energy Security, Reindustrialization

British land-consuming FDI projects in Sub-Saharan Africa are part of multiple strategies to profit from the economic reforms and rapidly growing consumer markets in the host countries, to respond to international and domestic energy and climate policies and the markets created for biofuels, and/or to "seek alpha" through alternative investments in the primary sector in Africa at a time of the financial crisis and economic stagnation back home. Increasingly, land-consuming FDI activities in Sub-Saharan Africa are also part of a (long-term) political strategy to use OFDI as a means to economic recovery and international political power through rising exports and industrial activity.

From the official perspective, land-consuming FDI projects are benefitting from a liberal policy stance towards capital exports that was adopted back in the 1970s. Only recently has OFDI to Sub-Saharan Africa also become an explicit component of the UK's foreign economic policy, which reflects the country's self-identification as a "cosmopolitan" economy and major political and economic power (and former empire). This policy frames overseas investments (alongside trade and IFDI) as a way to facilitate home country growth, thereby generating wealth, welfare, political stability, and international recognition. In this view, the overseas economic networks associated with OFDI can be used to sustain or expand the country's "soft power" at the international level.

From the project-level perspective, British land-consuming FDI in Sub-Saharan Africa mirrors the interests of a highly diverse private sector characteristic of the UK's liberal political economy. Some actors with long histories of operating on the continent have exploited the opportunities presented to them through divestiture programs, while others, such as the financial sector, have just begun to engage in land-consuming investments in the wake of multiple crises. Also, the adoption of biofuels and CO_2 emission targets provided incentives to newcomers to invest in agricultural projects and produce for the related markets. Early-stage companies have started to invest in Jatropha plantations, and actors of the aviation industry—affected by the CO_2 emission targets— have become involved and have offered these companies medium-term offtake agreements for their seemingly clean energy products. Despite the predominance of food and biofuel production projects in the "land grab" databases, British land-consuming investments cover a wide range of other sectors, including mineral extraction and construction services.[8]

---

8 | In this context, official UK OFDI data reminds us that financial services (43%) and mining (42.5%) were the largest sectors (measured by value) in Sub-Saharan Africa, pointing at the UK investor legacy with its focus on natural resources, as well as its economic constitution with a strong financial-sector orientation back home.

Most British projects produce for export to international markets or the UK. In many cases, however, the export-oriented business models designed by British companies did not materialize due to pricing problems, funding issues, and/or inexperienced plantation management, to name just a few of the problems encountered on the ground. As a result, many projects ended up selling their products in the host country or regionally; or went into administration. Land has been perceived primarily as a resource or financial asset, and again in contrast to the Chinese case, less often as a space for productive activities.

On the subject of timelines, three trends are observable in the 2000 to 2015 period. The first trend comprises investments made around the year 2000. The empirical details of British land-consuming investment projects indicate that at that time, host country divestiture programs and private sector perceptions of Africa as a new growth region were fundamental factors impacting investor decisions. Importantly, these factors emerged when economic growth in Britain and its major trading and investment partners was stagnant. The related investments were conducted by companies that had a long presence in the host countries, and/or they involved companies with the financial capacity and international experience and mindset to respond to these national and international incentives.

The second trend comprises land-consuming FDI projects that took place between 2000 and 2007. Most of these were related to international, European, or domestic renewable energy and climate policies, namely directives, targets, and carbon credits developed to achieve energy security and/or CO_2 emissions-reduction targets.[9] Specifically, they were operated primarily by new business actors, such as the early-stage companies that often had little prior experience in agriculture, and whose business models aimed to profit from these new policy regimes and related markets—they frequently failed to do so.

The third bulk of British land-consuming investments started after 2007. These projects have been strongly linked to the financial crisis, the economic recession in the UK, and the Eurozone crisis. These economic shocks have led financial actors to seek new investment outlets, often in the form of primary commodities. They have done this either as a hedge against inflation or, given the dire economic situation in the UK, the partner countries of continental Europe, and the crisis-ridden US, in pursuit of new growth markets. Since 2011, the British government has also tended to jump on this corporate trend by trying to promote British OFDI in African countries as a way to revive its manufacturing sector and develop new export and business opportunities.

The following paragraphs will review the core empirical elements of British OFDI in SSA in the context of the social, ecological, and economic dimensions

---

9 | UK Department of Energy &Climate Change (2006) and (2007).

of the UK's development trajectory, as well as in view of the country's political economy, institutional frameworks, and ideological context.

Compared to the Chinese example, the UK case study findings highlight that in a country with an open economy, host country dynamics and international events play out more prominently. Notably, the UK's investor legacy and long history as a liberal economy, as well as its long-term promotional OFDI policy stance, explain why a significant share of British land-consuming investments have been made in response to particular pull factors, such as host country reforms and international policy regimes. At the same time, the sectoral composition of British land-consuming FDI with its focus on resources echoes the country's investor legacy, as do the highly unequal investment patterns across different recipient countries. In fact, the land-consuming investments are concentrated in a few countries and focus on the same sectors that have characterized British-African economic relations for over a century. The limited number of manufacturing projects also mirrors the (financial-) service-sector orientation of the home country and the "embedded financial orthodoxy" of its political economy.

At the same time, the specific home country setting, namely the actor constellation, development context, and ideological superstructure, remains central to the explanation of how these investments take place. Take, for example, the dysfunctional system of industrial finance that is characteristic of the British political economy. Its effects are evidenced by the lack of patient capital that has plagued British biofuel and agricultural projects, often leading to their failure. Moreover, the strong presence of financial actors in British land-consuming OFDI projects reflects the "intellectual capture," as well as the overlapping interests of seemingly distinct public and private sector actor groups, that are characteristic of the UK's political economy of growth.

The relatively recent involvement of the British government in land-consuming OFDI activities in SSA has concurred with changes in the guiding ideology. In fact, the set of ideas that promote, rationalize, and legitimize (land-consuming and other) FDI in Africa has been modified in outlook and emphasis. The UK government now emphasizes the "mutually beneficial" nature of UK-Africa business relations, explicitly associating overseas investments more with national and foreign economic interests rather than unilateral humanitarianism. In the context of the 2007 financial crisis and ensuing economic recession, the UK government identified the financialization-led development approach, with its focus on financial services and its dependency on credit-financed public and private consumption, as posing a key challenge to economic recovery and the operative functioning of the state.[10] The core

---

10 | Confederation of British Industry (2011), 6; Pettinger (3 January 2014); Pettinger (8 January 2014).

problems of that approach include reduced and increasingly volatile government revenue; the country's declining industrial base, which has gone hand in hand with the loss of decent jobs and deteriorating terms of trade, particularly since the country became a net importer of energy sources;[11] economic recession at a time of international financial crisis; and rising socioeconomic inequality and the associated risk of social disintegration. Against this background, the Conservative government (since 2010) has begun to frame and re-engage in OFDI activities as a means to stimulate growth, access resources, improve industrial competitiveness, and provide for socioeconomic essentials such as jobs.

Official documentation also references realist assumptions and geopolitical considerations and suggests that the country's economic expansion—through further extension of the international economic networks comprising OFDI, IFDI, and trade—correlates with political power in international relations. Land-consuming (and other) FDI to SSA is framed as an important component of the government's ambition to play an influential role in world politics by sustaining the country's economic and political presence overseas and in multilateral institutions. On an institutional level, this rhetoric is matched both by an increase in the UK's commercial diplomacy and by the aligning of UK development finance and programs with the country's foreign policy goals. As a result of this "grand strategy" approach, development finance is increasingly being invested in the private sector operations of British companies currently active in African countries.

It remains to be seen how successful British land-consuming FDI in SSA turns out to be in meeting the multiple expectations associated with it. While trade and investment has increased significantly, the investment activities are spread very uneven, both with regards to countries and sectors. Moreover, the high project failure rate, regular involvement of fraudulent actors, and danger of capital flight all point at the challenges confronting these investments, on the project level as well as from a home country perspective. Overall, the official rhetoric seems overly optimistic regarding the utility of OFDI for the home country while no long-term strategy exists regarding the UK's engagement with Africa. At the same time, government efforts have so far hardly addressed the dysfunctional features of the home country political economy, such as the lack of patient capital or the effects of financialization on the state and society. From a host country perspective, the impact is strongly dependent on the steering of these investments to the benefits of the affected populations and societies. Anecdotal evidence suggests that the attraction of large-scale land-consuming

---

11 | On the implications and reasons for Britain's industrial decline, see Skidelsky (24 January 2013).

FDI often comes at a high cost for the affected populations and ecologies, with no safeguards in place.

3. Difference as Variation: A Country-Case Comparison

Given the complexity of Chinese and British land-consuming FDI described above, what does the comparative study of the contrasting cases tell us about the country-specific as well as cross-country features and dynamics at play? In this section, three (interrelated) arguments are made. Firstly, multiple differences exist regarding Chinese and British land-consuming OFDI. However, these differences are not necessarily significant in explaining why these investments happen, nor are they antithetic. Instead, differences are best understood as variations of the particular composition of actors and interests involved. Secondly, the complexity of (f)actors at play forbids any monocausal explanations of what is happening. Thirdly, it is important to note the similarities that exist regarding Chinese and British land-consuming OFDI. From a home country perspective, land-consuming OFDI is backed by relatively similar policy frameworks, and sets of ideas that associate OFDI with particular socioeconomic and geopolitical interests. On the project level, the investments apply the same managerial economics. The following paragraphs will explicate the comparative findings under the headings of difference, complexity, and similarity.

In view of difference, firstly, the particular mix of home-country-specific conditions explains how and why land-consuming investments occur, and ultimately highlights what makes them *Chinese* or *British*. In other words: differences do not refer to any sort of (antithetic) absolute difference in how and why these investments occur from a home country perspective. Moreover, not every difference is inevitably significant in the comparative explanation of how and why land-consuming OFDI occurs—a circumstance that holds for both the project level and the aggregate one.

In practice, the sectoral composition of Chinese investments reveals a focus on manufacturing and infrastructure projects, as well as energy resources, while British investments are largely resource and service-oriented and include a significant share of agricultural projects aimed at biofuel and food production. Regarding the role of land, Chinese investors prioritize its use as a resource and space for productive activities, whereas British investors use it mostly as a resource and, increasingly, as an asset. This does not, however, imply that all of these investment projects are related to the 2007/2008 resource and financial crises. In both cases, a large share of land-consuming OFDI projects began prior to the 2007/2008 timeline. Chinese projects often build on, or rehabilitate former aid projects, particularly in the agricultural sector where some projects can be traced back to the 1970s. Moreover, a large share of Chinese investments involves equity investments in existing projects, often in the form of a Chinese SOE investing in an African company that is itself an SOE or has close ties to the host government. Many British investments also go into existing enterprises (such as plantations) and involve companies which have had a long presence on the continent. At the same time, the bulk of early-stage companies are involved in greenfield investments, specifically the operation of plantations for export purposes.

The most obvious difference can be observed in the actor composition of both countries' land-consuming FDI projects. In spite of the great diversity of public and private actors from the host and home countries that are involved during a project's lifecycle, in the Chinese case, the investigated projects were predominantly executed by SOEs. British investments, in contrast, were undertaken primarily by private companies and financial investors, with the exception of the CDC Group. However, the case study has also shown that the British government has become involved through commercial diplomacy and/or the provision of investment-related development finance to British investors operating in African countries.

Moreover, different events, investor legacies, and political economies play important roles. In the Chinese case, the country is a relatively new source of FDI in Africa. The OFDI policy supporting this trend has emerged since the 1990s in response to particular events, such as the country's rising resource dependency in the 1990s, the Asian crisis in the late 1990s, and WTO accession in 2001. This means that Chinese land-consuming OFDI is strongly related to political reforms that have occurred since the 1990s and led to fundamental change and partial liberalization of the country's industrial and foreign economic policies and related administrative procedures. Contrastingly, in the British case, the country's long investor legacy and presence on the continent is of importance. Consequently, investments made prior to 2007/2008 were largely related to external pull factors, such as reforms in the host economies, the perception that African countries provided profitable business opportunities, or the international climate regime. Political reforms and home country strategies have come into play only more recently, in the form of a revised foreign policy regarding the British presence in African countries.

In the Chinese case, public sector reforms seem to have set the ground for the investments to occur as they do, however, in the British case it has been the private sector that has triggered the government to reconsider its engagement with African countries at a time of stagnant growth back home. In both cases, the public and private sectors overlap greatly, either through the strong role of SOEs in the domestic economy (China); the guiding ideology shared by public and private actors involved in the political economy of growth relevant for overseas investments in Africa (UK and China); or though revolving doors and the dependency of capitalist states on the economy to generate the revenues and jobs that are necessary for societal reproduction.

It is also noteworthy that most Chinese investment projects produce for domestic or regional markets in Africa, while most British investors planned to export to international markets or the UK. In the Chinese case, investors have just begun globalizing their activities and are producing largely for local and regional markets in the host countries. In the UK case, this export orientation is largely a continuation of historical investment patterns, as well as a reflection of the capacities of relevant actors.

Additionally, the rationales embedded in relevant official documentation and policies reflect another way in which Chinese and British land-consuming OFDI projects differ. In the case of China, these investments cater to the interests of a political economy of growth characterized by a very resource-intensive and export-oriented manufacturing sector, the marketization of power by state representatives, and the official interest in improving China's position and influence in the international political and economic landscape. Consequently, these investments open new markets, form part of a globalization process of Chinese companies, focus on the diversification of energy supplies, and are embedded in an official strategy to intensify political and economic networks. Contemporary agricultural projects have largely been motivated by reputational concerns and stem from the "mutual benefit" principle of China's Africa policy, i.e. they are intended to give something back in exchange for the increased, yet highly asymmetric trade and investment relations, thereby fostering good relations. Moreover, many investment projects have a medium-term profit strategy built in to their operations. The core actors in the Chinese political economy are government officials, SOEs, and the private sector, all of which pursue the same expansionist agenda, albeit for different reasons. Documented rationalizations range from considerations of political stability and resource security to access to new markets and the hope of finding profitable business opportunities overseas in light of the fierce competition back home.

In the case of the UK, the political economy comprises private actors seeking profitable investments in established sectors and, more recently, new actors trying to profit from newly created markets for renewable energy or the presence in new growth markets. The important role of the financial sector as a source of industry finance in these investments also reflects on the service-sector-driven growth strategy that has been pursued by British governments since the 1980s. More recently, in the face of the financial crisis, public actors have re-engaged with the industrial sector in pursuit of a source of growth. However, it remains to be seen what this implies for land-consuming FDI in SSA. At the same time, the dominance of the financial sector in British OFDI in general reflects the problems generated by the country's political economy, namely the lack of patient capital, which is needed, for instance, in the agricultural and industrial sectors.

Together, these details of Chinese and British land-consuming FDI in SSA highlight the core differences between the predominant trends, particularly in view of their actor composition, sectoral distribution, timelines, events, and strategic rationalizations. These differences relate to home country-specific aspects of the political economy, development context, investor legacy, and institutional setting. However, a closer look at how Chinese and British investments transpire also shows that many of these differences are not useful in explaining the purpose of these investments. Clearly, there are more public actors involved in the Chinese case, and a greater presence of financial investors in the UK case. At the same time, Chinese investments are largely for-profit, and are rationalized using mainstream economic thought. This means that the important role of public actors reflects China's role as a newcomer to the international economic realm, and not the final purpose of these investments. Accordingly, the country has to rely more strongly on inter-governmental cooperation to open new markets for industrial expansion and to diversify the country's supply of industrial resources. Moreover, the findings refer back to the Chinese domestic set-up, which clearly favors state enterprises.

In the UK case, meanwhile, this difference in actor composition does not mean that private investments appear in a vacuum. Instead, the less frequent involvement of public actors seems related to the UK's long-established ties with the African continent and private actors' correspondingly lengthy operational histories there. Moreover, these investments are embedded in national and international public policy frameworks and supported by home country measures. The huge number of financial actors is reflective of the "embedded financial orthodoxy" that has guided UK's domestic development policies since the Thatcher era.

Secondly, in view of the causal mechanisms at play in each case, the comparison accentuates that the interrelation of the country-specific conditions and outcomes is characterized by complexity. It is impossible to ascribe any of the domestic undercurrents in the form of agency, ideology, structure, and events a precise function as independent or dependent variables or to give a single (f) actor primary importance in explaining the outcome, namely land-consuming FDI ventures. Instead, these domestic undercurrents are co-determinant over time. The example of China shows this most clearly. Since the country's opening up, its socioeconomic and ecological dimensions of development have changed fundamentally and, as a result, so have the guiding ideology and actor constellations. China today embraces the type of overseas investments it termed exploitative four decades ago, and it has fundamentally reformed its administration, political system, and aid system in order to foster the newly adopted manufacturing and export-oriented growth strategy that matches the interests and international ambitions of its bureaucratic entrepreneurs.

Finally, thirdly, the comparative study of these two cases reveals institutional and ideological similarities between these rather different countries that highlight the important role of OFDI in contemporary development approaches of home countries. Over the past three decades, China has adopted an elaborate system of home country measures and is in the process of catching up with policy frameworks that are standard in OECD countries. This means that the countries only differ with regard to the degree (high/low) of stimulus and control exercised in their home country FDI policies.[12] While China applies high stimulus and control, the UK is characterized by high stimulus and low control.

Additionally, both countries have changed the guiding ideology underlying their foreign economic policies and overseas operations; however, the alterations differ in scale. On the one hand, China has fundamentally shifted from an earlier focus on autarky towards embracing open system features and factoring in other countries' land and resources in its development policy. In this process, a previous set of ideas on development and international relations has been replaced by another. On the other hand, the UK has (slightly) shifted the emphasis of its foreign policy towards Africa, and it has recently stepped up its commercial diplomacy to profit from the new growth region. The former guiding narrative of unilateral humanitarianism is increasingly complemented by a rationale of "mutual benefit" and "delivering prosperity together" that seems strikingly similar to the rhetoric commonly applied in South-South cooperation.

In fact, the two countries share a similar outlook on foreign economic policy when it comes to the role of OFDI promotion in accessing markets, securing resources, promoting exports, or strengthening the country's "soft power" and position in the international political and economic landscape (also see concluding discussion in Section 5). However, the detailed explanations of why both countries promote OFDI in Africa are rather different, and they reflect the particular political economies in the two countries at certain points in time. On the project level, both countries' investment projects pursue a for-profit rationale, and involve a rather diverse range of actors.

---

12 | See, for instance, Buckley et al. (2010), 243-277.

4. CHINESE AND BRITISH "LAND GRABS" IN HISTORICAL PERSPECTIVE

A remaining question is the novelty of contemporary Chinese and British land-consuming investments when compared to large-scale land acquisitions in the late 19th century. Broad references to colonialism made by some in the "land grab" debate often oversimplify the past and/or the present; for instance, such critiques' narrow focus on resources as the sole determining factor can have this effect. On the contrary, large-scale land acquisitions in the past and present are highly similar in terms of the complexity of their main empirical characteristics. In the late 19th century, and again today, land-consuming investment activities serve(d) a variety of purposes aside from that of securing resources. These purposes include opening markets, acquiring strategic assets, expanding spheres of influence, and searching for profitable business opportunities. Moreover, the 19th century investments, just like the contemporary ones, involved a diverse range of agents; and instead of being a total success story, many were confronted with insurmountable problems on the ground which led to their ultimate failure.

But what does a more detailed historical comparison of large-scale land acquisitions in the South tell us about the similarity of key elements over time? This section will look more closely at a selected range of aspects to highlight the co-existence of path-dependent and new aspects of Chinese and British land-consuming OFDI activities in SSA since 2000 (and until 2015)—making them both novel and old, to a certain degree. To narrow down the historical comparison of differences and similarities to a manageable size and concentrate on this co-existence argument, the discussion will revolve around three aspects: ideology, uneven development geographies, and institutions. These aspects have been central to the analysis of land-consuming OFDI from a home country perspective, and they evidence the importance of the events of the 19th century for our contemporary world.[13] In fact, the "global transformation" that was the industrial revolution in the 19th century has brought about particular ideologies and structures and a range of significant events that are still visible today.[14]

In terms of similarities, firstly, it is striking to see that in both China and the UK, the guiding ideology supporting capital exports uses basically the same narrative that was common during the Scramble for Africa in the 19th century. Together with trade and IFDI, OFDI is said to improve the home country's economic setting, to secure access to resources, to open export markets, and to sustain or reach a favorable position in the international economic landscape.

---

13 | Buzan and Lawson (2013), 1-17.
14 | Buzan and Lawson (2013), 1-17.

Overall, the official narrative during the Scramble, as well as today, promotes land-consuming investments as "not a choice, but a necessity."[15]

However, a closer look at this ideological conformity also shows the development of new aspects regarding the official rationalization and implementation of land-consuming investment activities—in the form of an ideological turn. During the Scramble, overseas investments were part of the "doctrinal, quasi-religious [...]" free trade doctrine, but this has changed since WWII.[16] While its core principles of multilateralism and non-discrimination persist, trade and investments have come to belong "to the more technical pages of economic theory and the diplomatic fineprint of international rules" under the protection of the WTO and/or bilateral consultations.[17] Accordingly, contemporary land-consuming OFDI is rationalized, legitimized, and promoted using the frames of mainstream economic theory, and it is an ordinary component of both home countries' industrial and foreign policies. Furthermore, host governments apply this technical frame too, and are actively involved in many of the Chinese and British OFDI activities, welcoming them as another source of capital that can be used to progressively finance national development plans – a narrative that also greatly resembles the rhetoric of colonial governments during the Scramble.[18]

The book has argued that this technical framing of international economic exchanges in general, and of (land-consuming and other) OFDI in particular, together with the institutionalization and legalization of the principles of multilateralism and non-discrimination, has enabled China to pursue a "peaceful development" approach. The institutions and strategies that have supported China's economic expansion since the 1990s, and its globalization since 2000, are fairly similar to those of the OECD countries; indeed, they are catching up with those standard measures, even though the Chinese government claims that they are innovative.[19] At the same time, we see that the rising Chinese involvement on the African continent has alerted "old" investor countries such as the UK. In fact, an increasing number of OECD countries have started to re-engage with OFDI promotion beyond the formal frameworks they have in place. Also, the UK has stepped up its commercial diplomacy via official visits and bilateral investment fora, but it has also refocused its development programs to Africa (and Asia).

Secondly, another comparison can be made regarding the uneven economic development geography. Vis-à-vis the international economic context, Chinese

---

15 | Compare Hobson (1965), 73.
16 | Trentmann (2008), 7.
17 | Trentmann (2008), 7.
18 | See Cottrell (1975), 28.
19 | State Council (2011b).

and British land-consuming OFDI activities clearly reflect—and most likely sustain—an international division of labor that emerged during the industrial revolution and the European imperial age of the 19th century. Unless African governments proactively engage with and steer capital imports to support economic diversification, their countries will continue to occupy the lowest positions in this order as primary commodity exporters and/or markets for industrialized goods in the world economy.

At the same time, the cases of China and the UK also reveal that these land-consuming investments are part of some relatively novel processes of global economic restructuring that might lead to an alteration of this development geography. In fact, as an emerging economy, China has become a major investor in Africa within the last two decades, and it is currently aiming to strengthen and improve its positional status within this international division of labor through upgrading. At the same time, the UK is trying to hold onto its favorable international position. To that end, it has started promoting land-consuming OFDI as a way to remain visible internationally, as well as rebalance its economy and profit from overseas growth markets.

From the viewpoint of uneven national development geographies, it is worth noting that certain conditions in the home countries are remarkably similar to those of the past. Now, as it did in the late 19th century, rising OFDI takes place in a home country context of high socioeconomic and wealth asymmetries. This observation is particularly interesting when recalling Hobson's argument that the concentration of wealth might have been one reason why capital was 'free' and available in home countries for profitable investment overseas.[20] At the same time, the UK case highlights that due to the realization of particular social security rights through financial market instruments, the situation is now more complex than in the 19th century. For instance, the rising aspiration of pension funds and public investors to invest in land-consuming overseas investment projects means that a diverse range of actors, including workers, have been implicated as implicit shareholders in this phenomenon since 2000.

Thirdly and finally, a core social institution rooted in the 19th century remains central to land-consuming OFDI today: the corporation.[21] During the era of colonialism, exploration, and free trade, chartered companies operated on the basis of a royal or government charter that outlined the terms and goals of their activities and granted them the right to military engagement and land governance. Importantly, institutions like the chartered company facilitated costly overseas enterprises by bringing together multiple investors and their capital resources through the practice of shareholding. As early as 1855, such companies were granted limited liability, which greatly reduced the risk carried

---

20 | Hobson (1965), 85-92; also see Chapter 3 (Section 2).
21 | Sukhdev (2012), 37-46.

by their shareholders.[22] At the same time, provisions such as the *ultra-vires* doctrine forbid the companies to act outside the charter rights assigned to them by the government.[23]

While the corporation has remained an important institution regarding trade and capital exports until today, state-market contexts have changed significantly. Most countries have subscribed to the open system economy and liberal principles. Furthermore, the charter has been replaced by a formal administrative process, and the legal means of protection available to corporations have been strengthened as a result of BITs, domestic reforms, and multilateral institutions. Plus, government provisions, such as the *ultra-vires* doctrine, have been cut, and trade and capital flows deregulated in many countries. In addition, both the relevant infrastructure (communication, transport) and the international economic governance structure have been improved. Overall, corporations' operational freedom vis-à-vis the state has been augmented as a result of these changes. In fact, the favorable economic context and the reduction of the risk associated with overseas operations also explain the rise of capital exports in the form of OFDI.[24]

In view of these altered state-market relations, the case studies have highlighted that the Chinese and British governments try to influence corporate decision making through compulsory, institutional, and productive forms of power in their interactions with economic actors. Accordingly, material, symbolic, and normative resources are applied by state agents in these investment processes through regulations (e.g., energy and climate policies); home country measures ranging from commercial diplomacy to financial incentives; and discursive framings. The fact that political and economic elites in both countries are closely interlinked on an individual, as well as intellectual, level helps to exert sway in both directions: from the public to the private sector and the private sector to the public sector. However, compared to the prevalence of government doctrines that companies had to obey in the 19th century, the public sector's influence on corporate behavior has decreased fundamentally, and corporate operations now tend to be associated with the representation of narrow shareholder values.[25]

Against this background, it is surprising to note the multiple ways in which the Chinese and British governments promote overseas investments using political and economic narratives similar to those popular in the late 19th century. In practice, foreign land, in its function as resource, marketplace, pro-

---

22 | Sukdhev (2012), 37-46.
23 | Mack (1930).
24 | See the rise of IFDI and OFDI in the World Bank's country data (http://data.worldbank.org).
25 | Sukdhev (2012), 37-46.

ductive space, strategic location, and/or financial asset, features prominently in the development policies and foreign economic policies of these two home countries. Moreover, overseas FDI stock in areas deemed to be of the utmost importance to the functioning of the home country's economy and society is considered to belong to that country's core infrastructure; it is often referred to as critical infrastructure (that needs protection).[26]

Thus, the two governments argue and act on the presumption that foreign lands are available to realize their national development objectives, as well as that their support for corporate overseas activities will be of economic, social, and political advantage to their countries. The involvement of state actors in OFDI activities highlights that these serve to open new markets, access cheap resources, and improve the relative trade and foreign exchange position of the home country, thereby enhancing its competitiveness, creating jobs, improving the terms of trade, and strengthening economic and political spheres of influence. It follows from this line of official reasoning that land-consuming OFDI in SSA is framed as an important step in ensuring the stability of the existing political and economic regimes.

It remains to be seen whether the rhetoric and expectations surrounding land-consuming OFDI will materialize, either on the project level or in the aggregate. At a minimum, the limited leeway that governments have to ensure that the accessed resources are sold back home, that profits are repatriated, or that corporate activity contributes to the prosperity and security of the home country in other ways, raises serious doubts about the core presumptions of the two countries' official rationalizations. The case of China highlighted some instances in which corporate actors acted in conflict with the central government's foreign ambitions. In the case of the UK, the prevailing dominance of the financial sector and the focus on shareholder value in overseas operations does not seem to be conducive to strengthening the productive sector. However, it is too early to judge the cumulative impact of OFDI on China and the UK.

Overall, this historical comparison has underlined the fact that broad references to historical events are not meaningful in explaining the quality of contemporary phenomena such as "land grabbing." Instead, a detailed assessment is necessary to apprehend the changes and continuities over time, and thereby to learn more about what is unique today.

---

26 | Wikileaks (2009b).

5. LAND GRABBING FOR HOME COUNTRY DEVELOPMENT? A SYNTHESIS OF OBSERVATIONS

Throughout this book, the argument has been made that land-consuming OFDI and home country development are closely interrelated. In conclusion, this section will synthesize findings and reflect upon the role of OFDI for home country development.

From an official line of reasoning, these investments are part of public policies that count on foreign lands to meet national development goals; as well as of foreign economic and diplomatic strategies to access resources, enter new markets, restructure the economy, and/or expand/sustain the sphere of influence using industrial activities and economic power. The investments are supported in both countries by political elites that are closely interlinked with dominant economic actors, on a personal level, by way of "intellectual capture," or through political institutions, like, for instance, the opening up of China's CCP to entrepreneurs and/or party finance in the UK.

OFDI, together with trade, is framed and perceived by the managerial and economic elites of the UK and China to advance their macro-level development agenda and address the structural problems they face. On the Chinese policy level, concerns about the rising dependency on external resources and markets, together with the fear of unsustainable levels of pollution, social welfare, and crowding out effects on indigenous industry have led to the adoption of an elaborate OFDI policy framework promoting overseas investment. In the British case, the main issues that yielded the establishment of a promotional and increasingly state-supported OFDI strategy included the EU accession and interests in market access shortly after the oil crisis; concerns about energy security; and the search for growth markets following the financial crisis and prolonged economic recession.

Concurrently, both countries' political elites pursue geopolitical ambitions in their cooperation with Africa, a continent that in their eyes has much to offer, namely resources, growth markets, and business opportunities. The intensification of economic networks and cooperation in this new growth region is said to build and/or sustain the home country's favorable (relative) position in the international political landscape and increase its economic strength at a time of global restructuring.

In this context, this research identified particular clusters of ideas linked to land-consuming OFDI (referred to throughout as the 'guiding ideology'). These have proven important in the associated perceptions, as well as policy and decision-making processes of countries and individuals. They shape the expectations and imagined futures of a wide range of diverse actors. Specifically, they reflect, justify, and obscure powerful interest structures, mobilize support, and create the institutions and purposeful agencies at play in OFDI activities in Africa. In line with the nature of ideologies, these clusters of ideas are "intended to be believed in by those affirming them publicly and by all men, because they are "true," and they thus have universal character."[27]

In both country cases, firstly, mainstream economic theory is at the core of the guiding ideology that frames these investments as an economic "necessity" and technical management issue. It informs the official language and normative narrative on land-consuming FDI in Africa, and parts of it are also taken up by private actors, and reflected in the overly optimistic expectations. In addition, secondly, China and the UK reference modern development prescriptions that focus on economic expansion as a way to prosperity, international political status, and domestic security. Propagated in significant white papers, as well as official documents and speeches, the framing of development in both cases comes close to President Truman's 1949 declaration that increases in the productivity and activity of an economy are "key to prosperity and peace" and preconditions of a progressively "higher standard of living."[28] This policy prescription towards development is, however, nothing unusual. To the contrary, "economic growth has maintained its position at or near the top of policy priorities in most countries," and is commonly framed as *conditio sine qua non* for prosperity, wellbeing, progress, and security.[29] Other policy objectives, like "free trade, increased competitiveness, lower taxes, reducing government's deficit, innovation and higher productivity" are referred to as a way to provide for "increases in economic output."[30]

This means that both countries share a global "quest for modernity [...] all wrapped in distinctive economic and political structures."[31] Consequently, contemporary land-consuming OFDI from China and the UK does not mark a turning point away from old development prescriptions or "free market" ideas, as is assumed by some authors who apply a narrow resource-security framing in their analyses.[32] Rather, OFDI from these countries reflects the assertion of existing practices and ideologies, namely the uneven development geographies with regard to the processes of value creation and consumption; and the prevalence of mainstream economic theory which promotes capital exports due to their framing as a technical management issue (rather than contentious control grabbing issue), and their macro-economic explanation as a rational choice to foster exports, access resources, expand skills and know-how, create employment, and ultimately sustain a country's economic growth.

---

27 | Gouldner (1976), 33.
28 | Gillespie (2001), 1.
29 | Victor (2008), 18.
30 | Victor (2008), 18-18.
31 | Gillespie (2001), 1. Also see Victor (2008), 18-19.
32 | E.g., IISD (2013).

At the same time, land-consuming OFDI projects present several inconsistencies of the expansionist development paradigm, the difficulties and violence of which have been at the heart of development studies. For instance, the expectation of unlimited economic expansion accompanying these capital movements (as found in official documentation) tends to disregard the existence of ultimate physical or territorial limits, the perception of which has influenced zero-sum mercantilist policies during previous eras.[33] Yet, the materiality of land-consuming projects is in many cases the very expression of such limits, meaning that (ideally) these are facilitating international economies of scale in spite of the problem of domestic diseconomies of space, or advance a country's growth in spite of the decline of the national resource base.[34]

Moreover, the development paradigm hides the asymmetric cost and benefit distribution of uneven development geographies by using technical terms, such as international division of labor;[35] or by suggesting that the location, not the ownership, of capital matters. Yet, by its very definition, foreign direct investment (land-consuming or not) is about "establish[ing] a long-lasting interest and significant control over a particular enterprise overseas."[36] Therefore, land-consuming FDI can be understood "as an interest in the *power* to consume or control land-based wealth (stemming from different land uses and activities)."[37] In fact, many "grabs" occur silently, through majority shareholding of a company.

Some land-consuming FDI projects are part a corporation's attempt to incorporate fragments of the supply chain—for instance, by acquiring business operations within the same production vertically or horizontally. Together with the uneven development geographies involved, the practice of land-consuming FDI projects thus points to the many neo-illiberal advances in and aspects of the host and home country economies, such as the concentration of ownership and control through forms of majority shareholding, conglomeration, and/or the aforementioned processes of integration of production processes within a single company.

In conclusion, it seems important to remember that this book has aimed to provide a meaningful account of Chinese and British land-consuming investments from 2000 until 2015; pointing to the necessity to study the co-dependency and -determinacy of actors, structures, ideas, events, including contingencies, of the global "land grab" from the home country perspective.

---

33 | Sornarajah (2010), 49-53; and Moran (2011), 1-9
34 | Bunker and Ciccantell, 2003.
35 | See, for instance, Lavoie (2014), 1-30; Sornarajah (2010), 49-53; Moran (2011), and 1-9; Denisia (2010).
36 | Goetz (2015), 180-181.
37 | Goetz (2015), 180-181; GRAIN (2008); Borras and Franco (2010).

Since then, the UK has decided by way of a referendum to exit the European Union, the terms of which are still being negotiated; China has stepped up its upgrading efforts by way of mergers and acquisitions in other regions, while beginning to invest in African industrialization, and establishing a development finance infrastructure that rivals the Bretton Woods system; and the current US government seems to turning away from previous forms of *American* multilateralism. The effects of these developments for OFDI policy in general, and land-consuming FDI in particular, were at the time of writing largely unforeseeable and at the time of publication, unpredictable. If anything, these constant changes underline that OFDI from a home country perspective remains in flux, and so do related policy paradigms.

APPENDICES

APPENDIX A: CHINESE INVESTMENTS IN AFRICA (19 INVESTIGATED PROJECTS)

Company/Project/Activity (Note: Several activities listed in the "land grab" databases turned out to be agreements, or projects, not companies. Therefore, this rubric also comprises agreements and project names.)	Recipient Country	Size (ha)			Purpose, Approach, and Goal	Project Development	Project Announced	Sources
		Announced	Acquired	Under Production				
Sino Cam Iko The company is a subsidiary of the Chinese state-owned (provincially managed) Shaanxi Land Reclamation General Corporation and part of the Chinese State Farm System. (Note: This project is run by a manager named *Wang Jianjun*. Several databases list the project as a separate project by "business man Wang Jianjun," like, for instance, GLP (2010: 31, 35)).	Cameroon	10.000 (long-term)		100-150 (in 2011)	*Project Purpose:* Food production for local markets.	After bilateral negotiations and an exploratory visit in 2005, the project was announced at the FOCAC 2006 Summit. An investment agreement of over USD 62 million was signed by both countries' governments. Funding took place through the China EXIM Bank, which transferred USD 40 million in 2009. In 2010, the contract for land was awaiting approval from Cameroon's Prime Minister. The project's current status (as of 2014) is unclear. The project was launched as part of China's technical co-operation framework. The overarching goal was to reduce rice imports to Cameroon by increasing the country's output from 50.000 to 400.000 tonnes per year. Apart from rice, the project also comprised maize, fruits, vegetables, and cassava production. One location, the Nanga-Eboko Rice Station, was formerly a Taiwanese cooperation farm (until 1972). According to available information, no consultation with local authority took place, with the exception of one location. The investment faced local opposition as well as organized urban civil society opposition due to fears that the produce would not be sold locally (as there was no such legal guarantee). The operationalization of this MoU began in 2008 on the preliminary 120 ha site. However, as of 2011, the investor was still waiting for the concession license to be approved by the Ministry of Agriculture. To gain access to the fertile ground in a moderate climate zone of the preliminary site, the investor cut down trees, which might result in problematic changes to the regional micro-climate, but the local Ministry of the Environment had not been allowed to access the site and conduct the mandatory environmental impact assessment. In addition, local residents complained about the lack of sufficient compensation.	2006	Brautigam and Zhang (2013), 1684-1685; Li (2010); Khan and Baye (2008), 7, 15; Wikileaks (2010a); World Bank (1998); Putzel et al. (2011), 31; Afriquinfos (2011, October 4); GLP (2010), 31, 35; Grain (2010, October 22).
Resettlement of Chinese farmers This project has been one of the very few explicit Chinese land lease requests.	Mozambique	Unknown scale			*Project Purpose:* Resettlement of farmers from China to Mozambique, worth RMB 700 million.	The resettlement project was first proposed in 1997. It was later discontinued due to political sensitivities, but negotiations were reportedly resumed in 2010. The current status of the project is unknown.	1997	Ekman (2010); Jansson and Kiala (2009).

Company	Country	Area (ha)	Project Purpose/Approach	Description	Year	Sources
China International Fund - MOZ The company is a joint venture between the China International Fund and SPI. The latter is a holding of the Frelimo Party, whereas China International Fund is a Hong Kong real estate company.	Mozambique		4.1	*Project Purpose:* Mining and production of cement for the local market.	The background of the project is the shortage of cement and the related high prices in Mozambique, together with Chinese commitments to rebuild infrastructure. (Other Chinese companies also applied for licenses to survey for suitable terrain to mine and produce cement). The mining concession in Matutuine (Maputo province) was approved in 2011; it is valid until 2036. The total investment for the cement factory amounts to USD 72 million. Allegedly, the factory construction took place without a prior environmental impact assessment. Moreover, the project commenced without a prior resettlement of the 230 families affected by the construction.	By 2011	Brautigam (2010, June 2); Duran 2012: Cementchina.net (2011, May 31).
ZTE Energy Established in 2007, the company focuses on R&D of bio-energy, R&D of energy saving and system services, and palm cultivation and oil processing trade. It is a subsidiary of the ZTE Corporation (its largest shareholder), a Shenzhen-based corporation with previous links to the China Ministry of Aerospace.	Democratic Republic of Congo	3,500	10 to 600 ha are used as an experimental plot.	*Project Purpose:* Food production for local use. *Project Approach:* Training farmers in food production techniques and planting high yielding crops.	ZTE Energy started producing food in 2008 on an experimental plot of 10 ha near Kinshasa, in cooperation with the DRC Ministry of Agriculture. According to the corporate website, ZTE Energy was also accredited as a supplier of the UN World Food Programme. In 2010, the company became involved in the effort to rehabilitate Domaine agropastoral industriel de la N'Sele (DAIPN), a former Sino-Congolese cooperation project dating back to 1972. The area of 600 ha was granted for the new project by the Ministry of Agriculture in 2010.The project – focused on maize, soybean, kidney, cassava, and vegetables – was supposed to involve Chinese investors as well as other foreign companies and the African Development Bank. This project is one of several agricultural projects in the DRC that is operated by a subsidiary of the ZTE Corporation.	2007	Baende (2010, March 29); Braeckmann (2009, September); CAITEC (2010); ZTE Energy (n.d.b); ZTE Energy (n.d.a); Putzel and Kabuyaya (2011), 34-35; ZTE Energy. (n.d.c).
ZTE Agribusiness Company Ltd. This company is a subsidiary of the Shenzhen- based ZTE Corporation with previous links to the China Ministry of Aerospace. It invests in agriculture and palm oil projects, and is part of the ZTE Corporation's decision to diversify its operations.	Democratic Republic of Congo	100.000	256	*Project Purpose:* Palm oil production for local use. *Project Approach:* Plantation.	The ZTE project in the DRC would have consumed up to 100.000 ha. It was negotiated in 2007 between the DRC Ministry of Agriculture and the ZTE Corporation. It intended to convert palm oil into biofuels, reportedly in abandoned plantations in Bandundu and Equateur. However, the project did not materialize. Instead, as of 2013, the company operated a 256 ha farm that produced maize, soy, meat, chicken, and eggs. Officially, the company has said that high transport costs made the palm oil project unprofitable.	Negotiations in 2007	Brautigam (2009); Brautigam and Zhang (2013), 1686; Putzel and Kabuyaya (2011), 34-35; Beiping, (2009, July 10); Koswanage (2011, April 29); Sun (2011), 15.

Company	Country	Land	Project details	Year	Sources
Malawi Cotton Company The company is a joint venture of the *China-Africa Development Fund* and the *Qingdao Ruichang Cotton Corporation*.	Malawi	Access to land through 110.000 rural households.	*Project Purpose:* Cotton production, including agriculture and processing for export to China. *Project Approach:* Central farming contract scheme ("company + rural household")	The Malawi Cotton Company involves over 110.000 rural households under a central farming contract scheme. The farmers produce cotton, and the company provides inputs as well as takes the harvest and processes it at a spinning and ginning plant in Balaka for export to China. In 2011, the company harvested close to 40.000 tonnes of cotton. To ensure sufficient cotton supply for domestic ginneries, Malawi put an export ban in place for unprocessed cotton. At the same time, a China Restraint Agreement was negotiated to reduce textile imports.	2008	China Development Bank (2012, May 31); Chirombo (2009, December 29).
SUKALA SA The company is a China-Mali joint venture with a 70% majority stake by the Chinese state-owned *CLETC*.	Mali	5.000	*Project Purpose:* Biofuels production (ethanol) for domestic and regional markets (Burkina Faso). The molasses is used as animal feed. *Project Approach:* Sugar cane plantation and processing activities.	The China-Mali joint venture owns a sugarcane plantation of approximately 5.000 ha. It started in the form of a debt-equity-swap between the Chinese state-owned company CLETC and the Malian government. The arrangement gave the Chinese side control over operations due to its majority stake (70%) in the project. The project dates back to 1996, but it has changed significantly over time. Prior to the joint venture with a Chinese majority stake, it was part of an aid and technical cooperation program under cooperative and transitional management. Also, precursor factories were built and renovated by the Chinese government in the 1960s and 1980s.	1996	Diaz-Chavez et al. (2010), 41, 50, 53, 113; Baxter and Mousseau (2011); Nolte and Voget-Kleschin (2013), 16-17; World Trade Organization (2004), 50; Xinhuanet.com (2009, February 11).
N-SUKALA SA A China-Mali joint venture created in 2009.	Mali	19.142 [long-term vision of leasehold for sugar production] 857 ha titled land for factory premises	*Project Purpose:* Sugar cane production for consumption (candy). *Company Goal:* Producing 103.680 tonnes of sugar and 9,6 million liters of ethanol per year.	The creation of the company, dedicated to growing and processing sugar for food production, was approved by the Malian parliament in 2009. The company has a renewable 50-year land lease for an area of 19,142 ha. The China EXIM Bank financed the construction of a processing factory based on a preferential loan which covers less than the overall costs. Main competitors have been complaining about the preferential position of this venture. For example, the US Company Schaeffer has alleged that N-SUKALA SA plans to expand on land originally reserved for Schaeffer in an attempt to preserve its quasi-monopolistic position in Mali. The project provides 639 permanent and 10.000 seasonal jobs.	2009	Diaz-Chavez et al. (2010), 50, 53, 113; Baxter and Mousseau (2011); Wikileaks (2009a); Xinhuanet.com (2009, February 11).

Project	Country	Size	Project Purpose / Approach	Description	Year	References
ChongQing Seed Corporation — The state-owned (municipal) company runs one of the Agricultural demonstration centers that were announced during the 2006 FOCAC meeting.	Tanzania	62–300	*Project Purpose:* Food production, mostly for domestic markets; training local farmers. *Project Approach:* Centralized out-grower scheme with local farmers.	The company grows and processes hybrid rice (its own intellectual property). The company's seeds are said to double the usual output. Some of the rice might be sold to China. The project is expected to profit from the Chinese experience and boost the Tanzanian agricultural development.	2006	ChinaDaily.com.cn (2008, May 17); Tanzanian Affairs (n.d.); Moshi and Mutui (2008), 5-7.
Intergovernmental Agreement — The two countries allegedly signed an agreement stipulating that China would deliver fertilizers and provide other forms of assistance, while Senegal would grow peanuts for export to China.	Senegal	100.000	*Project Purpose:* Food production.	It has been reported that the farmers' association of Senegal organizes the production of peanuts on 100.000 ha, with 30% of the yield to be shipped to China and the rest processed at local factories. It should be noted that while China imports significant amounts of peanuts from Senegal, the details of this particular case has not been confirmed.		Smaller et al. (2012), 16; China DSIC International Trade Co. Ltd. (2014); The Japan Times (2013, March 26).
Datong Enterprises — The private Chinese company invested in sesame production.	Senegal	35.000	*Project Purpose:* Food (sesame) production for export to China, Latin America, and Europe. *Project Approach:* Out-grower scheme eventually involving up to 200.000 people.	The Chinese private company announced plans to invest USD 5 million and produce 150.000 tonnes of sesame per year. It is not clear whether those plans came to fruition. It has been reported that the company received credit from Caisse Nationale and subsidies from the Senegalese state, and that the project is part of the Senegalese Growth Plan ("GOANA"). This plan resulted from the food crisis, and it includes the promotion of foreign investments in agriculture through the free repatriation of profit and tax breaks. Allegedly, the project faced problems because farmers sold their harvest to other buyers at a better price.	2008	Smaller et al. (2012), 17; Lewis (2009, February 11); Aiddata.org (n.d.a); People's Daily (2009, February 20).
Jonken Farm — The former friendship farm is operated by Jiangsu Agricorp (Jiangsu State Farms Group Corporation) and Zhongguo Agricorp (China National Agricultural Development Group Corporation) since 2003.	Zambia	3,500	*Project Purpose:* Food production (crops, husbandry, animal breeding) for local markets.	The Chinese project in Zambia employs 200 people. The project dates back to 1994, when the company began to rehabilitate a former China-Zambia friendship farm. The farm was an assistance project, but it was privatized in 1990 because it was not economically viable. Since 2003, Jiangsu Agricorp (Jiangsu State Farms Group Corporation) and Zhongguo Agricorp (China National Agricultural Development Group Corporation) now hold 40% and 60% respectively of the Friendship Farm.	1994/2003	Mwanawina (2008); Freeman et al. (2008), 17; Liu (n.d.), 1-2, 12-14; China National Agricultural Development Group Corporation (n.d.).

Company	Country	Scale	Project	Description	Sources
Chipata Cotton Company The company (now the *China Africa Cotton Company*) is a subsidiary of *Qingdao New Textiles Ltd*, a Chinese SOE that has been present in Zambia since 2004.	Zambia	2,500 contract farmers, with a vision of 20,000 contract farmers	*Project Purpose:* Cotton production. *Project Approach:* Intermediate contract farming, which involves three actor groups, i.e. the company, the agent, and the farmer.	The Chipata Cotton was renamed into the China Africa Cotton Company, following a 2008 investment by the China Development Bank. It is a subsidiary of Qingdao New Textiles Ltd., which has been operating in Zambia since 2004. Originally, only 2,500 out of the envisioned 20,000 contract farmers were involved. The project is one of several investments by the Chinese companies in the Zambian cotton sector. These investments have increased competition in this sector.¹ The project conforms well with the plans of Qingdao province to upgrade its domestic textile industry.	China Development Bank (2012, May 31); Chinese Embassy in the Republic of Zambia (2013, September 10); Phiri (2013, September 11); Schoneveld et al. (2014), 25-27; Times of Zambia (2004, June 14); Tschirley and Kabwe (2009); Wang (2014, June 30); Pedersen (2009).
SUCOCOMA The Chinese state-owned company, *Complant*, a wholly-owned subsidiary of the state-owned *State Investment and Development Corporation* (SDIC). SDIC relies on Complant to implement Chinese foreign cooperation programs, particularly in the area of construction.	Madagascar	unclear	*Project Purpose:* Land restoration, and construction of a sugar refinery	It has been reported that SUCOCOMA's project revolved around restoring irrigated land formerly used by a state-owned sugar company for sugar cane production. The current status of the project is unclear. However, a cable from the U.S. Embassy in Antananarivo, as well as corporate information, suggests that the Chinese SOE Complant manages two sugar refineries in Ambilobe and Namakia since 2008, under a twenty-year management contract. Complant also built a sugar refinery in Morondava, financed by the Chinese government. While this was turned over to the government of Madagascar in 2008, Complant continued to manage operations in 2012.	Üllenberg (2009); Wikileaks (2010b); Complant (n.d.); SDIC (n.d.); SDIC (n.d.a); Tossa (2012, August 25).

Company	Country	Area	Project Purpose	Description	Year	Sources
Viscount Energy Officially, the company presents itself as a "Chinese supported Nigerian firm."	Nigeria		*Project Purpose:* Biofuel factory construction.	In 2006, the Ebonyi State Government and the Chinese company signed a MoU about building a factory for producing biofuel. The factory was built as a turnkey project by Tianjin Energy Resources Ltd., a Chinese construction company. The project by Viscount Energy is intended to improve domestic energy security. However, while it matches Nigeria's National Biofuel Development Policy, the project is problematic in terms of food security and (the lacking) land use rationale. The ethanol plant intends to produce 20.000 gallons of ethanol per year, based on the input of 150.000 tonnes of a mix of cassava and sugar cane.	2006	Biopact (2006, August 14); Isiguzo (2006, August 28); Rothkopf (2007), 336; Oyeranti et al. (2010); McDowell (2012).
Hebei Hanhe Investment Company This is a state-owned provincial company.	Uganda	17.000 (10-year target)	*Project Purpose:* Food (maize, rice, vegetables) production for local and international markets.	173	The Hebei Company's 10-year target is to develop around 17.000 ha. In 2010, it was growing maize, vegetables, and trees on the total area of only 173 ha. Hebei Hanhe Investment Company has started in Uganda in 2009.	2009	Wang (2011, October 10); Aiddata.org (n.d.b).
China International Water and Electric Corporation The state-owned company is attached to the *Chinese Ministry of Commerce.*	Zimbabwe	100.000	*Project Purpose:* Irrigation system construction.	The company's cooperation with the government of Zimbabwe was not successful, and the project never got off the ground. Initially, the company had been approached by the Zimbabwean government to build an irrigation system and boost agricultural production. In the process of implementing the project, the company discontinued its operations due to political difficulties.		The Herald (2013, December 4); SW Radio Africa (2003, August 1).
SUCOBE The company is an affiliate of COMPLANT, a Chinese SOE. COMPLANT is a wholly-owned subsidiary of the state-owned *State Investment and Development Corporation (SDIC).*	Benin	4.800	*Project Purpose:* Biofuel production (ethanol) for export to Europe. *Project Approach:* The company uses sugar cane from its own land plot, plus cassava from local farmers in the production of biofuels.	Since 2003, SUCOBE runs the Savé Factory, which was established in 1973 by Benin and Nigeria. After a period of mismanagement and economic crisis, the factory had undergone several management changes. The factory produces and processes sugar cane into sugar and alcohol. It employs approx. 5.000 workers, of which 4.637 are casual and seasonal workers, mostly women. The company relies on external harvests to complement its own agricultural output. In addition to the sugar cane produced on 4,800 ha of land, which the company is leasing for 99 years (renewable), the company uses cassava bought from local farmers for its plant operation. As a result, there has been a cassava price hike in Benin. SUCOBE Company in Benin is an affiliate of the Chinese SOE COMPLANT.	2003	Nonfodji (2011); Tossa (2012, August 25).

Special Economic Zone (SEZ)	Mauritius	200-500	Project Purpose: Build a manufacture hub in the form of a Special Economic Zone, including light industrial products, medicines, textiles, and electronics.	Negotiations began in 2007, development in 2009, and completion is expected in 2016. Comprising an area of 200 to 500 ha, this SEZ is headed by Chinese companies. It is intended to become a major manufacturing hub for Chinese light industrial products, medicines, textiles, and electronics. It is expected to accommodate 40 Chinese companies and create 34,000 jobs, of which 8,000 will be given to Chinese contractors. The SEZ is expected to generate USD 220 million through exports and to attract investments worth USD 750 million. On a global scale, China plans to build 50 Special Economic Zones.	By 2009		Alves (2011); Brautigam and Tang (2011); Dwinger (2010, August 2).
The project is headed by the *Taiyuan Iron & Steel Group*, the *Shanxi Group*, and the *Tianli Group*.							

Appendix B: British Investments in Africa (22 investigated projects)

Company	Recipient Country	Size (ha)			Purpose, Approach, and Goal	Project Development	Timelines			Sources
		Announced	Acquired	Under Production			Project Announced	Land Transfer	Harvest	
SunBiofuels (SBF) SBF is a UK-based company with several subsidiaries across Africa. It was established in 2005. In 2008, it came under majority control (shareholding) of *Trading Emissions Plc* (TE), a carbon trading fund managed by EEA Fund Management Ltd. In 2011, SBF went into administration, and its operations were closed or sold off to investors.	Ethiopia	80.000	5.000	1.000	*Project Purpose:* Production of biodiesel, using Jatropha (originally on marginal land, later on prime land). *Project Approach:* Plantation and outgrower scheme. *Company Goal:* SBF: to become the largest provider of biofuel, first for export markets, later for the African market. TE: to profit from climate change mitigation policy by producing "clean" and renewable energy.	In 2005, SBF signed a lease with Benshangul Gumuz Regional State Government for 80.000 ha and purchased 80% of National Biofuel Corporation (Ethiopia) to strengthen presence in Ethiopia. SBF was also involved in the drafting of the Ethiopian Biofuels Strategy. SBF Ethiopia was not economically viable due to poor soil conditions, limited seed input, and the lack of third party finance (in addition to TE). The company used seed input from DiOils (UK) and Diligent Tanzania Ltd. (the Dutch subsidiary uses 3.500 ha through outgrower scheme to produce seeds for planting). SBF went into administration in 2011, when TE, its majority shareholder, denied it additional funds. It is unclear what happened to the Ethiopian operation of SBF.	2005	2005		Bergius (September 2012); Trading Emissions Plc (2008); Trading Emissions Plc (2011), 7; Hawkins and Chen (2011), 29-30; Sosovele (2010), 120; Trading Emissions Plc (2009).
	Tanzania	8-9.000		2.000		SBF Tanzania negotiated a 99-year government-backed lease in 2006. The 8-9.000 ha were spread over 11 villages with 11,200 people. This land was formerly used by charcoal makers and also included a swamp area important for local water security. The affected population was promised a compensation of USD 250 per household. After SBF went into administration, the Tanzanian subsidiary was sold to Lion's Head Global Partners (in 2011). There have been allegations that this company only employs 50 of the previous 700 workers, and that it has abstained from addressing the problem of the incomplete process of compensating the affected population.	2006			Bergius (September 2012), 3; Hawkins and Chen (2011), 29-30, 88, 96, 196.
	Mozambique	4.854 plus two farms of 607 ha and additional 3.000 ha under negotiation		2.310		SBF Mozambique secured land under a 50-year DUAT lease that was backed by the host government. The land is considered to be of prime quality regarding the combination of climate, location, soil quality, and infrastructure. The company also signed a MoU to supply the state-owned enterprise Petróleos de Moçambique SA with Jatropha crude oil, and it planned to export biofuel to Europe and India. In 2010, crude oil was sold to UOP Houston for experiments in the aviation sector, and in 2011, a lot of 30 tonnes of biofuel was sold to Lufthansa for trials. After SBF went into administration in 2011, the Mozambique subsidiary was sold to Highbury Finance. This is a project development and investment advisory firm, founded in 2004, that focuses on "alternative investment opportunities." The new investor claims to have 2,310 ha (of the total area of 4,854 ha) under operation, focusing on food production.	2006		2010	Highbury Finance (2013); Hawkins and Chen (2011), 29-30, 93, 225, 227; Sun Biofuels Mozambique (2011).

Vepower Ltd. The UK-incorporated bioenergy company operates plantations in Ghana and Malaysia, and power plants in the UK, and provides related services.	Ghana	50,000	50,000	*Project Purpose:* Provision of bioenergy through the planting of Jatropha and the production of fuel.	The company has leased a 50,000 ha plantation to grow Jatropha. It is in the process of securing finance. It signed a feedstock acquisition agreement with Jatropha Africa in 2010. The current status (as of 2014) of operations is unclear. The company's major partner, Jatropha Africa, allegedly went into administration in 2013 (see below).	BioZio (2011), 110, 127; Vepower (n.d.).
Unilever (UK-Netherlands) The company, which has long been present in Ghana, operated a plantation from 1999 to 2010.	Ghana		7,200	*Project Purpose:* Production of palm oil.	Unilever Ghana operated plantations in Ghana that it acquired in 1999 through the host government's divestiture program. In 2010, Unilever sold its majority share in the 7,200 ha Benso Oil Plantation Ltd. (which is listed on the Ghana Stock Exchange, and on which more than 9,000 people's livelihoods depend) to Wilmar Africa.	Ntsiful (2010), 129-137.
Jatropha Africa Jatropha Africa is an industry partner of the EU funded program "Capacity Building in South Africa, Namibia and Ghana to Create Sustainable, Non-food Bio-oil Supply Chains." Its current status regarding ownership structures and operations is unclear.	Ghana	50,000	100	*Project Purpose:* To grow Jatropha seedlings in the nurseries, and produce Jatropha crude oil for biodiesel refining companies. *Company Goal:* To provide renewable energy sources, whilst working in partnership with rural African communities to support economic development.	Jatropha Africa was invited to support the development of the Renewable Energy Policy for the Ghanaian Ministry of Energy in 2010. The bioenergy project started out with a pilot farm of 100 ha with 100,000 trees and aimed to expand to 50,000 ha in partnership with three villages in Ghana (no timeline). The latest project status is unclear. A report by Antwi-Bediako (31 October 2013) mentions that Jatropha Africa went into administration, due to the lack of funding and difficult policy environment. Personal communication with the Ghanaian farm manager in 2012 indicated that the company had come under Ghanaian ownership and was listed as a company with limited liability in Ghana.	Jatropha Africa (2010, August 22); Jatropha Africa (n.d.d); Jatropha Africa (n.d.a); Jatropha Africa (n.d.b); Jatropha Africa (n.d.c); Antwi-Bediako (2013, October 31).

Company	Location	Hectares	Project details	Year started	Sources
D1 Oils The UK-based share company was founded in 2005. In March 2012, it changed the name to *NEOS Resources Plc*. As of 2014, it is in the process of developing a new business strategy.	Zambia (subsidiaries also in Malawi, Ghana, South Africa, Swaziland, and Asia)	220,000 (total for India, Indonesia, Malawi and Zambia)	155,000-174,000 in Zambia (including outgrower schemes)	2,411 planted and 20,760 used through contract farming (in Zambia in 2007)	*Project Purpose:* Biofuel production for export and domestic use. *Project Approach:* Selling Jatropha oil for direct use in diesel engines or to companies producing biodiesel. D1 Oils, founded in 2005, used to be the biggest Jatropha producer worldwide, with several subsidiaries in Africa and Asia. However, the company has been struggling with economic viability of its operations throughout its existence, and has never paid any dividends to its shareholders. D1 Oils abandoned its plan to sell Jatropha crude oil internationally, after its partner Beyond Petroleum (BP, formerly British Petroleum) withdrew from a joint venture project on Jatropha production in 2009. Since then the oil has only been sold domestically. From 2007 to 2012, the company's share value drastically decreased; by 2012, operational losses amounted to more than GBP 1 million. To indicate a fresh beginning, the company changed its name to NEOS Resources in 2012, shifted its focus to India, and announced a diversification beyond Jatropha production in African countries. However, severe financial difficulties have continued. As of 2014, the company is in the process of selling off its assets, while negotiating its future business outlook with major shareholders.	2005	StockMarketWire.com (2012, March 13); Hawkins and Chen (2011), 21-23; Mitchell (2010), 118-125; NEOS Resources Plc. (2012, October 12); NEOS Resources Plc. (2012, November 15); NEOS Resources Plc. (2012, March 15); Investigate.co.uk (2014, January 30). Data on total hectares secured or operated remains unclear. See also GEXSI LLP (2008), 50, 55; Investigate.co.uk (2006, June 14); Reuk.co.uk (2007, January 15).
Cru Investment Management This investment company was indirectly involved in operations in Malawi through shareholding (14.54%) in the Malawi-based *Africa Invest Fund* (running from 2006-2008). The fund and other Cru's operations went into administration in 2011.	Malawi	6,000	*Project Purpose:* Investment in agricultural land for food and land management, with a focus on paprika and chilies grown for export. *Company Goal:* Profiting from growing scarcity (related to the rising global demand for food production) by investing in agricultural land; generating income from efficient management of land and from holding direct stakes in agricultural land.	Cru Investment Management managed the Africa Investment Fund from 2006 to 2008. The fund operated five to seven farms covering 6,000 acres in Malawi. It had a commercial farm workforce of more than 1,450 workers, and it cooperated with more than 5,000 outgrower farmers. In 2010, the auditor PricewaterhouseCoopers found that it was unlikely for Cru Investment Management to recuperate the money it had received as loans, due to the overvalued asset base. The Cru trustee, Capital, froze the money of the six funds managed by Cru. The operations managed by Africa Invest Fund in Malawi were sold in 2010 for GBP 175,000. The money was used for fees and liabilities, while investors hardly recovered their investments. Moreover, a fraud investigation took place, due to the alleged misappropriation of funds. Money from Arch funds managed by Cru had been lent to Africa Invest without shareholder notification, and Africa Invest and Cru chairman Maguire had allegedly withdrawn money without following proper procedure. Cru's case even resulted in a briefing to the UK Parliament.		BBC (2010, February 6); Grote (2009, March 24); Grote (2009, April 14); Grote (2010, March 16); Merian Research and CRBM (2010, 28; Merrett (2013, November 29); Miller (2011, July 7); Ntsiful (2010), 129-137; Paler (2010, July 14).

Company	Country	Hectares	Project Purpose/Approach/Goal	Description	Year	Sources
CAMS Agri-Energy Tanzania CAMS Agri-Energy belongs to the CAMS group, established in 1972. In the 1970s, the group focused on airport and port operators; now it invests in emerging market growth sectors, such as renewable energy, oil and gas, carbon credits, housing, project finance, technology, infrastructure. CAMS Agri-Energy started operating in 2008. Its current status (as of 2014) is unclear.	Tanzania	45,000	*Project Purpose:* Sweet sorghum-based ethanol production that does not undermine food security. *Project Approach:* Food and Fuel: farmers already grow sweet sorghum; the tall stalks can be used for ethanol production, without using food grain. Project will be profitable due to rising fuel prices and CO2 reduction finance schemes.	The project in Tanzania was set up in 2008, using 45,000 ha of land in two county districts. The aim is to develop ethanol and power production from sweet sorghum stalks, with distribution centers in rural Tanzania. Funds have been raised through equity financing and from a commercial bank in London. To produce ethanol, the project intends to use Chinese technology of fermentation and distillation in each village. The company cooperates with the Tanzanian seed authority and with an Indian NGO to reach out to farmers.	2008	Obulutsa (2008, September 19); Oakland Institute (2011b), 4, 18-19, 30; WWF-TPO (2009), 14-15, 23, 26, 29-36; Locher et al. (2013), 6-7, 13-14, 32, 36.
Lonrho Lonrho – a formerly UK listed company with operations in agriculture, infrastructure, transport, and support services in SSA dating back to 1909 – was taken over by two Swiss investors in 2013, and it has restored its status as a private company.	Angola	2	*Project Purpose:* Construction of a John Deere equipment dealership. *Company Goal:* Profiting from African growth markets.	Lonrho, a formerly UK-listed company with an ambiguous reputation, was taken over by a Swiss investor in 2013. Two years before that takeover Lonrho described the attractiveness of investments in land and agriculture in Africa as a composite of the following factors: Africa hosts a large share of the world's arable land; it remains the major continent for oil and gas reserves as well as the primary source for minerals; and African countries have relatively low external debt levels. The current status (as of 2014) and the timelines of the project are unclear.		Bloomberg News (2011, July 20); Lonrho (2012), 1-5.
	Angola	25,000	*Project Purpose:* Food production (rice) for domestic consumption.	In 2009, Lonrho Agriculture announced it had signed a deal with the Angolan government to carry out agricultural projects on 25,000ha of land in the provinces of Uige, Zaire and Bengo. The company secured a 50-year lease. The project was to be implemented within the scope of government initiatives to promote agricultural reconstruction and development. The agreement, signed on the Angolan side by the Agriculture and Rural Development Minister, Afonso Pedro Canga, and by the director of Gesterra, Gestão de Terras Ataveis, Carlos Alberto Jaime, anticipated rice production. This deal would have used up the bulk of the planned spending on agricultural projects in 2009 (USD 6 million), and would have been leveraged with Angolan financing. As of 2014, it is unclear what has become of this particular investment. The website of the now Swiss company, however, suggests that the company is still active in the farming sector, stating that it has "60% of [agricultural, A.G.] production coming from our own farming operations, and 40% from out growers (including commercial farms and Lonrho organised local cooperatives and small farmer programs)."	2009	Burgis (2009, January 16); Lonrho Fresh (n.d.); Lonrho Ltd. (2014, January 24); Macauhub (2009, January 14).

Procana	Mozambique	30,000	30,000	--	Project Purpose: Production of biofuel from sugar cane ethanol.	In 2007, after negotiations and a signed contract with the Mozambican government, the British-based company Bio-energy Africa decided not to follow through with its biofuel investment in southern Mozambique. Consequently, the government cancelled the contract, assigning 30,000ha in Gaza province for the development of a sugar cane plantation for the production of ethanol. Earlier in 2007, Procana had also announced its plans to invest an additional USD 510 million in construction of a new plant for the production of ethanol, sugar, electricity and fertilizers.	2007	Allafrica.com (2009, December 23); Biopact (2007, September 4).
The 2007 bioenergy project of Procana, a subsidiary company of the British-based firm *Bioenergy Africa*, did not get off the ground.								
Central African Mining and Exploration Company Plc (CAMEC)	Mozambique		300,000 in 2005; plus 67,620 in 2007		Project Purpose: Mining (coking and thermal coal).	During 2002-2009, CAMEC was active in mining projects in DRC, South Africa, Zimbabwe and Mozambique. In 2005, the company acquired ten licenses, covering 300,000ha, to explore for coal in Mozambique's northern Tete Province. In 2007, CAMEC acquired the majority share of Belde Empreendimentos Mineiros Limitada (Belde) of South Africa. Through the joint venture, CAMEC attained three additional mining licenses (coal), covering 67,620ha altogether.

CAMEC also held approximately 54.84% of Agriterra Ltd., a British agribusiness active in Mozambique (see below) and had common directors with this company (as of 2009). In 2009, CAMEC was sold to Eurasian Natural Resources Corporation, a Kazakh firm. Thereafter the company changed its management and withdrew from the London-based AIM Stock Exchange. | 2005 | Agriterra Ltd. (2009, January 12); Creamer Media (2009, November 11); Marima (2012, August 20); Refractories Window (n.d.); Webb (2009, September 18); Macauhub (2009, April 22). |
| CAMEC was listed at the AIM Stock Exchange during 2002-2009. Its Mozambican operations started in 2005. The company delisted from AIM once it was bought by a Kazakh firm in 2009. | | | | | | | | |

Agriterra Ltd Since 2009, Agriterra has been an AIM-listed agricultural business active in the production, processing and trading of multiple commodities in Africa. It has been aiming to "build itself into a multi-commodity African focused agricultural business." Until 2008, the company was active in the oil exploration business and named White Nile.	Mozambique	17,050 (since 2008/2009), plus 2,500 (since 2013)	*Project Purpose:* Food production, namely livestock (beef ranch) and feedlot; intended for domestic consumption and export.	Agriterra Ltd.'s subsidiary, Mozbife Ltd., runs the Mavonde Stud Ranch and the Dombe Ranch that altogether comprise 16,000ha. The 1000ha Mavonde Stud Ranch is envisioned to expand both with regard to land and herd size; the company is in negotiations about additional 3,000ha. The 15,000ha Dombe Ranch has a lease (DUAT) until 2061 that was granted by the Mozambican government. In addition, as of 2012, the comapny operated the 1,050ha Vanduzi Feedlot and managed maize processing facilities. The company's objective is to build a total herd in excess of 10,000 head by 2015. In January 2013, the company acquired the 2,500ha Inhazonia Ranch.	Agriterra Ltd. (2012, February 29); Agriterra Ltd. (n.d.b); Verdin (2009, March 26).
	Sierra Leone	Access to 3,500 farmers, and 45,000ha	*Project Purpose:* Cocoa production and trading; palm oil production. *Project Approach:* Buying a trading company with a buying register of 3,500 farmers to access cocoa; securing a lease on brownfield agricultural land suitable for palm oil plantations.	Agriterra operates multiple businesses in Sierra Leone. It bought a Sierra Leone-based trading and agricultural company to expand its operations in cocoa production and trading, including storage, a buying register of 3,500 farmers, and a 3,200ha cocoa plantation. There are also plans to include coffee and palm oil production. As of 2014, negotiations are in place to acquire an additional 1,600ha of land adjacent to this plantation. The project management aims to plant a total of 4,000ha by 2017, with the ultimate aim of producing a minimum of 8,000 tonnes of cocoa per annum by 2020/2021. Agriterra also bought control over a lease of 45,000ha brownfield agricultural land that is suitable for palm oil production with highest levels of rainfall (as of 2012). According to the Sierra Leone Investment and Export Promotion Agency (SLIEPA), the "President and Cabinet have identified oil palm as a priority growth sector and are prepared to provide support in the highest levels to accelerate investment." In this context, SLIEPA is "earmarking and preparing a number of suitable sites for 10,000ha+ palm plantations." Companies are able to lease land up to 71 years, for USD 20-30 per ha per year, with basic labor costs of USD 2-3 per day, flexible labor regulation, and 0% taxes for some investors.	Agriterra Ltd. (2012, February 29); Agriterra Ltd. (n.d.a); Carrere (2013).
	Liberia			In 2009, Agriterra signed a memorandum of understanding to acquire Equatorial Biofuels (Guernsey) Limited, a palm oil producer based in Liberia. Equatorial Biofuels Ltd. (now named Equatorial Palm Oil Company, see next project) has a total land holding of 169,000ha granted by the Liberian government in the form of concessions. However, the deal did not materialize and Agriterra decided to withdraw from it (see below).	Macauhub (2009, October 28); Public Ledger (2009, September 22).

Equatorial Palm Oil Company The company was founded in 2005 as Equatorial Biofuels, and changed its name to Equatorial Palm Oil Plc in 2008. It has been a publicly listed (AIM) crude oil producer since 2010.	Liberia	89,000 (concession), plus 80,000ha (Memorandum of Understanding).	*Project Purpose:* Palm oil production for export. *Project Approach:* Large-scale oil palm plantation.	The Equatorial Palm Oil Company has been granted concessions for three palm oil plantations in Liberia, all of which are located in a favorable climatic zone, close to cities, and in proximity to ports with facilities that can accommodate export operations. In 2009, Agriterra Ltd. was interested in acquiring the Equatorial Palm Oil Company, however, decided against it. As of September 2014, the UK incorporated company is a subsidiary of the parent company and ultimate controlling company Kuala Lumpur Kepong Berhad ("KLK"), a company incorporated in Malaysia. KLK owns and controls 62.86% of the Equatorial's share capital. Both, Equatorial Palm Oil and KLK have made significant losses in their operation in 2013 and 2014. The Equatorial Palm Oil Company's 169,000ha holding, of which 89,000ha are concessions granted by the government and 80,000ha are part of an MoU with the county district and tribal communities, is embedded in a plan by the Liberian government to re-establish export-oriented plantations as a growth sector and foreign exchange earner.	2005	Equatorial Palm Oil (2015): Investigate.co.uk (2009, August 18); Public Ledger (2009, September 22); Equatorial Palm Oil 2011; Equatorial Palm Oil (2013); Global Witness (2013, December 20); Equatorial Palm Oil (2011); Equatorial Palm Oil (2013); The Rights and Resources Group (2013), 267; Equatorial Palm Oil. (2014); Ejatlas.org (2014).

Company / Description	Country	Size (ha)		Project	Year		Sources
GEM Biofuels Founded in 2005, Green Energy Madagascar (GEM) has been active in establishing Jatropha plantations. Since 2007, it has been listed at the AIM London Stock Exchange. In 2013, the company changed its name (to *Hunter Resources Plc*) and operational focus.	Madagascar	495,000	55,700	*Project Purpose:* Jatropha crude oil production for export to the EU, North America, and Australasia. *Project Approach:* Plantation and outgrower scheme. *Company Goal:* Focus on Jatropha because it meets European criteria as a non-edible oil seed (since food-based biofuel industry faces sustainability challenges); become the largest producer of biofuels in Madagascar and the region.	The company was founded in 2004, and it has been AIM listed since 2007. Focusing on Jatropha production, GEM managed to secure over 495,000ha in Madagascar. According to its reports, the company secured this land – which included over 40,000ha natural forest – in the period from 2005 to 2011 through a 50-year lease, with parcel size ranging from 2,500ha to 50,000ha. Moreover, the company concluded 18 agreements with local communes for exclusive plantation rights as well as informal agreements about wild seed delivery. In 2007/2008, GEM was employing 4,500 local farmers in nine locations. The original plan was to plant 200,000ha by 2010. Yet, planting operations came to a halt in 2009, when tied up capital markets and bad plantation management forced the company to focus on maintaining existing plantations rather than (re)investing in their planned expansion. In 2010, the first revenues of GBP 18,000 from Jatropha oil were made, with shipments to Germany and Australia. These came largely from the harvest of a 40,000ha forest with many Jatropha trees, allowing the company to start harvesting earlier. During 2011, GEM concentrated on letting the plantations mature, and it did not engage in any further planting. It also reduced the number of staff. By the end of 2011, it had planted Jatropha on a total of 55,737ha. Still, the share value did not recover, nor did the company manage to attract additional funding. Unable to profit from its land bank, the company changed its name to Hunter Resources PLC in January 2013 to indicate its new investing policy and board changes. A corporate notice from December 2013 stated that share trading had been suspended as the company did not become an investment company in time to meet AIM London Stock Exchange requirements. The same notice announced that the management was in negotiations to become active in Peruvian mining projects 563km from the city of Lima, in an area where eight exploration concessions (a total of 3,500ha) are located. What has happened to the Jatropha production is unclear.	2005		Ullenberg (2008); ADVFN.com (2013, August 1); Investigate.co.uk (2008, September 20); GEMBioFuels (2011, September 28); GEMBioFuels (2012, April 12); GEMBioFuels (2012, December 5); Gerlach and Pascal (2010), 7; Hawkins and Chen (2011), 3, 24-25; Hunter Resources Plc (2013, December 30); OnVista.de (2014); Bloomberg News (2009, September 30).
Madabeef Madabeef appears to be a UK company which intends to raise beef cattle on 200,000ha for the export market. Status unclear.	Madagascar	200,000		*Project Purpose:* Livestock (cattle) for export.	No details available.		Douguet (2013, September 5); Hamelinck (2013), 87; International Land Coalition (n.d.); Ullenberg (2008); Van Der Werf (2012), 95, 179.

Avana Resources This Malagasy subsidiary of the UK-based Avana Group was set up in 2008 to hold and manage Avana's assets in Madagascar. *Avana Group* was founded in 2007 to develop uranium opportunities. For some time it was also active in the production of biofuels, but those activities seem to have been terminated.	Madagascar	30,000 ha (mining). plus plans to establish a 10,000ha biofuels plantation	*Projects Purpose:* Minerals exploration and exploitation (uranium), as well as biofuels production. *Company Goal:* "Investment in energy sources that improve supply security and diversity while reducing carbon emissions per unit of energy used," namely, uranium (nuclear power) and biofuels.	2008 license agreement	2009 and 2010 exploration of uranium	Avana Uranium (n.d.); Energy-Profile (2009); 53; GEXSI LLP (2008), Slide 58; Matthews (2010), 117-119.
G4Industries Ltd (UK) The company withdrew from the biofuel project in 2011 due to environmental concerns.	Kenya	28,000	*Project purpose:* Biofuel production based on sweet sorghum. *Project Approach:* Field to fuel and field to power model.			G4 Industries Ltd., a British-based company active in power, fuel and equipment projects, participated in the writing of the UEMA biofuel strategy for West Africa 2008. The company used to have two subsidiaries. The only one still active is G4 International (Denmark). This subsidiary benefits from Danish government to provide farming solutions in Africa that are approved by the UN. The second subsidiary used to be G4 International Kenya, but G4 Industries Ltd. abandoned its 28,000ha biofuel project in Kenya before operations begun. This decision was taken in response to pressure from NGOs over the potential negative impact on wildlife in the wetlands of the Tana River Delta.	Cernansky (2011, October 26); Business and Human Rights Resource Centre (n.d.).
Equatoria Teak Company (ETC) The company has operated since 2006, together with its sister company *Central Equatoria Teak Company*. From 2007 to 2010 it was run by governmental development funds, the *CDC* and *Finnfund*; then it was sold to unknown investors.	Sudan	18,649	*Project Purpose:* Timber (for export).		2007-2010	In 2006, a concession agreement between the Sudanese government and the ETC was signed relating to a 18,640ha forest reserve. Thus, ETC and its sister company gained control over the total area of 20,450ha forest reserves that were granted as concessions by the government for 32 years. The agreement stipulates royalty payment of USD 100 per cubic meter of exported sawn board; 80% of this amount goes to Western Equatoria State Ministry of Agriculture and 20% to Yambo County local government. ETC sold some consignments between 2007 and 2010, while its sister company never harvested timber. From 2007 to 2010, the company was represented by the CDC, after the CDC and Finnfund – two governmental development funds associated with the British and Finnish governments – had obtained a majority interest. In 2010, Finnfund and CDC sold the two companies. This followed controversies due to protests from local communities, and it being impossible to make the forest plantation economically viable in an environmentally and socially sustainable way.	Concession Agreement (2006, June 28); Deng and Mittal (2011), 2, 4, 28-29.

References

ActionAid. (2011, October 31). How a biofuels landgrab has destroyed the life of an African village [Press release]. Retrieved from http://www.actionaid.org/2011/10/how-biofuels-landgrab-has-destroyed-life-african-village

Action for South Africa. (2011). *Angola Monitor, 2*(11). Retrieved from http://www.actsa.org/Pictures/UpImages/pdf/Angola%20Monitor%20Issue_2_11.pdf

Actis. (2014a). Our history [Corporate website]. Retrieved from http://www.act.is/content/OurHistory

Actis. (2014b). Current investments [Corporate website]. Retrieved from http://www.act.is/content/CurrentInvestments

ADVFN.com. (2013, August 1). GEM Biofuels Plc change of name & directors shareholding. Retrieved from http://www.advfn.com/news_GEM-BioFuels-Plc-Change-of-Name-Directors-Shareh_55741577.html

Africa Confidential. (2013, October 18). Security crises threaten economic success. *Africa Confidential, 54*(21). Retrieved from http://www.africa-confidential.com/article-preview/id/5080/Security_crises_threaten_economic_success

Africa Confidential. (2014). Who is who: Hu Deping, China. *Africa Confidential*. Retrieved from http://www.africa-confidential.com/whos-who-profile/id/3101

African Development Bank. (2011, June 9). AfDB signs multi-million cooperation agreements with China and Brazil [Press release]. Retrieved from http://www.afdb.org/en/news-and-events/article/afdb-signs-multi-million-cooperation-agreements-with-china-and-brazil-8144/

[AfDB/OECD/UNDP/UNECA (2011)] African Development Bank, Development Centre of the Organisation for Economic Cooperation and Development, United Nations Development Programme, & United Nations Economic Commission for Africa. (2011). *African economic outlook 2011: Special theme Africa and its emerging partners*. Retrieved from http://www.undp.org/content/dam/undp/library/corporate/Reports/UNDP-Africa-2011-Economic-Outlook.pdf

African Development Bank. (2012, February 8). AfDB identifies key challenges to address through Agriculture Strategy [Press release]. Retrieved from http://africasd.iisd.org/news/afdb-identifies-key-challenges-to-addres s-through-agriculture-strategy/

African Development Bank (AfDB) (2014). Programme for infrastructure development in Africa (PIDA) [Press release]. Retrieved from http://www.afdb.org/en/topics-and-sectors/initiatives-partnerships/programme-for-infrastructure-development-in-africa-pida/

African Labour Research Network. (2009). *Chinese investments in Africa: Opportunity or threat for workers?* Retrieved from http://www.worldlabour.org/eng/node/243

Africa Research Institute. (2012, October). Between extremes: China and Africa (Briefing Note 1202). Retrieved from http://www.google.de/url?sa=t&rct=j&q=&esrc=s&source=web&cd=1&ved=0CCEQFjAA&url=http%3A%2F%2Fwww.africaresearchinstitute.org%2Ffiles%2Fbriefing-notes%2Fdocs%2FBetween-extremes-China-and-Africa-P2E56236DQ.pdf&ei=wyCDVNWuCMO9Ua2ngvAP&usg=AFQjCNENVY9pIWDc9LGI-BelRqp558YsMw&bvm=bv.80642063,d.d24

Afriquinfos.com (2011, October 4). Coopération Chine-Afrique: un centre pilote agricole bientôt fonctionnel au Cameroun. Retrieved from http://www.afriquinfos.com/articles/2011/10/4/brevesdafrique-188166.asp

Agriculture Council of America. (2014). Agricultural fact sheet [Blog post]. Retrieved from http://www.agday.org/media/factsheet.php

Agriterra Ltd. (2009, January 6). White Nile Ltd. extraordinary general meeting statement. Retrieved from http://www.agriterra-ltd.com/News.aspx?ArticleId=2539886

Agriterra Ltd. (2009, January 12). Schedule one: Agriterra Limited. RNS Number: 4657L. Retrieved from http://www.agriterra-ltd.com/News.aspx?ArticleId=2547831

Agriterra Ltd. (2012, February 29). Interim results, RNS number: 3254Y. Retrieved from http://www.agriterra-ltd.com/News.aspx?ArticleId=19919842

Agriterra Ltd. (n.d.a). Tropical Farms Ltd. Retrieved from http://www.agriterra-ltd.com/operation-tropical.aspx

Agriterra Ltd. (n.d.b). Mozbife Limitada. Retrieved from http://www.agriterra-ltd.com/operation-mozbife.aspx

Agritrade. (2012, February 6). New era dawning for palm oil producers. Retrieved from http://agritrade.cta.int/Agriculture/Commodities/Oil-crops/New-era-dawning-for-palm-oil-producers

Aiddata.org. (n.d.a). Sesame processing enterprise. ID: 1941. Retrieved from http://china.aiddata.org/projects/1941

Aiddata.org. (n.d.b). CDB funds construction of Hebei farm in Uganda. ID: 30011. Retrieved from http://china.aiddata.org/projects/30011

Aiddata.org. (n.d.c). Preferential loan for construction of sugar refinery. ID: 1506. Retrieved from http://china.aiddata.org/projects/1506

Aigaforum. (2011, June 9). Ethiopian investment, trade and tourism forum in London [Press release]. *Aigaforum.com*. Retrieved from http://www.aigaforum.com/news/trade_and_investment_forum_london_2011

Alden, C. (2007). *China in Africa*. London: Zed Books Ltd.

Alden Wily, L. (2012). Looking back to see forward: the legal niceties of land theft in land rushes. *The Journal of Peasant Studies, 39*(3-4), 751-775.

Allafrica.com. (2009, December 23). Mozambique: Investors decided to pull out of Procana months ago. *Allafrica.com*. Retrieved from http://allafrica.com/stories/200912230711.html

Allen, G. (2012, October 8). *UK trade statistics* (Standard Note SNEP 6211). London: House of Commons Library. Retrieved from http://www.parliament.uk/business/publications/research/briefing-papers/SN06211/uk-trade-statistics

Allen, G., & Dar, A. (2013, March 14). *Foreign direct investment* (Briefing paper SN/EP/1828). London: House of Commons Library. Retrieved from http://www.parliament.uk/briefing-papers/sn01828.pdf

AltAssets.net. (2006, April 26). CDC commits $100m to African agribusiness. Retrieved from http://www.altassets.net/private-equity-news/cdc-commits-100m-to-african-agribusiness-fund.html)

Alves, C. (2011). *Chinese economic and trade cooperation zones in Africa: The case of Mauritius* (SAIIA Occasional Paper No. 74). Johannesburg: South African Institute of International Affairs. Retrieved from http://www.saiia.org.za/occasional-papers/chinese-economic-and-trade-co-operation-zones-in-africa-the-case-of-mauritius

Amanor, K.S. (2012). Global resource grabs, agribusiness concentration and the smallholder: Two West African case studies. *The Journal of Peasant Studies, 39*(3-4), 731-49.

Analysis for Economic Decisions. (2010). *Mid-term evaluation of the Investment Facility and EIB own resources operations in ACP countries and the OCTs* (Final report, vol. I, ref. 1285). Retrieved from http://ec.europa.eu/europeaid/how/evaluation/evaluation_reports/reports/2010/1285_vol1_en.pdf

Andersson, J.O., & Lindroth. M. (2001). Ecologically unsustainable trade. *Ecological Economics, 37*(1), 113-122.

Anghie, A. (2006). The Evolution of International Law: colonial and postcolonial realities. *Third World Quarterly, 27*(5), 739-753.

Anghie, A. (2007). *Imperialism, sovereignty and the making of international law*. Cambridge: Cambridge University Press.

Anseeuw, W., Lay, J., Messerli, P., Giger, M., & Taylor, M. (2013). Creating a public tool to assess and promote transparency in global land deals: the experience of the Land Matrix. *Journal of Peasant Studies, 40*(3), 521-530.

Antwi-Bediako, R. (2013, October 31). Land grabbing and Jatropha boom in Ghana [Beahrs environmental leadership program, blog post]. Retrieved from http://beahrselp.berkeley.edu/blog/land-grabbing-and-jatropha-boom-in-ghana/

Arezki, R., Deininger, K., & Selod, H. (2013). What drives the global "land rush"? *The World Bank Economic Review*, 1–27.

Ariza-Montobbio, P., Lele, S., Kallis, G., & Martinez-Alier, J. (2010). The political ecology of Jatropha plantations for biodiesel in Tamil Nadu, India. *The Journal of Peasant Studies, 37*(4), 875-897.

Asche, H., & Schueller, M. (2008). *China's engagement in Afrika—Chancen und Risiken für Entwicklung*. Hamburg: German Institute of Global and Area Studies. Retrieved from http://www.giga-hamburg.de/sites/default/files/publications/studie_chinas_engagement_in_afrika.pdf

Atkin, J. (1970). Official regulation of British overseas investment, 1914–1931. *The Economic History Review, 23*(2), 324–334.

Augar, P. (2001). *The death of gentlemanly capitalism: The rise and fall of London's investment banks*. London: Penguin.

Augar, P. (2006). *The greed merchants: How the investment banks played the free market game*. London: Penguin.

Austin, G. (2010). African economic development and colonial legacies. *International Development Policy/Revue internationale de politique de développement, (1),* 22-32. Retrieved from http://poldev.revues.org/78?lang=en&v=1392752313000/_/jcr:system/jcr:versionStorage/ec/2d/01/ec2d01e0-1490-4077-89f3-abod48c9e15a/1.4/jcr:frozenNode

Avana Uranium. (n.d.). Get in touch with us [Corporate website]. Retrieved from http://avanauranium.com/contact.php

Ayoob, M. (2005). Security in the age of globalization. In J. Rosenau, & E. Aydinli (Eds.), *Globalization, security, and the nation state: Paradigms in transition* (pp. 9-26). New York: State University of New York Press.

Aziz, N. (2011, April 15). The neo-colonial land grab in Africa. *Commons Magazine*. Retrieved from http://onthecommons.org/neo-colonial-land-grab-africa

Baah, A. & Jauch, H. (Eds.). (2009). *Chinese investments in Africa: A labour perspective*. Retrieved from http://www.cebri.org/midia/documentos/315.pdf

Baende, L. (2010, March 29). Agriculture: Les chinois reprennent le site de la N'Sele. *L'Avenir Quotidienne*. Retrieved from http://www.afriqueredaction.com/article-agriculture-les-chinois-reprennent-le-site-de-la-n-sele-47588654.html

Bairoch, P., & Kozul-Wright, R. (1996). *Globalization myths: some historical reflections on integration, industrialization and growth in the world economy* (Discussion paper no. 113). Geneva: United Nations Conference on Trade and Development. Retrieved from http://unctad.org/en/docs/dp_113.en.pdf

Bangura, V. (2011). Sierra Leone Investment and Export Promotion Agency (SLIEPA). Presentation at the Food and Agriculture Organisation (FAO) technical workshop and roundtable meeting on promoting investment in agribusiness, 12-14 December 2011, Rome, Italy. Retrieved from http://www.fao.org/fileadmin/user_upload/tcsp/docs/Session11_Bangura_SLIEPA_Presentation.pdf

Barder, O. (2005). *Reforming development assistance: Lessons from the UK experience* (Working Paper 70). Washington, DC: Center for Global Development. Retrieved from http://www.cgdev.org/publication/reforming-development-assistance-lessons-uk-experience-working-paper-70

Barnett, M., & Duvall, R. (2005). Power in international politics. *International Organization, 59*(1), 39-75.

Baumann, M. (2013). *The political economy of land grabbing*. Paper presented at the conference Competition between Conflict and Cooperation, 13-14 June 2013, University of Freiburg, Germany. Retrieved from https://www.google.de/search?q=Baumann,+M.+%282013%29.+The+political+economy+of+land+grabbing&ie=utf-8&oe=utf-8&gws_rd=cr&ei=sW-NVOTwKYL6aIGEgcgD

Baxter, J., & Mousseau, F. (2011). *Understanding land investment deals in Africa: Country report Mali*. F. Mousseau & G. Sosnoff (Eds.). Oakland: The Oakland Institute. Retrieved from http://allafrica.com/download/resource/main/main/idatcs/00021029:0d0f31641207deae38bb314ff8a1bccd.pdf

BBC. (2010, February 6). Statements on Arch cru funds. *BBC.co.uk*. Retrieved from http://news.bbc.co.uk/2/hi/programmes/moneybox/8501831.stm

Beiping, T. (2009, July 10). Chinese agribusiness company in DR Congo to offer thousands of jobs for locals. *Xinhuanet.com*. Retrieved from http://news.xinhuanet.com/english/2009-07/10/content_11686244.htm

Belchior, M. J. (2010). China and Angola. *Macao Magazine, 40*(5). Retrieved from http://www.macaomagazine.net/index.php?option=com_content&view=article&id=119:china-and-angola&catid=40:issue-5

Bellingham, H. (2010). *UK and Africa: Delivering prosperity together*. Speech presented at Lancaster House, Foreign & Commonwealth Office, London, United Kingdom, 16 December 2010. Retrieved from https://www.gov.uk/government/speeches/uk-and-africa-delivering-prosperity-together--2

Bellingham, H. (2011). *The UK prosperity agenda—growth, open markets and good governance*. Speech presented at the Commonwealth Business Council business roundtable, Lagos, Nigeria, 17 February 2011. Retrieved from https://www.gov.uk/government/speeches/the-uk-prosperity-agenda-growth-open-markets-and-good-governance

Bergius, M. (2012, September). *Understanding land investment deals in Africa: Tanzanian villagers pay for Sun Biofuels investment disaster* (Land deal brief). Oakland: The Oakland Institute. Retrieved from http://www.oaklandins

titute.org/sites/oaklandinstitute.org/files/OI_Land_Deals_Brief_Sun_ Biofuels.pdf

Bergius, M. (2013, July 5). Kisarawe villagers to be paid compensation [Blog post]. Retrieved from http://mikaelbergius.wordpress.com/2013/07/05/kisa rawe-villagers-to-be-paid-compensation/

Bernasconi-Osterwalder, N., Johnson, L., & Zhang, J. (Eds.). (2013). *Chinese outward investment: An emerging policy framework*. Manitoba: The International Institute for Sustainable Development. Retrieved from http://www.iisd.org/pdf/2012/chinese_outward_investment.pdf

Bernstein, H. (1977). Notes on capital and peasantry. *Review of African Political Economy* 4(10), 60-73.

Bernstein, H., & Byres, T.J. (2001). From peasant studies to agrarian change. *Journal of Agrarian Change,1*(1), 1–56.

Bernstorff, J. v. (2013). The global "land grab,"sovereignty and human rights. *ESIL Reflections, 2*(9). Retrieved from http://www.esil-sedi.eu/node/426

Besada, H., & Goetz, A. (2012). The land crisis in southern Africa: Challenges for good governance. In B. Chigara (Ed.), *Southern African development community land issues: Towards a new sustainable land relations policy* (pp. 169-194). New York: Routledge.

Bessant, L. L. (1992). Coercive development: Land shortage, forced labor, and colonial development in the Chiweshe Reserve, colonial Zimbabwe, 1938-1946. *International Journal of African Historical Studies*, 39-65.

Biney, A. (2009). Land grabs: Another scramble for Africa. *Pambazuka News*, (144). Retrieved from http://pambazuka.org/en/category/features/58809

Biofuelsdigest.com. (2010, June 25). GEM Biofuels renamed Terra Rossa Plantations, as jatropha developer seeks image change. *Biofuelsdigest.com*. Retrieved from http:// www.biofuelsdigest.com/bdigest/2010/06/25/gem-biofuels-renamed-terrarossa-plantations-as-jatropha-developer-seeks-image-change/

Biofuelsdigest.com. (2010, July 1). Jatropha pioneer GEM Biofuels suspends share trading, delays audit. *Biofuelsdigest.com*. Retrieved from http://www.biofuelsdigest.com/bdigest/2010/07/01/jatropha-pioneer-gem-biofuels-sustpends-share-trading-delays-audit/ (accessed March 2011).

Biopact. (2006, August 14). Nigeria, China sign agreement on ethanol production. Retrieved from http://news.mongabay.com/bioenergy/2006/08/nigeria-china-sign-agreement-on.html

Biopact. (2007, September 4). Pro-Cana to invest $510 million in integrated ethanol, power, sugar and fertilizer plant in Mozambique. Retrieved from http://news.mongabay.com/bioenergy/2007/09/pro-cana-to-invest-510-million-in.html

BioZio. (2011). *Comprehensive Jatropha report: A detailed report on the Jatropha industry* (Updated February 2011). Chennai: BioZio. Retrieved from www.biozio.com/ref/report/jat/jatropha_biodiesel_report_feb_2011.pdf

Bird, F. (1998). *A defense of objectivity on the social sciences, rightly understood.* Paper presented at The Society of Christian Ethics. St. Cloud, United States.

Bird, F., & Velasquez, M. (Eds.). (2006). *Just business practices in a diverse and developing world: Essays on international business and global responsibilities.* London: Palgrave Macmillan.

Biron, C. (2012, April 23). World Bank overseeing global land grab. *Inter Press Service.* Retrieved from http://www.ipsnews.net/2012/04/world-bank-overseeing-global-land-grab/

BIS. (2010). *UK trade performance: Patterns in UK and global trade growth* (BIS economics paper no. 8). London: Skills. Retrieved from https://www.gov.uk/government/uploads/system/uploads/attachment_data/file/32114/10-803-uk-trade-performance-growth-patterns.pdf

BIS. (2011a). *Trade and investment for growth* [Whitepaper]. London: The Stationary Office. Retrieved from https://www.gov.uk/government/uploads/system/uploads/attachment_data/file/228941/8015.pdf

BIS. (2011b). Britain open for business [Press release, 10 May 2011]. Retrieved from https://www.gov.uk/government/news/britain-open-for-business

BIS. (2011c). *International trade and investment. The economic rationale for government support* (BIS economics paper no. 13). London: UK Trade and Investment (UKTI). Retrieved from https://www.gov.uk/government/uploads/system/uploads/attachment_data/file/32106/11-805-international-trade-investment-rationale-for-support.pdf

BIS. (2012). *The trade and investment for growth white paper: Progress and achievements in year one.* London: The Stationary Office. Retrieved from https://www.gov.uk/government/uploads/system/uploads/attachment_data/file/32473/12-623-trade-investment-for-growth-progress-year-one.pdf

BIS, FCO, UK Trade and Investment. (2012). Strengthening UK relationships in Asia, Latin America and Africa to support UK prosperity and security (12 December 2012) [Government website entry]. Retrieved from http://www.gov.uk/government/policies/strengthening-uk-relationships-in-asia-latin-america-and-africa-to-support-uk-prosperity-and-security

Bizikova, L., Roy, D., Swanson, D., Venema, H., & McCandless, M. (2013). *The water-energy-food security nexus: Towards a practical planning and decision support framework for landscape investment and risk management.* Manitoba: International Institute of Sustainable Development. Retrieved from http://www.iisd.org/pdf/2013/wef_nexus_2013.pdf

Black, J., Hashimzade, N., & Myles, G. (Eds.). (2009). *A dictionary of economics.* Oxford University Press [Online version]. Retrieved from http://www.

oxfordreference.com/view/10.1093/acref/9780199237043.001.0001/acref-9780199237043-e-2898

BloombergBusinessweek.com. (2005, August 21). China is a private sector economy. Retrieved from http://www.businessweek.com/stories/2005-08-21/online-extra-china-is-a-private-sector-economy

Bloomberg News. (2009, July 17). BP exits jatropha biofuel project to focus on ethanol. Retrieved from http://www.chron.com/business/energy/article/BP-exits-jatropha-biofuel-project-to-focus-on-1729179.php

Bloomberg News. (2009, September 30). GEM Biofuels Plc. Interim Results for the six months ended 30 June 2009. RNS Number: 9393Z. Retrieved from http://www.bloomberg.com/apps/news?pid=newsarchive&sid=aLGWD-mZBYujQ

Bloomberg News. (2011, July 20). Lonrho PLC LONR acquisition of Grindrod PCA. RNS Number: 7114K. Retrieved from http://renergieadvancedbiofuel.blogspot.com/2009/07/bp-exits-jatropha-biofuel-project-to.html

Bo, K. (2011). Governing China's energy in the context of global governance. *Global Policy, 2*(Issue Supplement 1), 51-65.

Bo, X. (2017, May 3). China becomes single largest contributor of Africa's FDI: report. *Xinhuanet*. Retrieved from http://www.xinhuanet.com/english/2017-05/03/c_136254183.htm

Boamah, F. (2011). *The relationship between land grabbing for biofuels and food security, a bane or Boon? The food security implications of jatropha biodiesel project in northern Ghana.* Presentation at the international conference Global Land Grabbing 2011, Brighton, United Kingdom.

Boamah, F. (2014). How and why chiefs formalize land use in recent times: The politics of land dispossession through biofuels investments in Ghana. *Review of African Political Economy*, (ahead-of-print), 1–18.

Borras, S., & McKinley, T. (2006). *The unresolved land reform debate: Beyond state-led or market-led models* (Policy research brief nr. 2). Brasilia: UNDP International Poverty Center. Retrieved from http://www.ipc-undp.org/pub/IPCPolicyResearchBrief2.pdf

Borras, S., & Franco, J. (2010). Towards a broader view of the politics of global land grab: rethinking land issues, reframing resistance. *Initiatives in Critical Agrarian Studies Working Paper Series, 1*. Retrieved from http://www.google.de/url?sa=t&rct=j&q=&esrc=s&source=web&cd=2&ved=0CCsQFjAB&url=http%3A%2F%2Framshorn.ca%2Fsites%2Fdefault%2Ffiles%2FBorras%2520%2526%2520Franco%2C%2520Politics%2520of%2520Land%2520Grab.pdf&ei=-x6DVJPaMYmBU_r5gwg&usg=AFQjCNHtuWaTUgqktluZq1OnE-oXxp_dBg&bvm=bv.80642063,d.d24

Borras, S., McMichael, P., & Scoones, I. (2010). The politics of biofuels, land and agrarian change: editors' introduction. *The Journal of Peasant Studies*, 37(4), 575-592

Borras, S., & Franco, J. C. (2012). Global land grabbing and trajectories of agrarian change: A preliminary analysis. *Journal of Agrarian Change*, 12(1), 34–59.

Borras. S., Hall, R., Scoones, I., White, B., & Wolford, W. (2011). Towards a better understanding of global land grabbing: an editorial introduction. *The Journal of Peasant Studies*, 38(2), 209-216.

Borras, S., Franco, J. C., Gómez, S., Kay, C., & Spoor, M. (2012). Land grabbing in Latin America and the Caribbean. *The Journal of Peasant Studies*, 39(3-4), 845-872.

Bosshard, P. (2008). *China's environmental footprint in Africa* (SAIIA China in Africa Policy Briefing Number 3). Johannesburg: South African Institute of International Affairs (SAIIA). Retrieved from http://www.saiia.org.za.

Bow, M. (2012, March 13). Farmland hindered as asset class. *Professional Pensions*. Retrieved from http://farmlandgrab.org/20180

Bowden, B. (2009). *The empire of civilization*. Chicago: University of Chicago Press.

Braeckmann, C. (2009, September). Le Congo et Ses Amis Chinois. *Le Monde Diplomatique*. Retrieved from http://www.monde-diplomatique.fr/2009/09/BRAECKMAN/18100

Brass, T. (1997). The agrarian myth, the new populism and the new right. *Economic and Political Weekly*, 32(4), 27–42.

Brautigam, D. (2008). Chinese Business and African Development: 'Flying Geese' or 'Hidden Dragons'?. In D. Large, J. C. Alden, & R. M. S. Soares de Oliveira (Eds.), *China Returns to Africa: A Rising Power and a Continent Embrace* (pp. 51-68). New York: Columbia University Press and London: Christopher Hurst.

Brautigam, D. (2009). *Dragon's gift: The real story of China in Africa*. Oxford: Oxford University Press.

Brautigam, D. (2010, June 2). China International Fund's new Bellzone-Kalia Guinea deal [Blog post]. Retrieved from http://www.chinaafricarealstory.com/2010/06/china-international-funds-new-bellzone.html

Brautigam, D. (2010). *China, Africa and the international aid architecture* (Working papers series no. 107). Tunis: African Development Bank. Retrieved from http://www.afdb.org/fileadmin/uploads/afdb/Documents/Publications/WORKING%20107%20%20PDF%20E33.pdf

Brautigam, D. (2011a). *Testimony on China's growing role in Africa before the United States Senate Committee on Foreign Relations Subcommittee on African Affairs*. Washington, DC: United States Senate. Retrieved from http://www.foreign.senate.gov/imo/media/doc/Deborah_Brautigam_Testimony.pdf

Brautigam, D. (2011b). Chinese development aid in Africa: What, where, why and how much?. In J. Golley, & L. Song (Eds.), *Rising China: Global challenges and opportunities* (pp. 203-223). Canberra: Australia National University Press.

Brautigam, D. (2011, February). China's special economic zones in Africa [Blog post]. Retrieved from http://www.chinaafricarealstory.com/2011/02/chinas-special-economic-zones-in-africa.html

Brautigam (2011, October 19). China International Fund in Africa: Caixin's new revelations [Blog post]. Retrieved from http://www.chinaafricarealstory.com/2011/10/china-international-fund-in-africa.html

Brautigam, D., & Tang, X. (2011). African Shenzhen: China's special economic zones in Africa. *Journal of Modern African Studies, 49*(1), 27–54.

Brautigam, D. (2012, January 12). The Zambezi Valley: China's first agricultural colony? Fiction or fact? [Blog post]. Retrieved from http://www.chinaafricarealstory.com/

Brautigam, D., & Ekman, S.-M. S. (2012). Briefing: Rumours and realities of Chinese agricultural engagement in Mozambique. *African Affairs 111*(444), 483-492.

Brautigam, D., & Tang, X. (2012). *An overview of Chinese agricultural and rural engagement in Tanzania* (IFPRI Discussion Paper 01214). Washington, DC: International Food Policy Research Institute. Retrieved from http://www.ifpri.org/sites/default/files/publications/ifpridp01214.pdf

Brautigam, D., & Zhang, H. (2013). Green dreams: Myth and reality in China's agricultural investment in Africa. *Third World Quarterly, 34*(9), 1676–1696.

Broadman, H. (2010). Multinational enterprises from emerging markets: Implications for the North and South. In K. P. Sauvant, G. McAllister, & W. Maschek (Eds.), *Foreign direct investments from emerging markets: The challenges ahead* (pp. 325-334). New York: Palgrave Macmillan.

Broughton, A. (2012, November 6). Land grabbing: A new colonialism. *International Journal of Socialist Renewal*. Retrieved from http://links.org.au/node/3099

Brown, G. (2002). *Mansion House speech*. Speech presented at the Mansion House, London, United Kingdom, 26 June 2002. Retrieved from http://www.theguardian.com/politics/2002/jun/27/economy.uk

Brown, G. (2004). *Mansion House speech*. Speech presented at the Mansion House, London, United Kingdom, 17 June 2004. Retrieved from http://www.theguardian.com/politics/2004/jun/17/economy.uk

Brown, L. (2013). Food, Fuel, and the Global Land Grab. *The Futurist, 47*(1). Retrieved from http://www.wfs.org/futurist/january-february-2013-vol-47-no-1/food-fuel-and-global-land-grab

Bryant, D. (2011). *Agriculture as an asset class 2011*. Canberra: Rural Funds Management Ltd.

Bruinsma, J. (2003). *World agriculture: towards 2015/2030. An FAO perspective*. London: Earthscan.
BT Pension Scheme. (2013). *Report and accounts 2013*. Retrieved from http://www.btpensions.net/41/scheme-report-and-accounts.
Buckley, L. (2011). *Eating bitter to taste sweet: An ethnographic sketch of a Chinese agriculture project in Senegal*. Paper presented at the international conference Global Land Grabbing 2011, Brighton, United Kingdom.
Buckley, P.J., Clegg, J.L., Cross, A. R., & Voss, H. (2010). What can emerging markets learn from outward direct investment policies of advanced countries? In K.P. Sauvant, G. McAllister, & W.A. Maschek, *Foreign direct investments from emerging market: the challenges ahead* (pp. 243-276). New York: Palgrave Macmillan.
Burgis, T. (2009, January 16). Lornho secures rice land deal in Angola. *Financial Times*. Retrieved from http://www.ft.com/cms/s/0/63460024-e342-11dd-a5cf-0000779fd2ac.html#axzz3EEC2JiD2
Burnett, P. (2014, April 7). Teak forest exploitation, South Sudan [Blog post]. Retrieved from http://ejatlas.org/conflict/teak-forest-exploitation-south-sudan
BusinessDaylive.co.za. (2014, January 30). Zimbabwe adopts Chinese Yuan as legal currency. *Bdlive.co.za*. Retrieved from http://www.bdlive.co.za/africa/africanbusiness/2014/01/30/zimbabwe-adopts-chinese-yuan-as-legal-currency
Business and Human Rights Resource Centre. (n.d.). Kenya: Villagers are being displaced as large swathes of land is turned over to companies for biofuel production, article alleges. Retrieved from http://business-humanrights.org/en/kenya-villagers-are-being-displaced-as-large-swathes-of-land-is-turned-over-to-companies-for-biofuel-production-article-alleges#c59938
Buzan, B., & Lawson, G. (2013). The global transformation: The nineteenth century and the making of modern international relations. *International Studies Quarterly*, 57(3), 620-634.
Cabinet Office, S. U. (2008). *Food matters: Towards a strategy for the 21st century*. London: The Cabinet Office. Retrieved from http://www.ifr.ac.uk/waste/Reports/food%20matters,%20Towards%20a%20Strategy%20for%20the%2021st%20Century.pdf
CADF. (2014). *CADFund* [Corporate website]. China Africa Development Fund. Retrieved from http://www.cadfund.com/en/
Caffentzis. G. (2002). Neoliberalism in Africa, apocalyptic failures and business as usual practices. *Alternatives—Turkish Journal of International Relations*, 1(3), 89-104.
Cain, P. J., & Hopkins, A. G. (1987). Gentlemanly capitalism and British expansion overseas II: New imperialism, 1850-1945. *The Economic History Review*, 40(1), 1-26.

Cain, P. J., & Hopkins, A. G. (2001). *British imperialism: 1688-2000* (2nd edition.). New York, NY: Routledge.

CAITEC. (2010). *China-Africa trade and economic relationship: Annual report 2010.* Beijing: Chinese Academy of International Trade and Economic Cooperation. Retrieved from http://www.fahamu.org/downloads/China-Africa_Trade_and_Economic_Relationship_Annual_Report_2010.pdf

Campbell, B., & Clapp, J. (1995). Guinea's economic performance under structural adjustment: Importance of mining and agriculture. *The Journal of Modern African Studies, 33*(3), 425–449.

Campbell, H. (2011, December 1). Angola: Fifty years of continued uprisings. *AllAfrica.com.* Retrieved from http://allafrica.com/stories/201112020892.html

Cargill. T. (2011). *More with less: Trends in UK diplomatic engagement in Sub-Saharan Africa* (Africa programme paper AFP PP 2011/03). London: Chatham House. Retrieved from http://www.chathamhouse.org/publications/papers/view/174359#

Carnell, R. (1996). *Overseas investment and the UK: Explanations, policy implications, facts and figures* (HM Treasury Occasional Paper No. 8). London: HM Treasury.

Carrere, R. (2013). *Oil palm in Africa: Past, present and future scenarios* (WRM series on tree plantations no. 15). World Rainforest Movement. Retrieved from http://wrm.org.uy/wp-content/uploads/2014/08/Oil_Palm_in_Africa_2013.pdf

Cato, S. M. (2011). *Environment and economy.* New York: Routledge.

Caulker, P. (2010). *Sierra Leone investment outreach campaign: Opportunities for investors in the oil palm sector.* Freetown: Sierra Leone Investment and Export Promotion Agency (SLIEPA). Retrieved from http://www.investsierraleone.biz/download/SL_OilPalm_Investment_Opp.pdf

Confederation of British Industry. (2011). *A vision for rebalancing the economy. A New approach to growth.* London: Confederation of British Industry. Retrieved from http://www.cbi.org.uk/campaigns/a-vision-for-rebalancing-the-economy/

CDC. (2012, May 9). *CDC announces USD 15m investment* [Press release]. Retrieved from http://www.cdcgroup.com/uploads/20120509_cdc_sgi_pressrelease_final.pdf (last accessed March 2013).

CDC. (2013, November 8). *CDC invests USD 18.1m in agribusiness in the Democratic Republic of Congo* [Press release]. Retrieved from http://www.cdcgroup.com/Media/News/CDC-invests-US181m-in-agribusiness-in-the-Democratic-Republic-of-Congo/

Cementchina.net. (2010, August 27). *Chinese business operators seek to build cement factory in Mozambique.* Retrieved from http://www.cementchina.net/newsdetail.aspx?id=7727

Cementchina.net. (2011, May 31). Cement production in Mozambique to triple through Chinese investment. Retrieved from http://www.cementchina.net/newsdetail.aspx?id=8812

Cernansky, R. (2011, October 26). UK company pulls out of controversial Kenya biofuel project. Retrieved from http://www.treehugger.com/renewable-energy/uk-company-pulls-out-controversial-kenya-biofuel-project.html

Cerny, P. G., & Evans, M. (2004). Globalisation and public policy under New Labour. *Policy Studies, 25*(1), 51–65.

Chafer, T. (2002). Franco-African relations: No longer so exceptional? [Pre-copy-edited version of the similar article, published in *African Affairs*, 101: 343-363]. Retrieved from http://eprints.port.ac.uk/60/1/African_Affairs_Article.pdf

Chafer, T. (2010). *The role of the FCO in UK Government* [Written evidence for the Foreign Affairs Committee]. London: House of Commons. Retrieved from http://www.publications.parliament.uk/pa/cm201012/cmselect/cmfaff/665/665vw10.htm

Chandler, A. D., & Mazlish, B. (Eds.). (2005). *Leviathans: Multinational corporations and the new global history*. Cambridge: Cambridge University Press.

Chang, H.-J. (2003). Kicking away the ladder: Infant industry promotion in historical perspective. *Oxford Development Studies, 31*(1), 21–32.

Chang, H.-J. (2004). Regulation of foreign investment in historical perspective. *European Journal of Development Research, 16*(3), 687–715.

Chaponniere, J-R., Gabas, Jean J-J., & Zhen, Q. (2010). *China Africa in agriculture: A background paper on trade, investment and aid in agriculture*. Bamako: China-DAC Study Group on Agriculture, Food Security and Rural Development. Retrieved from http://www.iprcc.org/userfiles/file/Jean-Raphael%20Chaponniere%20and%20Zheng%20Qi-EN.pdf

Chasukwa, M. (2013). *An investigation of the political economy of land grabs in Malawi*. (Land Deal Politics Initiative working paper no. 30). Retrieved from http://www.plaas.org.za/sites/default/files/publications-pdf/LDPI30%20Chasukwa.pdf

Chen, C., Goldstein, A., & Orr, R. J. (2009). Local operations of Chinese construction firms in Africa: An empirical survey. *International Journal of Construction Management, 9*(2), 75-89.

Chen, Z., & Jian, J. (2009). *Chinese provinces as foreign policy actors in Africa* (SAIIA Occasional Paper No. 22). Johannesburg: South African Institute of International Affairs. Retrieved from http://www.saiia.org.za/occasional-papers/chinese-provinces-as-foreign-policy-actors-in-africa

Cheng, L. (2001). Diversification of Chinese entrepreneurs and cultural pluralism in the reform era. In Shiping Hua (Ed.), *Chinese Political Culture, 1989-2000* (pp. 219–245). London: M.E. Sharpe.

Chichava, S. (2013). Xai-Xai Chinese rice farm and Mozambican internal political dynamics: A complex relation. (LSE IDEAS Occasional Paper 2). London: London School of Economics. Retrieved from http://www.lse.ac.uk/IDEAS/programmes/africaProgramme/pdfs/Sergio-Chichava---Occasional-Paper-2.pdf

Chinafrica.asia. (2009). Angola's laudable oil trade with China: China and Africa Meeting Point. *Chinafrica.asia*. Retrieved from http://www.chinafrica.asia/angola-laudable-oil-trade-with-china/

ChinaDaily.com.cn. (2008, May 17). Firms will grow rice in Africa. *Chinadaily.com.cn*. Retrieved from http:// www.chinadaily.com.cn/bizchina/2008-05/09/content_6674352.htm

ChinaDaily.com.cn (2012, November 12). Entrepreneurs' presence grows at CPC congress. *Chinadaily.com.cn*. Retrieved from http://www.chinadaily.com.cn/china/2012cpc/2012-11/12/content_15919473.htm

China Development Bank (CDB). (2012, May 31). $57 mn invested in agriculture by China-Africa Development Fund [Corporate website]. Retrieved from http://www.cdb.com.cn/english/NewsInfo.asp?NewsId=4159

China DSIC International Trade Co. Ltd. (2014). Our business: Trade department 3 [Corporate website]. Retrieved from http://www.sdictrade.com/en/Business/ywjg/default159.shtml

China International Fund. (CIF). (2011). CIF Space 2011/1 [Company brochure]. Retrieved from www.chinainternationalfund.com/UserFiles/Upload/20113255022533.pdf

China National Agricultural Development Group Corporation. (n.d.). Basic Information [corporate website]. Retrieved from http://www.chinacsrmap.org/Org_Show_EN.asp?ID=1416

China.org.cn. (2003, December 10). Fruitful agricultural cooperation. *China.org.cn*. Retrieved from http://www.china.org.cn/english/features/China-Africa/82040.htm

Chinese Embassy in the Republic of Zambia. (2013, September 10). Chinese Ambassador commended China-Africa Cotton Zambia Limited [Press release]. Retrieved from http://zm.chineseembassy.org/eng/sgzxdthxx/t1074797.htm

Chinese Government. (2006). 11th Five-Year Plan, 2006-2010. Retrieved from Chinese Government's Official Web Portal: http://english.gov.cn/special/115y_index.htm

Chinese Government. (2011). 12th Five-Year Plan, 2011-2015. Retrieved from Chinese Government's Official Web Portal: http://english.gov.cn/special/115y_index.htm

Chinese Academy of Social Sciences, & UNDP China. (2013). *China national human development report 2013: Sustainable and liveable cities: Toward ecological civilization*. Beijing: China Publishing Group Corporation. Retrieved from http://www.cn.undp.org/content/dam/china/docs/Publications/UNDP-CH_2013%20NHDR_EN.pdf

Chirombo, R. (2009, December 29). Malawi: Cotton production gets a boost [Blog post]. Retrieved from http://zachimalawi.blogspot.de/2009/12/malawi-cotton-production-gets-boost.html

Clapp, J., & Fuchs, D. (Eds.) (2009). *Corporate power in global agrifood governance*. Cambridge: MIT.

Clapp, J. (2013). *Financialisation, distance, and global food politics*. Paper presented at the international conference Food Sovereignty: A Critical Dialogue, 14-15 September 2013, New Haven, Yale University.

Clapp, J. (2015). Food security and food sovereignty. Getting past the binary. *Dialogues in Human Mispelling-Geography*, 4(2), 206-211.

Clapp, R. A. J. (1988). Representing reciprocity, reproducing domination: Ideology and the labour process in Latin American contract farming. *The Journal of Peasant Studies*,16(1), 5–39.

Cleantech Investor. (2007, March). London Cleantech IPOs: Rush of AIM listings ends 2006. *Cleantech Magazine*. Retrieved from http://www.cleantechinvestor.com/portal/mainmenucomp/companiesc/1381-clean-energy-brazil/7496-london-cleantech-ipos-rush-of-aim-listings-ends-2006.html

Cleantech Investor. (2008, May). UK Quoted Jatropha: Gem Biofuels. *Cleantech Investor*. Retrieved from http://www.cleantechinvestor.com/portal/mainmenucomp/companiesg/1562-gem-biofuels/1021-uk-quoted-jatropha-gem-biofuels.html

Cleveland, C., & Tietenberg, T. (2009, August 29). European Union Emissions Trading Scheme (EU ETS). *The Encyclopedia of Earth online*. Retrieved from http://www.eoearth.org/view/article/152687/

Clover, J., & Eriksen, S. (2009). The effects of land tenure change on sustainability: Human security and environmental change in southern African savannas. *Environmental Science & Policy*, 12(1), 53–70.

Cohn, S. (2003). Common ground critiques of neoclassical principles texts. *Post-autistic economics review, 18*.

Collier, D. (2011). Understanding process tracing. *PS: Political Science & Politics*, 44(04), 823-830.

Collins English Dictionary (5th edition, first published in 2000), & Collins A-Z Thesaurus (1st edition, first published in 1995). Imperialism. Retrieved from http://dictionary.reverso.net/english-definition/imperialism

Collinson, P. (2010, July 24). Is agriculture the next big investment thing? *The Guardian*. Retrieved from http://www.theguardian.com/money/2010/jul/24/agriculture-next-big-investment

Commission for Africa. (2005). *Our common interest: Report of the Commission for Africa*. London: Commission for Africa. Retrieved from http://www.commissionforafrica.info/2005-report

Commission for Africa. (2010). *Still our common interest: Commission for Africa report 2010*. London: Commission for Africa. Retrieved from http://www.commissionforafrica.info/wp-content/uploads/2010/09/cfa-report-2010-full-version.pdf

Congressional-Executive Commission on China. (CECC). (2005). *Special topic paper: China's household registration system: Sustained reform needed to protect China's rural migrants*. Washington, DC: CECC. Retrieved from http://www.cecc.gov/publications/issue-papers/cecc-special-topic-paper-chinas-household-registration-system-sustained

Coonan, C. (2008, December 28). China's new export: farmers. *The Independent*. Retrieved from http://www.independent.co.uk/news/world/asia/chinas-new-export-farmers-1215001.html

Complant (China National Complete Plant Import & Export Corporation). (n.d.). Overseas institutions [Corporate website]. Retrieved from http://www.complant.com/ejigou2.htm

Concession Agreement. (2006, June 28). Management and development of teak plantation agreement, 2006, between the Government of Western Equatoria State (Ministry of agriculture, environment and rural development) as principal partner and the Government of Southern Sudan (Ministry of agriculture and forestry) on one party and Equatoria Teak Company Ltd. Western Equatoria State, Yambio on the other. Retrieved from http://www.oaklandinstitute.org/sites/oaklandinstitute.org/files/Management_and_Development_of_Teak_Plantation_Agreement.pdf

Cottrell, P. L. (1975). *British overseas investment in the nineteenth century*. London: The Macmillan Press.

Cotula, L. (2011). *Land deals in Africa: What is in the contracts?* London: International Institute for Environment and Development. Retrieved from http://pubs.iied.org/pdfs/12568IIED.pdf

Cotula, L. (2012) The international political economy of the global land rush: A critical appraisal of trends, scale, geography and drivers. *The Journal of Peasant Studies 39*(3-4), 649-680.

Council of Ministers/Republic of Bulgaria. (2013, November 26). *Plamen Oresharski: We invited Chinese companies to invest in the processing industry* [Government website entry]. Retrieved from http://www.government.bg/cgi-bin/e-cms/vis/vis.pl?s=001&p=0137&n=74&g=

Creamer Media. (2009, November 11). Edmonds, Groves resign from Camec board after ENRC takeover. *Mining Weekly*. Retrieved from http://www.miningweekly.com/article/edmonds-groves-resign-from-camec-board-after-enrc-takeover-2009-11-11

Craggs, R. (2014). Development in a global-historical context. In V. Desai & R. Potter (Eds.), *The Companion to Development Studies* (Third edition, pp. 5–9). London: Routledge.
D1 Oils Plc. (2011). Growing energy solutions [Corporate website]. Retrieved from http://www.jatropha.pro/PDF%20bestanden/D1%20Oils%20Zambia.pdf
D1 Oils Plc. (2010). *Annual report and accounts 2010*. Retrieved from http://www.neosplc.com/wp-content/uploads/2011/07/D1-Oils-annual-report-and-accounts-2010.pdf
Dahlbeck, A. (2012). *Fuel for thought: Addressing the social impacts of EU biofuel policies*. Action Aid International. Retrieved from http://www.actionaid.org/sites/files/actionaid/fuel_for_thought.pdf
Daudin, G., Morys, M., & O'Rourke, K. (2010). Globalization, 1870-1914. In S. Broadberry & K. H. O'Rourke (Eds.), *The Cambridge Economic History of Modern Europe, volume 2: 1870 to the Present* (pp. 5-29). Cambridge: Cambridge University Press.
Davies, K. (2013). *China investment policy: An update* (OECD Working Papers on International Investment No. 2013/01). Paris: OECD. Retrieved from http://www.oecd.org/china/WP-2013_1.pdf
Davis, L. (1999). The late nineteenth century British imperialist: specification, quantification and controlled conjectures. In R. Dumett (Ed.), *Gentlemanly capitalism and British imperialism: The new debate on Empire* (pp.82-112). New York: Longman.
Davis, M. (2002). *Late Victorian holocausts*. London: Verso.
Davis, T. (2003). *Agricultural water use and river basin conservation*. Gland: WWF. Retrieved from http://assets.panda.org/downloads/agwaterusefinalreport.pdf
De Angelis, M. (2005). The political economy of global neoliberal governance. *Review (Fernand Braudel Center), 28*(3), 229-257.
De Beule. F., & Van den Bulcke. D. (2010). Changing policy regimes in outward foreign direct investment: From control to promotion. In K. P. Sauvant, G. McAllister, & W. Maschek (Eds.), *Foreign direct investments from emerging markets: The challenges ahead* (pp. 227-304). New York: Palgrave Macmillan.
Department for Environment, Food and Rural Affairs. (DEFRA). (2008). *Ensuring the UK's food security in a changing world* (Discussion paper). London: Department for Environment, Food and Rural Affairs. Retrieved from http://www.ifr.ac.uk/waste/Reports/DEFRA-Ensuring-UK-Food-Security-in-a-changing-world-170708.pdf
De Master, K. (2013). *Navigating de- and re-peasantisation: Potential limitations of a universal food sovereignty approach for polish smallholders*. Paper presented at the international conference Food Sovereignty: A Critical Dialogue, 14-15 September 2013, New Haven, Yale University.

Deming, S. (2011). The economic importance of Indian opium and trade with China on Britain's economy, 1843-1890 (pp. 1-17). *Economic Working Papers 25*.

Deng, D., & Mittal, A. (2011). *Understanding land investment deals in Africa: Country Report Sudan*. Oakland: The Oakland Institute. Retrieved from http://www.oaklandinstitute.org/sites/oaklandinstitute.org/files/OI_country_report_south_sudan_1.pdf

Deng, X. (1974). *Speech by Chairman of the delegation of the People's Republic of China, Teng Hsiao-Ping*. Speech presented at the Special Session of the U.N. General Assembly, New York, 10 April 1974. Retrieved from http://www.marxists.org/reference/archive/deng-xiaoping/1974/04/10.htm

Denisia, V. (2010). Foreign direct investment theories: An overview of the main FDI theories. *European Journal of Interdisciplinary Studies*, (3).

Department for International Development. (DFID). (1997). *Eliminating world poverty: A challenge for the 21st century: White paper on international development*. London: Stationary Office. Retrieved from http://www.bristol.ac.uk/poverty/downloads/keyofficialdocuments/Eliminating%20world%20poverty%20challenge.pdf

Department for International Development. (DFID). (2000). *Eliminating world poverty: Making globalisation work for the poor: White paper on international development*. London: Department for International Development. Retrieved from http://webarchive.nationalarchives.gov.uk/+/http:/www.dfid.gov.uk/Documents/publications/whitepaper2000.pdf

Department for International Development. (DFID). (2012, May 9). Business: CDC backs first Ethiopian fund [Press release]. Retrieved from https://www.gov.uk/government/news/business-cdc-backs-first-ethiopian-fund

Department for International Development. (DFID). (2013, March 25). The Investment Climate Facility for Africa [Guidance]. Retrieved from https://www.gov.uk/the-investment-climate-facility-for-africa-icf

Department for Transport. (2012, November 5). Renewable transport fuels obligation [Guidance]. Retrieved from https://www.gov.uk/renewable-transport-fuels-obligation

Department of Trade and Industry. (DTI). (2003). *Our energy future—creating a low carbon economy: Energy white paper*. London: Stationary Office. Retrieved from http://fire.pppl.gov/uk_energy_whitepaper_feb03.pdf

Department of Trade and Industry. (DTI). (2004). *Making globalization a force for good: Trade and investment white paper*. London: Department of Trade and Industry. Retrieved from http://www.tips.org.za/files/White_Paper_Trade_and_Investment_2004.pdf

DeRouen, K., & Mintz, A. (2010). *Understanding foreign policy decision making*. Cambridge: Cambridge University Press.

De Schutter, O. (2009, June 11). Large-scale land acquisitions and leases: A set of core principles and measures to address the human rights challenge [Briefing note]. Geneva: UN Office of the High Commissioner for Human Rights. Retrieved from http://www2.ohchr.org/english/issues/food/docs/BriefingNotelandgrab.pdf

De Schutter, O. (2011a). How not to think of land-grabbing: Three critiques of large-scale investments in farmland. *Journal of Peasant Studies, 38*(2), 249-279.

De Schutter, O. (2011b). Green rush: The global race for farmland and the rights of land users. *Harvard International Law Journal, 52*(2), 503-559.

Dhillon, S. (2014, February 3). Africa rising. British Chambers of Commerce [Blog post]. Retrieved from http://exportbritain.org.uk/blogs/africa-rising.html

Diaz-Chavez, R., Mutimba, S., Watson, H., Rodriguez-Sanchez, S., & Nguer, M. (2010). *Mapping food and bioenergy in Africa*. Accra: Forum for Agricultural Research in Africa. Retrieved from http://www.globalbioenergy.org/uploads/media/1005_Imperial_College_-_Mapping_food_and_bioenergy_in_Africa.pdf

Dicken, P. (2007). *Global shift: Mapping the changing contours of the world economy*. New York: Guilford Press.

Dietrich-O'Connor, F. (2011). *Decision impact assessment: Promotion of biofuel production in Ghana* (RPD 6080 Environment and Development). Guelph: University of Guelph. Retrieved from http://www.academia.edu/3696959/Decision_Impact_Assessment_for_the_Promotion_of_Biofuel_Production_in_Ghana

Dore, R. (2000). *Stock market capitalism: Welfare Capitalism: Japan and Germany versus the Anglo-Saxons*. New York: Oxford University Press.

Douguet, V. (2013, September 5). Madagascar: To eat or to be eaten. Retrieved from http://www.ejolt.org/2013/09/madagascar-to-eat-or-to-be-eaten/

Duignan, P., & Gann, L.H. (Eds.). (1969). *Colonialism in Africa, 1870-1960* (Vol. I). London: Cambridge University Press.

Duignan, P., & Gann, L.H. (1969a). Introduction. In P. Duignan & L.H. Gann (Eds.), *Colonialism in Africa, 1870-1960* (Vol. I, pp. 1-26). London: Cambridge University Press.

Duignan, P., & Gann, L. H. (1969b). Reflections on imperialism and the scramble for Africa. In P. Duignan & L. H. Gann (Eds.), *Colonialism in Africa, 1870-1960* (Vol. I, pp. 100-131). London: Cambridge University Press.

Dumett, R. (Ed.). (1999). *Gentlemanly capitalism and British imperialism: The new debate on Empire*. New York: Longman.

Dunning, J., & Narula, R. (Eds.). (1996). *Foreign Direct Investment and governments: Catalysts for economic restructuring*. London: Routledge.

Duran, J. (2012). *China International Fund-SPI: The Chinese Frelimo connection*. Paper presented at the international conference Moçambique: acumulação e transformação num contexto de crise internacional 2012, Maputo, Mozambique.

Dutta, M. (2005). *China's industrial revolution and economic presence*. Hackensack:World Scientific.

Dwinger, F. (2010, August 2). Special economic zones (SEZs) in Africa: China's economic development model comes to Mauritius. Retrieved from http://www.consultancyafrica.com/index.php?option=com_content&view=article&id=490:special-economic-zones-sezs-in-africa-chinas-economic-development-model-comes-to-mauritius&catid=58:asia-dimension-discussion-papers&Itemid=264

Eastwood, R., Lipton, M., & Newell, A. (2004). *Farm Size*. Paper prepared for Volume III of the Handbook of Agricultural Economics, University of Sussex. Retrieved from http://www.sussex.ac.uk/Units/PRU/farm_size.pdf

Economic Commission for Africa, & Africa Union. (2011). *Minerals and Africa's Development: The International Study Group Report on Africa's Mineral Regimes*. Addis Ababa: Economic Commission for Africa. Retrieved from http://repository.uneca.org/bitstream/handle/10855/21569/Bib-69220.pdf?sequence=1

Economic Observer. (2012, February 11). Nongye buju "zou chuqu" san da yanqi quanding zhongdian. *Economic Observer*. Retrieved from http://www.eeo.com.cn/2012/0211/220696.shtml

Edelman, M. (2013). Messy hectares: questions about the epistemology of land grabbing data. *Journal of Peasant Studies*, 40(3), 485-501.

Edelman, M., Oya, C., & Borras, S. Jr. (Eds.). (2013). Global land grabs [Special issue]. *Third World Quarterly, 34*(9).

EdificeCapital.com. (2014). Agriland. Retrieved from http://edificecapital.com/en/investment-funds/agriland-2.html

Ejatlas.org. (2014). Equatorial palm oil project stalls in Bassa, Liberia. *Environmental Justice Atlas*. Retrieved from http://ejatlas.org/conflict/equatorial-palm-oil-project-stalls-in-bassa-liberia

Ekins, P. (1993). "Limits to growth" and "sustainable development": Grappling with ecological realities. *Ecological Economics, 8*, 269–288.

Ekman, S.-M. S. (2010). *Leasing land overseas: A viable strategy for Chinese food security? Opportunities and risks of Chinese agricultural investments in Mozambique* [Master thesis]. Shanghai: Fudan University, School of Economics. Retrieved from http://www.google.de/url?sa=t&rct=j&q=&esrc=s&source=web&cd=1&ved=0CCMQFjAA&url=http%3A%2F%2Fomrmz.org%2Findex.php%2Fbiblioteca%2Fcategory%2F52-china%3Fdownload%3D944%3Achina&ei=6q-EVK6VBtKtaZrpgZgN&usg=AFQjCNHHlZZguNEHNic7y8c4ZfVH7dpVWQ&bvm=bv.80642063,d.d2s

Energy-profile.com. (2009). *A man in the know* [Interview with Sam Malin]. *Energy Profile 2009:* (2), 50–55. Retrieved from https://s3.amazonaws.com/files3.peopleperhour.com/uploads/Portfolio-19880-SAM%20MALIN.pdf

English.news.cn. (2010, August 18). Chinese vice president calls for stronger agricultural cooperation. *English.news.cn.* Retrieved from http://www.focac.org/eng/ltda/dsjbzjhy/t725057.htm

English.news.cn. (2011, June 21). Communist Party organizations play important role in China's private enterprises. *English.news.cn.* Retrieved from http://news.xinhuanet.com/english2010/indepth/2011-06/21/c_13941961.htm

Equatoria Teak Company. (2014). Plantations [Corporate website]. Retrieved from http://www.equatoriateak.com/plantations/http://www.equatoriateak.com/plantations/

Equatorial Palm Oil. (2010, February 23). *Equatorial Palm Oil Plc.: Placing and admission to AIM* [Admission document]. Retrieved from http://www.epoil.co.uk/uploads/epo-admission-document.pdf

Equatorial Palm Oil. (2011). About us [Corporate website]. Retrieved from http://www.epoil.co.uk/aboutus.aspx

Equatorial Palm Oil. (2013). *Annual report and accounts: For the year ended 31 December 2013.* Retrieved from http://www.epoil.co.uk/uploads/epofinancialstatements2013v16.pdf

Equatorial Palm Oil. (2014). *Annual report and accounts: For the period ended 30 September 2014.* Retrieved from http://www.epoil.co.uk/corporate-documents.aspx

Equatorial Palm Oil. (2015). About us [Corporate website]. Retrieved from http://www.epoil.co.uk/ (accessed 13 January 2015).

Ernst & Young. (2011a). *It's time for Africa: Ernst & Young's 2011 Africa attractiveness survey.* London: Ernst &Young Global Ltd. Retrieved from http://www.ey.com/ZA/en/Issues/Business-environment/2011-Africa-attractiveness-survey

Ernst & Young. (2011b). *Destination UK: Sustaining success in the new economy.* London: Ernst & Young Global Ltd. Retrieved from http://www.ey.com/UK/en/Issues/Business-environment/2011-European-attractiveness-survey

Ernst & Young. (2012). *Building bridges: Ernst & Young's 2012 Africa attractiveness survey.* London: Ernst & Young Global Ltd. Retrieved from http://emergingmarkets.ey.com/wp-content/uploads/downloads/2012/05/attractiveness_2012_africa_v16.pdf

Ernst & Young. (2013). *Getting down to business: Ernst & Young's Attractiveness Survey: Africa 2013.* London: Ernst & Young Global Ltd. Retrieved from http://www.ey.com/Publication/vwLUAssets/The_Africa_Attractiveness_Survey_2013/$FILE/Africa_Attractiveness_Survey_2013_AU1582.pdf

[ESG/ICTSD/Le Hub/UEMOA/UN Foundation] Energy and Security Group, International Center for Trade, Le Hub, UEMOA, & UN Foundation. (2008).

Sustainable bioenergy development in UEMOA member countries. Retrieved from http://www.compete-bioafrica.net/publications/publ/UNF_Bioenergy_full_report-10-2008.pdf

EthiopianReview.com. (2011, February 2). Woyanne agricultural minister dismisses president's request. *Ethiopian Review*. Retrieved from http://www.ethiopianreview.com/content/31359

European Commission. (1997). Energy for the future: renewable sources of energy. White paper for a community strategy and action plan (Whitepaper). COM(97)588 final. Retrieved from http://europa.eu/documents/comm/white_papers/pdf/com97_599_en.pdf

European Commission. (2012, May 18). Food security: EU supports G8 initiative for a "New Alliance" with partner countries, donors and the private sector [Press release, EC-IP/12/490]. Retrieved from http://europa.eu/rapid/press-release_IP-12-490_en.htm

[European Directive 2003/30/EC] Directive 2003/87/EC of the European Parliament and of the Council of 13 October 2003 establishing a scheme for greenhouse gas emission allowance trading within the Community and amending Council Directive 96/61/EC. Retrieved from http://eur-lex.europa.eu/legal-content/EN/TXT/?uri=CELEX:32003L0087

[European Directive 2009/28/EC] Directive 2009/28/EC of the European Parliament and of the Council of 23 April 2009, on the promotion of the use of energy from renewable sources and amending and subsequently repealing Directives 2001/77/EC and 2003/30/EC. Retrieved from http://eur-lex.europa.eu/legal-content/EN/TXT/PDF/?uri=CELEX:32009L0028&from=EN

European Investment Bank. (2010, December 9). European Financing Partners replenished with EUR 225 million [Press release]. Retrieved from http://www.eib.org/infocentre/press/releases/all/2010/2010-226-european-financing-partners-replenished-with-eur-225-million.htm

European Union, External Action. (2014a). EU relations with the African, Caribbean and Pacific Group of States (ACP) [Official website]. Retrieved from http://eeas.europa.eu/acp/index_en.htm

European Union, External Action. (2014b). The EU's relations with Africa [Official website]. Retrieved from http://eeas.europa.eu/africa/index_en.htm

Executive Research Associates Ltd. (2009). *China in Africa. A strategic overview*. Retrieved from http://www.ide.go.jp/English/Data/Africa_file/Manualreport/pdf/china_all.pdf

Ezeoha, A., & Cattaneo, N. (2011). FDI flows to Sub-Saharan Africa: The impact of finance, institution and natural resource endowment. Retrieved from http://www.csae.ox.ac.uk/conferences/2011-edia/papers/294-ezeoha.pdf

Fahrmeir, A., & Steller, V. (2013). Wirtschaftstheorie, Normsetzung und Herrschaft: Freihandel, "Rule of Law" und das Recht des Kanonenboots. In A. Fahrmeir & A. Imhausen (Eds.), *Die Vielfalt normativer Ordnungen: Konflikte und Dynamik in historischer und ethnologischer Perspektive* (Vol. 8, pp. 165-197). FFM: Campus.

Fairhead, J., Leach, M., & Scoones, I. (Eds.) (2012). Green Grabbing: a new appropriation of nature? *The Journal of Peasant Studies, 39*(2) [Special issue].

Fairbairn, M. (2013). Indirect dispossession: domestic power imbalances and foreign access to land in Mozambique. *Development and Change, 44*(2), 335-356.

Falleti, T. (2006). Theory-guided process-tracing in comparative politics: Something old, something new. *Newsletter of the Organized Section in Comparative Politics of the American Political Science Association, 17*(1), 9-14.

FAO. (2009). How China stabilized grain prices during the recent global food price crisis. *Crop Prospects and Food Situation, 4* (November 2009). Rome, Italy: FAO. Retrieved from http://www.fao.org/docrep/012/ak340e/ak340e06b.htm

FAO. (2012a). *The state of food and agriculture*. Rome: FAO. Retrieved from http://www.fao.org/docrep/017/i3028e/i3028e.pdf

FAO. (2012b). *Voluntary guidelines on the responsible governance of tenure of land, fisheries and forests in the context of national food security*. Rome: FAO. Retrieved from http://www.fao.org/docrep/016/i2801e/i2801e.pdf

FCO. (2011a). *Business plan 2011-2015* (May 2011). London: Foreign & Commonwealth Office. Retrieved from https://www.gov.uk/government/uploads/system/uploads/attachment_data/file/32855/FCO-Business-Plan1.pdf

FCO. (2011b). *A charter for business*. London: Foreign & Commonwealth Office. Retrieved from https://www.gov.uk/government/uploads/system/uploads/attachment_data/file/35438/business-charter.pdf

Feng, S. (2010). Mali Sugar Conglomerate: CLETC project case in Mali [PowerPoint presentation]. Retrieved from the website of the International Poverty Reduction Center in China: http://www.iprcc.org/userfiles/file/Feng%20Sheyong-EN(1).pdf

Feng, X. (2009). The emergence of temporary staffing agencies in China. *Comparative Labor Law & Policy Journal, 30*(2), 431–462.

Fewsmith, J. (2001). *China since Tiananmen: The politics of transition*. Cambridge: Cambridge University Press.

Finance.jrj.com.cn. (2011, May). Haiwai zhong liang xu raoguo "di er dai zhimin zhuyi" menkan. *Finance.jrj.com.cn*. Retrieved from http://finance.jrj.com.cn/industry/2011/05/1120149943746.shtml

Forum on China-Africa Cooperation (FOCAC). (2012). The fifth ministerial conference of the Forum on China-Africa Cooperation Beijing action plan

(2013-2015). Beijing: MOFA. Retrieved from http://www.focac.org/eng/ltda/ dwjbzjjhys/t954620.htm

Foster, V., Butterfield, W., Chen, C., & Pushak, N. (2008). *Building bridges: China's growing role as infrastructure financier for Sub-Saharan Africa* (Trends and policy options, no. 5). Washington, D.C.: World Bank.

Foucault, M. (2008). *The birth of biopolitics: Lectures at the Collège de France, 1978-79*. M. Senellart (Ed.). Houndmills: Palgrave Macmillan.

Franco, J., Levidow, L., Fig, D., Goldfarb, L., Hönicke, M., & Luisa Mendonça, M. (2010). Assumptions in the European Union biofuels policy: Frictions with experiences in Germany, Brazil and Mozambique. *The Journal of Peasant Studies, 37*(4), 661–698.

Freeman, D., Holslag, J., & Weil, S. (2008). China's foreign farming policy: can land provide security?. *Asia Paper, 3*(9).Retrieved from http://www.vub.ac.be/biccs/documents/Freeman,%20Holslag%20and%20Weil%20%282008%29,%20China%27s%20foreign%20farmong%20policy,%20BICCS%20Asia%20Paper,%20vol.%203%20%289%29..pdf

Fritz, T. (2010). *Peak Soil: Die globale Jagd nach Land*. Berlin: FDCL.

Gadzala, A., & Hanusch, M. (2010). *African perspectives on China-Africa: Gauging popular perceptions and their economic and political determinants* (Working paper no. 117). Afrobarometer. Retrieved from http://www.afrobarometer.org/publications/working-papers/item/167-african-perspectives-on-china-africa-gauging-popular-perceptions-and-their-economic-and-political-determinants

Galadima, A., Garba, Z. N., Ibrahim, B. M., Almustapha, M. N., Leke, L., & Adam, K. (2011). Biofuels production in Nigeria: The policy and public opinions. *Journal of Sustainable Development, 4*(4), 22-31.

Gardner, L. A. (2012). *Taxing colonial Africa: the political economy of British imperialism*. Oxford: Oxford University Press.

Gasparatos, A., & Stromberg, P. (2012). *Socioeconomic and environmental impacts of biofuels: Evidence from developing nations*. Cambridge: Cambridge University Press.

Gaullier, G., Lemoine, F., & Ünal-Kesenci, D. (2006). *China's emergence and the reorganization of trade flows in Asia*. Paris: Centre d'Etudes Prospectives et d'Information Internationale.

GEM Biofuels. (2010). Biofuels, such as biodiesel and ethanol, are being developed as a response to climate change, high oil prices and an increasing lack of secure energy supplies.[Corporate website]. Retrieved from http://www.gembiofuels.com (last accessed March 2010).

GEM Biofuels. (2011, September 28). *GEM BioFuels Plc—Half yearly report* (RNS Number 0289P). Retrieved from http://www.bloomberg.com/apps/news?pid=newsarchive&sid=amNZtOWYET80

GEM Biofuels. (2012, April 12). GEM Biofuels Plc. [Corporate notice]. Retrieved from http://www.hunter-resources.com/PDF/rns/12042012-Investors-update.pdf

GEM Biofuels. (2012, December 5). Notice on AGM, proposed investing policy, share capital reorganisation, change of name, subscription for new shares and board changes [Corporate notice]. Retrieved from http://www.hunter-resources.com/PDF/rns/05122012-AGM-and-Subscription.pdf

George, A. L., & Bennett, A. (2005). *Case studies and theory development in the social sciences*. Cambridge: MIT Press.

Gerlach, A.-C. & Pascal, L. (2010). *Resource-seeking foreign direct investment in African Agriculture: A review of country case studies* (FAO commodity and trade policy research working paper No. 31). Rome: FAO. Retrieved from http://www.fao.org/fileadmin/templates/est/PUBLICATIONS/Comm_Working_Papers/EST-WP31.pdf

GEXSI LLP. (2008). Global market study on Jatropha [PowerPoint presentation prepared for the WWF]. Retrieved from http://www.jatropha-alliance.org/fileadmin/documents/GEXSI_Jatropha-Project-Inventory_AFRICA.pdf

Gillespie, A. (2001). *The illusion of progress: Unsustainable development in international law and policy*. Sterling: Earthscan.

Giovanetti, G., & Ticci, E. (2011). *Sub-Saharan Africa in global trends of investment in renewable energy: Drivers and the challenge of the water-energy-land nexus*. London, United Kingdom/Bonn, Germany/Brussels, Belgium: Overseas Development Institute, German Development Institute, Europe Centre for Development Policy Management. Retrieved from http://erd-report.eu/erd/report_2011/documents/dev-11-001-11researchpapers_giovannetti-ticci.pdf

Global Policy Forum. (2014). Multilateral agreement on investment [NGO website]. Retrieved from http://www.globalpolicy.org/globalization/globalization-of-the-economy-2-1/multilateral-agreement-on-investment-2-5.html

Global Witness. (2013, December 20). UK's Equatorial Palm Oil accused of human rights abuses in Liberia. *GlobalWitness.org*. Retrieved from http://www.globalwitness.org/Liberia/EPO

[GLP (2010)] Friis, C., & Reenberg, A. (2010). *Land grab in Africa: Emerging land system drivers in a teleconnected world* (Global Land Project report no. 1). Copenhagen: GLP-IPO.

Goetz, A., Searchinger, T., Beringer, T., German, L., McKay, B., de LT Oliveira, G., & Hunsberger, C. (2018). Reply to commentary on the special issue Scaling up biofuels? A critical look at expectations, performance and governance. *Energy Policy*, *118*, 658-665.

Goetz, A. (forthcoming, 2018). Somewhere between mutual development and cooperative exploitation: Forms and impact of China-Africa cooperation. In L. Chabelle, E. Tok, & H. Besada (Eds.), *Innovating South-South cooperation: Challenges, modalities and policies*. Ottawa: University of Ottawa Press.

Goetz, A. (2015): How different are the UK and China? Investor countries in comparative perspective. *Canadian Journal for Development Studies/ Revue canadienne d'études du développement*, Vol. 36, No. 2, 179–195.

Golay, C., & Biglino, I. (2013). Human rights responses to land grabbing: A right to food perspective. *Third World Quarterly*, 34(9), 1630-1650.

Goldsmith., E. (1993). Development and social destruction. *Ecoscript*, 35(June). Retrieved from http://www.edwardgoldsmith.org/36/development-and-social-destruction/

Goldstone, J.A. (2008). Comparative historical analysis and knowledge accumulation in the study of revolution. In D. Rueschemeyer, D., & J. Mahoney, J. (Eds.), *Comparative historical analysis in the social sciences* (pp. 40-90). Cambridge: Cambridge University Press.

Goldthau, A., & Witte, J. M. (Eds.). (2010). *Global energy governance: The new rules of the game.* Washington, D.C: Brookings Institution.

Gouldner, A.W. (1976). *The dialectic of ideology and technology: The origins, grammar and future of ideology.* London: MacMillan Press.

Gouraud, J.-L. (2011, October 18). The records of Jeune Afrique's interview with Director-General Lu Shaye. *Jeune Afrique*. Retrieved from http://www.focac.org/eng/zfgx/t885029.htm

GRAIN. (2008). *Seized: The 2008 land grab for food and financial security.* Barcelona: GRAIN. Retrieved from http://www.grain.org/article/entries/93-seized-the-2008-landgrab-for-food-and-financial-security

GRAIN. (2010, September 8). World Bank report on land grabbing: beyond the smoke and mirrors. Barcelona: GRAIN. Retrieved from http://www.grain.org/article/entries/4021-world-bank-report-on-land-grabbing-beyond-the-smoke-and-mirrors

GRAIN. (2010, October 22). Unpacking a Chinese company's land grab in Cameroon. Barcelona: GRAIN. Retrieved from http://farmlandgrab.org/16485

GRAIN. (2012, February 23).GRAIN releases data set with over 400 global land grabs. Barcelona: GRAIN. Retrieved from http://www.grain.org/article/entries/4479-grain-releases-data-set-with-over-400-global-land-grabs

GRAIN. (2013). Collating and dispersing: GRAIN's strategies and methods. *Journal of Peasant Studies*, 40(3), 531-536.

Green, E.H.H. (1999). Gentlemanly capitalism and British economic policy, 1880–1914: The debate over bimetallism and protectionism. In R. Dumett (Ed.), *Gentlemanly capitalism and British imperialism: The new debate on Empire* (pp.44-67). New York: Longman.

Greenaironline.com. (2012, January 23). Availability and sustainability key challenges, says Lufthansa, as biofuel trials end with first commercial transatlantic flight. *Greenaironline.com*. Retrieved from http://www.greenaironline.com/news.php?viewStory=1507

Grote, D. (2009, March 24). Cru staff to move to Maguire's Africa Invest initiative. *Citywire.it.* Retrieved from http://citywire.co.uk/new-model-adviser/news/cru-staff-to-move-to-maguires-africa-invest-initiative/a334198

Grote, D. (2009, April 14). Cru confirms fund loans went to Africa and defends investment. *Citywire.co.uk.* Retrieved from http://citywire.co.uk/new-model-adviser/news/cru-confirms-fund-loans-went-to-africa-and-defends-investment/a336599

Grote, D. (2010, March 16). Africa Invest bids to rescue business with £6 million rights issue. *Citywire.it.* Retrieved from http://citywire.it/news/africa-invest-bids-to-rescue-business-with-6-million-rights-issue/a388024?section=new-model-adviser

[GTZ (2009)] Görgen, M., Rudloff, B., Simons, J., Üllenberg, A., Väth, S., & Wimmer, L. (2009). *Foreign Direct Investment (FDI) in land in developing countries.* Bonn: GTZ. Retrieved from http://www.giz.de/expertise/downloads/Fachexpertise/giz2010-en-foreign-direct-investment-dc.pdf

Gyasi, E. A. (1996). The environmental impact and sustainability of plantations in Sub-Saharan Africa: Ghana's experiences with oil-palm plantations. In G. Benneh, W. B. Morgan, & J. I. Uitto (Eds.), *Sustaining the future: Economic, social and environmental change in Sub-Saharan Africa* (pp. 342-357). Tokyo: The United Nations University.

Hague, W. (2010). *Britain's foreign policy in a networked world.* Speech delivered at the Locarno Room, The Foreign and Commonwealth Office, London, UK, 1 July 2010. Retrieved from https://www.gov.uk/government/speeches/britain-s-foreign-policy-in-a-networked-world--2

Haigh, C. (2014). *Carving up a continent: How the UK government is facilitating the corporate takeover of African food systems.* London: World Development Movement.

Hall, D. (2011). Land grabs, land control, and Southeast Asian crop booms. *The Journal of Peasant Studies, 38*(4), 837–857.

Hall, D. (2012). *Where is Japan in the global land grab?* Paper presented at the International Conference Global Land Grabbing II, Ithaca, USA.

Hall, D. (2013). Primitive accumulation, accumulation by dispossession and the global land grab. *Third World Quarterly, 34*(9), 1582–1604.

Hall, P. (1990). *Policy paradigms, social learning and the State: The case of economic policy-making in Britain* (Working paper 1990/4). Madrid: Centro de Estudios Avanzados en Ciencias Sociales, Fundación Juan March.

Hall, P. A., & Soskice, D. (2001). *Varieties of capitalism: The institutional foundations of comparative advantage.* Oxford: Oxford University Press.

Hall, R. (2011). Land grabbing in Southern Africa: The many faces of the investor rush. *Review of African Political Economy, 38*(128), 193–214.

Hall, R., & Sulle, E. (2013). Reframing the New Alliance Agenda: A Critical Assessment based on Insights from Tanzania (Policy brief no. 56). Brighton:

University of Sussex, Future Agricultures. Retrieved from http://r4d.dfid. gov.uk/pdf/outputs/Futureagriculture/Policy_Brief_056.pdf

Haller, P. (2014). The Political Economy of Large-Scale Land Acquisitions: Water Security and Food Sovereignty [Announcement of panel 369 at the ECPR general conference 2014, Glasgow). Retrieved from http://ecpr.eu/ Events/PanelDetails.aspx?PanelID=3289&EventID=14

Halperin, S. (2004). *War and social change in modern Europe: the great transformation revisited.* Cambridge: Cambridge University Press.

Halperin, S. (2005). Trans-local and trans-regional socio-economic structures in global development: a 'horizontal' perspective. *Research in Rural Sociology and Development, 11,* 19-55.

Hamelinck, C. (2013). *Land grabs for biofuels driven by EU biofuels policies* (Project number: BIENL13469).: Ecofys Netherlands B.V. Retrieved from http://www.ecofys.com/files/files/ecofys-2013-report-on-land-grabbing-for-biofuels.pdf

Harcourt, W. (Ed.). (2011). Global land grabs. *Development, 54*(1) [Special issue].

Harris, C. (2004). How did colonialism dispossess? Comments from an edge of empire. *Annals of the Association of American Geographers, 94*(1), 165-182.

Harrison, J. (2010). United Kingdom national report: The protection of foreign investment (Rapporteur report). International Academy of Comparative Law, University of Edinburgh. Retrieved from http://www.law.ed.ac.uk/includes/remote_people_profile/remote_staff_profile?sq_content_src=%2BdXJsPWhodHAlMoElMkYlMkZ3d3cyLmxhdy5lZC5hYy51ayUyR mZpbGVfZG93bmxvYWQlMkZwdWJJsaWNhdGlvbnMlMkYxXzYyOF91b mloZWRraW5nZG9tcmVwb3J0X3aGVwcm9oZWNoaW9uX29ub2ZmcmlL nBkZiZhbGw9MQ%3D%3D

Harrison, J. (2013). International Law Commission and the development of international investment law. *The. Geo. Wash. Int'l L. Rev., 45,* 413.

Harvey, D. (2003). *The new imperialism.* Oxford: Oxford University Press.

Harvey, D., & Rivera, H.A. *(2010, September). Explaining the crisis. International Socialist Review, 73.* Retrieved from http://isreview.org/issue/73/explaining-crisis

Harvey, M. (2011). *Perspectives on the UK's place in the world* (European programme paper no. 1). London: Chatham House. Retrieved from http://www.chathamhouse.org/sites/files/chathamhouse/public/Research/Europe/1211pp_harvey.pdf

Harvey, P. (2010). *Capacity building in South Africa, Namibia and Ghana to create sustainable, non-food bio-oil supply chains. ACP Science & Technology Programme* (Factsheet). Brussels: African, Caribbean and Pacific Group of States (ACP). Retrieved from http://www.acp-st.eu/content/capacity-building-south-africa-namibia-and-ghana-create-sustainable-non-food-bio-oil-supply-

Hauswirth, I. (2006). *Effective and efficient organisations? Government export promotion in Germany and the UK from an organisational economics perspective*. Heidelberg: Physica-Verlag.
Hawkins, D., & Chen, Y. (2011). *Plant with a bad name*. London: Hardman & Co. Retrieved from http://www.google.de/url?sa=t&rct=j&q=&esrc=s&source=web&cd=1&ved=0CCUQFjAA&url=http%3A%2F%2Fwww.jatropha.pro%2FPDF%2520bestanden%2FPlant%2520with%2520a%2520bad%2520name.pdf&ei=a7qEVMyNJ9LYapLOguAI&usg=AFQjCNGlA804VBCRj2hRhW53kns36B4DgQ&bvm=bv.80642063,d.d2s
He, Q. (2002). *The pitfalls of modernization*. Tokyo: Soshisha.
He, Q. (2012, November 13). Open alliance of power and money meets in Beijing. *The Epoch Times*. Retrieved from http://www.theepochtimes.com/n2/opinion/open-alliance-of-power-and-money-meets-in-beijing-314232.html
Headey, D., & Fan, S. (2010). *Reflections on the global food crisis: How did it happen? How has it hurt? And how can we prevent the next on?* (Research monograph no. 165). Washington, DC: International Food Policy Research Institute.
Hein, W. (2001). *Global Governance and the Evolution of a New Role of International Finance and Economic Institutions for Sub-Saharan Africa*. (Working Paper). Hamburg: Deutsches Übersee-Institut. Retrieved from http://www.google.de/url?sa=t&rct=j&q=&esrc=s&source=web&cd=1&ved=0CCYQFjAA&url=http%3A%2F%2Fkms1.isn.ethz.ch%2Fserviceengine%2FFiles%2FISN%2F46956%2Fipublicationdocument_singledocument%2Fb849f32d-fd81-489b-a02f-80d4c83c18e9%2Fen%2F2001-01-Global%2BGovernance.pdf&ei=iCSDVKygO0avUZ2hgdgP&usg=AFQjCNEsIYip9HrNbb5ammTPPQkU_2LtCQ&bvm=bv.80642063,d.d24
Heires, M., Nölke, A. (2014). Finanzialisierung. In *Theorien der Internationalen Politischen Ökonomie* (pp. 253-266). Springer VS, Wiesbaden.
Heumesser, C. & Schmid, E. (2012). *Trends in Foreign Direct Investment in the agricultural sector of developing and transition countries: A review*. Vienna: Universität für Bodenkultur Wien. Retrieved from http://www.gffa-berlin.de/images/stories/GFFA2013/studie%20der%20universitt%20owien.pdf
Highbury Finance. (2013). Sun Biofuels Mozambique [Corporate website]. Retrieved from http://sunbiofuelsmz.com/joomla/site-map/aboutusm1 (last accessed March 2013).
Hills, J., Brewer, M., Jenkins, S., Lister, R., Lupton, R., Machin, S., Mills, C., Modood, T., Rees, T., & Riddell, S. (2010). *An anatomy of economic inequality in the UK: Report of the National Equality Panel*. London: Government Equalities Office and Centre for Analysis of Social Exclusion, London School of Economics and Political Science. Retrieved from http://www.google.de/url?sa=t&rct=j&q=&esrc=s&source=web&cd=1&ved=0C

CgQFjAA&url=http%3A%2F%2Feprints.lse.ac.uk%2F28344%2F1%2F CASEreport60.pdf&ei=vrqEVMr2D4Kzae2wgWA&usg=AFQjCNEP w2IvSMJsFfx387jU-jIyek7V3g&bvm=bv.80642063,d.d2s

Hirsch, F. (2005). *Social limits to growth*. New York: Routledge.

Hirsch, S. (2012). Nation states and nationality of MNEs. *Columbia FDI Perspectives*, 57. New York: Vale Columbia Center on Sustainable International Investment. Retrieved from http://www.vcc.columbia.edu/content/nation-states-and-nationality-mnes

HM Government. (2010). *A strong Britain in an age of uncertainty: The national security strategy* [Whitepaper]. London, United Kingdom: Cabinet Office. Retrieved from https://www.google.de/search?q=HM+Government.+%282 010%29.+A+strong+Britain+in+an+age+of+uncertainty%3A+The+nation al+security+strategy+&ie=utf-8&oe=utf-8&aq=t&rls=org.mozilla:de:offi cial&client=firefox-a&channel=sb&gfe_rd=cr&ei=IbuEVLrtNIiJ8Qfo5Y DAAw

HM Treasury and BIS. (2011). *The plan for growth*. London, United Kingdom: HM Treasury and Department for Business, Innovation & Skills. Retrieved from https://www.google.de/search?q=HM+Treasury+and+BIS.+%282011% 29.+The+plan+for+growth.+&ie=utf-8&oe=utf-8&aq=t&rls=org.mozil la:de:official&client=firefox-a&channel=sb&gfe_rd=cr&ei=WruEVPinB4i J8Qfo5YDAAw

HM Treasury and Osborne, G. (2013, July 9). Reducing the deficit and rebalancing the economy [Policy]. Retrieved from https://www.gov.uk/govern ment/policies/reducing-the-deficit-and-rebalancing-the-economy

Hobsbawm, E. (1989). *Age of Empire: 1875-1914*. New York: Vintage.

Hobson, J. A. (1965). *Imperialism: A study*. Ann Arbor: University of Michigan Press.

Home, F., & Mittal, A. (2011). *Understanding land investments in Africa: Country report Zambia*. F. Mousseau & A. Mittal (Eds.). Oakland: The Oakland Institute. Retrieved from http://www.oaklandinstitute.org/sites/oaklandinstit ute.org/files/OI_country_report_zambia.pdf

Home, R. (2009). Land ownership in the United Kingdom: Trends, preferences and future challenges. *Land Use Policy, 26*, S103–S108.

Home, R. (2012). The colonial legacy in land rights in Southern Africa. In B. Chigara (Ed.), *Southern African Development Community Land Issues* (pp. 8–26). London: Routledge.

Hood, C., James, O., Scott, C., Jones, G. W., & Travers, T. (1999). *Regulation inside government: Waste watchers, quality police, and sleaze-busters*. Oxford: Oxford University Press

Hunsberger, C., German, L., & Goetz, A. (2017). "Unbundling" the biofuel promise: Querying the ability of liquid biofuels to deliver on socio-economic policy expectations. *Energy Policy, 108*, 791-805.

Hunter Resources Plc. (2013, December 30). Hunter Resources Plc.: Suspension of trading, update on the implementation of the company's investing strategy, granting of convertible loan facility and reverse takeover discussions [Statement]. Retrieved from http://www.hunter-resources.com/PDF/rns/20131230-Prospective-RTO.pdf

Hyam, R. (2010). *Understanding the British empire*. Cambridge: Cambridge University Press.

[IAASTD 2008] McIntyre, B. D., Herren, H.R., Wakhungu, J.W.&, Robert, T. (Eds.). (2008). *Agriculture at the crossroads* (Synthesis report). Washington, DC: International Assessment of Agricultural Knowledge, Science and Technology for Development (IAASTD). Retrieved from http://www.fao.org/fileadmin/templates/est/Investment/Agriculture_at_a_Crossroads_Global_Report_IAASTD.pdf

[IDE-JETRO (n.d.)] Institute of Developing Economies –Japan External Trade Organization. (n.d.). Unilever Tea Kenya.Africa Growing Enterprises File. Retrieved fromhttp://www.ide.go.jp/English/Data/Africa_file/Company/kenya06.html

[IFPRI 2009] von Braun, Joachim, and Ruth Meinzen-Dick. (2009). "Land Grabbing" by foreign investors in developing countries: Risks and opportunities. *IFPRI Policy Brief, 13*. Washington, D.C.: International Food Policy Research Institute. Retrieved from http://www.ifpri.org/publication/land-grabbing-foreign-investors-developing-countries

[IIED/FAO/IFAD 2009] Cotula, L., Vermeulen, S., Leonard, R., & Keeley, J. (2009). *Land grab or development opportunity? Agricultural investment and international land deals in Africa*. London, Rome: IIED/FAO/IFAD. Retrieved from http://www.fao.org/3/a-ak241e.pdf

[IISD 2013] Bizikova, L., Roy, D., Swanson, D., Venema, H. D., & McCandless, M. (2013). *The water-energy-food security nexus: Towards a practical planning and decision-support framework for landscape investment and risk management*. New York: International Institute for Sustainable Development.

[ILC 2011] International Land Coalition. (2011). *Securing land access for the poor in times of intensified natural resources competition*. Rome: International Land Coalition. Retrieved from http://www.landcoalition.org/sites/default/files/publication/1146/AOM%202011%20report_web_EN.pdf

[ILC 2012] Anseeuw, W., L. Alden Wily, L., Cotula, L. & Taylor, M. (2012). *Land rights and the rush for land: Findings of the global commercial pressures on land research project*. Rome: International Land Coalition. Retrieved from http://www.landcoalition.org/sites/default/files/publication/1205/ILC%20GSR%20report_ENG.pdf

Ince, O. U. (2013). Primitive accumulation, new enclosures, and global land grabs: A theoretical intervention. *Rural Sociology, 79*(1), 104–131.

Ingwe, R., Okoro, J., & Ukwayi, J. K. (2010). The new Scramble for Africa: How large-scale acquisition of Sub-Saharan Africa's land by multinational corporations and rich countries threaten sustainable development. *Journal of Sustainable Development in Africa, 12*(3), 28-50.

Insight Group Plc. (2011, October 26). Mozambican Biofuel exports to German airline Lufthansa. *Insight Group*. Retrieved from http://insightgroupplc.wordpress.com/2011/10/26/mozambican-biofuel-exports-to-german-airline-lufthansa/

InSouth.org. (2014). South-South Cooperation: China [Blog post]. Retrieved from http://www.insouth.org/index.php?option=com_content&view=article&id=62:china&catid=31:country-windows&Itemid=86

International Energy Agency. (2013). World Energy Outlook 2013. Paris: IEA.

International Land Coalition. (n.d.). Deal number 267. Retrieved from http://www.commercialpressuresonland.org/land-deals/267

Investigate.co.uk. (2006, June 14). D1 Oils Plc – Agreements in India & Zambia. *Investigate.co.uk*. Retrieved from http://www.investegate.co.uk/article.aspx?id=200606140856045458E

Investigage.co.uk. (2008, September 20). GEM Biofuels Plc. Interim results for the six months ended 30 June 2008 (RNS Number 5328E). *Investigage.co.uk*. Retrieved from http://www.investegate.co.uk/article.aspx?id=200809291009205328E

Investigate.co.uk. (2009, August 18). Agriterra Ltd. Proposed acquisition of palm (RNS Number 5780X). *Investigate.co.uk*. Retrieved from http://www.investegate.co.uk/agriterra-ltd/rns/proposed-acquisition-of-palm/200908180700055780X/

Investigate.co.uk. (2014, January 30). NEOS Resources PLC: Update (RNS Number 8853Y). *Investigate.co.uk*. Retrieved from http://www.investegate.co.uk/neos-resources-plc--neos-/rns/update/201401301046278853Y/

Isiguzo, C. (2006, August 28). Nigeria: Ebonyi to build N10.4 billion ethanol plant. Retrieved from http://allafrica.com/stories/200608280673.html

Ismail, M., & Rossi, A. (2010). *A compilation of bioenergy sustainability initiatives*. Rome: Food and Agriculture Organization (FAO).

Jackson, P. (2011). *Prosperity without growth: Economics for a finite planet*. Oxford: Taylor & Francis Ltd.

Jansen, K. (2014). The debate on food sovereignty theory: agrarian capitalism, dispossession and agroecology. *The Journal of Peasant Studies* (ahead of print: http://www.tandfonline.com/doi/pdf/10.1080/03066150.2014.945166).

Jansson, J. (2009). *Patterns of Chinese Investment, Aid and Trade in Central Africa (Cameroon, the DRC and Gabon)* (A briefing paper by the Centre for Chinese Studies, prepared for World Wide Fund for Nature). Stellenbosch:

University of Stellenbosch. Retrieved from http://www.ccs.org.za/wp-content/uploads/2009/11/CCS-Central-Africa-Briefing-Paper-August-2009.pdf

Jansson, J., & Kiala, C. (2009). *Patterns of Chinese Investment, Aid and Trade in Mozambique* (A briefing paper for the Centre for Chinese Studies, prepared for WWF). Stellenbosch: University of Stellenbosch. Retrieved from http://assets.wwf.org.uk/downloads/ccs_mozambique_briefing_paper_october_2009.pdf

Jatropha Africa. (n.d.a). Capacity building in South Africa, Namibia and Ghana to create sustainable, non-food bio-oil supply chains. Retrieved from http://www.jatrophaafrica.com/ACP-Project

Jatropha Africa. (n.d.b). Jatropha Seeds. Reducing Carbon Dioxide. Retrieved from http://www.jatrophaafrica.com/seeds

Jatropha Africa. (n.d.c). News. Retrieved from http://www.jatrophaafrica.com/News

Jatropha Africa. (n.d.d). Jatropha Africa [Corporate website]. Retrieved from http://www.jatrophaafrica.com/

Jatropha Africa. (2010, August 22). Jatropha Africa input to Ghana Biofuel Committee [Press relase]. Retrieved from http://www.jatrophaafrica.com/ourwork/view/httpwww.jatrophaafrica.comourworkviewGhana-Biofuel-Committee

Jauch, H. (2011). Investments in Africa: Twenty-first century colonialism? *New Labour Forum, 20(2),* 49-55.

Jiang, J., & Sinton, J. (2011). *Overseas investments by Chinese national oil companies.* Paris: International Energy Agency. Retrieved from http://www.google.de/url?sa=t&rct=j&q=&esrc=s&source=web&cd=1&ved=0CCgQFjAA&url=http%3A%2F%2Fwww.iea.org%2Fpublications%2Ffreepublications%2Fpublication%2Foverseas_china.pdf&ei=DCCDVLzAN8eqUdWzhPAP&usg=AFQjCNHDxOwJw1ucorhKF0VJsfWe2N6rvg&bvm=bv.80642063,d.d24

Jiang, W. (2009). Fuelling the dragon: China's rise and its energy and resources extraction in Africa. *The China Quarterly, 199,* 585–609.

Joint Nature Conservation Committee. (2009). The biodiversity footprint of UK Foreign Direct Investment. Peterborough: JNCC. Retrieved from http://jncc.defra.gov.uk/pdf/pub09_biodiversityfootprint.pdf

Jones, G. (2005a). *Multinationals and global capitalism: From the nineteenth to the twenty-first century.* Oxford: Oxford University Press.

Jones, G. (2005b). *Renewing Unilever: Transformation and tradition.* Oxford: Oxford University Press.

Jones, J. (2014). The French in West Africa. Retrieved from website of the West Chester University: http://courses.wcupa.edu/jones/his312/lectures/fren-occ.htm

Kahrl, F., Roland-Holst, D., & Zilberman, D. (2005). New horizons for rural reform in China: Resources, property rights, and consumerism. *Agricultural and Resources Economics Update*, 9(1), 11-15.

Kariuki J. (1999). Tobacco cultivation threatens food security in Kenya. Retrieved from http://lists.essential.org/intl-tobacco/msg00111.html (accessed 3 April 2012).

Katzenstein, P. J. (Ed.). (1977a). *Between power and plenty: Foreign economic policies of advanced industrial states*. Madison: University of Wisconsin Press.

Katzenstein, P. J. (1977b). Introduction: Domestic and international forces and strategies of foreign economic policy. *International Organization*, 31(04), 587–606.

Katzenstein, P. J. (2005). *A world of regions: Asia and Europe in the American Imperium*. Ithaca: Cornell University Press.

Kaul, C. (2011, March 3). From empire to independence: The British Raj in India 1858-1947. *BBC History*. Retrieved from http://www.bbc.co.uk/history/british/modern/independence1947_01.shtml

Kautsky, K. (1907). Socialism and colonial policy. *Workers' Liberty Magazine* 2(3), 83-130.

Kegley, C. W., & Raymond, G. A. (2011). *The global future: A brief introduction to world politics*. Boston, MA: Wadsworth/Cengage Learning.

Khan, A., & Baye, F. M. (2008). *China-Africa economic relations: The case of Cameroon*. Nairobi, Kenya: African Economic Research Consortium (AERC). Retrieved from http://dspace.africaportal.org/jspui/bitstream/123456789/32048/1/Cameroon-China.pdf?1

Khan, S. & VanWynsberghe, R. (2008). Cultivating the under-mined: cross-case analysis as knowledge mobilization. *Forum Qualitative Sozialforschung/(Forum: Qualitative Social Research)*, 9(34). Retrieved from http://www.qualitative-research.net/index.php/fqs/article/view/334/729

King and Wood Mallesons. (2014, May). Offshore RMB Backflow Channels (Banking newsletter). Retrieved from http://www.kingandwood.com/bankingnewsletter.aspx?id=banking-newsletter-2014-05-09&language=en

Knaup, H., & Mittelstaedt, J. von. (2009, July 30). The new colonialism: Foreign investors snap up African farmland. *Spiegel Online*. Retrieved from http://www.spiegel.de/international/world/the-new-colonialism-foreign-investors-snap-up-african-farmland-a-639224.html

Konefal, J., Mascarenhas, M., & Hatanaka, M. (2005). Governance in the global agro-food system: Backlighting the role of transnational supermarket chains. *Agriculture and Human Values*, 22(3), 291-302.

Konijin, P. (2013). *International cooperation in a multilateral world: The role of emerging powers*. The Hague: Society for International Development, Netherlands Chapter.

Korniyenko, Y., & Sakatsume, T. (2009). *Chinese investment in the transition countries* (Working paper no. 107). London: European Bank for Reconstruction and Development. Retrieved from http://www.ebrd.com/downloads/research/economics/workingpapers/wp0107.pdf

Koswanage, N. (2011, April 29). Factbox—Major and emerging palm oil player in Africa. *Reuters* (UK). Retrieved from http://uk.reuters.com/article/2011/04/29/uk-palmoil-africa-firms-factbox-idUKTRE73S27020110429

Kotschi, J., & Association for AgriCulture and Ecology. (2013). *A soiled reputation. Adverse impacts of mineral fertilizers in tropical agriculture*. Berlin: Heinrich Böll Foundation and WWF Germany. Retrieved from http://www.google.de/url?sa=t&rct=j&q=&esrc=s&source=web&cd=1&ved=0CCYQFjAA&url=http%3A%2F%2Fwww.wwf.de%2Ffileadmin%2Ffm-wwf%2FPublikationen-PDF%2FWWF-Study_Adverse_impacts_of_mineral_fertilizers_in_tropical_agriculture.pdf&ei=PjCDVIGFFoXrUqKJgugP&usg=AFQjCNEs1NzKG6gn5S75uGmN9zMb5ajGRA&bvm=bv.80642063,d.d24

Kotz, D. M. (2002). Globalization and neoliberalism. *Rethinking Marxism*, 14(2), 64-79.

KPMG. (2014). Oil and gas in Africa. Reserves, potential and prospects of Africa. KPMG Africa. Retrieved from http://www.kpmg.no/arch/_img/9843212.pdf

Kragelund, P. (2009). Knocking on a wide-open door: Chinese investments in Africa. *Review of African Political Economy*, 36(122), 479-497.

Krausmann, F., Fischer-Kowalski, M., Schandl, H., & Eisenmenger, N. (2008). The global sociometabolic transition. *Journal of Industrial Ecology*, 12(5-6), 637–656.

Krausmann, F., Gingrich, S., Eisenmenger, N., Erb, K.-H., Haberl, H., & Fischer-Kowalski, M. (2009). Growth in global materials use, GDP and population during the 20th century. *Ecological Economics*, 68(10), 2696–2705.

Kugelman, M. (2009): Introduction and acknowledgments. In M. Kugelman, S. L. Levenstein (Eds.), *Land grab? The race for the world's farmland* (pp. 1-27). Washington, DC: Woodrow Wilson International Center for Scholars.

Kuhnen, F. (1986). Causes of underdevelopment and concepts for development. An introduction to development theories. *The Journal of Institute of Development*, Vol.III, University of Peshawar. Retrieved from http://www.google.de/url?sa=t&rct=j&q=&esrc=s&source=web&cd=3&ved=0CD0QFjAC&url=http%3A%2F%2Fwww2.fiu.edu%2F~ereserve%2F010029280-1.pdf&ei=s4yNVIrXG5PKaILmgbAD&usg=AFQjCNErGIrXjo4aZWpPrEo_i3G7vr2xSg&bvm=bv.81828268,d.d2s

Kumar, B. N., & Graf, I. (1998). Globalization, Development and Ethics: Moral Responsibility and Strategies of International Management in the Perspective of „Sustainable Development ". Kumar, Bri Nino/Steinmann, Horst (Eds.), *Ethics in international management* (pp.127-160). Berlin: Walter de Gruyter.

Kuzemko, C. (2010). UK energy governance change and the "Russian Bear": 2003-2007. Paper presented at the ECPR Conference 2010, Stockholm, Sweden.

Lahiff, E. (2012). The land question in southern Africa: a political economy perspective. In B. Chigara (Ed.), *Re-conceiving property rights in the new millennium: Towards a new sustainable land relations policy* (pp. 103-124). New York: Routledge.

Lall, S. (1996). The investment development path: some conclusions. In J. H. Dunning, & R. Narula (Eds.), *Foreign direct investment and governments. Catalysts for economic restructuring* (pp. 322-335). New York: Routledge.

Lang, T., & Heasman, M. (Eds.). (2004). *Food wars: the global battle for mouths, minds and markets*. New York: Earthscan.

Lapavitsas, C. (2014). *State and finance in financialised capitalism* (Think piece). London: Centre for Labour and Social Studies. Retrieved from http://classo nline.org.uk/docs/2014_Think_Piece_-_financialisation_-_Costas_Lapav itsas.pdf

Lavers, T. (2011). *The role of foreign investment in Ethiopia's smallholder-focused agricultural development strategy* (Working paper no. 2). The Hague: International Institute of Social Studies. Retrieved from http://www.plaas.org.za/sites/default/files/publications-pdf/WP%2002.pdf

Lavers, T. (2012). "Land grab" as development strategy? The political economy of agricultural investment in Ethiopia. *The Journal of Peasant Studies, 39*(1), 105–132.

Lavoie, M. (2014). *Post-Keynesian economics: New foundations*. Northampton: Edward Elgar Publishing.

Lazonick, W., & O'Sullivan, M. (1997). Finance and industrial development: Part I: the United States and the United Kingdom. *Financial History Review, 4*(01), 7–29.

Lee, S.-K., & Riel Müller, A. (2012). *South Korean external strategy qualms: Analysis of Korean overseas agricultural investment within the global food system*. Paper presented at the international conference Global Land Grabbing II, Ithaca, USA. Retrieved from http://www.google.de/url?sa=t&rct=j&q=&esrc=s&source=web&cd=1&ved=0CCMQFjAA&url=http%3A%2F%2Fwww.cornell-landproject.org%2Fdownload%2Flandgrab2012papers%2Flee.pdf&ei=r3-NVNvKJ4r3ap3hgagD&usg=AFQjCNGDOT4gQo_oMCBx 6gs02v06gyvpTA&bvm=bv.81828268,d.d2s

Lee, V. (2000). *Unemployment insurance and assistance systems in mainland China*. Hong Kong: Legislative Council Secretariat, Research and Library Services Division. Retrieved from http://www.legco.gov.hk/yr99-00/english/sec/library/e18.pdf

Lemke, T. (2010). "The birth of bio-politics"—Michel Foucault's lecture at the Collège de France on neo-liberal governmentality. *Economy and Society*, 30(2), 190–207.

Lenin, W.J. (1975). *Der Imperialismus als hochstes Stadium des Kapitalismus*. Beijing: Verlag für Fremdsprachige Literatur.

Lepenies, P. (2008). An inquiry into the roots of the modern concept of development. *Contributions to the History of Concepts*, 4(2), 202–225.

Leung, A. (2010). *A new China-Africa financial, investment and business partnership*. Presentation prepared for the international conference China and the World: Crisis Adjustment and Global Prosperity 2010, Beijing, China. Retrieved from http://www.google.de/url?sa=t&rct=j&q=&esrc=s&source=web&cd=2&ved=0CC8QFjAB&url=http%3A%2F%2Fwww.andrewleunginternationalconsultants.com%2Ffiles%2Fbeijing-university-presentation---a-new-china-africa-financial-investment-and-business-partnership.pdf&ei=dsCEVKjVB4ruaP_agtgI&usg=AFQjCNFZWyTqBurVD5XZzzBnH0HxL5mrsA&bvm=bv.80642063,d.d2s

Levy, D. L., & Prakash, A. (2003). Bargains old and new: Multinational corporations in global governance. *Business and Politics*, 5(2), 131–150.

Lewis, D. (2009, February 11). Chinese back Africa's farms but want greater support. *Reuters*. Retrieved from http://farmlandgrab.org/post/view/2760

Li, J.L. (2010). *Sino-Africa agricultural cooperation experience sharing*. Paper presented at the Seminar on Agriculture, Food Safety and Rural Development for Growth and Poverty Reduction, organized by OECD and IPRCC, Paris, France. Retrieved from http://iprcc.org/userfiles/file/Li%20Jiali%EF%BC%8DEN.pdf

Li, T. (2011). Centering labor in the land grab debate. *The Journal of Peasant Studies*, 38(2), 281-298

Li, T. (2012). *What is land? Anthropological perspectives on the global land rush*. Paper presented at the international conference Global Land Grabbing II, 17-19 October 2012, Ithaca, Cornell University. Retrieved from http://www.cornell-landproject.org/download/landgrab2012papers/li.pdf

Li, X. (2006). *China's foreign aid and aid to Africa: Overview* [PowerPoint presentation]. Retrieved from http://www.oecd.org/dataoecd/27/7/40378067.pdf

Liang, J. (2010, June 24). Mozambican PM visits Hubei, highlights agricultural cooperation. *People's Daily Online*. Retrieved from http://english.people.com.cn/90001/90776/90883/7032148.html

Liberti, S. (2012). *Landraub: Reisen ins Reich des neuen Kolonialismus*. Berlin: Rotbuch.

Lion's Head Global Partners. (n.d.). Partners [Corporate website]. Retrieved from http://www.lhgp.com/partners.htm (accessed 31 November 2013).

Lion's Head Global Partners. (2013). Agriculture: Mtamba Farm [Corporate website]. Retrieved from http://www.lhgp.com/agriculture.html (accessed 13 March 2013)

Liu, P. H. (n.d.). How China's "Trade Not Aid" Strategy Became Construed As Charitable Help: Deconstructing the "Touching" Idyll of Li Li's Investment in Africa. *Identity, Culture, and Politics: An Afro-Asian Dialogue*, 12(2), 1-18. Retrieved from http://tkuir.lib.tku.edu.tw:8080/dspace/handle/987654321/80490

Liu, Q. (2011, November 4). Chinese enterprises look to Africa. *Chinatoday.com.cn*. Retrieved from http://www.chinatoday.com.cn/ctenglish/se/txt/2010-11/04/content_309582.htm

Liu, J., Zhan, J., & Deng, X. (2005). Spatio-temporal patterns and driving forces of urban land expansion in China during the economic reform era. *Ambio,34*(6), 450-455.

Locher, M., & Sulle, E. (2013). Foreign land deals in Tanzania: An update and a critical view on the challenges of data (re)production (LDPI Working Paper 31). The Land Deal Politics Initiative, Netherlands. Retrieved from http://www.plaas.org.za/sites/default/files/publications-pdf/LDPI31Locher%26Sulle.pdf

Lonrho Fresh. (n.d.). Sourcing: Where every creation starts [Corporate website]. Retrieved from http://www.lonrhofresh.com/sourcing.html

Lonrho Plc. (2012). *Annual report and accounts for the 15 month period to 31 December 2011*. Retrieved from http://www.lonrho.com/Doc/Lonrho%20Annual%20Report%202011.pdf

Lonrho Ltd. (2014, January 24). History [Corporate website]. Retrieved from http://www.lonrho.com/About_Lonrho/History/Default.aspx?id=744

Loots, E., & Kabundi, A. (2012). Foreign Direct Investment to Africa: Trends, dynamics and challenges. *SAJEMS NS 13*(2), 128-141.

Lopes, C. (2014). We need more agribusiness in Africa. *Africa Renewal* [Special Edition on Agriculture], p. 20. Retrieved from http://www.un.org/africarenewal/magazine/special-edition-agriculture-2014/we-need-more-agribusiness-africa

Luckmann, T., & Berger, P. L. (1966). *The social construction of reality: A treatise in the sociology of knowledge*. London: Penguin Books.

Lufthansa. (2014). All about biofuels [Corporate website]. Retrieved from http://www.puresky.de/en/#/all-about-biofuels/jatropha/

Luxemburg, R. (1913). *Die Akkumulation des Kapitals*. Berlin: Buchhandlung Vorwärts Paul Singer. Retrieved from http://www.marxists.org/deutsch/archiv/luxemburg/1913/akkkap/

Macauhub. (2009, January 14). Angola: Lonrho Agriculture to carry out agricultural projects in Uíge, Zaire and Bengo provinces. Retrieved from http://www.macauhub.com.mo/en/2009/01/14/6396/

Macauhub (2009, April 22). Mozambique: Mining company CAMEC discovers 1.03 billion-tonne coal deposit. Retrieved from http://www.macauhub.com.mo/en/2009/04/24/6951/

Macauhub. (2009, October 28). Agriterra Ltd to expand cattle business in Mozambique. Retrieved from http://www.macauhub.com.mo/en/2009/10/28/8007/

Mack, F.A. (1930). The Law on Ultra Vires Acts and Contracts of Private Corporations. *Marquette Law Review,14*(1).

Macquarie University and Free University Amsterdam Project. (2011, May 15). More support for Chinese agricultural investment abroad as manufacturing investment matures [Blog post]. Retrieved from Exporting China's Development to the World: http://mqvu.wordpress.com/2011/05/15/more-support-for-chinese-agricultural-investment-abroad/

Magdoff, F. (2013). Twenty-First-Century Land Grabs. Accumulation by Agricultural Dispossession. *Monthly Review. 65*(6). Retrieved from http://monthlyreview.org/2013/11/01/twenty-first-century-land-grabs/

Makki, F., & Geisler, C. (2011). *Development by dispossession: Land grabbing as new enclosures in contemporary Ethiopia*. Paper presented at the international conference Global Land Grabbing 2011, Brighton, United Kingdom.

Mamonova, N. (2012). *Challenging the dominant assumptions about peasants' responses to land grabbing: A study of diverse political reactions from below on the example of Ukraine*. Paper presented at the international conference Global Land Grabbing II, Ithaca, USA. Retrieved from http://www.cornell-landproject.org/download/landgrab2012papers/mamanova.pdf

Mann, M. (2012). Return of the empire. A new agency of the Old East India Company? *Südasien-Chronik—South Asia Chronicle, 2*, 398-415. Retrieved from http://edoc.hu-berlin.de/suedasien/band-2/398/PDF/398.pdf

Manson, K. (2012, 8 March). East Africa: Development funds put $40m into private equity for microfinance [Blog post]. Retrieved from Financial Times: Beyond BRICS: http://blogs.ft.com/beyond-brics/2012/03/08/east-africa-development-funds-put-40m-into-private-equity-for-microfinance/

Margulis, M., McKeon, N., & Borras, S. M. (Eds.). (2013). *Land grabbing and global governance*. New York: Routledge.

Marima, T. (2012, August 20). Rautenbach's controversial mining deals. *Zimbabwe Independent*. Retrieved from http://www.theindependent.co.zw/2012/08/20/rautenbachs-controversial-mining-deals/

Marks, R. B. (2007). *The origins of the modern world: A global and ecological narrative from the fifteenth to the twenty-first century*. Lanham: Rowman & Littlefield.

Marmo, L. (2013). The policy aspects around "Virtual Land Imports." Presentation at the international conference Global Soil Week 2013, Berlin, Germany.

Martin, M.F. (2010). *China's Sovereign Wealth Fund: Developments and Policy Implications* (CRS Report for Congress 7-5700). Washington, DC: U.S. Congress. Retrieved from http://www.google.de/url?sa=t&rct=j&q=&esrc=s&source=web&cd=1&ved=0CCgQFjAA&url=http%3A%2F%2Fdigitalcommons.ilr.cornell.edu%2Fcgi%2Fviewcontent.cgi%3Farticle%3D1760%26context%3Dkey_workplace&ei=-B2DVNDaCeK_ywPao4FQ&usg=AFQjCNFl8NCRKaJXJWtX1bCLwR_oIS9SeA&bvm=bv.80642063,d.bGQ

Martin, W., & Manole, V. (2004, June). *China's emergence as the Workshop of the World* (Working paper no. 216). Stanford: Stanford Center for International Development. Retrieved from http://web.stanford.edu/group/siepr/cgi-bin/siepr/?q=system/files/shared/pubs/papers/pdf/SCID216.pdf

Matondi, P. B., Havnevik, K., & Beyene, A. (2011). *Biofuels, land grabbing and food security in Africa*. London, United Kingdom: Zed Books.

Matthews, D. (2010). *The new rules of business*. Hampshire: Harriman House.

McCarthy, J. F., Vel, J. A., & Afiff, S. (2012). Trajectories of land acquisition and enclosure: development schemes, virtual land grabs, and green acquisitions in Indonesia's Outer Islands. *Journal of Peasant Studies, 39*(2), 521-549.

McDowell, M. A. (2012). *China in Nigeria*. Newport: Naval War College Newport, Joint Military Operations Dept. Retrieved from http://www.google.de/url?sa=t&rct=j&q=&esrc=s&source=web&cd=1&ved=0CCMQFjAA&url=http%3A%2F%2Fwww.dtic.mil%2Fcgi-bin%2FGetTRDoc%3FAD%3DADA570334&ei=0e2BVKukDoGwPaXYgbgF&usg=AFQjCNHNil9Bq-6-ib4Go54IzoUDaJdXFA&bvm=bv.80642063,d.ZWU

McKinsey Global Institute. (2010). *Lions on the move: The progress and potential of African economies*. McKinsey & Company. Retrieved from http://www.mckinsey.com/insights/africa/lions_on_the_move

McMichael, P., & Scoones, I. (Eds.). (2010). The politics of biofuels, land and agrarian change [Special issue]. *The Journal of Peasant Studies, 37* (4).

McMichael, P. (2012). The land grab and corporate food regime restructuring. *The Journal of Peasant Studies, 39*(3-4), 681-701.

McNellis, P. (2009). *Foreign Investment in developing country agriculture: The emerging role of private sector finance* (FAO commodity and trade policy research working paper no. 28). Rome: FAO. Retrieved from http://www.fao.org/fileadmin/templates/est/INTERNATIONAL-TRADE/FDIs/mcnellis.pdf

Merian Research and CRBM. (2010). *The vultures of land grabbing: The involvement of European financial companies in large-scale land acquisition abroad*. London: Regulate Finance for Development. Retrieved from http://farmlandgrab.org/wp-content/uploads/2010/11/VULTURES-completo.pdf

Merrett, J. (2013, November 29). Cru case: Arch under fire over disclosure to advisers. *Citywire.co.uk*. Retrieved from http://citywire.co.uk/new-model-adviser/cru-case-arch-under-fire-over-disclosure-to-advisers/a721319

Miller, C., Richter, S., McNellis, P., & Mhlanga, N. (2010). *Agricultural investment funds for developing countries*. Rome: FAO. Retrieved from http://www.fao.org/fileadmin/user_upload/ags/publications/investment_funds.pdf

Miller, L. (2011, July 7). Maguire yanked pension out of Arch cru weeks before collapse. *Investment Week*. Retrieved from http://www.investmentweek.co.uk/investment-week/news/2086466/maguire-yanked-pension-arch-cru-weeks-collapse

Ministry of Agriculture, Republic of Mali. (2009). *National strategy for the development of rice growing*. Bamako: Ministry of Agriculture, General Secretariat. Retrieved from http://www.jica.go.jp/english/our_work/thematic_issues/agricultural/pdf/mali_en.pdf

Ministry of Energy, Republic of Ghana. (2010). *National energy policy*. Accra: Ministry of Energy. Retrieved from http://ghanaoilwatch.org/images/laws/national_energy_policy.pdf

Ministry of Foreign Affairs (MOFA). (2006). *China's Africa policy* [Whitepaper]. Beijing: MOFA. Retrieved from http://www.focac.org/eng/zt/zgdfzzcwj/t230479.htm

Ministry of Foreign Affairs. (2010, October 15). China-Africa trade volume set to hit new record high this year: report [Press release]. Retrieved from MOFA website: http://www.focac.org/eng/zxxx/t761304.htm

Ministry of Commerce (MOFCOM), Department of Western Asian and African Affairs. (2010). An interpretation of new measures on economic and trade cooperation from 4th ministerial conference. Beijing: Ministry of Foreign Affairs (MOFA). Retrieved from http://www.focac.org/eng/dsjbzjhy/t696509.htm

Ministry of Commerce (MOFCOM). (2011a). *2010 Statistical bulletin of China's outward Foreign Direct Investment*. Beijing: Ministry of Commerce. Retrieved from http://english.mofcom.gov.cn/article/statistic/foreigninvestment/201109/20110907742320.shtml

Ministry of Commerce (MOFCOM). (2011b). Introduction to the special loan for the development of African SMEs. 18 June 2011. Beijing: Ministry of Commerce. Retrieved from http://english.mofcom.gov.cn/article/policyrelease/Cocoon/201106/20110607621336.shtml

Ministry of Commerce (MOFCOM). (2011c). Notice on doing the work of funding applications for the Foreign Economic and Technical Cooperation Programme in 2011 (Guanyu zuo hao 2011 nian duiwai jingji jishu hezuo zhuanxiang zijin shenbao gongzuo de tongzhi). 29 April 2011. Beijing: Ministry of Commerce. Retrieved from http://www.mofcom.gov.cn/article/b/bf/201104/20110407525027.shtml

Mitchell, D. (2010). *Biofuels in Africa: Opportunities, prospects, and challenges*. Washington, DC: The World Bank. Retrieved from http://elibrary.worldbank.org/doi/abs/10.1596/978-0-8213-8516-6

Modern Ghana.com. (2005, January 23). India edge out UK in FDI to Ghana. *Modernghana.com*. Retrieved from http://www.modernghana.com/news/70616/1/india-edge-out-uk-in-fdi-to-ghana.html

Moosa, I. A. (2002). *Foreign Direct Investment: Theory, evidence and practice*. Houndmills: Palgrave Macmillan.

Moran, T. H. (2011). *Foreign Direct Investment and development: Launching a second generation of policy research: Avoiding the mistakes of the first, reevaluating policies*. Washington, DC: Institute for International Economics.

Morgenthau, H.(2005). *Politics among nations* (7th ed.). Boston: McGraw-Hill.

Moshi, H.P.B., & Mutui, J.M. (2008) *Scoping Studies on China–Africa Economic Relations: The Case of Tanzania*. Nairobi: African Economic Research Consortium (AERC) (mimeo).

Mosley, J. (2012). *Peace, bread and land: Agricultural investments in Ethiopia and the Sudans* (AFP BP 2012/01). London: The Royal Institute of International Affairs. Retrieved from http://www.chathamhouse.org/sites/files/chathamhouse/public/Research/Africa/bp0112_mosley.pdf

Moss, T., Ramachandran, V., & Shah, M. (2004). *Is Africa's skepticism of foreign capital justified? Evidence from East African firm survey data* (Working paper no. 41). Washington, DC: Center for Global Development. Retrieved from www.cgdev.org/files/2748_file_cgd_wp041rev.pdf

MRL Public Sector Consultants (2014). Renewable transport fuel obligation [Corporate website]. Retrieved from http://www.mrl.uk.com/rtfo.html.

Murphy, C. (1994). *International organization and industrial change: Global governance since 1850*. Cambridge: Polity Press.

Murphy, R., & Tao, R. (2006). No Wage and No Land: New Forms of Unemployment in Rural China. In G. Lee, & M. Warner (Eds.), *Unemployment in China* (pp. 128-149). New York: Routledge.

Murrin, D. (2009). Emergent [Personal website]. Retrieved from http://www.davidmurrin.co.uk/emergent

Mushi, D. (2012, May 18). Tanzania: How biomass use fuels rapid deforestation [Opinion]. *Tanzania Daily News*. Retrieved from http://allafrica.com/stories/201205180044.html.

Mwanawina, I. (2008). *China-Africa economic relations: the case of Zambia*. AERC Scoping Studies on China-Africa Economic Relations (mimeo).

Mwega, F. & Ngugi, R.W. (2006). Foreign direct investment in Kenya. In S.I. Ajayi (Ed.), *Foreign direct investment in Sub-Saharan Africa: Origins, targets, impact and potential* (pp. 119-143). Nairobi: Africa Economic Research Consortium. Retrieved from http://dspace.africaportal.org/jspui/bitstream/123456789/32165/3/FDI_papers_booklength_volume.pdf?1#page=133

Nagle, G. (2000). *Advanced geography*. Oxford: Oxford University Press.

National People's Congress. (2011). 12th Year Plan (2011-2015): The full English version [translated by Delegation of the European Union in China]. Retrieved from http://www.britishchamber.cn/content/chinas-twelfth-five-year-plan-2011-2015-full-english-version

Nelson, S. R. (2008). The Real Great Depression (Panic of 1873). *The Chronicle of Higher Education, 17.*

NEOS Resources Plc. (2011, October 12). Notice of general meeting [Corporate website]. Retrieved from http://www.neosplc.com/2011/10/12/notice-of-general-meeting/

NEOS Resources Plc. (2011, November 15). Change of auditors and accounting reference date [Corporate website]. Retrieved from http://www.neosplc.com/2011/12/15/change-of-auditors-and-accounting-reference-date/

NEOS Resources Plc. (2012, March 15). Change of name to NEOS Resources plc. [Corporate website]. Retrieved from http://www.neosplc.com/2012/03/15/change-of-name-to-neos-resources-plc/

Nicholas, T. (1999). Businessmen and land ownership in the late nineteenth century. *The Economic History Review, 52*(1), 27-44.

[NIEO Declaration 1974]. United Nations General Assembly. Declaration on the Establishment of a New International Economic Order. Resolution adopted by the General Assembly, A/RES/S-6/3201 (1974, May 1). New York: United Nations. Retrieved from http://www.un-documents.net/s6r3201.htm

Nolte, K., & Voget-Kleschin, L. (2013). *Evaluating consultation in large-scale land acquisitions: Spotlight on three cases in Mali* (Working paper no. 28). Land Deal Politics Initiative. Retrieved from http://www.plaas.org.za/sites/default/files/publications-pdf/LDPI28Nolte%26VogetKleschin.pdf

Nonfodji, P. (2011). *China's farmland rush in Benin: Toward a win-win economic model of cooperation?* Paper presented at the international conference on Global Land Grabbing I, Brighton, United Kingdom.

North, D. (1990). *Institutions, institutional change and economic performance.* Cambridge: Cambridge University Press.

North, D., Wallis, John J., & Weingast, B. (2009). *Violence and social orders: A conceptual framework for interpreting recorded human history.* Cambridge: Cambridge University Press.

Ntsiful, A. (2010). *Outgrower oil palm plantations scheme by private companies and poverty reduction in Ghana* [Dissertation]. Retrieved from St. Clements University: http://www.stclements.edu/grad/gradntsi.pdf

Nunnenkamp, P. (2006). Was von ausländischen Direktinvestitionen zu erwarten ist: unbegründete Ängste in den Heimatländern, übertriebene Hoffnungen in den Gastländern? *Zeitschrift Für Wirtschaftspolitik, 55*(1), 20–44.

[Nyéléni 2007]. Declaration of the Forum for Food Sovereignty. Nyéléni 2007. Published on 27 February 2007, Sélingué, Mali. Retrieved from http://www.nyeleni.org/spip.php?article290

Oakland Institute. (2011a). *Understanding land investments in Africa: Deciphering Emergent's investments in Africa* (Land Deal Brief). Oakland: The Oakland Institute. Retrieved from http://www.oaklandinstitute.org/land-deal-brief-deciphering-emergent%E2%80%99s-investments-africa

Oakland Institute. (2011b). *Understanding land investment deals in Africa. Country report Tanzania*. F. Mousseau & A. Mittal (Eds.). Oakland: The Oakland Institute. Retrieved from http://www.oaklandinstitute.org/understanding-land-investment-deals-africa-tanzania

Obulutsa, G. (2008, September 19). UK firm eyes ethanol plant in Tanzania. *Reuters*. Retrieved from http://uk.reuters.com/article/2008/09/19/uk-tanzania-biofuels-interview-idUKLJ5231720080919

Odusola, A. F. (2014). *Land grab in Africa: A review of emerging issues and implications for policy options* (Working paper no.124). Brasilia: International Policy Centre for Inclusive Growth.

Olukoju, A. (2002). "Getting too great a grip": European shipping lines and British West African lighterage services in the 1930s. *Afrika Zamani, 9&10*, 19–40.

Oman, W. (2011, July 1). China, the West, and the rebalancing of global growth [Blog post]. *Global Policy Journal*. Retrieved from http://www.globalpolicyjournal.com/blog/01/07/2011/china-west-and-rebalancing-global-growth.

OnVista.de. (2014). GEM Biofuels Plc Aktie. Retrieved from http://www.onvista.de/aktien/GEM-BIOFUELS-PLC-Aktie-IM00B24F0V53

Organisation for Economic Co-operation and Development. (OECD). (2015a). OECD Inclusive Growth Initiative [Website]. Retrieved from http://www.oecd.org/inclusive-growth/

Organisation for Economic Co-operation and Development. (OECD). (2015b). Social and welfare issues: Inequality [Website]. Retrieved from http://www.oecd.org/social/inequality.htm

Osei, C. (2011). UK FDI in emerging markets: The case of Blue Skies Holding Limited. In A. Patterson & S. Oakes (Eds.), *Academy of Marketing Conference 2011: Marketing Field Forever*. Liverpool: Academy of Marketing. Retrieved from https://www.google.de/search?q=Osei%2C+C.+%282011%29.+UK+FDI+in+emerging+markets%3A+The+case+of+Blue+Skies+Holding+Limited&ie=utf-8&oe=utf-8&aq=t&rls=org.mozilla:de:official&client=firefox-a&channel=sb&gfe_rd=cr&ei=QMmEVLiCAoqI8QfOm4G4AQ#rls=org.mozilla:de:official&channel=sb&q=The+case+of+Blue+Skies+Holding+Limited

Osterhammel, J. (2009). *Kolonialismus: Geschichte, Formen, Folgen*. Munich: C.H. Beck.

Oya, C. (2013a). The land rush and classic agrarian questions of capital and labour: A systematic scoping review of the socioeconomic impact of land grabs in Africa. *Third World Quarterly, 34*(9), 1532-1557.

Oya, C. (2013b). Methodological reflections on 'land grab'databases and the 'land grab'literature 'rush'. *Journal of Peasant Studies, 40*(3), 503-520.

Oyeranti, O. A., Babatunde, M. A., Ogunkola, E. O., & Bankole, A. S. (2010). The impact of China-Africa investment relations: The case of Nigeria. *AERC Collaborative Research China-Africa Project Policy Brief,* (8), 6.

Pakenham, T. (1992). *Scramble for Africa*. London: Abacus.

Paler, N. (2010, July 14). Africa Invest Malawi farming business sold for just £175.000. *Cityqire.co.uk.* Retrieved from http://citywire.co.uk/new-model-adviser/news/africa-invest-malawi-farming-business-sold-for-just-175000/a414102

PANAP (Pesticide Action Network Asia & the Pacific). (2013). Food sovereignty: Resource materials. Retrieved from http://www.panap.net/en/fs/page/food-sovereignty/77

Park, Y. J. (2009). *Chinese migration in Africa* (Occasional paper no. 24). Johannesburg: South African Institute for International Affairs. Retrieved from https://www.google.de/search?q=Park%2C+Y.+J.+%282009%29.+Chinese+migration+in+Africa+%28Occasional+paper+No.+24%29.+Johannesburg%2C+South+Africa%3A+South+African+Institute+for+International+Affairs+%28SAIIA%29.+Retrieved+from&ie=utf-8&oe=utf-8&aq=t&rls=org.mozilla:de:official&client=firefox-a&channel=sb&gfe_rd=cr&ei=8_g3VMeYHsiG8QeOiYDIDw

Park, Y.J. (2012, January 4). Living in between: The Chinese in South Africa [Feature]. *Migration Information Source* [The Online Journal of the Migration Policy Institute, Washington, DC.]. Retrieved from http://www.migrationinformation.org/Feature/display.cfm?id=875

Patel, R. (2012). *Stuffed and starved: The hidden battle for the world food system.* Brooklyn: Melville House.

Patton, D. (2008, April 7). Africa at large: China eyes idle farmland in continent. *Business Daily* (Kenya). Retrieved from http://www.afrika.no/Detailed/16472.html

Payi, X. (2011, September). Nigeria diversifies reserves into Renminbi. *Stanlib. com.* Retrieved from http://www.stanlib.com/EconomicFocus/Pages/NigeriadiversifiesreservesintoRenminbi.aspx

Pearce, F. (2012). *The land grabbers: The new fight over who owns the earth.* Boston: Beacon Press.

Pearce, R. (1984). The Colonial Office and planned decolonization in Africa. *African Affairs, 83*(330), 77–93.

Pedersen, C. T. (2009). *Harvesting next to poverty. An analysis of the cotton industry's impact on small scale farmers in Zambia* (Doctoral dissertation). Retrieved from http://rudar.ruc.dk/bitstream/1800/4402/1/Thesis%5B1%5D.pdf

People's Daily. (2005, July 13). China has socialist market economy in place. *People's Daily*. Retrieved from http://english.people.com.cn/200507/13/eng20050713_195876.html

People's Daily. (2009, February 20). Chinese private enterprises pioneer in Africa. *People's Daily*. Retrieved from http://en.people.cn/90001/90778/90857/90861/6597615.html

Pettinger, T. (2014, January 3). UK balance of payments. *Economicshelp.org*. Retrieved from http://www.economicshelp.org/blog/5776/trade/uk-balance-of-payments/

Pettinger, T. (2014, January 8). UK national debt. *Economic.help.org*. Retrieved from http://www.economicshelp.org/blog/334/uk-economy/uk-national-debt/

Phiri, J. (2013, September 11). Zambia: Chinese firm to boost East cotton output. *Times of Zambia*. Retrieved from http://allafrica.com/stories/201309120765.html

Pohl, C. (2010). Jatropha: Money doesn't grow on trees. *Friends of the Earth International* (120). Retrieved from https://www.foeeurope.org/sites/default/files/publications/jatropha_FoEIreport_Jan2011.pdf

Potter, S. J. (2002). British overseas expansion, 1815-1880. In S. Ellis (Ed.), *Empires and states in European perspective* (pp. 123-143). Pisa: Università di Pisa.

Prahalad, C. K., & Lieberthal, K. (2003). The end of corporate imperialism. *Harvard business review, 81*(8), 109-17.

Private Equity. (2012, February 10). Em Vest gets funds from Truestone. Retrieved from http://www.privateequityafrica.com/wp/sectors-2/agriculture/emvest-gets-funds-from-truestone/

Proactiveinvestors.co.uk. (2009, November 25). GEM Biofuels commences commercial production of jatropha oil in Madagascar. *Proactiveinvestors*. Retrieved from http://www.proactiveinvestors.co.uk/companies/news/10574/gem-biofuels-commences-commercial-production-of-jatropha-in-madagascar-10574.html

Public Ledger. (2009, September 22). Agriterra pulls out of proposed African palm oil project. *The Public Ledger* (Editorial). Retrieved from https://www.agra-net.net/agra/public-ledger/agriterra-pulls-out-of-proposed-african-palm-oil-project--1.htm

Putzel, L., & Kabuyaya, N. (2011). *Chinese aid, trade and investment and the forests of the Democratic Republic of Congo* (Working paper no. 82). Bogor: Center for International Forestry Research. Retrieved from http://www.oenz.de/fileadmin/users/oenz/PDF/Putzel_et_al_China_DRC_forests_2011.pdf

Putzel, L., Assembe Mvondo, S., Ndong, L.B.B., Banioguila, R.P., Cerutti, P.O., Tieguhong, J.C., Djeukam, R., Kabuyaya, N., Lescuyer, G., & Mala, W.A. (2011). *Chinese trade and investment and the forests of the Congo Basin: Synthesis of scoping studies in Cameroon, Democratic Republic of Congo and Gabon* (CIFOR working paper no. 67). Bogor, Indonesia: Center for International Forestry Research (CIFOR). Retrieved from http://www.cifor.org/publications/pdf_files/wpapers/wp67putzel.pdf

Raghavan, C. (2000). After Seattle, world trade system faces uncertain future. *Review of International Political Economy, 7*(3), 495-504.

Rasmussen, R., Chow, J.Y., Nelson, D., Hendriks, E., & Savanti, P. (2011). *Chinese investments in South American agribusiness: An overview of an ongoing expanding process* (Rabobank industry note 276-2011). Utrecht: Rabobank Group, Food & Agribusiness Research and Advisory. Retrieved from http://www.institutionalinvestorchina.com/arfy/uploads/soft/110808/1_1504229371.pdf

Refractories Window. (n.d.). Central African Mining & Exploration Company Plc (CAMEC). Retrieved from http://www.refwin.com/company/companynr.asp?id=13030

Renard, M.-F. (2011). *China's trade and FDI in Africa* (Series Nr. 126). Tunis: African Development Bank. Retrieved from http://www.afdb.org/filead min/uploads/afdb/Documents/Publications/Working%20126.pdf

Renewable Fuels Agency. (2008). *The Gallagher review of the indirect effects of biofuels production.* East Sussex: Renewable Fuels Agency. Retrieved from https://www.unido.org/fileadmin/user_media/UNIDO_Header_Site/Subsites/Green_Industry_Asia_Conference__Maanila_/GC13/Gallagher_Report.pdf

Renewable Fuels Agency. (2011). Renewable Fuels Agency 2009/2010 annual report to Parliament on the Renewable Transport Fuel Obligation (January 2011). London: The Stationary Office. Retrieved from http://webarchive.nationalarchives.gov.uk/20110407094507/http:/www.renewablefuelsagency.gov.uk/sites/rfa/files/Year_Two_RTFO_v2.pdf

Reppert-Bismarck, J. von. (2011, January 21). Biofuel jatropha falls from wonder-crop pedestal. *Reuters.* Retrieved from http://www.reuters.com/article/2011/01/21/us-eu-africa-jatropha-idUSTRE70K4VU20110121

Reuk.co.uk. (2007, January 15). D1 Oils Plc biodiesel. *Reuk.* Retrieved from http:www.reuk.co.uk/D1-Oils-PLC-Biodiesel.htm

Robbins, P. (2004). *Political ecology: A critical introduction.* Malden: Blackwell Publishing.

Rodt, A.P. (2012). *From plan to action? The joint Africa-EU strategy.* Paper presented at the conference Dansk Selskab for Statskundskab Vejle 2012, Årsmøde, Denmark.

Rogers, M.; & Ruppersberger, D. (2012). *Investigative report on the U.S. national security issues posed by Chinese telecommunication companies Huawei and ZTE.* A report by Chairman Mike Rogers and Ranking Memer M.A. Dutch Ruppersberger of the Permanent Select Committee on Intelligence (112th Congress), 8 October 2012. Washington, DC: U.S. House of Representatives. Retrieved from https://intelligence.house.gov/sites/intelligence.house.gov/files/documents/Huawei-ZTE%20Investigative%20Report%20%28FINAL%29.pdf

Romei, V. (2015, December 3). China and Africa: Trade relationship evolves [Blog post]. *Financial Times Online.* Retrieved from https://www.ft.com/content/c53e7f68-9844-11e5-9228-87e603d47bdc

Romei, V., & Jopson, B. (2010, December 14). Chart of the week: China-Africa trade [Blog post]. *Financial Times Online.* Retrieved from http://blogs.ft.com/beyond-brics/2010/12/14/chart-of-the-week-the-china-africa-trade/#axzz1jkcJRVjE

Rosen, D.H., & Hanemann, T. (2009). *China's changing outbound Foreign Direct Investment profile: Drivers and policy implications* (Policy brief no. PB09-14). Washington DC: Peterson Institute for International Economics. Retrieved from http://www.iie.com/publications/pb/pb09-14.pdf

Rosset, P. (2011). Food sovereignty and alternative paradigms to confront land grabbing and the food and climate crises. *Development,* 54(1), 21–30.

Rothkopf, G. (2007). *A blueprint for green energy in the Americas: Strategic analysis of opportunities for Brazil and the hemisphere.* Washington, DC: Inter-American Development Bank. Retrieved from www10.iadb.org/intal/intalcdi/PE/2008/01212.pdf

Rudman, S. (2006). *The multinational corporation in China: Controlling interests.* Malden: Blackwell Publishing.

Rueschemeyer, D., & Mahoney, J. (Eds.). (2003). *Comparative historical analysis in the social sciences.* Cambridge: Cambridge University Press.

Rui, H.C., Yip, G.S., & Prashantham, S. (2010). How different are Chinese foreign acquisitions? Adding an Indian comparison. In K.P. Sauvant, G. McAllister, & W.A. Maschek, *Foreign direct investments from emerging market: the challenges ahead* (pp. 173-196). New York: Palgrave Macmillan.

Rulli, M. C., & D'Odorico, P. (2013a). The science of evidence: the value of global studies on land rush. *The Journal of Peasant Studies,* 40(5), 907-909.

Rulli, M. C., & D'Odorico, P. (2013b). Reply to 'The politics of evidence: a response to Rulli and D'Odorico'. *The Journal of Peasant Studies,* 40(5), 913-914.

Rulli, M. C., & D'Odorico, P. (2014). Food appropriation through large scale land acquisitions. *Environmental Research Letters,* 9(6), 064030 (8 pp).

Sadeque, N. (2012). *From colonial to corporate landgrabbing—the case of Pakistan.* Paper presented at the international conference Asia Land Forum—Democratizing Governance of Land 2012, Phnom Penh, Cambodia. Retrieved from http://www.landcoalition.org/sites/default/files/publication/1348/2012Asia LandForumNajmaSadeque.pdf

Saeed, K. (2008). Limits to growth concepts in classical economics. *Social Science Research Network* 2008. Retrieved from http://www.wpi.edu/Images/CMS/SSPS/LIMITS_08.pdf

Sakellaris, P. (2010, October 4). Development financing instruments of the European Investment Bank. [Presentation at the IMF/WB Annual Meetings, Lisbon]. Retrieved from https://www.bcplp.org/pt-PT/Encontros Lisboa/2010Lis/Documents/EncLx_2010_Apresentacao_Sakellaris.pdf

Salidjanova, N. (2011). *Going out: An overview of China's outward Foreign Direct Investment* (USDCC staff research report, 30 March 2011). Washington, DC: U.S.-China Economic and Security Review Commission. Retrieved from http://www.uscc.gov/sites/default/files/Research/GoingOut.pdf

Salvaterra, N. (2013, May 13). Angola looks to China as Oil sales to U.S. Decline. *The Wall Street Journal*. Retrieved from http://online.wsj.com/news/articles/SB10001424127887323716304578481402547990718

Sandrey, R. (2009). *The impact of China-Africa trade relations: The case of Angola*. Nairobi, Kenya: African Economic Research Consortium (AERC). Retrieved from http://dspace.africaportal.org/jspui/bitstream/123456789/32375/1/Angola-TradeStudy.pdf?1

Sauvant, K. P., McAllister, G., & Maschek, W. (Eds.). (2010). *Foreign Direct Investments from emerging markets: The challenges ahead*. New York: Palgrave Macmillan.

Schenk, C.R. (2005). Britain in the world economy. In P. Addison, & Jones, H. (Eds.) *A Companion to Contemporary Britain: 1939-2000* (pp. 463-468). Oxford: Blackwell.

Schmitt, H. O. (1979). Mercantilism: A Modern Argument. *The Manchester School*, 47(2), 93–111.

Schoneveld, G., German, L., & Gumbo, D. (2014). *The developmental implications of SinoAfrican economic and political relations: A preliminary assessment for the case of Zambia* (Working paper no. 133). Bogor: Center for International Forestry Research. Retrieved from http://www.cifor.org/library/4486/the-developmental-implications-of-sino-african-economic-and-political-relations-a-preliminary-assessment-for-the-case-of-zambia/

Schroder. (2008). *Agricultural Land Fund Limited* [Commercial flyer, August 2014]. Retrieved from http://www.schroders.com/staticfiles/schroders/Sites/UKRetail/Discretionary%20Asset%20Manager/Schroder%20Agricultural%20Land%20Fund%20Flyer.pdf

Schroder. (2014). *Schroder Alternative Solutions: Agriculture Fund* [Corporate performance report, September 2014]. Retrieved from http://www.schroders.com/getfunddocument?oid=1.9.221088

Scoones, I., Hall, R., Borras, S. M., White, B., & Wolford, W. (2013a). The politics of evidence: methodologies for understanding the global land rush. *The Journal of Peasant Studies, 40*(3), 469-483.

Scoones, I., Hall, R., Borras, S. M., White, B., & Wolford, W. (2013b). The politics of evidence: A response to Rulli and D'Odorico. *The Journal of Peasant Studies, 40*(5), 911-912.

SDIC. (n.d.). Wholly-owned companies [Corporate website]. Retrieved from http://www.sdic.com.cn/en/InvestEnt/wholly/A020401index_1.htm

SDIC. (n.d. a). International Business [Corporate website]. Retrieved from http://www.sdic.com.cn/en/ourbusiness/stateawned/A020203index_1.htm)

Sege, M., & Beuret, M. (2009). *China safari: On the trail of Beijing's expansion in Africa*. New York: Nation Books.

Seiwald, M., & Zeller, C. (2011). Die finanzielle Inwertsetzung des Waldes als CO_2-Senke: Nutzungsrechte und Nutzungskonflikte im Rahmen der nationalen Entwicklungsstrategie in Ecuador. *Peripherie, Zeitschrift für Politik und Ökonomie in der Dritten Welt, 124*(31), 421-446.

Shaad, B., & Wilson, E. (2009). *Access to sustainable energy: What role for international oil and gas companies? Focus on Nigeria*. London: IIED. Retrieved from http://pubs.iied.org/pdfs/16022IIED.pdf

Shelton, G. (2009, December 22). FOCAC IV: New opportunities for Africa [Press release]. Retrieved from the Forum on China-Africa Cooperation website: http://www.focac.org/eng/ltda/dsjbzjhy/t647035.htm

Shengjin, W. (1995). China's export of labor and its management. *Asian and Pacific Migration Journal, 4*(2-3), 429-447.

Shepard, D. & Mittal, A. (2009). *The great land grab: Rush for world's farmland threatens food security for the poor*. Oakland: The Oakland Institute. Retrieved from http://www.oaklandinstitute.org/sites/oaklandinstitute.org/files/LandGrab_final_web.pdf

Shih, T. H. (2010, January 18). Beijing distances itself from CIF. *South China Morning Post* (Hong Kong). Retrieved from http://www.scmp.com/article/704013/beijing-distances-itself-cif

Shokpeka, S. A., & Nwaokocha, O. (2009). British colonial economic policy in Nigeria, the example of Benin Province 1914-1954. *Journal of Human Ecology, 28*(1), 57–66.

Siegelman, P. (1965). Introduction. In J.A. Hobson, *Imperialism* (pp. v-xx). Ann Arbor: The University of Michigan Press.

Sikor, T. (2012). Tree plantations, politics of possession and the absence of land grabs in Vietnam. *Journal of Peasant Studies, 39*(3-4), 1077-1101.

SilverStreet Capital. (2010, June 20). Sir Bob warns pensions may miss out on Africa [Corporate website]. Retrieved from http://www.silverstreetcapital.

com/Articles/204859/SilverStreet_Capital_Home/Analysis_and_Reports/Market_Commentary/Sir_Bob_warns.aspx

Silver Street Capital. (2010, August 9). Grains prices. Comments on recent price moves [Power point presentation]. Retrieved from http://www.google.de/url?sa=t&rct=j&q=&esrc=s&source=web&cd=1&ved=0CCMQFjAA&url=http%3A%2F%2Fwww.silverstreetcapital.com%2FPublisher%2FFile.aspx%3FID%3D56121&ei=9oWIVJWZDYvcPeWZgPAG&usg=AFQjCNHePP3bOy9Itx2boMBMwBRf-187Ww&bvm=bv.81456516,d.ZWU

Silver Street Capital (2015, March 12). Home [Corporate website]. Retrieved from http://www.silverstreetcapital.com/Groups/106181/SilverStreet_Capital_Home.aspx

Simantke, E. (2013, August 12). Land Grabbing: Wettrennen um Nahrungsmittel in der Zukunft. *Der Tagesspiegel*. Retrieved from http://www.tagesspiegel.de/politik/landgrabbing-wettrennen-um-nahrungsmittel-in-der-zukunft/8621946.html

Skidelsky, R. (2013, January 24). Meeting our makers: Britain's long industrial decline. *Newstatesmen.com*. Retrieved from http://www.newstatesman.com/culture/culture/2013/01/meeting-our-makers-britain%E2%80%99s-long-industrial-decline

Skinner, J., & Cotula, L. (2011). Are land deals driving "water grabs"? *Briefing: The Global Land Rush*. IIED, London. Retrieved from http://pubs.iied.org/17021IED.html

Smallbusiness.co.uk. (2011, October 13). The African dream. Retrieved from http://www.smallbusiness.co.uk/running-a-business/business-management/1661623/the-african-dream.thtml

Smaller, C., & Mann, H. (2009). *A thirst for distant lands: Foreign investment in agricultural land and water*. Manitoba: International Institute for Sustainable Development. Retrieved from http://www.iisd.org/pdf/2009/thirst_for_distant_lands.pdf

Smaller, C., Wie, Q., & Liu, Y. (2012). *Farmland and water: China invests abroad*. Manitoba: International Institute for Sustainable Development. Retrieved from http://www.iisd.org/pdf/2012/farmland_water_china_invests.pdf

Smalley, R. (2013). Plantations, contract farming and commercial farming areas in Africa: a comparative review (Working paper no. 55). *Land and agricultural commercialization in Africa*. Future Agricultures Consortium. University of Sussex, Brighton, UK. Retrieved from http://bdsknowledge.org/dyn/bds/docs/854/FAC_Working_Paper_055.pdf

Snyder, J. (1991). *Myths of Empire: Domestic politics and international ambition*. Ithaca: Cornell University Press.

Solberg, C. (1974). Farm workers and the myth of export-led development in Argentina. *The Americas, 31*(2), 121-138.

Solimano, A., & Watts, N. (2005). *International migration, capital flows and the global economy: a long run view, 35*. Santiago: United Nations Publications.

Somaliland Press. (2013, May 19). Africa: Land grab a new concept invented to implement a neo-colonialism in African country. Retrieved from http://www.oaklandinstitute.org/africa-land-grab-new-concept-invented-implement-neo-colonialism-african-country

Soque, M. (2014, June 30). U.K. companies eye Angolan deals as trade soars, Simmonds says. *BloombergBusiness*. Retrieved from http://www.bloomberg.com/news/articles/2014-06-30/u-k-companies-eye-angolan-deals-as-trade-soars-simmonds-says

Sornarajah, M. (2010). *The international law of foreign investment*. Cambridge: Cambridge University Press.

Sosovele, H. (2010), Policy challenges related to biofuel development in Tanzania. *Africa Spectrum*, 45(1), 117-129.

Soy, S. K. (1997). *The case study as a research method*. Unpublished paper, University of Texas at Austin. Retrieved from https://www.ischool.utexas.edu/~ssoy/usesusers/l391d1b.htm

Spillius, A. (2013, September 25). China ‚land grab' sees it given control of 5% of Ukraine, accused of ‚neo-colonialism'. *National Post* (Canada). Retrieved from http://news.nationalpost.com/2013/09/25/china-land-grab-sees-it-given-control-of-5-of-ukraine-accused-of-neo-colonialism/

Spilsbury, L. (2012/2013). Can Michael Sata tame the dragon and channel Chinese investment towards development for Zambians? *Journal of Politics & International Studies, 8* (Winter 2012/13), 238-278.

Stads, G.-J., & Sène, L. (2011). *Private-sector agricultural research and innovation in Senegal: Recent policy, investment, and capacity trends*. Washington, D.C.: International Food Policy Research Institute. Retrieved from http://www.ifpri.org/sites/default/files/publications/senegal-ps-note-full.pdf

Starr, E. (2013). *Rethinking investment dynamics: An alternative framework of the global land rush*. Paper presented at the international conference Food Sovereignty: A Critical Dialogue, 14-15 September 2013, New Haven, Yale University.

State Council. (2005) *China's peaceful development road*. Whitepaper. Beijing: Information Office of the State Council. Retrieved from http://www.china.org.cn/english/2005/Dec/152669.htm

State Council. (2010). *China-Africa economic and trade cooperation*. Whitepaper. Beijing: Information Office of the State Council. Retrieved from http://bw.china-embassy.org/eng/jmwl/t785012.htm

State Council. (2011a). *China's foreign aid* (Whitepaper). Beijing: Information Office of the State Council. Retrieved from http://www.eu-china.net/upload/pdf/nachrichten/2011-04-21Chinas-ForeignAid-WhitePaper.pdf

State Council. (2011b). *China's peaceful development* (Whitepaper). Beijing: Information Office of the State Council. Retrieved from http://news.xinh uanet.com/english2010/china/2011-09/06/c_131102329.htm

State Council. (2012). *China's energy policy*. Beijing: Information Office of the State Council. Retrieved from http://www.gov.cn/english/official/2012-10/24/content_2250497.htm

State Council. (2013, August). *China-Africa economic and trade cooperation*. Beijing: Information Office of the State Council. Retrieved from http://news.xinhuanet.com/english/china/2013-08/29/c_132673093.htm

Steggerda, M., & Visser, O. (2012). *"A farm manager should get his hands dirty." Global land acquisitions and the export of western farm models to Russia*. Paper presented at the international conference Global Land Grabbing II, Ithaca, USA. Retrieved from http://www.cornell-landproject.org/download/landg rab2012papers/steggerda.pdf

Steinmo, S. (2008). What is historical institutionalism? In D. D. Porta & M. Keating (Eds.), *Approaches in the Social Sciences* (pp. 150–178). Cambridge: Cambridge University Press.

Steps Centre. (2012, April 25). "Green Grabs": Appropriating nature [Blog post]. *Steps Centre*. Retrieved from http://steps-centre.org/2012/project-related/green-grabs-appropriating-nature/

StockMarketWire.com. (2012, March 13). D1 Oils losses rise. *StockMarketWire.com*. Retrieved from http://www.stockmarketwire.com/article/4327513/D1-Oils-losses-rise.html

Stuchtey, B. (2010). Colonialism and imperialism, 1450–1950. *European History Online* (EGO). Retrieved from http://www.ieg-ego.eu/stuchteyb-2010-en

Suárez, S. M., Osorio, L. M., & Langford, M. (2009). *Voluntary guidelines for good governance in land and natural resource tenure: Civil society perspectives*. Rome: Food and agriculture organization of the United Nations (FAO).

Sukhdev, P. (2012). *Corporation 2020*. Munich: Oekom.

Sun, H. L. (2011). Understanding China's agricultural investments in Africa (Occasional paper no. 122). Johannesburg: South African Institute of International Affairs. Retrieved from http://dspace.africaportal.org/jspui/bitst ream/123456789/32504/1/saia%20OP%20102.pdf?1

Sun Biofuels Mozambique. (2011, August 26). About us [Corporate website]. Retrieved from http://sunbiofuelsmz.com/joomla/site-map/aboutusm1 (accessed March 2013)

Svedberg, P. (1981). Colonial enforcement of foreign direct investment. *The Manchester School, 49*(1), 21-38.

SW Radio Africa. (2003, August 1). Chinese Nuanentsi. Retrieved from http://www.swradioafrica.com/News_archives/files/2003/August/01%20Aug/chinese-nuanentsi.html

Takman, L. (2004). Enter the Dragon IV: China's proliferating investment treaty program. Retrieved from The University of New South Wales website: http://www.clmr.unsw.edu.au/article/deterrence/public-v-private-enforcement/enter-dragon-iv-chinas-proliferating-investment-treaty-program

Tan-Mullins, M., Urban, F., Mang, G. (2017). Evaluating the behaviour of Chinese stakeholders engaged in large hydropower projects in Asia and Africa. *The China Quarterly, 230*, 464-488.

Tanzanian Affairs. (n.d.). Archive for business & the economy. *Tanzanian Affairs*. Retrieved from http://www.tzaffairs.org/category/business-the-economy/

Tanzanian Affairs. (2013, January 1). Progress in Agriculture. *Tanzanian Affairs*. Retrieved from http://www.tzaffairs.org/2013/01/progress-in-agriculture/

Tây Sơn News Wire. (2011, September 27). China's richest man to join Central Committee of Communist Party [Blog post]. Retrieved from http://www.eyedrd.org/2011/09/the-richest-chinese-man-to-join-central-committee-of-communist-party.html

Te Velde, D.W. (2002). *Foreign Direct Investment for development: Policy challenges for Sub-Saharan African countries*. London: Overseas Development Institute. Retrieved from http://www.odi.org/sites/odi.org.uk/files/odi-assets/publications-opinion-files/2416.pdf

Te Velde, D.W., & Bilal, S. (2003). *Foreign Direct Investment and home country measures in the Lomé Conventions and Coutonou Agreement*. New York: UNCTAD.

Te Velde, D. W. (2006). *Foreign Direct Investment and development: An historical perspective*. Background paper for World Economic and Social Survey for 2006, commissioned by UNCTAD. London: Overseas Development Institute. Retrieved from http://www.odi.org/sites/odi.org.uk/files/odi-assets/publications-opinion-files/850.pdf

Te Velde, D.W., & Calì, M. (2006). *A political economy perspective of UK trade policy*. London: Overseas Development Institute. Retrieved from http://www.odi.org/sites/odi.org.uk/files/odi-assets/publications-opinion-files/4675.pdf

Te Velde, D. W. (2007). Understanding developed country efforts to promote Foreign Direct Investment to developing countries: The example of the United Kingdom. *Transnational Corporations, 16*(3), 83–104.

The African Business Journal. (2013, May). *The African Business Journal, 4*(5). A. Tubanos (Ed.). Retrieved from http://www.conceptlink.com/wp-content/uploads/2013/04/May-2013.pdf

The Africa Report (2014, September 29). Governance across Africa improving more slowly—Ibrahim survey. Retrieved from http://www.theafricareport.com/North-Africa/governance-across-africa-improving-more-slowly-ibrahim-survey.html

The Equality Trust. (2012). *The Equality Trust research digest: Inequality and the 2011 England riots*. London: The Equality Trust. Retrieved from http://www.equalitytrust.org.uk/sites/default/files/riots-2-august-2012.pdf

The Herald. (2013, December 4). Government consults on water project. *The Herald*. Retrieved from http://www.herald.co.zw/84829/

The Japan Times (2013, March 26). China makes peanuts new 'gold' in Senegal. *The Japan Times Online*. Retrieved from http://www.japantimes.co.jp/news/2013/03/26/business/china-makes-peanuts-new-gold-in-senegal/#.VIGRsFf5E4I

The National Archives. (2005). *Operational selection policy OSP23: Records of Britain's overseas representation, 1973 –*. London: The National Archives. Retrieved from http://www.nationalarchives.gov.uk/documents/information-management/osp23.pdf

The New Political Economy Network. (NPEN). (2010). *Britain's broken economy—and how to mend it*. London: NPEN. Retrieved from http://www.lwbooks.co.uk/ebooks/BritainsBrokenEconomy.pdf

The New York Times. (2013, July 26). Goldman Sachs's aluminum pile (Editorial). *The New York Times*. Retrieved from http://www.nytimes.com/2013/07/27/opinion/goldman-sachss-aluminum-pile.html?_r=0

Theodora.com. (2014, January 31). United Kingdom: Economy. *Theodora.com*. Retrieved from http://www.theodora.com/wfbcurrent/united_kingdom/united_kingdom_economy.html

The Renewable Transport Fuel Obligation Order 2007, No. 3072. (2007). Retrieved from http://www.legislation.gov.uk/uksi/2007/3072/contents/made

The Rights and Resources Group. (2013). *Investments into the agribusiness, extractive, and infrastructure sectors of Liberia: An overview*. Washington, D.C.: RRI. Retrieved from www.rightsandresources.org/documents/files/doc_5772.pdf

The Wall Street Journal. (2014, March17). Feronia Inc. commences 5.000 hectare replanting for 2014. *The Wall Street Journal Online*. Retrieved from http://online.wsj.com/article/PR-CO-20140317-902636.html

This Day. (2006, August 28). Nigerian Ebonyi state to build ethanol plant. *Gas&Oil.com*. Retrieved from http://www.gasandoil.com/news/2006/09/cna63969

Thomas, L. J. (1994). Neoclassical development theory and the Prebisch doctrine: A Synthesis. *The American Economist*, 75-81.

Times of Zambia. (2014, June 14). Zambia: Chipata Cotton Company woos more growers. Retrieved from http://allafrica.com/stories/200406140584.html

TopForeignStocks.com. (2009, June 13). The top net capital importers and exporters of capital in 2008. *Topforeignstocks.com*. Retrieved from http://

topforeignstocks.com/2009/06/13/the-top-net-capital-importers-and-ex porters-of-capital-in-2008/

Tortajada, C. (2013). *Corporate land grabs: Policy implications on water management in the South*. Mexico: Third World Centre for Water Management. Retrieved from http://www.post2015hlp.org/wp-content/uploads/2013/10/Corporate-Land-Grabs-Policy-Implications-on-Water-Resources-Cecilia-Tortajada-FINAL-Sep-27-2013.pdf

Tossa, G. (2012, August 25). Benin: An overview of Complant Sugar Company in Benin (SUCOBE). The International Union of Food, Agricultural, Hotel, Restaurant, Catering, Tobacco and Allied Workers' Associations (IUF). Retrieved from http://www.iuf.org/sugarworkers/benin-an-overview-of-complant-sugar-company-in-benin-sucobe/

TradeInvestNigeria.com. (2009, October 10). UK-based company invests in $250 million tourism village. Retrieved from http://www.tradeinvestnigeria.com/news/277849.htm

TradeInvestNigeria.com. (2009, November 19). New leisure parks to attract tourists to Niger delta. Retrieved from http://www.tradeinvestnigeria.com/feature_articles/332020.htm

TradingEconomics.com. (2014). United Kingdom: Unemployment rate. Retrieved from http://www.tradingeconomics.com/united-kingdom/unemployment-rate (accessed 12 December 2014).

Trading Emissions Plc. (2008). *Report & accounts for the year ended 30 June 2008*. Retrieved from http://www.tradingemissionsplc.com/Report2008/

Trading Emissions Plc. (2009). *Consolidated interim financial statements*. Retrieved from http://www.tradingemissionsplc.com/Trading%20Emissions%20Interim%20Dec%202009.pdf

Trading Emissions Plc. (2010). *Report and accounts 2010*. Retrieved from http://www.tradingemissionsplc.com/Trading%20RA%20web.pdf

Trading Emissions Plc. (2011). *Report & accounts: Results for the year ended 30 June 2011*. Retrieved from http://www.tradingemissionsplc.com/Annual_Report_2011.pdf

Trentmann, F. (2008). *Free trade nation: Commerce, consumption, and civil society in modern Britain*. Oxford: Oxford University Press, USA.

Truestone Impact Investment Management. (n.d.). The world has changed and so could our investment choices [Corporate website]. Retrieved from http://www.truestoneimpactinvestment.co.uk/

Tschirley, D., & Kabwe, S. (2009). *The cotton sector of Zambia* (Africa region working paper no. 124). Washington, D.C.: World Bank. Retrieved from http://www.worldbank.org/afr/wps/WPS_124_Zambia_Cotton_Study.pdf

UK Climate Change Act 2008, Charter 27. (2008). Retrieved from http://www.legislation.gov.uk/ukpga/2008/27

UK Department of Energy & Climate Change (DECC). (2006). *The energy challenge: Energy review report 2006*. London: DECC. Retrieved from https://www.gov.uk/government/uploads/system/uploads/attachment_data/file/272376/6887.pdf

UK Department of Energy & Climate Change (DECC). (2007). *Meeting the energy challenge: A white paper on energy*. London: DECC. Retrieved from http://webarchive.nationalarchives.gov.uk/20121205174605/http:/www.decc.gov.uk/assets/decc/publications/white_paper_07/file39387.pdf

UK Trade and Investment. (2006). *Prosperity in a changing world* (Strategy paper). London: UKTI. Retrieved from http://images.chinwag.com/graphics/UKTI/UKTI%20Prosperity%20in%20a%20Changing%20World.pdf

UK Trade and Investment. (2011). *Britain open for business: Growth through international trade and investment* (Strategy paper). London: UKTI. Retrieved from https://www.gov.uk/government/uploads/system/uploads/attachment_data/file/294090/Britain_open_for_business_-_UKTI_s_five_year_strategy_1_.pdf

UK Trade and Investment. (2012): *UK Clean Energy: Key Facts 2012*. London: UKTI.

Üllenberg, A. (2008). *Jatropha à Madagascar: Rapport sur l'état actuel du secteur*. Madagascar, Gesellschaft für Technische Zusammenarbeit (GTZ). Retrieved from http://www.formad-environnement.org/Jatropha-Mada-2007-GTZ.pdf

Üllenberg, A. (2009). *Foreign direct investment (FDI) in land in Madagascar*. Eschborn: Gesellschaft für Technische Zusammenarbeit (GTZ). Retrieved from http://www2.gtz.de/wbf/4tDx9kw63gma/gtz2010-0063en-foreign-direct-investment-madagascar.pdf

UNCCD. (2010). *UNCCD News—A bi-monthly update on the work of the United Nations Convention to Combat Desertification* 2(3). Retrieved from www.unccd.int

UNCTAD. (2009). *World investment report: Transnational corporations, agricultural production and development*. New York: United Nations. Retrieved from http://unctad.org/en/docs/wir2009_en.pdf

UNCTAD and Arbeiterkammer Wien. (2011). *Price formation in financialized commodity markets. The role of information*. New York, Geneva: United Nations Conference on Trade and Development and Arbeiterkammer Wien. Retrieved from http://unctad.org/en/Docs/gds20111_en.pdf

UN DESA. (2010). Foreign land purchases for agriculture: What impact on sustainable development? *Sustainable development innovation briefs* (8). New York: UN DESA, Division for Sustainable Development. Retrieved from http://sustainabledevelopment.un.org/content/documents/no8.pdf

UN DESA. (2012). *Sustainable development in the 21st century (SD21): Review of implementation of Agenda 21 and the Rio Principles: Study prepared by the Stakeholder Forum for a Sustainable Future.* New York: UN DESA, Division for Sustainable Development. Retrieved from http://sustainabledevelopment.un.org/content/documents/641Synthesis_report_Web.pdf

UNECA. (2008). Biofuels: What strategies for developing the sector in West Africa? (CEA-AO/CIE.11/2008/4b). United Nations Economic Comission for Africa. Retrieved from http://np-net.pbworks.com/f/UN+Africa+%282008%29+Strategies+Biofuels+for+West+Africa.pdf

UNFCCC. (n.d.). Kyoto Protocol. Retrieved from http://unfccc.int/kyoto_protocol/items/2830.php

United Nations Human Rights, Office of the High Commissioner for Human Rights. (n.d.). Special rapporteur on the right to food. Retrieved from http://www.ohchr.org/EN/Issues/Food/Pages/FoodIndex.aspx

United States Senate Committee on Banking, Housing & Urban Affairs (2013, July 23). Hearings: Examining financial holding companies: Should banks control power plants, warehouses, and oil refineries? Financial institutions and consumer protection. Washington, DC Retrieved from http://www.banking.senate.gov/public/index.cfm?Fuseaction=Hearings.Hearing&Hearing_ID=cca72cb5-a8fd-427a-978a-a51140a75cb0

U.S. Central Intelligence Agency (2014, June 20). United Kingdom. *The World Factbook.* Retrieved from https://www.cia.gov/library/publications/the-world-factbook/geos/uk.html

U.S. Energy Information Administration. (2013). United Kingdom. Retrieved from http://www.eia.gov/countries/cab.cfm?fips=uk

Van Der Werf, W. (2012). *Large-scale foreign land investments in Africa with particular attention to the case of Zambia* (Doctoral dissertation). Retrieved from http://wiredspace.wits.ac.za/handle/10539/11579

Veit, P. (2010). *Biofuels and land use in Tanzania.* Seattle and Washington, D.C.: World Resource Institute and Landesa. Retrieved from http://www.focusonland.com/countries/biofuels-and-land-use-in-tanzania/

Vepower Ltd. (n.d.). Invest in VEPOWER projects [Corporate website]. Retrieved from http://www.vepower.com/inv_proj.html

Verdin, M. (2009, March 26). Agriterra heralds first revenues in five years. *Agrimoney.com.* Retrieved from http://www.agrimoney.com/news/agriterra-heralds-first-revenues-in-five-years--112.html

Victor, P. (2008). *Managing without growth.* Cheltenham; Northampton: Edward Elgar Publishing.

Visser, O., Mamonova, N., & Spoor, M. (2012). Oligarchs, megafarms and land reserves: understanding land grabbing in Russia. *Journal of Peasant Studies, 39*(3-4), 899-931.

Voget-Kleschin, L., & Stephan, S. (2013). The potential of standards and codes of conduct in governing large-scale land acquisition in developing countries towards sustainability. *Journal of agricultural and environmental ethics, 26*(6), 1157-1179.

Vissers, E. (2013, June). Crude World: China's Oil Diplomacy with Pariahs (BWP 13-1). *Berkeley APEC Study Center Working Paper Series.* Retrieved from http://basc.berkeley.edu/pdf/Working_Papers/BWP13-01.pdf

Walter, A. (2000). *British investment treaties in South Asia: Current status and future trends.* Tokyo: International Development Center of Japan (IDCJ). http://personal.lse.ac.uk/WYATTWAL/images/British.pdf

Wang, C. (2014, June 30). Chinese cotton firm harvests a bumper crop in Africa. *China Daily Asia.* Retrieved from http://www.chinadailyasia.com/business/2014-06/30/content_15145267.html

Wang, F. (2011, October 10). Agriculture in Africa new hope for private firms. Retrieved from http://www.ecns.cn/in-depth/2011/10-10/2859.shtml

Wang, X. (2002). The Prospect of Antimonpoly Legislation in China. *Washington University Global Studies Law Review, 1*(1), 201-231. http://openschol arship.wustl.edu/law_globalstudies/vol1/iss1/10

Watt, N. (2010, June 7). David Cameron readies UK for debt pain as he blames Labour "illusion." *The Guardian.* Retrieved from http://www.theguardian.com/politics/2010/jun/07/david-cameron-debt-interest-deficit

Webb, M. (2009, September 18). ENRC to make £584m offer for Camec. *Mining Weekly.* Retrieved from http://www.miningweekly.com/article/enrc-to-make-584m-offer-for-camec-2009-09-18Wei, Y. (2002). Corporatization and privatization: A Chinese perspective. *Northwestern Journal of International Law & Business, 22*(2), 219-234.

Wei, Y., & Balasubramanyam, V. N. (Eds.). (2004). *Foreign Direct Investment: Six country case studies.* Cheltenham: Edward Elgar Publishing.

Weingärtner, L. (2010). Assessment and appraisal of Foreign Direct Investments (FDI) in land in view of food security. Eschborn: Gesellschaft für Technische Zusammenarbeit. Retrieved from http://www.giz.de/expertise/downloads/gtz2010-en-foreign-direct-investment-food-security.pdf

Weis, T. (2007). *The global food economy: The battle for the future of farming.* Halifax: Fernwood Publishing.

Weisman, J. (1980). Restrictions on the acquisition of land by aliens. *The American Journal of Comparative Law, 28*(1), 39–66.

Wendimu, M. A. (2013). *Jatropha potential on marginal land in Ethiopia: Reality or myth?* (Working paper no. 17). Frederiksberg: Department of Food and Resource Economics. Retrieved from http://okonomi.foi.dk/workingpap ers/WPpdf/WP2013/IFRO_WP_2013_17.pdf

Wen, J. (2009). Building the new type of China-Africa strategic partnership. Speech at the 4th Ministerial Conference of FOCAC, Sharm el-Sheik, 9

November 2009. Retrieved from http://www.china.org.cn/world/2009-11/09/content_18849890.htm

White, B., Borras, S., Hall, R., Scoones, I., & Wolford, W. (2012). The new enclosures: Critical perspectives on corporate land deals. *The Journal of Peasant Studies, 39* (3-4), 619-647.

White, N. (1999). Gentlemanly capitalism and empire in the twentieth century; the forgotten case of Malaya, 1914-1965. In R. Dumett (Ed.), *Gentlemanly capitalism and British imperialism: The new debate on Empire* (pp.175-195). New York: Longman.

[Wikileaks 2009a] U.S. Embassy Bamako. (2009, September 23). Cable 09BAMAKO104, Status Confidential. Bamako, Mali. Retrieved from http://farmlandgrab.org/post/view/19206

[Wikileaks 2009b] U.S. Secretary of State. (2009, February 18). Cable 09STATE15113, Status SECRET7NOFORN. Subject: Request for Information: Foreign Critical Dependencies (Critical Infrastructure and Key Resources located abroad). Washington, DC: U.S. Secretary of State. Retrieved from https://wikileaks.org/cable/2009/02/09STATE15113.html

[Wikileaks 2010a] U.S. Embassy Yaounde. (2010, February 18). Cable 10YAOUNDE95, Status Unclassified. Yaounde, Cameroon. Retrieved from https://wikileaks.org/cable/2010/02/10YAOUNDE95.html

[Wikileaks 2010b] U.S. Embassy Antananarivo. (2010, February 12). Cable 10ANTANANARIVO72, Status Unclassified. Antananarivo, Madagascar. Retrieved from https://wikileaks.org/cable/2010/02/10ANTANANARIVO72.html

Wildau, G. (2013, May 10). China to simplify foreign exchange rules on foreign direct investment. *Reuters.* Retrieved from http://www.reuters.com/article/2013/05/11/us-china-fx-investment-idUSBRE94A01P20130511

Wilkes, A., & Huang, W. (2011). *Analysis of China's overseas investment policies* (Working paper no. 79). Bogor: Center for International Forestry Research (CIFOR). Retrieved from http://www.cifor.org/publications/pdf_files/wpapers/wp-79cifor.pdf

Wilmar International Ltd. (2011, February 7). Update on proposed acquisition of Benso Oil Palm Plantation Limited (Announcement no. 00078). Retrieved from http://media.corporate-ir.net/media_files/irol/16/164878/Media/20110207%20-%20News_Release_Update_on_Proposed_Acquisition_of_BOPP_by_Wilmar.pdf

Wilson, H. (2013, July 28). Goldman Sachs denies aluminium price-rigging. *The Telegraph* (UK). Retrieved from http://www.telegraph.co.uk/finance/newsbysector/industry/mining/10207764/Goldman-Sachs-denies-aluminium-price-rigging.html

Winkler, S. (2012, June). Taiwan's UN dilemma: To be or not to be. *The Brookings Institution*. Retrieved from http://www.brookings.edu/research/opinions/2012/06/20-taiwan-un-winkler

Woetzel, J. (2008, July 8). Reassessing China's state-owned enterprises. *Forbes.com*. Retrieved from http://www.forbes.com/2008/07/08/china-enterprises-state-lead-cx_jrw_0708mckinsey.html

Wolfe, P. (1997). History and imperialism: a century of theory, from Marx to postcolonialism. *The American Historical Review*, 388-420.

Wolford, W., Borras, S., Hall, R., Scoones, I., & White, B. (Eds.). (2013a). Governing Global Land Deals: The Role of the State in the Rush for Land. *Development and Change, 44*(2) [Special issue].

Wolford, W., Borras, S. M., Hall, R., Scoones, I., & White, B. (2013b). Governing global land deals: the role of the state in the rush for land. *Development and Change, 44*(2), 189-210.

World Bank. (1998). *China: State farm commercialisation project*. Washington, DC: The Word Bank. Retrieved from http://documents.worldbank.org/curated/en/1998/03/693672/china-state-farms-commercialization-project

World Bank. (2007). *World development report 2008: Agriculture for development*. Washington, DC: The World Bank. Retrieved from http://siteresources.worldbank.org/INTWDR2008/Resources/WDR_00_book.pdf

World Bank, & State Environmental Protection Agency (SEPA,China). (2007). *Cost of pollution in China: Economic estimates of physical damages*. Washington. DC: The World Bank. Retrieved from http://siteresources.worldbank.org/INTEAPREGTOPENVIRONMENT/Resources/China_Cost_of_Pollution.pdf

World Bank. (2009). What is inclusive growth?(Note). Retrieved from http://siteresources.worldbank.org/EXTPREMNET/Resources/WhatIsIG.pdf?resourceurlname=WhatIsIG.pdf

World Bank. (2010). *Investing across borders 2010: Indicators of foreign direct investment regulation in 87 economies*. Washington, DC: The World Bank. Retrieved from http://iab.worldbank.org/~/media/FPDKM/IAB/Documents/IAB-report.pdf

World Bank. (2010, September 7). New World Bank report sees growing global demand for farmland (Press release no. 2011/080/DEC). Retrieved from http://go.worldbank.org/XWESRO2MT0

[WB 2011] Deininger, K., Byerlee, D., Lindsay, J., Norton, A., Selod, H., & Stickler, M. (2011). *Rising global interest in farmland: Can it yield sustainable and equitable benefits?* Washington, DC: The World Bank. Retrieved from http://siteresources.worldbank.org/DEC/Resources/Rising-Global-Interest-in-Farmland.pdf

World Economic Forum. (2010). The future of industrial biorefineries (Whitepaper). D. King (Ed.). Retrieved from http://www3.weforum.org/docs/WEF_FutureIndustrialBiorefineries_Report_2010.pdf

World Wide Fund for Nature -Tanzania Programme Office (WWF-TPO). (2009). *Biofuel industry study, Tanzania: An assessment of the current situation.* Retrieved from http://www.tnrf.org/files/E-INFO-WWF-TPO_Biofuel_Industry_Study_Tanzania.pdf

World Rainforest Movement (2010, August 6). Oil palm in Ghana [Blog post]. Retrieved from http://oilpalminafrica.wordpress.com/2010/08/06/oil-palm-in-ghana/

World Rainforest Movement (2010, August 9). Sierra Leone [Blog post]. Retrieved from http://oilpalminafrica.wordpress.com/2010/08/09/oil-palm-in-sierra-leone/

World Trade Organization. (2004). *Trade policy review: Mali* (WT/TRP/S/133) [Report by the Secretariat, 24 May 2004]. Retrieved from http://www.wto.org/english/tratop_e/tpr_e/s133-0_e.doc

Xinhuanet.com. (2009, February 11). Backgrounder: China-Mali ties in continuous development. *Xinhuanet.com.* Retrieved from http://news.xinhuanet.com/english/2009-02/11/content_10802821.htm

Xue, H. (2010). *China-Africa cooperation on agricultural development and economy.* Presentation prepared for Chinese Academy of International Trade and Economic Cooperation, Ministry of Commerce, Beijing, China. Retrieved from http://www.iprcc.org/userfiles/file/Xue%20Hong-EN%281%29.pdf

Xue, Q., & Han, B. (2010). The role of government policies in promoting outward foreign direct investments from emerging markets. In K. P. Sauvant, G. McAllister, & W. Maschek (Eds.), *Foreign direct investments from emerging markets: The challenges ahead* (pp. 305-324). New York: Palgrave Macmillan.

Yi, L., & Yong, B. (2011).The expansion of Chinese construction companies in the global market. In *47th ASC annual international conference proceedings.* Retrieved from http://ascpro0.ascweb.org/archives/cd/2011/paper/CPRT348002011.pdf

Yu, K. (2008). *China's governance reform from 1978 to 2008* (No. 76/2008). Duisburg Working Papers on East Asian Studies. Duisburg, Essen: IN-EAST, Universität Duisburg Essen. Retrieved from https://www.uni-due.de/~hyo382/fileadmin/publications/gruen/paper76.pdf

Yuan Long Ping High-Tech Agriculture Ltd. (2014). Yuan Long Ping High-Tech Agriculture [Corporate website]. Retrieved from http://www.lpht.com.cn/eng/company/Company.htm

Zagema, B. (2011). Land and power: The growing scandal surrounding the new wave of investments in land. *Oxfam Policy and Practice: Agriculture, Food and Land* 11(6), 114-164.

Zebregs, H. (1998). *Can the neoclassical model explain the distribution of foreign direct investment across developing countries?* (IMF Working Paper 139). Washington, DC: International Monetary Fund. Retrieved from http://www.google.de/url?sa=t&rct=j&q=&esrc=s&source=web&cd=1&ved=0CCcQFjAA&url=http%3A%2F%2Fwww.imf.org%2Fexternal%2Fpubs%2Fft%2Fwp%2Fwp98139.pdf&ei=A4MNVf_BBoXiaPrVgJAD&usg=AFQjCNHu2ssM_tnvtonGVkGPFu_OxLoY5w&bvm=bv.88528373,d.d2s.

Zetterlund, Y. (2013). *Gender and land grabbing. A post-colonial feminist discussion about the consequences of land grabbing in Rift Valley Kenya* (Master thesis). Malmö University. Retrieved from http://dspace.mah.se/handle/2043/15718

Zhang, F. (2010). *Reforming China's state-owned farms: State farms in agrarian transition* (Conference paper). Research collection of School of Sciences, Singapore Management University. Retrieved from http://ink.library.smu.edu.sg/soss_research/1089/

Zhuang, J., Vandenberg, P., & Huang, Y. (2012). *Growing beyond the low-cost advantage. How the People's Republic of China can avoid the middle-income trap.* Manila, Beijing: Asian Development Bank, Peking University.

Zittoun, T., Duveen, G., Gillespie, A., Ivinson, G., & Psaltis, C. (2003). The use of symbolic resources in developmental transitions. *Culture & Psychology 9* (4), 415-448.

Zoomers, A. (2010). Globalisation and the foreignisation of space: Seven processes driving the current global land grab. *The Journal of Peasant Studies, 37*(2), 429–447.

ZTE Energy. (n.d.a). Agricultural experimental plot in Congo [Corporate website]. Retrieved from http://www.zte-e.com/en/case_js.aspx?Page=2&id=711

ZTE Energy. (n.d.b). Congo (Kinshasa) agricultural experimental plot [Corporate website]. Retrieved from http://www.zte-e.com/en/prod_js.aspx?ID=738

ZTE Energy. (n.d.c). Zonenergy Company Ltd. About us [Corporate website]. Retrieved from http://www.zte-e.com/en/about_js.aspx?ID=684

Conference documentation (online)

International Conference "Global Land Grabbing," organized by the Land Deals Politics Initiative (LDPI) in collaboration with the Journal of Peasant Studies and hosted by the Future Agricultures Consortium at the Institute of Development Studies, University of Sussex, 6-8 April 2011 (http://www.future-agricultures.org/events/global-land-grabbing).

International Conference "Global land Grabbing II," organized by the Land Deal Politics Initiative (LDPI), and co-organized and hosted by the Cornell Department of Development Sociology, Cornell University, 17-19 October

2012 (http://www.cornell-landproject.org/activities/2012-land-grabbing-co nference/).

Agrarian Studies Conference "Food Sovereignty—A Critical Dialog," Yale University, 14-15 September 2013 (http://www.yale.edu/agrarianstudies/ foodsovereignty/).

Colloquium "Food Sovereignty—A Critical Dialog," International Institute of Social Studies in The Hague, 24 Januar 2014 (http://www.iss.nl/ research/research_programmes/political_economy_of_resources_enviro nment_and_population_per/networks/critical_agrarian_studies_icas/ food_sovereignty_a_critical_dialogue/).